Knowledge Unbound

Knowledge Unbound

Selected Writings on Open Access, 2002–2011

Peter Suber

The MIT Press
Cambridge, Massachusetts
London, England

This book was set in ITC Stone by Toppan Best-set Premedia Limited. Printed and bound in the United States of America.

Library of Congress Cataloging-in-Publication Data.

Names: Suber, Peter, author.
Title: Knowledge unbound : selected writings on open access, 2002-2011 / Peter Suber ; foreword by Robert Darnton.
Description: Cambridge, MA ; London, England : The MIT Press, [2015] | Selection of writings, mostly from the author's SPARC open access newsletter. | Includes index.
Identifiers: LCCN 2015038285| ISBN 9780262029902 (hardcover : alk. paper) | ISBN 9780262528498 (pbk. : alk. paper)
Subjects: LCSH: Open access publishing. | Communication in learning and scholarship—Technological innovations.
Classification: LCC Z286.O63 S822 2015 | DDC 070.5/7973—dc23 LC record available at http://lccn.loc.gov/2015038285

10   9   8   7   6   5   4   3   2   1

Contents

Foreword

Robert Darnton

Venture into this book, and you will be swept up in a conversation about one of the most important and least understood aspects of the digital era: access to knowledge online. You could not choose a better interlocutor. Peter Suber is the leading advocate for open access—that is, the collective effort to overcome barriers that needlessly restrict the availability of digital resources. He was the principal author of the first manifesto of the open-access movement, the Budapest Declaration of 2002. In 2003 he left a tenured position as a professor of philosophy at Earlham College in order to devote himself full time to the cause. And he has published an online newsletter about OA issues since 2001. This book brings together the most important pieces of that running argument, which covers a crucial decade in the development of the internet.

It is no ordinary book. Do not expect a chronological narrative or a logical sequence of propositions. Instead, settle back for a good chat. Suber picks up ideas wherever he finds them, inspects them from different angles, and takes them apart, exposing their fault lines and explaining their strengths. He invites you to join him in the discussion. He addresses you in a straightforward manner, without a hint of professorial *Besserwisserei*. He appeals to your reason, tickles your funny bone on occasion, and always, at least implicitly, asks for your commitment to a common cause: the democratization of access to knowledge. For we are all in this together, Suber says. The Internet belongs to us. It is a public good, and as members of the public, we should debate all the issues that it has brought before us.

Most of us have never given them adequate thought. What, for example, is the extent, in scope and usage, of the dark, fenced-off sectors of the Internet in relation to the open expanses of the World Wide Web? Do OA editions of monographs undercut or stimulate the sale of print editions? Which journals get more hits, the closed (those requiring passwords and payments) or the open (OA and free of charge)? Are processing (or "author's") fees more common on the closed or the open journals? Which grows faster, the size of the web or the reach of search engines? Why is it more effective to take out a Creative Commons license for a text than simply to post it on a web site and make it freely available?

Some of these questions do not have adequate answers, but all of them deserve pondering. Suber takes you through them step by step and helps you enjoy their richness, thanks to his talent for treating complexity with clarity. Far from deprecating arguments opposed to his own, he dispatches them with respect, coolly and convincingly. You, the reader, remain at his side; and when you take leave of him at the end of the book, you feel that you have adventured into fertile, unmapped territory.

For make no mistake about it: the resolution of these questions will determine a large part of the digital future. By posing them in all their complexity, Suber cuts to the core of policy decisions. It is easy, in principle, to be in favor of free access to digitized resources, but digitization is expensive. How to resolve a case of public-domain works that a private enterprise proposes to digitize free of charge but with an exclusive right to exploit them commercially for a certain time? And what should that time limit be— one, five, or twenty years? What right, if any, does the public have to consult works that are covered by copyright but have been digitized with the use of public funds. And how should that consultation take place—one digital copy at a time to readers in a public library? Multiple copies restricted to designated locations? With or without the capacity to download and print out further copies?

Library directors, university administrators, and government officials must puzzle through problems like these every day. Suber provides guidance but few firm answers, because he takes full account of the complicating factors in the real world of learning— information overload, the escalation of journal prices, the growing importance of tools and apps, and the need for sustainability. Far from dismissing the commercial pressures on publishers of closed-access journals, he shows how self-interest and canny calculations can lead to a reversal ("flipping") of their business model. And to help the reader grasp the line of reasoning, he pursues useful analogies: open access is a public good, which can be made equally available to everyone after funding at the production end, like roads or radio broadcasts. Processing fees can be compared to the development of postage stamps, which replaced the standard, c.o.d. method of paying for letters in the 1840s: the sender instead of the receiver carried the cost, and the new system brought down prices while scaling up the service. But every analogy has its drawbacks, which Suber also discusses, intent on reaching the most rational conclusion, not on scoring points against his opponents. He does not conceal the identities of the opposition—publishers like Elsevier, lobbyists like the agents of the Association of American Publishers, and political allies of the lobbyists such as Congressman John Conyers. But he treats them respectfully, reserving his rare sardonic remarks for "the demented world of scholarship," where prestige tends to trump quality in dealings with academic journals.

Suber's scorn expresses repugnance at the irrationality of professors who fail to recognize their own self-interest. While indulging their vanity at being published in prestigious journals, they remain complicit in a system that exploits them and damages their universities; for they provide free labor—the research, writing, refereeing, and editing of articles—to publishers who charge exorbitant prices for access to their work. Not that the professors dig into their own pockets to pay for the journal subscriptions. They leave that to the university libraries. In fact, they often do not know who pays the bill, because they consult the journals online from their laboratories or studies without setting foot in a library.

In general, however, the tone of Suber's arguments remains cool and rational. He speaks with the voice of a philosopher. He weighs the pros and cons of every issue and reaches convincing conclusions. Along the way, he also provides plenty to ponder on the legal and technical side of the arguments, for he has acquired an extraordinary command of the esoteric aspects of the Interenet. With the help of Suber, you can detect copyfraud, distinguish between "gratis" and "libre" OA (not to mention the more common "green" and "gold" varieties), appreciate the advantages of FRPAA and the drawbacks of the "Ingelfinger Rule," the "Eigenfactor," and even the element of "ullage."

All of these considerations feed into the best informed and most effectively crafted case for open access that is currently available. But do not mistake Suber's arguments for disinterested ratiocination. They have a sharp, polemical edge. Suber slices into the counterarguments in order to clear a way for a cause: open knowledge for everyone, not merely the cultural elite and corporate insiders. He accepts the legitimacy of copyright and the importance of sustainable business plans. But he provides an arsenal of arguments for anyone who wants to democratize the world of learning within the surrounding world of economic and legal realities.

The democratic thrust of Suber's arguments deserves emphasis, because they sometimes seem to be directed at fellow academics. When he says "you," he often means collaborators in the OA movement, who need to adjust their strategy and modify their polemics according to contingencies. A tone of preaching to the converted seeps into some of the essays, because they were originally written as installments in a newsletter aimed primarily at OA sympathizers. Suber did not rewrite them in order to make them more palatable to a general public. Yet they deserve to be read by the unconverted, for they cover the whole gamut of OA-related issues, and they show how those issues arose, helter-skelter, over the past ten years. Although they are loosely grouped by subject matter, they do not link up in logical succession, and they need not be read one after the other in linear fashion. In fact, the table of contents can be used like a menu on a web site, permitting readers to jump around according to their shifting interests. They should make allowances for the original form of the essays, which resemble blogs more than chapters in a book.

Paradoxically, the blog-like quality of the essays makes them especially interesting, for they offer a running commentary on the digital scene while the scenery was changing. That they are now collected in a book after a previous existence on the web is testimony to the staying power of the printed codex—not as a substitute for communication online but as a supplement to it. The digital and the analog do not occupy opposite extremes along a technological spectrum. They intersect and overlap in ways that we are only beginning to understand. To enlarge your understanding, begin with Peter Suber. He will not have the last word, but his book provides the best possible portal for anyone who wants to navigate through the issues posed by open access.

Preface

In 2001–2002, I took a sabbatical from Earlham College, planning to complete two or three unfinished articles in philosophy. The web had been around for more than 10 years, and web browsers for more than eight. I was already in the habit of putting my philosophy writings and course hand-outs online for anyone, human or machine, to use for any purpose. I was already experiencing the benefits of that wider exposure: correspondence from serious readers, citations to my work, speaking invitations, online discussions of my ideas, and a steadily rising number of incoming links.

As a scholar, I was living through the rise of the internet as a medium for scholarship. It was transformative and intoxicating. To me it was like an asteroid crash, fundamentally changing the environment, challenging dinosaurs to adapt, and challenging all of us to figure out whether we were dinosaurs. Not every academic saw it that way. To some, it was just one more medium for junk mail, advertising, narcissism, and pornography.

Two figures stood in the background as I thought about the communications revolution going on around me. One was Plato, who said he was lucky to have been born in Greece at the time of Socrates. The other was Bob Dylan, who said, *Keep your eyes wide, the chance won't come again.*

I felt distinctly lucky to be alive and intellectually awake at the birth of the internet. I used the net for my own work in ways that felt serious and constructive, and not just geeky and playful. But I also indulged a geeky side to play with the internet's power and potential. I watched carefully as some fellow academics tried to use it in serious and constructive ways, and as other fellow academics tried just as seriously not to. I was surprisingly late to realize that I wasn't just watching. I was personally making the transition that whole institutions, industries, and cultures were making, or were soon to make, and I was trying to understand and advance this transition.

Plato and Dylan reminded me that I wasn't just using new technology or participating in profound change. I was benefiting from lucky timing. I kept thinking: *Poor Ben Franklin. He would have loved this revolution. I wish I could talk to him about it.* (Of course he was lucky about another revolution even if unlucky about this one.)

The internet was created by researchers to share research. It's the offspring of ARPA-NET, the digital network created by the Advanced Research Projects Agency (ARPA) to share computer-science research among ARPA labs. Tim Berners-Lee invented the World Wide Web 20 years later as an internet application to help researchers share research. Commerce was even prohibited on the internet until the web was about two years old. But as soon as the door opened, entrepreneurs raced to take advantage of the online environment for commerce and entertainment, and quickly overtook and over-shadowed its pioneering academic uses. Researchers who had been on board early didn't lose their momentum, but the larger academic world split into about four groups. One group raced ahead at least as fast as the commercial entrepreneurs, a second group moved ahead cautiously and experimentally, a third wondered whether sharing research online was a good idea, and a fourth noticed the hubbub but tried not to be distracted from their work, including the work of sharing research.

Scholars had always written cutting-edge, peer-reviewed journal articles for impact, not for money. Journals did not pay them for their articles, and yet scholars were eager to write new ones and give them to publishers, relinquishing both rights and revenue. They were keenly aware of the intangible benefits of publication, such as advancing knowledge and advancing their careers, and recognized that those incentives were more fitting for research articles, and far stronger, than royalties could ever be. In fact, they understood that they were paid salaries by universities in part to give away their research articles and avoid the need to write more popular and less specialized work for income. Royalties might come up for textbooks, but rarely for monographs and never for research articles. Scholars knew or should have known that a technology had just emerged to enlarge their audience and increase their impact without requiring any sacrifices they were not already making. They knew or should have known that this technology was entirely compatible with rigorous peer review. They knew or should have known that they were better positioned to use this new technology to their advantage than fellow authors, such as journalists and novelists, who depended on royalty income.

As academics, we knew what it was like to be held back by high prices and inade-quate technology, for example in reading research we needed to read or distributing our own research to everyone who could make use of it. We were soon going to know what it was like to be held back by inadequate imagination and slow-changing aca-demic customs.

By 2001 I was already using the web routinely for my own research and teaching, and thinking about how researchers and teachers could take better advantage of it. I saw some signs that other academics were doing the same, but I didn't see as many as I hoped to see. When I did notice that someone—anyone— took the internet seriously as a medium of scholarship, and especially as a revolutionary medium that could dis-tribute research to a worldwide audience free of charge, I fired off excited emails to a handful of colleagues. At first I wrote each colleague an individualized message. After a while I saved time by broadcasting one email to a list. I remember apologizing for shifting from personal messages to form letters. After another while, I realized that if I were willing to send depersonalized emails to a list of friends, I should be willing to send the same emails to a list of friends and willing strangers. So I moved the list online and let people sign up for it.

That's how my newsletter was born. I called it the Free Online Scholarship Newsletter (FOSN), starting in March 2001, and renamed it the SPARC Open Access Newsletter (SOAN) in July 2003 when SPARC (Scholarly Publishing and Academic Resources Coalition) became my sponsor and publisher. I wrote new issues of SOAN until June 2013.

But on that sabbatical in 2001, I really wanted to complete a few unfinished philosophy essays. I loved everything about my job as a philosophy professor except the frustrating way that teaching triggered ideas for more writing projects than I had time to finish. So as my sabbatical began, I was brimming with ideas and anticipation. But I was brimming with something else as well. My newsletter had just launched, and the public list of subscribers was growing with gratifying speed. Once I turned in my spring grades, I surprised myself by pushing the philosophy books off my desk and spending every hour of my work day, plus many other hours, on the topic of free online scholarship, better known today as open access or OA.

During that sabbatical, I published about one issue of the newsletter every week. When I returned to full-time teaching the next year, I suspended the newsletter and launched a blog—Open Access News—to take its place. Omitting a long story here, my wife and I used that year to arrange to leave our positions and move to the small town on the coast of Maine where we'd spent our sabbatical.

I've worked full-time on OA ever since leaving Earlham in 2003. I resumed my newsletter as soon as I could, and made it monthly. But I kept my blog and wrote the blog and newsletter together. For a variety of reasons, I had to lay down the blog in 2010, after eight years and 18,000+ posts, but the newsletter kept going for another three years.

This book is a selection of my writings on OA, mostly from the newsletter. The hardest part of putting it together was deciding what to omit. Our first whack at a selection was much too large for a single volume and we had to cut more than 20 whole essays. Our second whack was more feasible, but by the time we agreed on it I'd written half a dozen new articles and wanted to include a few of them.

In the end, we selected these 44 pieces published between March 2002 and March 2011. I've abridged some to minimize repetition, but haven't otherwise modified the texts.

For a more complete list of my writings on OA, here's an online bibliography that I keep up to date.

http://cyber.law.harvard.edu/~psuber/wiki/Writings_on_open_access

I don't have space here to thank everyone who has supported my work on OA. But I must thank Rick Johnson and Heather Joseph, two successive executive directors of SPARC. Rick invited me to move my newsletter to SPARC in 2003, and Heather ratified the arrangement when she took over in 2005. I showed them my drafts before publication, but neither ever told me to cut or reword something I wanted to say. Neither ever hinted that something I wanted to say might make their lives difficult. It's true that we agreed on the big things, such as the benefits of OA and the strategies for achieving it. We agreed on many small things as well. But I can't believe we saw eye to eye on every word every month for the 10 years that SPARC published the newsletter. Yet they were unstinting in their generosity in letting me put SPARC's good name at risk. I know that a writer rarely gets that kind of freedom, especially with a monthly check. It's a stroke of luck on a par with being alive and intellectually awake at the birth of the internet.

Above all, I thank my wife, Liffey Thorpe. Incredibly, she was ready to give up her tenured full professorship at the same time I was, so that we could move to Maine and start the next phase of our careers, in my case the OA phase. Without that, six years out of seven I'd still be waiting for my next sabbatical to finish the pieces I really wanted to write.

Introduction

Knowledge as a Public Good

From "Knowledge as a public good," SPARC Open Access Newsletter, November 2, 2009.

http://dash.harvard.edu/handle/1/4391171

One of the most durable arguments for OA is that knowledge is and ought to be a public good. Here I don't want to restate or evaluate the whole argument, which is complex and has many threads. But I do want to pull at a few of those threads.

What is a public good? In the technical sense used by economists, a public good is non-rivalrous and non-excludable. A good is non-rivalrous when it's undiminished by consumption. We can all consume it without depleting it or becoming "rivals." Radio broadcasts are non-rivalrous; my reception doesn't block yours or vice versa. A good is non-excludable when consumption is available to all, and attempts to prevent consumption are generally ineffective. Radio broadcasts are non-excludable for people with the right equipment in the right area. Breathable air is non-excludable for this purpose even though a variety of barriers, from pollution to suffocation, could stop people from consuming it.

Knowledge is non-rivalrous. Your knowledge of a fact or idea does not block mine, and mine does not block yours. Thomas Jefferson described this situation beautifully in an 1813 letter to Isaac McPherson: "If nature has made any one thing less susceptible than all others of exclusive property, it is the action of the thinking power called an idea. ... Its peculiar character ... is that no one possesses the less, because every other possesses the whole of it. He who receives an idea from me, receives instruction himself without lessening mine; as he who lights his taper at mine, receives light without darkening mine." (See H.A. Washington, ed., *The Writings of Thomas Jefferson*, printed by the United States Congress, 1853–54, vol. VI, p. 180.)

George Bernard Shaw also described it: "If you have an apple and I have an apple and we exchange apples then you and I will still each have one apple. But if you have an idea and I have an idea and we exchange these ideas, then each of us will have two ideas." (I can't find a source for the Shaw quotation and would appreciate any help.)

Knowledge is also non-excludable. We can burn books, but not all knowledge is from books. We can raise the barriers to knowledge, through prices or punishments, but that only creates local exceptions for some people or some knowledge. When knowledge is available to people able to learn it, from books, nature, friends, teachers, or their own senses and experience, attempts to stop them from learning it are generally unavailing.

The thesis that knowledge is a public good frequently shows up in critiques of copyright law for trying to privatize what is intrinsically public. But we should be more precise. Copyright law, even today in its grotesquely unbalanced form, recognizes that knowledge is a public good. It privatizes only the expression of ideas, and leaves the ideas themselves unprivatized, unregulated, and public.

Nonetheless, privatizing the expression of ideas, such as the texts which capture knowledge, seriously impedes the sharing of knowledge. But we should talk about that impediment clearly. It means that *texts* are not public goods, even if the knowledge they contain remains a public good. Hence, to remove impediments to knowledge-sharing, the job isn't to make knowledge a public good, which is already done. The job is to make texts into public goods as well.

Or the job is to make *some* texts into public goods. I want to focus on texts by authors who consent to make them public goods. One of the most important types will be royalty-free research articles. Because I believe that authors of royalty-producing monographs, novels, and journalism have a right to their royalties, I'm not interested in making *all* kinds of copyrighted texts into public goods or at least not without author consent.

Can we make *texts* into public goods?

Texts on paper, skin, clay, or stone are rivalrous material objects. Even when we use an inexpensive medium like paper and an inexpensive method of reproduction like xerography, the product is rivalrous. All texts were rivalrous before the digital age. But digital texts are non-rivalrous. With the right equipment we can all have copies of the same digital text without having to take turns, block one another, multiply our costs, or deplete our resources. This may be the deepest transformation wrought by the digital revolution. For the first time in the history of writing, we can record our non-rivalrous knowledge without turning it into a rivalrous material object. The same revolutionary liberation from rivalrous media affects sound, images, and video. No matter how we record knowledge today, the recording can be as non-rivalrous as the underlying knowledge itself, something new under the sun.

http://www.earlham.edu/~peters/fos/newsletter/07-02-07.htm#problems

Publishers sometimes object to the taxpayer argument for OA on the ground that public money supports many goods, such as buildings or wheat, which we cannot readily provide to the public free of charge. The problem with these objections is that they pick out rivalrous material goods as examples. It's true that we can't give everyone free access to a building without making them take turns, or free access to wheat without rationing. But the taxpayer argument for OA is about free access to a strictly non-rivalrous good where there is no risk of depletion and no need to take turns or ration. In fact, it would cost more to discriminate among users, and make this non-rivalrous good available to some and not others, than to give it freely and indiscriminately to all.

http://www.earlham.edu/~peters/fos/2005/09/another-critique-of-nih-policy-misses.html

http://www.earlham.edu/~peters/fos/2006/05/two-minds-about-frpaa.html

Note that digital texts are non-rivalrous not because they are publicly-funded, scholarly, or carry author consent, but because they are digital. Hence the public good argument is not limited to publicly-funded goods, and in that respect (and a few others) differs from the taxpayer argument. Here, though, I am deliberately limiting it to scholarly texts that carry author consent.

Texts on paper, skin, clay, or stone are not only rivalrous; they are also excludable. As we know too well, even digital texts online behind price or password barriers are excludable. However, when we choose to put digital texts online without price or password barriers, they are not excludable, just as roads are not excludable when we choose to build them without toll booths.

If we choose, then, we can make texts, not just the knowledge expressed in texts, into true public goods that are non-rivalrous and non-excludable. Or we could if it were not for copyright law, the one restriction on would-be public goods that doesn't arise from the good's material form. Free online texts can be copyrighted. Forms of sharing facilitated by revolutionary new technologies may be obstructed by copyright, and users not excluded by practical or technical barriers may be excluded by legal barriers.

I put it this way in order to highlight the anomalous situation in which we find ourselves. We possess a revolutionary technology for knowledge sharing but are often restrained from using it by laws which (in the relevant respects) have not changed for more than two centuries. It's not just that legal change is slower than technological change. The desire for legal change is either not sufficiently widespread or is dispersed among the comparatively powerless and opposed by the comparatively powerful. Some of us want to seize the opportunities created by digital media and lift the legal restrictions on new kinds of knowledge sharing. But many others want to keep the restrictions in place and force us to forego the full benefits of our revolutionary technology. We're divided on whether to seize or fear the opportunities created by the internet.

This is a good moment to remember that copyright law originated in the 18th century when full-text copying of any lengthy text was a time-consuming and error-prone job. When copyright arose, and for centuries after, it prohibited acts that were difficult to commit. But today it prohibits acts that are easy to commit. That doesn't invalidate copyright law, as law. But it reduces the law's effectiveness as a barrier of exclusion, even if it ought not to reduce its effectiveness. The compliance arising from the difficulty of violation is no longer quite so invisibly blended together with the compliance arising from respect for the law. Hence our understanding of the extent of respect for the law is not quite so distorted. In fact, compliance is down. Way down. Speaking for the US, I doubt that we've seen more widespread and conspicuous violation of any laws since Prohibition.

If the barriers that count against public goods are practical or technical, then digital goods of all sorts may already be public goods. But if legal barriers count as well, and they should, then we must address them as well.

Can we make *copyrighted* texts into public goods? Again, the answer is yes. With the copyright holder's consent, we can remove the legal barriers which obstruct free sharing. Without the copyright holder's consent, we can get the same or better result if we wait for the copyright to expire. But here I'll focus on methods that don't require delays of up to a century or more: the life of the author plus 70 years.

Both green OA and gold OA rely on copyright-holder consent. As a practical matter, the expiration of copyright is only a legal basis for OA when we are talking about digitizing old texts, not distributing new ones.

Authors are the copyright holders until they decide to transfer their rights away, for example, to a publisher. If they authorize OA while they are still the copyright holders, then authors can make their works into public goods. If they transfer their rights to an OA journal and the journal uses the rights to authorize OA, then the journal can make the works into public goods.

When journals don't provide OA on their own (gold OA), more often than not they are willing to let authors provide OA through a repository (green OA). When journals don't allow even that, authors can try to retain the right to authorize OA themselves.

Can we make copyrighted texts into public goods even when publishers are unwilling to authorize it and unwilling to let authors retain the right to authorize it?

Again the answer is yes. Even in this case there are several lawful ways to make texts into public goods. The most effective is the method pioneered by the Wellcome Trust and now used by the NIH and about a dozen other funding agencies. It rests on the simple fact that funders are upstream from publishers. Authors sign funding contracts before they sign publishing contracts. If the funding contract requires authors to retain key rights and use them to authorize OA, then the author's eventual publisher comes on the scene too late to interfere. Authors could always choose to avoid publishers unwilling to allow OA, but the Wellcome/NIH method tends to elicit publisher accommodation and therefore to keep all publishers within the circle of eligible destinations.

The trick is to keep the relevant rights in the hands of someone who will authorize OA. Publishers like to use the language of expropriation when protesting the NIH policy, as if publishers owned the relevant rights and the NIH seized them or blocked their exercise. But the beauty of the Wellcome/NIH method is that it prevents publishers from owning the relevant rights. Authors retain them, use them to authorize OA, and only transfer the rest of the bundle to publishers. Publishers have the right to refuse to publish work by Wellcome- or NIH-funded authors, but they choose not to exercise it. The NIH, for example, is putting publishers to the choice of accommodating the policy or refusing the publish NIH-funded research. This is hard bargaining, not expropriation. It's just what publishers have been doing to authors, in order to make research a private good, until some funders took the side of authors, in order to make research a public good.

Green OA mandates at universities represent one way to generalize the funder approach. Universities and funders are two different institutions, with different kinds of influence over publishing scholars, using their influence to make research texts into public goods. Instead of making OA a condition of funding, they can make it a condition of employment. Or faculty, seeing the benefits of OA, can self-impose this condition on themselves. At 16 universities, OA policies have been self-imposed by unanimous votes.

(In SOAN [SPARC Open Access Newsletter] for June 2009, I listed 12 universities where the relevant faculty bodies adopted green OA mandates by unanimous votes. Since then unanimous votes by the relevant bodies have occurred, or come to light, at University College London, Copenhagen Business School, the York University librarians, and Venezuela's Universidad de Oriente.)

http://www.earlham.edu/~peters/fos/newsletter/06-02-09.htm#maryland

But there's another way to generalize the funder approach, or a gold rather than green way: When you pay for something, insist on getting what you want. It's remarkable how little this method has been used by universities.

Roads are public goods which we generally succeed in treating as public goods. By contrast, knowledge is a public good whose most important embodiments and manifestations we treat as private commodities, despite the ease of taking a different course and despite the palpable harm our present course inflicts on research, health care, the environment, public safety, and every aspect of life which depends on research. How did we avoid this problem with roads? What can we learn from roads?

We treat roads as public goods when we don't require users to pay to use them, which would exclude drivers who can't afford to pay. (This, by the way, is what's wrong with the cost-recovery model for public data: it excludes people from access to something which is or ought to be a public good.) But we don't expect road builders to donate their labor and materials. Instead, we pay them upfront so that they don't have to decline the job, work as volunteers, or seek their compensation after the fact by installing toll booths. If we want a toll-free road and offer to pay for one, we can find usually find a first-class road builder willing to make one for us.

Governments get the kinds of roads they want because they ask for them. They contract for them. It helps that governments are just about the only entities buying roads. That inclines road builders to listen when governments describe what they want. Universities should be just as specific in saying what kinds of journals they want. It should help that universities are just about the only entities buying peer-reviewed scholarly journals.

When I say that universities buy journals, of course I mean university libraries. But want to spotlight the larger institution in order to broaden the responsibility for change. If we are going to take any deliberate steps toward the road-building model for journals, the steps will be more successful if approved by university administrators, not just librarians.

There are some important differences between road builders and publishers, of course. For example, road builders concentrate on custom work. Every job is a one-off, built to the specs of a client. Road builders don't make many copies of a new road and hope to sell different copies to different buyers —a model which, where it exists, reduces the bargaining power of individual buyers. As a result publishers have more bargaining power with universities than road builders have with governments. A related difference is that there are often many road builders bidding for the same job. Governments commissioning roads enjoy the benefits of a buyer's market. If a road builder insists on an unacceptable condition, the government can usually deny the bid, look elsewhere, and get what it wants. Another difference is that when several governments with a common interest commission a road together, they face no anti-trust problems. A final difference —to cut the list short— is that governments tend to care only about the quality and price of roads and road builders, not their prestige.

These differences are reasons not to expect the same solution for scholarship. But they don't foreclose an analogous solution.

Universities and libraries could demand change as a condition of their enormous annual layouts for journals. "If we're going to pay for your services, then we want the following terms. ..."If universities want toll-free journals, they could specify that in the purchasing contract, as governments do when they want toll-free roads.

There's no contradiction, by the way, in "paying for" a "toll-free" journal. I'm imagining that universities, individually or collectively, would pay for the production of a journal but insist that the journal be OA, or free even for those who don't pay. The situation is the same for a government "paying for" a "toll-free" road.

Here we have to work through some of the differences between road builders and publishers. Universities won't have much bargaining power as long as publishers put out "must-have" journals and universities are unwilling to cancel. We're still in that epoch, but we're in the late stages. Decades of hyperinflationary price increases are pushing us past it. Every year universities cancel journals that were "must-have" just a few years earlier. The longer subscription journal prices rise faster than inflation, the more universities will be forced to cancel valued titles, and the more realistically they can threaten to cancel others in the future. Though we're still moiling through this historical change, after a critical point universities will be able to tell publishers, "This is what we want. If you can't provide it, we'll find someone who will."

Today the converse is more common: publishers can tell universities, "This is what we're selling. If you don't want it, we'll sell to others who do."

Imagine a world in which for centuries all roads had been toll roads. The very idea of a toll-free road is new and unheard of. Then imagine a town trying to commission a toll-free road. The road builder might say, "No, sorry. That's not what I do. I can build you a toll road. Take it or leave it." Now imagine all the towns in a country or large region jointly commissioning a toll-free road.

It makes a huge difference who can say "take it or leave it" in a negotiation. Right now publishers tend to hold that privileged position. But as prices and cancellations keep rising, the positions are reversing. Even apart from the average balance of bargaining power, slowly shifting to universities, there is the bargaining power over specific titles. The desirability of journals is a matter of degree, despite the binary sound of "must-have." Some high-demand journals may be unthreatened by all recent developments. But the set of unthreatened journals is shrinking, and the set for which universities could modify basic terms to better serve research and researchers is growing. For a growing number of journals overall, universities could cancel, threaten to cancel, or bargain effectively, if they wanted to.

If we don't want to wait for slow processes to shift more bargaining power to universities, then concerted action could change the picture overnight. If anti-trust law blocks concerted action, universities could achieve much the same result by making individual, independent, convergent requests of publishers. This is feasible to the extent that universities really do have a common interest (say) in OA, and could start to demand what they want, separately and without coordination. In general, publishers have more bargaining power than universities today because they are more aggressive in acting on their own interests, not because they act as a cartel. Universities could be more aggressive in acting on their own interests and avoid any whiff of cartel.

(If concerted university action does raise anti-trust problems, on which I have no opinion, then note the irony that in this case anti-trust law would not block a private monopoly opposing the public interest but block a public good advancing the public interest.)

Universities that act alone for better terms from publishers are as unlikely to succeed as workers who ask for raises alone. But universities can act together without acting as a cartel if critical numbers of them become courageous about seeking their own interests at about the same time. Without critical numbers and critical timing, early requests will simply be rejected. But as soon as some large institutions or clusters of institutions start to win concessions, it will be easier for the next institutions to make the same requests and build on the momentum.

To adapt a point I made last December:

http://www.earlham.edu/~peters/fos/newsletter/12-02-08.htm#predictions

> If it's tried too soon, [early universities will be rejected]. But after a point, when other OA initiatives have had their effect, and more TA [toll access] publishers have adapted to an OA world, universities will encounter fewer flat refusals and the [university demands for better terms] will trigger more publisher accommodation than publisher resistance. Enlightened [universities] will be watching for that moment and testing the waters. Because the odds of success soar as more universities adopt similar policies, or because followers take fewer risks than leaders, [university demands for OA from publishers] may spread quickly once they are adopted.

Finally, as I argued elsewhere in the same piece, the recession adds a new layer of opportunity:

> [A]s the recession deepens, universities will face an opportunity similar to the one now faced by governments. It may sound strange to call the financial crisis an opportunity for governments. Certainly no government would mortgage its future with massive bailouts unless forced by the prospects of disaster. But the bailout of large banks and manufacturers is an opportunity to demand transformations from these banks and manufacturers that address long-term problems. Universities could seize the same opportunity. They could wake up to their power as buyers—virtually the only buyers—of scholarly journals and demand transformations that better serve the interests of the research community. ... They could offer to make future payments to publishers conditional upon friendlier access policies, and initiate a transition from reader-pays TA to institutionally-subsidized OA. ...

Another of the relevant differences is that a government would never reject a low bid, let alone relinquish its demand for a toll-free road, just because a certain road or road builder had prestige among drivers. There are no "must-have" roads that override a government's specs for a needed new freeway. This is part of the imbalance of bargaining power between universities and publishers, but the existence of prestige adds a new element. Journal prestige attracts authors, readers, and subscribers, and it's not changing as fast as the economics of library acquisitions. Universities may be increasing their cancellations of high-prestige journals, thanks to the price hikes instituted by the journals themselves, and this makes prestige less decisive at renewal time. But it doesn't reduce journal prestige itself or its role in attracting authors and readers.

Even if roads had prestige, drivers would not demand prestige over quality and access. That kind of thing only happens in the demented world of scholarship, where authors, publishers, and tenure committees all routinely put prestige ahead of quality, when the two differ, and ahead of access.

http://www.earlham.edu/~peters/fos/newsletter/09-02-08.htm#prestige

Because prestige or brand is not a factor in road building, road builders tend to be fungible to governments. For road builders willing to build a given road according to spec, the most relevant difference among them will be their bids. If their reputations come into play, it will be their reputations for finishing jobs on time and under budget. Prestige, brand, and reputation are much more significant in publishing. We shouldn't expect that to change on its own. But universities could change it if they exerted themselves. Every year universities cancel more high-prestige titles, giving them more bargaining power over the titles they renew. If this gradual shift of bargaining power is too little, too slow, concerted action can always make change sudden. Universities don't have to pretend that prestige, brand, and reputation don't exist or don't matter. They only have to realize that they are just about the only buyers of these journals and have untapped power to demand better terms.

Part of the road builder model is that road builders are adequately paid. Their bids cover their costs and some margin, and a scholarly analog to the road builder model should do the same. If we could do that, then it should answer most publisher objections about the transition to gold OA, which have been based on financial risk.

As the PLoS analogy of publishers as midwives always suggested, the idea is to stop the midwife from keeping the baby, not to avoid paying for services rendered.

Of course adequate payment won't answer the objection that publishers deserve 30% profit margins, or the objection that it's demeaning for publishers to work on spec. But if we can separate the publishers who only object to financial risk from the others, and eliminate financial risk by offering adequate remuneration, then universities could work with the publishers who are ready to work with them. As for rest, we can take advantage of a further difference between universities and publishers. Nearly all authors, referees, and editors of scholarly journals work in universities, and the internet allows us to distribute perfect copies of non-rivalrous digital files to a worldwide audience at zero marginal cost. When publishers are not willing to help, even when adequately paid, then we can work around them. Unfortunately for governments facing recalcitrant road builders and a dearth of effective competition, disintermediation is not an option.

Postscript

Fortuitously, I had already chosen this month's topic and was well into my draft when the Royal Swedish Academy of Sciences announced that Elinor Ostrom had won the Nobel Prize for economics.

http://nobelprize.org/nobel_prizes/economics/laureates/2009/press.html

Ostrom's lifework has focused on showing that commons need not be tragic, even when they consist of rivalrous and depletable resources like fish stocks or woodlands, and need not be privatized to be well-managed. She has also written extensively on knowledge commons, which are not rivalrous or depletable.

For a quick sense of how her work on common property connects with the special case of an information or knowledge commons, see her video press conference at Indiana University the day the prize was announced. At minute 18:40 she says, "The work of Garrett Hardin we tested in the lab. If you ... are facing a problem like a fishery, and no communication is allowed, people overharvest *drastically*. Simply allowing people to communicate and discuss what they can do—*simply* communication—makes a huge difference [in avoiding overharvesting]. When in addition people can design in a lab the rules that they will follow in the future, then they get up to 92% of optimal."

http://www.indiana.edu/~radiotv/asx/npe_20091012.asx

Here's some of her work on the commons of information, knowledge, and scholarly communication, all of it on deposit in the Digital Library of the Commons, the OA repository launched by her institute at Indiana University.

http://dlc.dlib.indiana.edu/dlc/

—Charlotte Hess and Elinor Ostrom, Artifacts, Facilities, and Content: Information as a Common-Pool Resource, a conference presentation at Duke Law School, October 17, 2001.

http://dlc.dlib.indiana.edu/dlc/handle/10535/1762

—Charlotte Hess and Elinor Ostrom, Ideas, Artifacts, and Facilities: Information as a Common-Pool Resource, *Law & Contemporary Problems*, 66 (2003) pp. 111ff. See esp. Section V, The Evolution of Scholarly Information.

http://www.law.duke.edu/shell/cite.pl?66+Law+&+Contemp.+Probs.+111+(WinterSpring+2003)

—Charlotte Hess and Elinor Ostrom (eds.), *Understanding Knowledge as a Commons: From Theory to Practice*, MIT Press, 2006.

http://mitpress.mit.edu/catalog/item/default.asp?ttype=2&tid=11012
(These are the revised proceedings of a small workshop she and her research group sponsored at Indiana University in 2004, in which I had the pleasure of participating.)

—Charlotte Hess and Elinor Ostrom, *Introduction: An Overview of the Knowledge Commons*

http://mitpress.mit.edu/books/chapters/0262083574intro1.pdf
(Their introduction to the 2006 MIT book above.)

An excerpt from the introduction:

First, open access to information is a horse of a much different color than open access to land or water. In the latter case, open access can mean a free-for-all, as in Hardin's grazing lands, leading to overconsumption and depletion. With distributed knowledge and information the resource is usually nonrivalrous. ... In this instance, instead of having negative effects, open access of information provides a universal public good: the more quality information, the greater the public good.

—Elinor Ostrom and Charlotte Hess, *A Framework for Analyzing the Knowledge Commons*

http://dlc.dlib.indiana.edu/dlc/handle/10535/632109/
(Their contribution, as opposed to their introduction, to the 2006 MIT book above.)

—Charlotte Hess and Elinor Ostrom, Studying Scholarly Communication: Can Commons Research and the IAD Framework Help Illuminate Complex Dilemmas? A conference presentation at Oaxaca, Mexico, May 10, 2004.

http://dlc.dlib.indiana.edu/dlc/handle/10535/2147

For my contribution to the 2006 MIT book above, see: Peter Suber, *Creating an Intellectual Commons Through Open Access*.

http://dash.harvard.edu/handle/1/4552055

For the other contributions to the book, search by author in the Digital Library of the Commons.

http://dlc.dlib.indiana.edu/dlc/

Note that most of Ostrom's work on knowledge commons was co-authored by Charlotte Hess, formerly a colleague at Indiana University but since September 2008 the Associate Dean for Collections and Scholarly Communication at Syracuse University Library. Here are a few relevant pieces Hess wrote without Ostrom:

—Charlotte Hess, Dilemmas of Building a Sustainable Equitable Information Resource, a conference paper at IASCP, Vancouver, June 10–14, 1998.

http://dlc.dlib.indiana.edu/dlc/handle/10535/559

—Charlotte Hess, The Knowledge Commons: Theory and Collective Action; or Kollektive Aktionismus? A conference paper at the Wizards of OS 2, June 10–12, 2004.

http://dlc.dlib.indiana.edu/dlc/handle/10535/2307

—Charlotte Hess, Resource Guide for Authors: Open Access, Copyright, and the Digital Commons, *The Common Property Resource Digest,* March 2005.

http://dlc.dlib.indiana.edu/dlc/handle/10535/3339

Here are some of the better articles and blog posts on Ostrom's work since her prize was announced, highlighting the features most relevant to OA and the knowledge commons.

—David Bollier, Elinor Ostrom And The Digital Commons, *Forbes*, October 13, 2009.

http://www.forbes.com/2009/10/13/open-source-net-neutrality-elinor-ostrom-nobel-opinions-contributors-david-bollier.html

—David Bollier, Putting People Back into Economics, On the Commons, October 13, 2009.

http://www.onthecommons.org/content.php?id=2540

—Andy Kaplan-Myrth, Elinor Ostrom's Theories Applied to Copyright: This Commons Is Certainly Not Tragic, Myrth on a Blog, October 27, 2009.

http://blog.kaplan-myrth.ca/elinor-ostroms-theories-applied-to-copyright?c=1

—Mike Linksvayer, Nobel Prize in Economics to Elinor Ostrom "for her analysis of economic governance, especially the commons," Creative Commons blog, October 12, 2009.

http://creativecommons.org/weblog/entry/18426

—Daniel Moss, Nobel Prize in economics a big boost to commons and blow to corporate control, *Grist*, October 13, 2009

http://www.grist.org/article/2009-10-13-nobel-economics-prize-a-big-boost-to-commons-and-blow-to-corpora/

—Jay Walljasper, Tragedy of the Commons R.I.P., On the Commons, October 13, 2009.

http://www.onthecommons.org/content.php?id=2542

Open Access, Markets, and Missions

From "Open access, markets, and missions," SPARC Open Access Newsletter, March 2, 2010.

http://dash.harvard.edu/handle/1/4322590

Do we want newspapers, TV newsrooms, and online news bureaus to maximize profits, or do we want them to serve a certain function in the community? Someone might object that these goals are compatible, and that a TV news station (for example) with the most profit is the one with the most viewers. Its incentives to maximize viewership are incentives to maximize service to the community. But we don't really know in advance what behavior will maximize profits; if we did, business and investment would be easy, not hard. The abstract confidence that maximizing profits will maximize service to the community will prove false if profit seeking leads the station to devote most of its coverage to crime, sports, celebrities, entertainment, and weather. We can admit that all-celebrities all-the-time meets real demand, serves the community in that particular way, and may be rewarded by revenue and market share. But it doesn't follow that it serves the function in the community that should be served by journalism. On the contrary.

We can ask the same question of education. Do we want schools to maximize profits, or do we want them to serve a certain function in the community? Again, someone might object that these goals are compatible, and that the school with the most profit, or at least the most voluntary enrollments, is the one best serving the community. But, again, this will be false if maximizing profit leads the school to teach creationism as science or expand football at the expense of writing. We can admit that telling students what their parents want them to hear, or promoting sports that the public likes to watch, meets real demand and serves the community in that particular way. But it doesn't follow that it serves the function in the community that should be served by education. On the contrary.

For these reasons, let me call journalism and education "mission-oriented" economic sectors, as opposed to "market-oriented" sectors like hat and hardware manufacturing. These are two ends of a spectrum, not airtight categories. In fact, I'm more interested in the complicated middle ground between the two poles than in the two poles themselves. When a newspaper's revenues decline, it may have to scale back on investigative stories about health insurance and scale up on stories about new-fledged ducklings at the zoo. When a university's endowment tanks, it may have to close some low-enrollment programs in favor of high-enrollment programs. Hard choices like these are commonplace in every organization. Tough times can nudge an organization temporarily closer to the market end of the spectrum, and better times can free it to give renewed priority to its mission.

Do we want scholarly journal publishers to maximize profits, or do we want them to serve a certain function in the community? Someone might object that these goals are compatible, and that the publisher with the most profit is the one with the most subscribers and hence the one serving the largest audience and providing the widest access. Its incentives to maximize subscribers are incentives to maximize service to the research community. But as elsewhere, we don't really know in advance what behavior will maximize profits. The abstract confidence that maximizing profits will maximize service to the community will prove false if profit seeking leads the publisher to:

(1) make its method of cost recovery function as an access barrier,
(2) produce fake journals to puff the products of drug companies,
(3) lobby the legislature to block public access to publicly-funded research,
(4) retain a business model that scales negatively for users (excluding more and more readers as the volume of published knowledge continues its exponential growth), or
(5) take advantage of the natural monopolies of individual journals to raise prices out of proportion to journal size, cost, impact, or quality, or to raise them faster than inflation and library budgets (maximizing margins over subscribers).

We can admit that artificial scarcity will protect a revenue stream for the existing array of conventional publishers, and serve the research community in that particular way. But it doesn't follow that it serves the function in the community that should be served by scholarly publishing. On the contrary.

Financial analysts at Credit Suisse First Boston pointed out that second-rate journals with low rejection rates have higher profit margins than first-rate journals with high rejection rates. Higher rejection rates increase the costs per published paper by requiring journals to perform peer review more times per published paper. This creates incentives for profit maximizers to lower their rejection rates, even if that means lowering standards. At the same time, it creates incentives for profit maximizers to bundle journals together and reduce the freedom of libraries to cancel low-quality titles.

http://www.earlham.edu/~peters/fos/newsletter/05-03-04.htm#creditsuisse

Scholarly publishing ought to be a mission-oriented economic sector, just as journalism and education ought to be. But it has evolved into a market-oriented sector. It ought to cluster toward the mission-oriented end of the spectrum, but since WWII has drifted toward the market-oriented end of the spectrum.

Three years ago (February 2007) the American Association of University Presses Statement on Open Access drew a similar conclusion about university presses:

http://aaupnet.org/aboutup/issues/oa/statement.pdf

http://www.earlham.edu/~peters/fos/2007/02/aaup-statement-on-open-access.html

> The core mission of university presses has always been to disseminate knowledge to the widest possible audience. ... For university presses, unlike commercial and society publishers, open access does not necessarily pose a threat to their operation and their pursuit of the mission to "advance knowledge, and to diffuse it ... far and wide."... But presses have increasingly been required by their parent universities to operate in the market economy. ...

Universities are themselves mission-oriented organizations. But when they face hard choices, they must find ways to shore up revenue in order to continue to serve their missions. One way they have done this is to ask their presses to behave more like market-oriented publishers. This may (or may not) help with institutional mission-goals like funding low-income students or enriching teacher-student ratios, but it subverts the mission-goals of advancing and disseminating research.

Scholarly societies are like universities in this respect. They are mission-oriented organizations confronting hard choices about their future. In the face of these pressures they often decide to shore up the revenues needed for their missions by encouraging their publishing arms to behave more like market-oriented publishers.

Last year (February 2009) four major organizations—the Association of American Universities, Association of Research Libraries, Coalition for Networked Information, and National Association of State Universities and Land Grant Colleges—made their own argument that universities should put missions before markets when thinking about how to share the knowledge they generate:

http://www.arl.org/bm~doc/disseminating-research-feb09.pdf

http://www.earlham.edu/~peters/fos/2009/02/calling-on-universities-to-maximize.html

> The production of new knowledge through the practices of research and scholarship lies at the heart of the university's mission. Yet, without effective and ongoing dissemination of knowledge, the efforts of researchers and scholars are wasted. Dissemination is thus a core responsibility of the university. ... Dissemination strategies that restrict access are fundamentally at odds with the dissemination imperative inherent in the university mission. ... Dissemination of knowledge is as important to the university mission as its production. ... [T]here is an inherent difficulty with relying on market forces alone to maximize dissemination. ...

Profit maximizing limits access to knowledge, by limiting it to paying customers. If anyone thinks this is just a side-effect of today's market incentives, then we can put the situation differently: Profit maximizing doesn't always limit access to knowledge, but is always ready to do so if it pays better. This proposition has a darker corollary: Profit maximizing doesn't always favor untruth, but is always ready to do so if it would pay better. It's hard to find another explanation for the fake journals Elsevier made for Merck and the dishonest lobbying campaigns against OA policies. (Remember "Public access equals government censorship"? "If the other side is on the defensive, it doesn't matter if they can discredit your statements"?)

http://www.earlham.edu/~peters/fos/2009/06/elsevier-fake-journal-tally-now-9.html

http://www.nature.com/news/2007/070122/full/445347a.html

http://www.earlham.edu/~peters/fos/2007/01/siege-mentality-at-aap.html

I don't exempt OA journals that charge publication fees as if for peer review and then provide little or no peer review. Readiness to put revenue ahead of mission can lead any publisher, OA or TA, or any business of any kind, to take shortcuts with quality or turn to deception.

http://www.earlham.edu/~peters/fos/2009/06/hoax-exposes-incompetence-or-worse-at .html

What if low-quality and even fake journals really are more profitable than honestly vetted journals, and disinformation campaigns really do protect the revenue stream? It wouldn't follow that most publishers are dishonest, any more than the existence of temptations means that resisting temptation is rare or futile. It would only mean that a minimal sort of service to mission or community requires a step back from profit maximizing. Most publishers take this step, including most subscription or TA journals, and many take more than this step. Nonprofit society publishers have missions other than profit seeking and generally put their missions ahead of extra revenue. Those with TA journals set their average subscription prices lower than their for-profit counterparts and provide greater quality and impact. And most of them allow author-initiated green OA. Neither for-profit status nor aggressive profit seeking prevent most TA publishers from providing honest peer review, even if it increases the costs per published article. If publishers were never willing to put mission before profit, all but the most profitable—and perhaps even they—would have shifted long ago from academic publishing to pornography.

But steps back from profit maximizing may still leave a publisher closer to the market-oriented end of the spectrum than the mission-oriented end. And that is where the industry remains clustered today, after several decades of migration. Today the mission is suffering far more than the profits.

A market-oriented organization is not a pure type at the far end of the spectrum. It may want to sell fine wine, or fine peer review, even though the margins would be higher if it reduced quality. The same considerations apply on the other side. A mission-oriented organization is not a pure type at the other end of the spectrum. It's not so lucky or wealthy that it is spared hard choices, and not so callow or idealistic that it is oblivious to their stakes. To be mission-oriented is a matter of degree, measuring an organization's willingness to reduce its take in order to advance its mission, or its determination to decide its hard cases, when it responsibly can, in favor of its mission.

It's wonderful when a company has the resources and resolve to make an expensive hard choice in favor its mission, for example when Google put its Chinese business at risk by deciding to stop censoring its Chinese search engine. But even companies with the resolve can lack the resources to do the same. Hence, it's understandable when, financially pinched, they must take a step back from their mission to insure their survival, for example when the Journal of Visualized Experiments converted from full OA to hybrid OA or Haematologica converted from no-fee OA to fee-based OA.

http://bit.ly/duprGH

http://www.earlham.edu/~peters/fos/2009/04/jove-retreats-from-oa.html

http://www.earlham.edu/~peters/fos/2009/06/oa-journal-introduces-publication-fees.html

The question is not whether a given publisher is pure, or how it can justify impurity. The question is whether we should conceive mission pressures as regrettable interference with market decisions or market pressures as regrettable interference with mission decisions. I don't want to suggest a common priority for all organizations across the economy. On the contrary, I'm arguing that different economic sectors differ in just this respect, and I want to resist the breezy assumption that all problems are best solved by markets. Arguments that journalism, education, and scholarly publishing should solve their problems by behaving like "other businesses" misunderstand how they differ from "other businesses." If their financial viability is sometimes at risk, so is their special service to the community.

The kind of argument I'm criticizing was put most strongly by the Professional & Scholarly Publishing Division of the Association of American Publishers in its press release for the ill-fated PRISM initiative: "The free market of scholarly publishing is responsive to the needs of scholars and scientists and balances the interests of all stakeholders."

https://mx2.arl.org/Lists/SPARC-OAForum/Message/3934.html

http://www.earlham.edu/~peters/fos/2007/08/publishers-launch-anti-oa-lobbying.html

The same theme has been prominent in the rhetoric of the publishing lobby before and after, including several submissions to the recent public consultation from the White House Office for Science and Technology policy. When the publishing lobby argues that OA policies interfere with the market, it presupposes that scholarly publishing is a market, or that it was a market before OA policies distorted it. But that position overlooks all the long-standing, mission-oriented modifications to this putative market. It overlooks all the ways in which scholarly publishing is permeated by state action and gift culture. It overlooks the fact that most scientific research is funded by taxpayers, the fact that most researcher salaries are paid by taxpayers, and the fact that most journal subscriptions are paid by taxpayers. It overlooks the fact that authors donate their articles and referees donate their peer-review reports. It overlooks the fact that copyright is a state-created monopoly.

Publishers benefit from all these traditional distortions or modifications of the market and only protest new ones that would benefit researchers. In formulating their objections, they position themselves as champions of the free market, not as beneficiaries of its many distortions and modifications.

Some stakeholders see scholarly publishing as the best of both worlds: a functional hybrid of public funding to produce research and private profit seeking to vet and distribute it. Others see it as the worst of both worlds: a dysfunctional monster in which research funded by taxpayers and donated by authors is funneled to businesses which lock it up and meter it out to paying customers. But there's no doubt that it's a cross of two worlds. To call it a market is like calling mule a horse.

The assumption that scholarly publishing is already a market is one kind of mistake. But the deeper mistake—and my primary concern here—is to argue or assume that it ought to be a market. Or since a "market" can be many things, let me be more precise. The abstract confidence that maximizing profits will maximize service to the community may be warranted in many economic sectors, or even most. But it's not warranted in journalism, education, and scholarly publishing, just as it's not warranted in law enforcement, disaster relief, or emergency medicine. In these sectors incentives to maximize profits can function as incentives to reduce quality and access, not to increase them.

A related mistake is to categorize this argument as socialist or to assume that the only solution is state ownership. Some mission-oriented organizations, like police and fire departments, work best when state-owned and government-run. But others, like schools, work well both ways and most people want a mix of both kinds. For others, like newspapers, state ownership would be a disaster. I don't want the state to control peer review any more than I want it control journalism. When the publishing lobby protested that the NIH policy would "nationalize science," it didn't go wrong by deploring the prospect of nationalizing science, only by failing to read the policy.

http://www.earlham.edu/~peters/fos/newsletter/09-02-07.htm#peerreview

The solution is much less dramatic. Researchers, their employers, and their funders, should act more decisively in their own interests. Publishers should remain free to publish any kind of journal they want and researchers should remain free to submit their work to the journals of their choice. But when researchers choose to publish in non-OA journals, they should retain the rights needed to authorize OA and they should use those rights to deliver OA. Their employers and funders should adopt policies to assure this.

If someone objects that these policies "interfere with the market," we can choose from several responses. We can concede the point, and even argue that interfering with the market is part of the purpose. We can argue that there is no market here to interfere with. Or we can argue that when stakeholders act in their own interests, that is the market at work, or that is a start at restoring balance to a one-sided half-market in which only publishers have been acting decisively in their own interests. No matter which response we choose, we needn't give up support for markets in other sectors.

If publishers object that these policies will undermine their revenues, we can give narrow answers focusing on what the evidence shows. But we can give broader answers as well, rejecting the assumption that the interests of the research community should be subordinated to the business interests of publishers. We can argue that scholarly publishing should never have been outsourced to market-oriented businesses and should gradually be recovered by mission-oriented institutions.

Markets do many things well but don't do everything well. Hard-core capitalists often defend that proposition unprompted, citing mission-oriented organizations like police and fire departments, the armed forces, the courts, and public schools, even apart from charities and nonprofits. The difficulty is that if we are generally inclined to support market solutions, then we are generally inclined to overlook the exceptions. In the end, my argument is simply that the stakeholders in scholarly communication—researchers, universities, libraries, societies, publishers, foundations, and governments—need to step back for perspective, remember the exceptions or at least remember that there *are* exceptions, and pick up the conversation again in light of that perspective.

Instead of hypnotically granting the primacy of markets in all sectors, as if there were no exceptions, we should remember that many organizations compromise profits or relinquish revenues in order to foster their missions, and that we all benefit from their dedication. Which institutions and sectors ought to do so, and how should we protect and support them to pursue their missions? Instead of smothering these questions for offending the religion of markets, we should open them for wider discussion. Should scholarly publishing, with all of its mixed incentives and hard choices, migrate closer to market-oriented end of the spectrum or to the mission-oriented end of the spectrum? For me the answer depends on a prior question. Do we want scholarly publishing to serve a certain function in the community?

(Note: This essay stands on its own but also serves as a sequel to "Knowledge as a public good" which appeared in the November 2009 issue.)

http://www.earlham.edu/~peters/fos/newsletter/11-02-09.htm#publicgood

What Is Open Access?

Open Access Overview

Focusing on open access to peer-reviewed research articles and their preprints

From "Open Access Overview."

http://www.earlham.edu/~peters/fos/overview.htm

This is an introduction to open access (OA) for those who are new to the concept. I hope it's short enough to read, long enough to be useful, and organized to let you skip around and dive into detail only where you want detail. It doesn't cover every nuance or answer every objection. But for those who read it, it should cover enough territory to prevent the misunderstandings that delayed progress in our early days.

If this overview is still too long, then see my very brief introduction to OA. It's available in 20+ languages and should print out on just one page, depending on your font size. If these pieces are too short, see my other writings on OA, including Open Access (MIT Press, 2012), my book-length introduction to OA. The book home page includes links to OA editions and a continually growing collection of updates and supplements.

http://legacy.earlham.edu/~peters/fos/brief.htm

http://cyber.law.harvard.edu/~psuber/wiki/Writings_on_open_access

http://cyber.law.harvard.edu/hoap/Open_Access_%28the_book%29

I welcome your comments and suggestions.

- Open-access (OA) literature is digital, online, free of charge, and free of most copyright and licensing restrictions.
  - OA removes *price barriers* (subscriptions, licensing fees, pay-per-view fees) and permission barriers (most copyright and licensing restrictions). The PLoS shorthand definition—"free availability and unrestricted use"—succinctly captures both elements.

    https://www.plos.org/

- There is some flexibility about which permission barriers to remove. For example, some OA providers permit commercial re-use and some do not. Some permit derivative works and some do not. But all of the major public definitions of OA agree that merely removing price barriers, or limiting permissible uses to "fair use" ("fair dealing" in the UK), is not enough.
- Here's how the Budapest Open Access Initiative put it: "There are many degrees and kinds of wider and easier access to this literature. By 'open access' to this literature, we mean its free availability on the public internet, permitting any users to read, download, copy, distribute, print, search, or link to the full texts of these articles, crawl them for indexing, pass them as data to software, or use them for any other lawful purpose, without financial, legal, or technical barriers other than those inseparable from gaining access to the internet itself. The only constraint on reproduction and distribution, and the only role for copyright in this domain, should be to give authors control over the integrity of their work and the right to be properly acknowledged and cited."

  http://www.budapestopenaccessinitiative.org/read

- Here's how the Bethesda and Berlin statements put it: For a work to be OA, the copyright holder must consent in advance to let users "copy, use, distribute, transmit and display the work publicly and to make and distribute derivative works, in any digital medium for any responsible purpose, subject to proper attribution of authorship. ..."

  http://legacy.earlham.edu/~peters/fos/bethesda.htm

  http://openaccess.mpg.de/Berlin-Declaration

- The Budapest (February 2002), Bethesda (June 2003), and Berlin (October 2003) definitions of "open access" are the most central and influential for the OA movement. Sometimes I refer to them collectively, or to their common ground, as the BBB definition.

  http://www.budapestopenaccessinitiative.org/

  http://legacy.earlham.edu/~peters/fos/bethesda.htm

  http://openaccess.mpg.de/Berlin-Declaration

  http://legacy.earlham.edu/~peters/fos/newsletter/09-02-04.htm#progress

- When we need to refer unambiguously to sub-species of OA, we can borrow terminology from the kindred movement for free and open-source software. Gratis OA removes price barriers alone, and libre OA removes price barriers and at least some permission barriers as well. Gratis OA is free of charge, but not free of copyright of licensing restrictions. Users must either limit themselves to fair use or seek permission to exceed it. Libre OA is free of charge and expressly permits uses beyond fair use. To adapt Richard Stallman's famous formulation (originally applied to software), gratis OA is free as in 'free beer,' while libre OA is also free as in 'free speech.'

http://en.wikipedia.org/wiki/Gratis_versus_libre

http://legacy.earlham.edu/~peters/fos/newsletter/08-02-08.htm#gratis-libre

http://www.gnu.org/philosophy/free-sw.html

- In addition to removing access barriers, OA should be immediate, rather than delayed, and should apply to full texts, not just abstracts or summaries.

- OA is compatible with copyright, peer review, revenue (even profit), print, preservation, prestige, quality, career-advancement, indexing, and other features and supportive services associated with conventional scholarly literature.

http://legacy.earlham.edu/~peters/writing/jbiol.htm

http://legacy.earlham.edu/~peters/fos/overview.htm#copyright

http://legacy.earlham.edu/~peters/fos/overview.htm#peerreview

http://legacy.earlham.edu/~peters/fos/overview.htm#journals

http://legacy.earlham.edu/~peters/fos/newsletter/09-02-08.htm#prestige

http://legacy.earlham.edu/~peters/fos/newsletter/09-02-08.htm#prestige

- The primary difference is that the bills are not paid by readers and hence do not function as access barriers.
- The legal basis of OA is the consent of the copyright holder (for newer literature) or the expiration of copyright (for older literature).
  - Because OA uses copyright-holder consent or the expiration of copyright, it does not require the reform, abolition, or infringement of copyright law.
  - One easy, effective, and increasingly common way for copyright holders to manifest their consent to OA is to use one of the Creative Commons licenses. Many other open-content licenses will also work. Copyright holders could also compose their own licenses or permission statements and attach them to their works (though there are good reasons not to do so without legal advice).

http://creativecommons.org/

http://web.archive.org/web/20130501234933/

http://digital-rights.net/wp-content/uploads/books/ocl_v1.2.pdf

https://www.plagiarismtoday.com/2009/05/28/why-to-not-write-your-own-license/

- When copyright holders consent to OA, what are they consenting to? Usually they consent in advance to the unrestricted reading, downloading, copying, sharing, storing, printing, searching, linking, and crawling of the full-text of the work. Most authors choose to retain the right to block the distribution of mangled or misattributed copies. Some choose to block commercial re-use of the work. Essentially, these conditions block plagiarism, misrepresentation, and sometimes commercial re-use, and authorize all the uses required by legitimate scholarship, including those required by the technologies that facilitate online scholarly research.

- For works not in the public domain, OA depends on copyright-holder consent. Two related conclusions follow: (1) OA is not Napster for science. It's about lawful sharing, not sharing in disregard of law. (2) OA to copyrighted works is voluntary, even if it is sometimes a condition of a voluntary contract, such as an employment or funding contract. There is no vigilante OA, no infringing, expropriating, or piratical OA.

  http://legacy.earlham.edu/~peters/fos/newsletter/10-02-03.htm#notnapster

- Of course OA can be implemented badly so that it infringes copyright. But so can ordinary publishing. With a little care it can be implemented well so that doesn't infringe copyright. Just like ordinary publishing.

- The campaign for OA focuses on literature that authors give to the world without expectation of payment.
  - Let me call this *royalty-free literature*. (It's interesting that there isn't already a standard term for this.)
  - There are two reasons to focus on royalty-free literature. First, it reduces costs for the provider or publisher. Second, it enables the author to consent to OA without losing revenue.
  - The most important royalty-free literature for our purposes is the body of peer-reviewed scientific and scholarly research articles and their preprints. (Non-academics are often surprised to learn that scholarly journals generally do not pay authors for their articles.)
  - Obviously no one writes royalty-free literature for money. Scholars write journal articles because advancing knowledge in their fields advances their careers. They write for impact, not for money. It takes nothing away from a disinterested desire to advance knowledge to note that it is accompanied by a strong self-interest in career-building. OA does not depend on altruistic volunteerism.

    http://opcit.eprints.org/oacitation-biblio.html

- Because scholars do not earn money from their journal articles, they are very differently situated from most musicians and movie-makers. Controversies about OA to music, movies, and other royalty-producing content, therefore, do not carry over to research articles.
- Royalty-free literature is the low-hanging fruit of OA, but OA needn't be limited to royalty-free literature. OA to royalty-producing literature, like monographs, textbooks, and novels, is possible as soon as the authors consent. But because these authors often fear the loss of revenue, their consent is more difficult to obtain. They have to be persuaded either (1) that the benefits of OA exceed the value of their royalties, or (2) that OA will trigger a net increase in sales. However, there is growing evidence that both conditions are met for most research monographs.
- Nor need OA even be limited to literature. It can apply to any digital content, from raw and semi-raw data to images, audio, video, multi-media, and software. It can apply to works that are born digital or to older works, like public-domain literature and cultural-heritage objects, digitized later in life.
- I refer to "peer-reviewed research articles and their preprints" in my subtitle because it's the focus of most OA activity and the focus of this overview, not because it sets the boundaries of OA.

- Many OA initiatives focus on publicly-funded research.
  - The argument for public access to publicly funded research is strong, and a growing number of countries require OA to publicly-funded research.

    http://legacy.earlham.edu/~peters/fos/newsletter/09-04-03.htm#taxpayer

    http://roarmap.eprints.org/

  - The campaign for OA to publicly-funded research usually recognizes exceptions for (1) classified, military research, (2) research resulting in patentable discoveries, and (3) research that authors publish in some royalty-producing form, such as books. Recognizing these exceptions is at least pragmatic, and helps avoid needless battles while working for OA to the largest, easiest subset of publicly-funded research.
  - The lowest of the low-hanging fruit is research that is both royalty-free and publicly-funded. The policy of the US National Institutes of Health (NIH) is a good example.

    http://publicaccess.nih.gov/

  - But the OA movement is not limited to publicly-funded research, and seeks OA to research that is unfunded or funded by private foundations (like the Wellcome Trust or Howard Hughes Medical Institute).

    http://www.wellcome.ac.uk/

    http://www.hhmi.org/

- OA literature is not free to produce or publish.
  - No serious OA advocate has ever said that OA literature is costless to produce, although many argue that it is much less expensive to produce than convention- ally published literature, even less expensive than priced online-only literature. The question is not whether scholarly literature can be made costless, but whether there are better ways to pay the bills than by charging readers and creating access barriers.
  - As the BOAI FAQ put it: "*Free* is ambiguous. We mean free for readers, not free for producers. We know that open-access literature is not free (without cost) to produce. But that does not foreclose the possibility of making it free of charge (without price) for readers and users."

    http://legacy.earlham.edu/~peters/fos/boaifaq.htm#wishfulthinking

  - The costs of producing OA literature, the savings over conventionally published literature, and the business models for recovering the costs, depend on whether the literature is delivered through OA journals or OA repositories. (Details below.)

    http://legacy.earlham.edu/~peters/fos/overview.htm#journals

    http://legacy.earlham.edu/~peters/fos/overview.htm#repositories

    http://legacy.earlham.edu/~peters/fos/overview.htm#green/gold

  - For those who do argue that OA literature costs less to produce than non-OA lit- erature of comparable quality, how does the argument run? In short: OA dispenses with print (but so do many non-OA journals nowadays). OA eliminates subscrip- tion management (soliciting, tracking, renewing subscribers, negotiating prices and site licenses, collecting fees). OA eliminates DRM (authenticating users, dis- tinguishing authorized from unauthorized users, blocking access to the unauthor- ized). OA reduces or eliminates legal expenses (drafting and enforcing restrictive licenses). Many OA journals eliminate marketing and rely solely on spontaneous aid from other players, such as search engines, bloggers, discussion forums, social tagging, and social networking. While reducing these expenses, OA adds back little more than the cost of collecting author-side fees or institutional subsidies.
  - As long as the full-text is OA, priced add-ons or enhancements are compatible with OA. If the enhancements are expensive to provide, then providers may have to charge for them. If they are valuable, then providers may find people willing to pay for them. At some OA journals, priced add-ons provide part of the revenue needed to pay for OA.
- OA is compatible with peer review, and all the major OA initiatives for scientific and scholarly literature insist on its importance.
  - Peer review does not depend on the price or medium of a journal. Nor does the value, rigor, or integrity of peer review.

- One reason we know that peer review at OA journals can be as rigorous and honest as peer review in conventional journals is that it can use the same procedures, the same standards, and even the same people (editors and referees) as conventional journals.
- Conventional publishers sometimes object that one common funding model for OA journals (charging fees to authors of accepted articles or their sponsors) compromises peer review. I've answered this objection at length elsewhere (1, 2).

  http://legacy.earlham.edu/~peters/fos/newsletter/03-02-04.htm#objreply

  http://legacy.earlham.edu/~peters/fos/newsletter/10-02-06.htm#quality

- OA journals can use traditional forms of peer review or they can use innovative new forms that take advantage of the new medium and the interactive network joining scholars to one another. However, removing access barriers and reforming peer review are independent projects. OA is compatible with every kind of peer review and doesn't presuppose any particular model.
- The reverse is not true, however. Some emerging models of peer review presuppose OA, for example models of "open review" in which submitted manuscripts are made OA (before or after some in-house review) and then reviewed by the research community. Open review requires OA but OA does not require open review.
- In most disciplines and most fields the editors and referees who perform peer review donate their labor, just like the authors. Where they are paid, OA to the resulting articles is still possible; it merely requires a larger subsidy than otherwise.
- Despite the fact that those exercising editorial judgment usually donate their labor, performing peer review still has costs—distributing files to referees, monitoring who has what, tracking progress, nagging dawdlers, collecting comments and sharing them with the right people, facilitating communication, distinguishing versions, collecting data, and so on. Increasingly these non-editorial tasks are being automated by software, including free and open-source software.

  http://oad.simmons.edu/oadwiki/Free_and_open-source_journal_management_software

- There are two primary vehicles for delivering OA to research articles, OA journals ("gold OA") and OA repositories ("green OA").

  http://legacy.earlham.edu/~peters/fos/overview.htm#journals

  http://legacy.earlham.edu/~peters/fos/overview.htm#repositories

- The chief difference between them is that OA journals conduct peer review and OA repositories do not. This difference explains many of the other differences between them, especially the costs of launching and operating them.

- There are other OA vehicles on which I won't focus here, such as personal web sites, ebooks, discussion forums, email lists, blogs, wikis, videos, audio files, RSS feeds, and P2P file-sharing networks. There will undoubtedly be many more in the future.
- Most activists refer to OA delivered by journals as *gold OA* (regardless of the journal's business model), and to OA delivered by repositories as *green OA*.
- The green/gold distinction is about venues or delivery vehicles, not user rights or degrees of openness. It is not equivalent to the gratis/libre distinction.

  http://legacy.earlham.edu/~peters/fos/2008/08/greengold-oa-and-gratislibre-oa .html

  http://legacy.earlham.edu/~peters/fos/newsletter/08-02-08.htm#gratis-libre

- OA journals ("gold OA"):
  - OA journals conduct peer review.

    http://legacy.earlham.edu/~peters/fos/overview.htm#peerreview

  - OA journals find it easier than non-OA journals to let authors retain copyright.
  - OA journals find it easier than OA repositories to provide libre OA. OA repositories cannot usually generate permission for libre OA on their own. But OA journals can.

    http://legacy.earlham.edu/~peters/fos/newsletter/08-02-08.htm#gratis-libre

  - Some OA journal publishers are non-profit (e.g. Public Library of Science or PLoS) and some are for-profit (e.g. BioMed Central or BMC).

    https://www.plos.org/

    http://www.biomedcentral.com/

  - OA journals pay their bills very much the way broadcast television and radio stations do: those with an interest in disseminating the content pay the production costs upfront so that access can be free of charge for everyone with the right equipment. Sometimes this means that journals have a subsidy from a university or professional society. Sometimes it means that journals charge a publication fee on accepted articles, to be paid by the author or the author's sponsor (employer, funding agency). OA journals that charge publication fees usually waive them in cases of economic hardship. OA journals with institutional subsidies tend to charge no publication fees. OA journals can get by on lower subsidies or fees if they have income from other publications, advertising, priced add-ons, or auxiliary services. Some institutions and consortia arrange fee discounts. Some OA publishers (such as BMC and PLoS) waive the fee for all researchers affiliated with institutions that have purchased an annual membership.

https://www.plos.org/

http://www.biomedcentral.com/

- A common misunderstanding is that all OA journals use an "author pays" business model. There are two mistakes here. The first is to assume that there is only one business model for OA journals, when there are many. The second is to assume that charging an upfront fee is an "author pays" model. In fact, most OA journals (70%) charge no author-side fees at all. Moreover, most conventional or non-OA journals (75%) do charge author-side fees. When OA journals do charge fees, the fees are usually (88%) paid by author-sponsors (employers or funders) or waived, not paid by authors out of pocket.

  http://oad.simmons.edu/oadwiki/OA_journal_business_models

  http://legacy.earlham.edu/~peters/fos/newsletter/11-02-06.htm#nofee

  http://www.alpsp.org/Ebusiness/ProductCatalog/Product.aspx?ID=47

  http://arxiv.org/abs/1101.5260

- A growing number of universities maintain funds to pay publication fees on behalf of faculty who choose to publish in fee-based OA journals.

  http://oad.simmons.edu/oadwiki/OA_journal_funds

- Some OA proponents use a color code to classify journals: *gold* (provides OA to its peer-reviewed research articles, without delay), *green* (permits authors to deposit their peer-reviewed manuscripts in OA repositories), *pale green* (permits, i.e. doesn't oppose, preprint archiving by authors), *gray* (none of the above).
- For details on the business side of OA journals, see the OAD list of Guides for OA journal publishers.

  http://oad.simmons.edu/oadwiki/Main_Page

  http://oad.simmons.edu/oadwiki/Guides_for_OA_journal_publishers

- We can be confident that OA journals are economically sustainable because the true costs of peer review, manuscript preparation, and OA dissemination are considerably lower than the prices we currently pay for subscription-based journals. There's more than enough money already committed to the journal-support system. Moreover, as OA spreads, libraries will realize large savings from the conversion, cancellation, or demise of non-OA journals.

- For a list of OA journals in all fields and languages, see the Directory of Open Access Journals.

  https://doaj.org/

- For news about OA journals, follow the oa.journals and oa.gold tags at the OA Tracking Project.

  http://tagteam.harvard.edu/hubs/oatp/tag/oa.journals

  http://tagteam.harvard.edu/hubs/oatp/tag/oa.gold

  http://cyber.law.harvard.edu/hoap/Open_Access_Tracking_Project

- OA repositories ("green OA"):
  - OA repositories can be organized by discipline (e.g. arXiv for physics) or institution (e.g. DASH for Harvard). When universities host OA repositories, they usually take steps to ensure long-term preservation in addition to OA.

    http://arxiv.org/

    http://dash.harvard.edu/

  - OA repositories do not perform peer review themselves. However, they generally host articles peer-reviewed elsewhere.
  - OA repositories can contain preprints, postprints, or both.
    - A preprint is any version prior to peer review and publication, usually the version submitted to a journal.
    - A postprint is any version approved by peer review. Sometimes it's important to distinguish two kinds of postprint: (a) those that have been peer-reviewed but not copy-edited and (b) those that have been both peer-reviewed and copy-edited. Some journals give authors permission to deposit the first but the not the second kind in an OA repository.
  - OA repositories can include preprints and postprints of journal articles, theses and dissertations, course materials, departmental databases, data files, audio and video files, institutional records, or digitized special collections from the library. Estimates of the costs of running a repository depend critically on how many different functions they take on. If the average cost of an institutional repository is now high, it's because the average institutional repository now does much more than merely provide OA to deposited articles.
  - OA repositories provide OA by default to all their contents. Most now also allow "dark deposits" which can be made OA at any later date. This is useful in working with publishers who permit green OA only after an embargo period. Authors may deposit new articles immediately upon publication and switch them to OA when the embargo period expires.

- Authors need no permission for preprint archiving. When they have finished writing the preprint, they still hold copyright. If a journal refuses to consider articles that have circulated as preprints, that is an optional journal-submission policy, not a requirement of copyright law. (Some journals do hold this policy, called the Ingelfinger Rule, though it seems to be in decline, especially in fields outside medicine.)
- If authors transfer copyright to a publisher, then OA archiving requires the publisher's permission. Most surveyed publishers (60+%) already give blanket permission for postprint archiving. Many others will do so on request, and nearly all will accommodate a mandatory green OA policy from the author's funder or employer. However, when authors retain the right to authorize green OA, then they may authorize green OA on their own without negotiating with publishers.

  http://sherpa.ac.uk/romeo/statistics.phpp

- When authors transfer copyright to publishers, they transfer the OA decision to publishers at the same time. Even if most publishers allow green OA, many do not. In addition, many qualify their permission and some add new restrictions over time, such as fees or embargo periods. For these reasons there is a growing trend among scholarly authors to retain the right to provide green OA and only transfer the remaining bundle of rights to publishers. Some do this through author addenda which modify the publisher's standard copyright transfer agreement. Some funders (like the Wellcome Trust and NIH) require authors to retain key rights when publishing journal articles. At some universities (like Harvard and MIT) faculty have granted the university the non-exclusive right to provide OA to their work.

  http://oad.simmons.edu/oadwiki/Author_addenda

  http://www.wellcome.ac.uk/About-us/Policy/Spotlight-issues/Open-access/Policy/index.htm

  http://publicaccess.nih.gov/

  https://osc.hul.harvard.edu/

  https://libraries.mit.edu/scholarly/mit-open-access/open-access-at-mit/mit-open-access-policy/

- Because rights-retention policies solve the green OA permission problem for future work, there's no need for green OA policies to create loopholes for dissenting publishers, for example requiring OA "subject to copyright" or "except when publishers do not allow it". There may be good reasons to create opt-outs for authors, as Harvard does, but there's no need to create opt-outs

for publishers. When authors authorize OA while they are still the copyright
holders, they needn't seek permission from publishers later on and needn't
worry about infringement. Funders and universities are upstream from
publishers and can adopt policies to ensure green OA and the permissions to
make it lawful.

https://osc.hul.harvard.edu/authors/waiver

- Because most publishers already permit green OA, and because green OA is a *bona
  fide* form of OA, authors who fail to take advantage of the opportunity are actually a greater obstacle to OA than publishers who fail to offer the opportunity.
  Funders and universities are in a position to close the gap and ensure green OA
  for 100% of published work by their grantees and faculty. Because authors cannot close this gap on their own, funders and universities who fail to close the gap
  have no one else to blame if fast-rising journal prices enlarge the fast-growing
  fraction of new research inaccessible to those who need it. All publishers could
  help the process along and some are actually doing so. But there's no need to
  depend on publishers when we could depend on ourselves.
- For a searchable database of publisher policies about copyright and archiving, see
  Project SHERPA.

  http://www.sherpa.ac.uk/romeo/

- Because most publishers and journals already give blanket permission for green
  OA, the burden is on authors to take advantage of the opportunity. This means
  that authors may publish in nearly any journal that will accept their work (OA or
  non-OA) and still provide OA to the peer-reviewed text through an OA repository.
  (Unfortunately, the compatibility of green OA with publishing in most non-OA
  journals is still one of the best-kept secrets of scholarly publishing.)

  http://sherpa.ac.uk/romeo/statistics.php

- The most useful OA repositories comply with the Open Archives Initiative (OAI)
  protocol for metadata harvesting, which makes them interoperable. In practice,
  this means that users can find a work in an OAI-compliant archive without knowing which archives exist, where they are located, or what they contain. (Confusing as it may be, OA and OAI are separate but overlapping initiatives that should
  not be mistaken for one another.)

  http://www.openarchives.org/

- Every university in the world can and should have its own open-access,
  OAI-compliant repository and a policy to encourage or require its faculty

members to deposit their research output in the repository. A growing number do precisely this.

http://roarmap.eprints.org/

- We can be confident that OA repositories are economically sustainable because they are so inexpensive. There are many systems of free and open-source software to build and maintain them. Depositing new articles takes only a few minutes, and is done by individual authors, not archive managers. In any case, OA repositories benefit the institutions that host them by enhancing the visibility and impact of the articles, the authors, and the institution.

  http://web.archive.org/web/20041204125834/

  http://www.arl.org/sparc/pubs/enews/aug01.html#6

  http://oad.simmons.edu/oadwiki/Free_and_open-source_repository_software

  http://eprints.soton.ac.uk/260688/

- The two leading lists of OA repositories around the world are the Directory of Open Access Repositories (OpenDOAR) and the Registry of Open Access Repositories (ROAR).

  http://www.opendoar.org/

  http://roar.eprints.org/

- For news about OA repositories, follow the oa.repositories and oa.green tags at the OA Tracking Project.

  http://tagteam.harvard.edu/hubs/oatp/tag/oa.repositories

  http://tagteam.harvard.edu/hubs/oatp/tag/oa.green

  http://cyber.law.harvard.edu/hoap/Open_Access_Tracking_Project

- The OA project is constructive, not destructive.
  - The purpose of the campaign for OA is the constructive one of providing OA to a larger and larger body of literature, not the destructive one of putting non-OA journals or publishers out of business. The consequences may or may not overlap (this is contingent) but the purposes do not overlap.
  - Even though journal prices have risen four times faster than inflation since the mid-1980's, the purpose of OA is not to punish or undermine expensive journals, but to provide an accessible alternative and take full advantage of new technology—the internet—for widening distribution and reducing costs. Moreover, for researchers themselves, the overriding motivation is not to solve the

journal pricing crisis but to deliver wider and easier access for readers and larger audience and impact for authors.

http://web.archive.org/web/20130617183513/

http://www.sparc.arl.org/bm~pix/journal-price-graph~s600x600.jpg

- Publishers are not monolithic. Some already provide full OA, some provide hybrid models, some are experimenting, and some are considering experiments. Among those not providing OA, some are opposed and some are merely unpersuaded. Among the unpersuaded, some provide more free online content than others. Among the opposed, some have merely decided not to provide it themselves, while others lobby actively against policies to encourage or require it. Some oppose gold but not green OA, while others oppose green but not gold OA. OA gains nothing and loses potential allies by blurring these distinctions.
- Promoting OA does not require the boycott of any kind of literature, any kind of journal, or any kind of publisher. Promoting OA need not cause publisher setbacks, and publisher setbacks need not advance OA. To focus on undermining non-OA journals and publishers is to mistake the goal.

  http://legacy.earlham.edu/~peters/fos/newsletter/05-03-04.htm#distractions

- Open-access and toll-access literature can coexist. We know that because they coexist now. We don't know whether this coexistence will be temporary or permanent, but the most effective and constructive way to find out is to work for OA and see what happens to non-OA providers, not to detour from building OA to hurt those who are not helping.

  http://legacy.earlham.edu/~peters/fos/newsletter/03-02-05.htm#coexistence

- Open access is not synonymous with universal access.
  - Even after OA has been achieved, at least four kinds of access barrier might remain in place:
    (1) *Filtering and censorship barriers.* Many schools, employers, and governments want to limit what you can see.
    (2) *Language barriers.* Most online literature is in English, or just one language, and machine translation is very weak.
    (3) *Handicap access barriers.* Most web sites are not yet as accessible to handicapped users as they should be.
    (4) *Connectivity barriers.* The digital divide keeps billions of people, including millions of serious scholars, offline.
  - Even if we want to remove these four additional barriers (and most of us do), there's no reason to hold off using the term "open access" until we've succeeded.

Removing price and permission barriers is a significant plateau worth recognizing with a special name.

- OA is a kind of access, not a kind of business model, license, or content.
  - OA is not a kind of business model.
    - There are many business models compatible with OA, i.e., many ways to pay the bills so that readers can reach the content without charge. Models that work well in some fields and nations may not work as well in others. No one claims that one size fits all.

      http://oad.simmons.edu/oadwiki/OA_journal_business_models

    - There are many differences among the disciplines that affect the funding of OA. We should not expect OA to make progress in all disciplines at the same rate, any more than we should expect it to make progress in all countries at the same rate. Most of the progress and debate is taking place in the STM fields (science, technology, and medicine), but OA is just as feasible and useful in the humanities.

      http://legacy.earlham.edu/~peters/fos/lists.htm#disciplines

      http://legacy.earlham.edu/~peters/writing/apa.htm

    - New OA business models are evolving, and older ones are being tested and revised, all the time. There's a lot of room for creativity in finding ways to pay the costs of a peer-reviewed OA journal or a general-purpose OA repository, and we're far from having exhausted our cleverness and imagination.

      http://oad.simmons.edu/oadwiki/OA_journal_business_models

  - OA is not a kind of license. There are many licenses compatible with OA, i.e. many ways to remove permission barriers for users and let them know what they may and may not do with the content. See the sections on permission barriers and licenses above.

    http://legacy.earlham.edu/~peters/fos/overview.htm#permissionbarriers

    http://legacy.earlham.edu/~peters/fos/overview.htm#licenses

  - OA is not a kind of content. Every kind of digital content can be OA, from texts and data to software, audio, video, and multi-media. The OA movement focuses on peer-reviewed research articles and their preprints. While most of these are just text, a growing number integrate text with images, data, and executable code. OA can also apply to non-scholarly content, like music, movies, and novels, even if these are not the focus of most OA activists.

- OA serves the interests of many groups.
  - *Authors*: OA gives them a worldwide audience larger than that of any subscription-based journal, no matter how prestigious or popular, and demonstrably increases the visibility and impact of their work.

    http://opcit.eprints.org/oacitation-biblio.html

  - *Readers*: OA gives them barrier-free access to the literature they need for their research, unconstrained by the budgets of the libraries where they may have access privileges. OA increases reader reach and retrieval power. OA also gives barrier-free access to the *software* they use in their research. Free online literature is free online data for software that facilitates full-text searching, indexing, mining, summarizing, translating, querying, linking, recommending, alerting, "mash-ups" and other forms of processing and analysis.
  - *Teachers and students*: OA puts rich and poor on an equal footing for these key resources and eliminates the need for payments or permissions to reproduce and distribute content.
  - Libraries: OA solves the pricing crisis for scholarly journals. It also solves what I've called the permission crisis. OA also serves library interests in other, indirect ways. Librarians want to help users find the information they need, regardless of the budget-enforced limits on the library's own collection. Academic librarians want to help faculty increase their audience and impact, and help the university raise its research profile.

    https://en.wikipedia.org/wiki/Serials_crisis

    http://legacy.earlham.edu/~peters/writing/acrl.htm

  - *Universities*: OA increases the visibility of their faculty and research, reduces their expenses for journals, and advances their mission to share knowledge.
  - *Journals and publishers*: OA makes their articles more visible, discoverable, retrievable, and useful. If a journal is OA, then it can use this superior visibility to attract submissions and advertising, not to mention readers and citations. If a subscription-based journal provides OA to some of its content (e.g. selected articles in each issue, all back issues after a certain period, etc.), then it can use its increased visibility to attract all the same benefits plus subscriptions. If a journal permits OA through postprint archiving, then it has an edge in attracting authors over journals that do not permit postprint archiving. Of course subscription-based journals and their publishers have countervailing interests as well and often resist or oppose OA. But it oversimplifies the situation to think that *all* their interests pull against OA.

    http://legacy.earlham.edu/~peters/fos/newsletter/10-02-06.htm#quality

http://opcit.eprints.org/oacitation-biblio.html

http://web.archive.org/web/20031115185846/

http://www.biomedcentral.com/openaccess/archive/?page=features&issue=6

- *Funding agencies*: OA increases the return on their investment in research, making the results of the funded research more widely available, more discoverable, more retrievable, and more useful. When funding agencies disburse public funds, OA helps in a second way as well, by providing fundamental fairness to taxpayers or public access to the results of publicly-funded research.
- *Governments*: As funders of research, governments benefit from OA in all the ways that funding agencies do (see previous entry). OA also promotes democracy by sharing non-classified government information as widely as possible.
- *Citizens*: OA gives them access to peer-reviewed research, most of which is unavailable in public libraries, and gives them access to the research for which they have already paid through their taxes. But even those with no interest in reading this literature for themselves will benefit indirectly because researchers will benefit directly. OA accelerates not only research but the translation of research into new medicines, useful technologies, solved problems, and informed decisions that benefit everyone.

- OA in historical perspective:
  - Scholarly journals do not pay authors for their articles, and have not done so since the first journals were launched in London and Paris in 1665. (See Jean-Claude Guédon, In Oldenburg's Long Shadow.)

    http://www.arl.org/component/content/article/6/25988

  - Journals took off because they were more timely than books. For readers, journals were better than books for learning quickly about the recent work of others. For authors they were better than books for sharing new work quickly with the wider world and for establishing priority over other scientists working on the same problem. Journals gave authors the benefit of a fast, public time-stamp on their work. Because authors were rewarded in these strong, intangible ways, they accepted the fact that journals couldn't afford to pay them. Over time, journal revenue grew but authors continued in the tradition of writing articles for impact, not for money.
  - OA was physically and economically impossible in the age of print, even if the copyright holder wanted it. Prices were not only unavoidable for print journals, they were even affordable until the 1970's, when they began to rise faster than inflation. Journal subscription prices have risen nearly four times faster than inflation since 1986. Fortuitously, just as journal prices were becoming unbearable, the internet emerged to offer an alternative.

http://web.archive.org/web/20130617183513/

http://www.sparc.arl.org/bm~pix/journal-price-graph~s600x600.jpg

http://oad.simmons.edu/oadwiki/Timeline

- It doesn't matter whether we blame unaffordable journals on excessive publisher prices or inadequate library budgets. If we focus on publishers, it doesn't
  matter whether we blame greed or innocent market forces (rising costs and new
  services). Blame is irrelevant and distracting. The volume of published knowledge
  is growing exponentially and will always grow faster than library budgets. In
  that sense, OA scales with the growth of knowledge and toll access does
  not. We've already (long since) reached the point at which even affluent
  research institutions cannot afford access to the full range of research literature.
  Priced access to journal articles would not scale with the continuing, explosive
  growth of knowledge even if prices were low today and guaranteed to remain
  low forever.

http://legacy.earlham.edu/~peters/fos/newsletter/03-02-04.htm#scaling

http://legacy.earlham.edu/~peters/fos/2008/02/three-on-harvard-oa-mandate.
html

- The pricing crisis itself is just one factor in the rise of OA. Even if scholars did not
  turn to OA in order to bypass unaffordable access fees, they'd turn to it in order to
  take advantage of the internet as a powerful new technology for sharing knowledge instantly, with a worldwide audience, at zero marginal cost, in a digital form
  amenable to unlimited processing.
- For a schematic history of OA, see the OAD timeline of the OA movement.

http://oad.simmons.edu/oadwiki/Timeline

[...]
First put online June 21, 2004. Last revised June 28, 2015. [See the online version for
links to 10 translations.]

Removing the Barriers to Research: An Introduction to Open Access for Librarians

This essay was originally published in *College & Research Libraries News* 64 (February 2003): 92–94, 113. The original print edition was abridged. The edition reprinted here is from the unabridged online edition.

http://dash.harvard.edu/handle/1/3715477

The serials pricing crisis is now in its fourth decade. We're long past the point of damage control and into the era of damage. Prices limit access, and intolerable prices limit access intolerably. Every research institution in the world suffers from intolerable access limitations, no matter how wealthy. Not only must libraries cope by canceling subscriptions and cutting into their book budgets, but researchers must do without access to some of the journals critical to their research.

One might expect relief from digital technologies that allow the distribution of perfect copies at virtually no cost. But so far these technologies have merely caused panic among traditional publishers, who have reacted by laying a second crisis for libraries and researchers on top of the first. The new crisis is still in its first decade and doesn't yet have a name. Let me call it the *permission crisis*. It's the result of raising legal and technological barriers to limit how libraries may use the journals for which they have so dearly paid. The legal barriers arise from copyright law and licensing agreements (statutes and contracts). The technological barriers arise from digital rights management (DRM): software to block access by unauthorized users, sometimes with the help of special hardware. The permission crisis is a complex quadruple-whammy arising from statutes, contracts, hardware, and software.

I bring up these two crises because I will argue that *open access* will solve them both. Since the pricing crisis is already well-known, let me elaborate for a moment on the permission crisis. You know what you could do in a world in which the pricing crisis were solved. Here's what you could do in a world in which the permission crisis were solved:[1]

- You would own, not merely license, your own copies of electronic journals.
- You would have the right to archive them forever without special permission or periodic payments. Long-term preservation and access would not be limited to the actions taken by publishers, with future market potential in mind, but could be supplemented by independent library actions.
- If publishers did not migrate older content, such as the back runs of journals, to new media and formats to keep them readable as technology changed, then libraries would have the right to do it on their own.
- Access and usage would not be limited by password, IP address, usage hours, institutional affiliation, physical location, a cap on simultaneous users, or ability to pay. You would not have to authenticate users or administer proxy servers.
- You would have the right to lend and copy digital articles on any terms you liked to any users you liked. You could offer the same services to users affiliated with your institution, walk-in patrons, users at home, visiting faculty, and ILL users.
- Faculty and others could donate digital literature and software without violating their licenses, and you could accept them without limiting their usability.
- All use would be non-infringing use, and all use allowed by law would also be allowed by technology. There would be no need for fair-use judgment calls and their accompanying risk of liability. There would be no need to err on the side of non-use. Faculty could reproduce full-text for students without the delays, costs, or uncertainties of seeking permission.
- You would not have to negotiate, either as individual institutions or consortia, for prices or licensing terms. You would not have to remember, consult, or even retain, complex licensing agreements that differ from publisher to publisher and year to year.
- Users who object to cookies or registration would have the same access privileges as other users. Anonymous inquiry would be possible again for every user.
- You would never have to cancel a subscription due to a tight budget or unacceptable licensing terms. Researchers would not encounter gaps in the collection corresponding to journals with unacceptable prices or licensing terms.

The pricing crisis means that libraries must pay intolerable prices for journals. The permission crisis means that, even when they pay, libraries are hamstrung by licensing terms and software locks that prevent them from using electronic journals in the same full and free way that they may now use print journals. (In general, the pricing crisis applies to both print and electronic journals, while the permission crisis only applies to e-journals.)

Together the two crises mean that libraries are paying much more in order to get much less. Together the two crises severely impede research. This is not just a problem for libraries and researchers. When research is impeded, so are all the benefits of research—from medicines and technologies to environmental health, economic prosperity, and public safety.

Thesis 1. Both the pricing and permission crises can be solved at one stroke by open access.

Open-access literature is defined by two essential properties. First, it is free of charge to everyone. Second, the copyright holder has consented in advance to unrestricted reading, downloading, copying, sharing, storing, printing, searching, linking, and crawling.[2] The first property solves the pricing crisis. The second property solves the permission crisis.

Both properties depend on the will of the copyright holder. Most copyright holders want to charge for access to their work (erect price barriers) and block access to those who haven't paid (erect permission barriers). But this is dictated by their economic interests, not by copyright law. They have the right to make price and permission barriers disappear if they wish. The secret of open access is to keep copyright in the hands of those who desire open access. There is no need to abolish, reform, or violate copyright law. (Because open access carries the copyright holder's consent, it should never be described as "Napster for science.")

If scientists and scholars transfer their copyright to a traditional publisher, then the publisher will typically not consent to open access. On the contrary, traditional publishers erect price and permission barriers precisely to prevent open access. However, if authors retain copyright, then they will consent to open access, at least for the research articles for which they expect no payment. If they write for impact and not for money, then they want the widest possible dissemination of their work, which requires that their work be online free of charge and free of the usage limitations imposed by most licensing terms. Copyright holders who consent to open access will dispense with price and dispense with DRM.[3]

If open access reduces pricing and permission barriers to zero, then it clearly solves both crises. Moreover, it does so efficiently, completely, and lawfully. Other remedies to the same problems are either legally dubious, such as circumventing DRM, or arduous and incomplete, such as copyright reform or anti-trust action against publishing conglomerates.

If open access provides such an elegant solution to these otherwise intractable problems, then one may well wonder whether it is too good to be true. Can we put this theory into practice? Is it feasible? Is it quixotic?

Thesis 2. Open access is definitely attainable for scientific and scholarly journal literature, the body of literature primarily affected by the pricing and permission crises. It has already been attained for a growing portion of this literature.

Three facts make open access attainable for this special body of literature. First, authors of scientific and scholarly journal articles do not demand payment for their work. They willingly publish in journals that pay no royalties, and they have done so for three centuries. Second, the internet allows distribution of perfect copies at virtually no cost to a worldwide audience. We can seize rather than fear the opportunities it creates. Third, when the author retains copyright and consents to open access, then there are no legal barriers whatsoever to open access.

The only thing new here is the internet. In the age of print, open access was physically and economically impossible, even if the copyright holder wanted it. The cost of print publication was substantial and had to be recovered, so that journals necessarily existed behind a price barrier. Insofar as this limited access, the limitations were forgivable, even if harmful to research. But these limitations are no longer necessary, and hence, no longer excusable. As the Budapest Open Access Initiative[4] puts it, "An old tradition and a new technology have converged to make possible an unprecedented public good."

If it still sounds quixotic, consider what open-access proponents are *not* advocating. We do not call on scholars to shun priced or printed journals, either as authors, editors, referees, subscribers, or readers, nor do we call on libraries to cancel or deaccession them. We do not call for research literature to be put into the public domain or for the abolition of copyright. (For the narrow purpose of attaining open access, we do not even call for the reform of copyright.) We do not call for open access to anything other than scientific and scholarly research literature. For example, we do not call for open access to music, movies, or software. We do not even call for open access to all forms of scholarly literature, for example, books which their authors hope will generate revenue. The call is limited to peer-reviewed research articles and their preprints. We do not call for self-publishing to the internet, if that bypasses peer review. We do not call on libraries to change their serials policies, since they already take price into account alongside other criteria like usage and impact. We do not call for readers or libraries to boycott any kind of literature or any kind of publisher.

The attainability of open access depends on the key distinction between literature that authors consent to distribute without payment and literature on which authors hope to make money. All authors, artists, and creators have a right to make money from their work, and we do not criticize anyone for trying. But when authors choose to give their work away, then readers should get the full benefit of their generosity. Opening access to readers would also repay authors by giving them the enlarged audience and impact for which they sacrificed revenue. Intermediaries wishing to erect price and permission barriers between authors and readers serve neither, harm both, and enrich only themselves. Authors and readers should bypass them.

The internet makes this possible for the first time in history. This is true partly because of the nature of the internet and partly because of the nature of journal literature. Scholars write the articles, edit the journals, and provide the peer review. We can create the archives and launch the journals that finally give life to open access. Bypassing the price and permission barriers that obstruct research is entirely in our hands. If we had to persuade publishers to give up their revenue streams, or legislatures to reform copyright law, then we'd be no further along than we were in the age of print. But with the internet now at hand, open access depends only on the initiative of scholars.

In short, there is a serious problem, known best to librarians, and a beautiful solution, within the reach of scholars.

[...]

[O]pen-access archives and journals provide open access because the copyright holder authorizes it, not through a vigilante action that violates the copyright holder's will.

We do not call for open access to research articles because they are useful (as if everything useful should be free) or because their costs are low (as if everything inexpensive should be free). We call for open access to research articles because they have the relevant peculiarity that their authors write for impact, not for money, want the widest possible dissemination for their work, and consent to open access. Here is a body of work that is *very useful and very inexpensive*. It's not free to produce, but a very small subsidy will make possible a very large public good.

Who will pay this subsidy? Open-access archives can easily be supported by the institutions hosting them. The cost is trivial, and there is a direct benefit to any institution that hosts an archive for the research output of its faculty. Open-access journals have more substantial costs, but can cover them by charging the author's sponsor (employer or funder) rather than the reader's sponsor (library). It's novel for an institution to pay for outgoing articles rather than incoming articles, but it's natural to consider the cost of dissemination just another cost of research, and in the long run paying for dissemination will cost institutions much less than paying for access. Moreover, of course, the result is that the full cost of dissemination is covered so that worldwide access can be free of charge.

BioMed Central[10] is just one publisher proving that this business model can work for authors, readers, and their institutions. BMC proves that institutions will pay dissemination fees in order to enhance the impact of their employees' research, and to be spared access or subscription fees to the same literature. It also proves that open-access publishing can do more than cover its costs: it can actually generate a profit. Open-access publishers can also sell priced add-ons to the essential literature, provided that the essential full-text literature is still free of pricing and permission barriers.[11]

Open-access methods of funding journals are novel but already in use and proving themselves. However, if the novelty causes trepidation, then by all means compare these methods carefully to the "tried and true" model we are using today, which takes literature written by authors donating their labor, and vetted by editors donating their labor, and locks it away behind price and permission barriers so that even the world's wealthiest institutions cannot assure their faculty full access to it. This is not done for the sake of long-term preservation, since the permission barriers worsen the problems of preservation. It's not done to profit authors, readers, or their institutions, since it harms all three, but to profit third parties with no creative role in the research or the writing.

The benefit of open access to libraries is solving the pricing and permission crises. The benefit to scholars, beyond the benefit to libraries, is giving readers barrier-free access to the literature they need, and giving authors larger audiences and greater impact. Because the benefits on both sides are immense, librarians and scholars should work together to bring open access, step by step, to every institution and discipline.

There's a lot that librarians can do[12] and a lot that scholars can do[13] to help this cause. If I'm right that librarians have the best understanding of the problem, and that scholars control the solution, then collaboration is highly desirable. Journal publishers have shrewdly seen an opportunity to make money even in the age of the internet, and have seized it. However, their business strategy limits access to knowledge and slows research. In response, let's be as shrewd as the publishers. The internet has given scholars and librarians an unprecedented opportunity to save money and advance their interests at the same time. We should simply seize it. What are waiting for?

Notes

1. This list only applies to the literature *for which* the permission crisis is solved. In my terms, it only applies to open-access literature, not to all literature. The items in the list overlap somewhat, not only with one another, but with items bearing on the solution to the pricing crisis.

2. The only constraint that authors might want to enforce is that no one should distribute mangled or misattributed copies. This is a reason for authors to retain copyright. Authors who don't care to enforce these constraints, or who live in moral-rights countries where they are enforceable even without copyright, could put their works into the public domain.

3. Some friends of open access want to use DRM in harmless forms—forms that do not restrict access—in order to measure traffic and provide data for usage and impact analysis.

4. Budapest Open Access Initiative.

http://www.soros.org/openaccess/

10. BioMed Central.

http://www.biomedcentral.com/

11. For more on the funding model for open-access journals, see Budapest Open Access Initiative FAQ

http://www.earlham.edu/~peters/fos/boaifaq.htm

Peter Suber, "Where Does the Free Online Scholarship Movement Stand Today?" *Cortex*, 38, 2 (April 2002), pp. 261–264.

http://www.earlham.edu/~peters/writing/cortex.htm

Excerpt: "There are many successful and sustainable examples in our economy in which some pay for all, and those who pay are moved by generosity, self-interest, or some combination. Either way, they willingly pay to make a product or service free for everyone rather than pay only for their own private access or consumption. This funding model, which works so well in industries with much higher expenses [such as television and radio], will work even better in an economic sector with the nearly unique property that producers donate their labor and intellectual property, and are moved by the desire to make a contribution to knowledge rather than a desire for personal profit."

Peter Suber, "Open Access to the Scientific Journal Literature," *Journal of Biology* 1 (1) (June 2002): 3f.

http://www.earlham.edu/~peters/writing/jbiol.htm

Excerpt: "Publishers adopt open access not to make a charitable donation or political statement, but to provide free online access to a body of literature, accelerate research in that field, create opportunities for sophisticated indexing and searching, help readers by making new work easier to find and retrieve, and help authors by enlarging their audience and increasing their impact. If these benefits were expensive to produce, they would nevertheless be worth paying for —but it turns out that open access can cost much less than traditional forms of dissemination. For journals that dispense with print, with subscription management, and with software to block online access to non-subscribers, open access can cost significantly less than traditional publication, creating the compelling combination of increased distribution and reduced cost."

12. Details on what librarians can do:
What librarians can do to facilitate open access in general

http://www.soros.org/openaccess/help.shtml#libraries

What librarians can do to facilitate eprint archiving in particular

http://www.eprints.org/self-faq/#libraries-do

Answering some library-specific questions and objections about open-access, reprinted in Walt Crawford's Cites and Insights, November, 2002, pp. 12–14,

http://citesandinsights.info/civ2i14.pdf

[*Added 2/1/03*. The BioMed Central open-access advocacy kit for librarians

http://www.biomedcentral.com/info/about/advocacy?for=librarians]

[*Added 2/1/03*. When librarians write scholarly papers, they should post the preprints and if possible the postprints in open-access archives. There are two devoted to library and information science:

E-LIS (E-Prints in Library and Information Science)

http://eprints.rclis.org/

DLIST (Digital Library of Information Science and Technology)

http://dlist.sir.arizona.edu/]

13. Details on what scholars can do:
What scholars can do to facilitate open access in general

http://www.soros.org/openaccess/help.shtml#scholars

What scholars can do to facilitate eprint archiving in particular

http://www.eprints.org/self-faq/#researcher/authors-do

Two sources for both librarians and scholars (both already cited in note 11):
Answering questions and objections about open access in general (the BOAI FAQ)

http://www.earlham.edu/~peters/fos/boaifaq.htm

Answering the eight most common questions and objections about open access

http://www.earlham.edu/~peters/writing/jbiol.htm

[*Added 2/1/03*. The BioMed Central open-access advocacy kit for researchers

http://www.biomedcentral.com/info/about/advocacy?for=researchers]

I'd like to thank Neal Baker, Denise Troll Covey, Tom Kirk, Stephanie Orphan, and Vicky Reich for helpful comments on an earlier draft of this article.

I put this article online January 21, 2003. Subsequent additions are enclosed in brackets and dated.

http://www.earlham.edu/~peters/writing/acrl.htm

The Taxpayer Argument for Open Access

From "The taxpayer argument for open access," SPARC Open Access Newsletter, September 4, 2003.

http://dash.harvard.edu/handle/1/4725013

There are many arguments for open access. Let's focus here on just one: the argument that taxpayers have a right to open access to the results of the research funded by their taxes.

If the research papers based on taxpayer-funded research are locked away in conventional journals that require payments for access, then taxpayers will end up paying twice for the same research. The primary version of the argument is that it would be wrong to make taxpayers pay a second fee for access. A secondary version of the argument is that tax money should be spent in the public interest, not to create intellectual property for the benefit of private publishers, who acquire it and profit from it without paying the authors or compensating the public treasury. Both versions of the argument object that taxpayers are paying twice when they shouldn't have to. The first version of the argument focuses on overpayment, while the second focuses on misuse of one or both payments.

A third form of the argument holds that the current U.S. rule to put the works of tax-paid government employees into the public domain (Section 105 of the Copyright Act) should be extended to the works of tax-paid government contractors and grantees. It holds that the arguments for our current policy also apply to this extension of the policy, so that it would be inconsistent to support the current policy and oppose its extension. I won't examine this third form of the argument here. Other aspects of the argument take all my space, and I dealt with some of these issues in SOAN for 7/4/02.

http://www.earlham.edu/~peters/fos/newsletter/07-04-03.htm

Here are five objections to the taxpayer argument and at least five replies. My purpose is to clarify the argument, identify its strong and weak forms, and show where it comes to an end and must be supplemented by other arguments for open access.

(1) Objection: Taxpayers can walk into a library that has paid for access, and read journal articles without paying to do so. Or they can receive copies of the articles by interlibrary loan. We already have free access by taxpayers to taxpayer-funded research, and to most other research as well.

Reply: This is free public access to a paid copy. The subscribing library had to pay retail to make this access possible, and to do so it had to forgo many other purchases. Moreover, of course, the library payment is on top of the previous taxpayer payment.

So this kind of access is a red herring that does not answer the taxpayer argument or fill the need for open access. In addition, most public libraries don't subscribe to a good range of scientific and scholarly research journals, and most academic libraries (according to W. Wayt Gibbs) are cutting back the access privileges they accord to "walk-in" patrons not affiliated with the institution.

W. Wayt Gibbs, "Public Not Welcome: Libraries cut off access to scientific literature," *Scientific American*, August 11, 2003.

http://www.sciam.com/article.cfm?articleID=000380BE-160C-1F30-9AD380A84189F2 D7&pageNumber=1&catID=2

[...]

(2) Objection: Open access to federally funded research will only affect a subset of the scientific and scholarly journal literature. Federal funding supports the natural sciences much more than the social sciences and humanities, and some natural sciences much more than others. Why is open access to one field's results more important than open access to another field's results?

Reply: The taxpayer argument is that *at least* the government-funded research should be open access, not that *only* this research should be open access. It's about fairness to taxpayers, not fairness to the disciplines. Moreover, there's no harm in solving a large problem one step at a time, especially if different steps have different justifications. Finally, there are many arguments for open access, and some of them (as we all know) apply to all the disciplines even if the taxpayer argument does not.

The taxpayer argument does not intrinsically distinguish among the disciplines, and does not imply that some are more important than others. Instead, it applies to any research that is funded by taxes. It's contingent on what research falls into this category and the taxpayer argument, by itself, is indifferent to the policies that determine which disciplines and research projects get funded. If tax dollars only funded research in one narrow specialization, such as the history of the umbrella, then the taxpayer argument would only require open access to that narrow band of research. Conversely, if all research were funded by taxes, then the taxpayer argument would require open access to all of it.

(3) Objection: When the government gives a research grant, it is funding the research itself, and perhaps the writing of articles based on that research. But the journal is charging for value it adds to that research and writing: peer review, copy editing, manuscript preparation, marketing, and publishing. So while subscription fees are additional payments, they don't pay for the same thing as the government research grant.

Reply: This is true. If the taxpayer argument is that federal research grants and journal subscription fees pay for the very same product, then it's mistaken. Some who speak loosely might make this mistake. But most who use the argument take it in a slightly different direction. They argue that the primary value of a journal article lies in the research and writing. When taxpayers have already paid for this primary value, then their access to the resulting journal article should not be held hostage to secondary expenses, at least when some of these are unnecessary, some are overpriced, and the rest can be subsidized so that they needn't become access barriers for readers.

Note three particular aspects of this refinement of the argument.

First, even if all its assertions are true, it depends on open-access arguments (such as the adequacy of upfront funding) that go beyond the taxpayer argument. In that sense the taxpayer argument is limited in scope and must be combined with other open-access arguments to take us all the way to the conclusion.

Second, it concedes that journals add value to the author's research and writing. I only pause to point this out because publishers often overlook the fact that open-access proponents agree with them about this. Open-access proponents might even concede that journals add value in every way that publishers say they do. However, open-access proponents tend to argue that some of these journal services are more essential than others, even if all are valuable, that they cost less than most journals charge for them, that it's better to cover the costs of the essential services from the author's end of the transaction than the reader's end, and therefore that they do not justify access barriers. Open-access proponents and commercial publishers may never agree on these four propositions. But debating them takes us well beyond the taxpayer argument.

Third, when the taxpayer argument is applied to archives rather than journals, then it doesn't face the same limitation and doesn't need the support of other open-access arguments. Open-access archives don't perform peer review, copy editing, manuscript preparation, marketing, or publishing. [...]

Sometimes the taxpayer argument is restated so that it is about ownership rather than access. The Public Library of Science used to argue that parents should pay the midwife but then keep the baby, or that the midwife should accept payment but then return the baby. The analogous taxpayer argument is that taxpayers *own* the research they fund, and that the midwife-publisher should be paid for services rendered, not for access by the owner to what it owns. Moreover, the midwife can be fully compensated without transferring title to the baby. [...]

When refined to avoid an obvious mistake, then, the taxpayer argument concedes that subscription fees and government research grants do not pay for the same goods. Hence, it doesn't object that taxpayers pay twice for the same goods. It objects that one payment ought to suffice—and, under a better publishing system, would suffice. The second payment isn't a duplicate of the first, but either a needless access barrier (because the expenses it covers can recouped in other ways) or an improper one (because it gives midwives improper control of the baby, and private-sector enterprises improper control of a public investment).

Note how refining the argument has led us to shift from its primary form (about avoiding duplicate payments) to its secondary form (about spending tax money in the public interest).

[...]

(4) Objection: At best, the taxpayer argument supports open access for taxpayers, not open access for the whole world. If access can be open for one nation and closed to other nations, then that's as far as this argument compels us to go. In fact, if we could fine-tune access even further, and limit it to those citizens who actually paid taxes and deny it to fellow citizens who didn't, then the taxpayer argument would not stop us.

Reply: This is a fascinating objection whose strength depends on a complicated combination of other government policies and empirical facts about profit and loss. In short, if enforcing this access barrier costs less than it brings in, then the taxpayer argument has no objection to it; but otherwise, the taxpayer argument requires that we remove the barrier and provide open access to the whole world.

Leave aside the problem that "open access" to one country and not others isn't really "open access." The question is what the taxpayer argument implies, not what the term "open access" implies.

First note how this logic has been applied in Canada. The Canadian government supports the National Research Council (NRC), which supports the NRC Research Press, which publishes 15 peer-reviewed journals. On January 1, 2001, Canada adopted the policy that Canadians should have free online access to these 15 journals, while citizens of other countries would have to pay. The free access for Canadians is funded by the Depository Services Program, a public-private partnership funded in part by the Canadian Treasury Board.

I wish I knew whether the 15 NRC journals only publish research funded by Canadian taxpayers, whether the DSP has arranged the free online access by buying it from the NRC Press at retail prices, whether all or only some of the funding for Canadian access comes from Canadian taxpayers, and whether the cost of limiting open access to Canadians is offset by subscriptions from non-Canadians. Unfortunately, I don't know any of these things.

But what's interesting is that the taxpayer argument seems to entail no more than the nation-limited kind of open access that Canada has arranged. Moreover, there seem to be good reasons for the limitation. If the argument is that the taxpayers who funded certain research shouldn't pay twice, then it aims to protect those taxpayers, not foreigners and others who didn't pay to fund the research. If the argument is that tax money should be spent in the public interest, then it probably applies only to the national interest. The world interest may trump the national interest in ethics, but tax policy is a peculiar domain in which taxpayers can have good reasons to favor themselves over other and larger populations.

Against these arguments is the simple fact that it *costs less* to provide unrestricted access to all internet users than to discriminate between authorized and unauthorized users and block access to the unauthorized. If taxpayers deserve open access, then they deserve it without paying extra for the apparatus to block others.

Behind this we see the familiar reasons why open-access journals have lower expenses than conventional journals. They dispense with subscription management, password registration, and authentication filters.

Why should Canadians pay for open access by other countries? Here's an analogy. An insurance company might buy a radio advertisement that it knows will be broadcast to a cluster of states, including a state where it does no business. If the technology existed to block the transmission to states where it does no business, the company would have no interest in paying extra to use it. The company's interest is in saving money and getting its message to a certain audience. From its point of view, over-distribution is harmless, and only under-distribution is harmful. If over-distribution costs less than precise distribution, then it's a bargain. This line of reasoning should carry even more weight for nations funding open access to research papers, which are useful across all boundaries.

So this branch of the taxpayer argument—for worldwide rather than merely national access—reduces to the venerable one that, other things being equal, the government should take the lowest acceptable bid. It should not pay more than necessary for the goods that policy has decided the public should have. This direct, practical argument means that we don't even have to reach the more nuanced, ethical argument that we should always prefer to buy two goods for the price of one, when we can, even if one of the goods will be enjoyed by people other than ourselves. But the second argument is as valid as the first. We should not spitefully deny others a costless benefit or a benefit that costs no more than what we would have spent on ourselves.

But what if the cost isn't the same? What if the access-limiting apparatus paid for itself in subscription fees from non-citizens? That would mean that ordinary bean counting would entail nation-limited access, without a whiff of nationalism or spite.

When access-limiting apparatus pays for itself in subscription fees, then it does nullify the cost argument for worldwide access. In fact, it would even reverse the cost argument insofar as this apparatus would then be a means for reducing the cost of national open access.

Canadians who want free access to the 15 NRC journals must go to a certain Web site and register their IP address and ISP. Presumably software at the NRC journals then checks user IP addresses against this national registry. This is expensive compared to putting the same articles on the web without all this armor. Because Canadians could get open access without this extra investment, we should ask what the extra investment brings them. The answer is "nothing at all"—unless subscriptions bought by non-Canadians reduce the price that Canadians pay for their own open access.

A country that paid for its own open access through fees charged to outsiders would be putting economic efficiency ahead of the public good from public knowledge. This might run afoul of other policy-based arguments for open access, but we must acknowledge that it would not run afoul of the taxpayer argument.

Canada's National Research Council (NRC)

http://www.nrc-cnrc.gc.ca/

NRC Research Press journals

http://pubs.nrc-cnrc.gc.ca/cgi-bin/rp/rp2_jour_e

Canadian government's Depository Services Program (DSP)

http://web.archive.org/web/20030810183747/

http://dsp-psd.communication.gc.ca/index-e.htm

Web form for Canadians to fill out to get free online access through the DSP to the NRC Research Press journals

http://web.archive.org/web/20030826062654/

http://dsp-psd.communication.gc.ca/NRC-CNR/aide-e.html

FAQ on free access for Canadians

http://web.archive.org/web/20030805000908/

http://igci.gc.ca/NRC-CNR/faq_journals-e.html

Press release announcing the free online access for Canadians, June 18, 2000 (the free access began January 1, 2001)

http://web.archive.org/web/20031104164600/

http://dsp-psd.communication.gc.ca/INFODEP/Avis/00/0107-e.html

(5) Objection: Ordinary taxpayers don't need to read peer-reviewed scientific literature and wouldn't understand it if they did. Researchers would benefit from access to this literature, but they form a small subset of taxpayers.

Reply: This may be true (more below), but it's beside the point. The taxpayer argument doesn't say that taxpayers should have open access because they need it, or because it would be useful to them; it says they should have open access because they've paid for it. If you buy a house, you should be allowed to enter, even if someone can argue that you didn't really need to buy it.

Of course other open-access arguments assert that open access is useful. Indeed the usefulness or public good argument is the main argument. [...But] even the argument from usefulness or the public good needn't assert that open access is equally useful to every kind of person or that everything useful ought to be free.

When Martin Sabo and some PLoS members use the taxpayer argument, they emphasize the value of open access for individual patients suffering from serious diseases, or the value of open access for relatives and friends browsing on their behalf. This is a weak form of the argument that invites the present objection. Unfortunately it often crowds out a much stronger version of the argument that could have been used in its place.

This form of the argument is weak because, in fact, most individuals don't need to read peer-reviewed medical literature and wouldn't be able to understand it. It's even weaker if it puts more weight on the emotional drama of one person's story rather than the evidence added by that story to the total case for the conclusion. It's a judgment call whether a given rendering of the argument crosses this fine line.

Rick Weiss opened his August 5 story in the *Washington Post* with an anecdote about an ill child in a poor family. In the following days, participants on the SSP discussion list ripped Weiss for making such a bald appeal to emotion. Quoting one post: "I find it disgusting and reprehensible that certain proponents of open access are preying on the fears of families and holding out the false hope that cures for devastating chronic illness may lie in the pages of hard-to-find medical journals." The problem is not that open-access proponents are opening themselves to this kind of criticism, or that the SSP list is predominantly pro-publisher and anti-OA. The problem is that for some open-access rhetoric, the criticism is justified.

The argument from individual sufferers is only a fallacious appeal to hope and fear if it puts more than an anecdote's worth of weight on the emotional anecdotes it tells. But it needn't be fallacious at all. There are individuals without medical training who can understand some peer-reviewed medical literature and who benefit from reading it first-hand, and it's undeniably true that open access will help realize this benefit.

I am one such person. I've used online medical research (some open access, some through the licenses bought by my college) for myself and for close relatives. I've used it for serious illnesses and for a slew of minor questions ranging from diet to fitness. I often learn more from this first-hand reading than I learned from my family doctor, and often explore issues that I wouldn't bother to raise with my doctor. I'm grateful for the access that made this research and exploration possible. The point is not that I'm rare, but that this benefit is small compared to the benefit of open access *for researchers*.

It's small even if there are a lot of people like me who benefit from doing their own online research. It's small even if we place a great value, as I do, on the benefits of first-hand reading and research.

The reason is simply that open access by medical researchers will help everyone by accelerating the progress of medicine, while open access by individual sufferers will only help a much smaller number of people and in much less significant ways. Both benefits are real. But when making the case for open access, let's lead with the strongest version of the argument, not the most sentimental. We don't have to be silent about other, lesser benefits. But we invite misunderstanding and criticism when we lead with the lesser benefits and leave the impression that there are no larger ones.

Rick Weiss, "A Fight for Free Access To Medical Research Online Plan Challenges Publishers' Dominance," *Washington Post,* August 5, 2013.

http://www.washingtonpost.com/wp-dyn/articles/A19104-2003Aug4.html

The SSP list (from the AAP)

http://lists.resourcenter.net/read/?forum=ssp-

[...]

Conclusion

The taxpayer argument can be misleading. It seems to say that government research grants and journal subscription fees duplicate one another. But they don't and a careful form of the argument will acknowledge this. It seems to imply that open access is required only for taxpayers, not the world, but this depends on some empirical contingencies that will differ from place to place and time to time. It can locate the benefit of open access in individual taxpayers who suddenly gain access to peer-reviewed medical literature, or it can locate it in the gain to everyone when open access accelerates the progress of medicine and the other sciences. When stripped of mistaken assertions and disentangled from other arguments for open access, the argument can answer the objections raised against it. It is stronger when cast as an argument about spending tax money in the public interest than when cast as an argument against duplicate payments or overspending. It is stronger still when combined with other arguments for open access. On its own, it is stronger for open-access archives than open-access journals. When combined with other arguments, it may be equally strong for both, depending on how you judge the other, non-taxpayer arguments for open access.
[...]

"It's the Authors, Stupid!"

From "'It's the authors, stupid!'" *SPARC Open Access Newsletter*, June 2, 2004.

http://dash.harvard.edu/handle/1/4391161

Of all the groups that want open access to scientific and scholarly research literature, only one is in a position to deliver it: authors. There are three reasons why:

- Authors decide whether to submit their work to OA journals.
- Authors decide whether to deposit their work in OA archives.
- Authors decide whether to transfer copyright.

If you support OA, then the good news is that authors don't need anyone else's permission or cooperation to provide OA to their own work. The bad news is that research authors are notoriously anarchical and do not act as a bloc. If you oppose OA, then simply switch the good news and the bad.

So even though readers, libraries, universities, foundations, and governments want OA for their own reasons, most of what they can do to promote OA takes the form of guiding, helping, or nudging authors. In this sense, authors have primacy in the campaign for OA, and the single largest obstacle to OA is author inertia or omission.

Once we recognize this, we will focus on four author-centric strategies for achieving OA:

(1) Educate authors about OA
(2) Help authors provide OA to their work
(3) Remove disincentives for authors to provide OA to their work
(4) Create incentives for authors to provide OA to their work

Let's consider these in order.

(1) Educate authors about OA

Author inertia or omission is not a sign of opposition. Usually it is a sign of ignorance or inattention. Most scientists and scholars are too preoccupied with their research to know what open access is—even today, after years of rising public recognition. This is harmful to OA, to science, and to the authors themselves, but it's hard to criticize directly. Research faculty are good at what they do because they are absorbed in their projects and have extraordinary talents for shutting out distractions. We're coping here with a side-effect of this strength, not with a simple weakness.

A new ALPSP study shows that 82% of senior researchers (4,000 thousand in 97 countries) knew "nothing" or just "a little" about OA. Even if the numbers are better for junior faculty, we clearly have a long way to go just to educate the scientists and scholars themselves.

http://web.archive.org/web/20041106175838/

http://ciber.soi.city.ac.uk/ciber-pa-report.pdf

Talk to your colleagues about OA. Talk to them on campus and at conferences. Talk to them to them in writing through the journals and newsletters that serve your field. Talk to your students, the authors of tomorrow.

If you have provided OA to your own work, talk to your colleagues about your experience. Firsthand testimonials from trusted colleagues are much more effective than policy arguments, even good policy arguments. They are also more effective with this audience than advice from librarians or university administrators, even good advice. The chief problem is getting the attention of busy colleagues and showing them that this matters for their research impact and career. Only researchers can do this for other researchers.

A surprising number of OA converts—I'm one—didn't go beyond understanding to enthusiasm until they provided OA to their own writings and saw for themselves, sometimes suddenly, the signs of rising impact. There is a discernible increase in email from serious readers, inclusions in course syllabi, links from online indices, invitations to important conferences, and citations from other publications. When you experience this in your own case, it's anecdotal but compelling. When you hear it from a trusted colleague, it makes a difference.

If you don't have time for sustained campaigning, then at least respond to misunderstandings. Don't let damaging myths circulate without correction. When someone says that OA bypasses peer review or violates copyright, correct them. When someone says that OA is naive because "there's no free lunch," point out that no OA advocate ever said that providing OA was without expense. (The question is whether there are better ways to cover those expenses than by charging readers or their libraries for access.)

The best compendium of common myths about OA, decisively corrected, is by BioMed Central.

http://www.biomedcentral.com/about/advocacy12/

Let's say that x is the percentage of publishing scientists and scholars who have already provided OA to at least some of their writings. To jumpstart progress significantly, we don't need x to rise to 100 or even 50. We need the percentage of publishing scientists and scholars *who have heard about the benefits of OA firsthand from a trusted colleague* to rise to 2x. If 5–10% of university faculty publish 80% of the articles, then a slight widening of the current circle will encompass a critical mass of authors.

Many scholars are not at all ignorant of OA, but say they are just too busy to take the steps to provide it for their own research articles. I'm sympathetic, because full-time teacher-researchers *are* very busy. But I'm not very sympathetic. Scholars who have time to do research and write it up don't begrudge this time, because this is work they love. But if they get this far, then they always find time for follow-up steps that they do not love: submitting the articles to journals and responding to referee comments. Finally, they always seem to have time to bring their published articles to the attention of department chairs, deans, promotion and tenure committees, and colleagues in the field. Scholars find the time for these steps because they are passionate about their research, because they want to share it with others, and (for the unloved steps) because they see the connection between them and career-building.

Providing OA to our work is career-building. The benefits to others are significant, but dwelling on them might have drawn attention away from the strong self-interest that authors have in OA. Get the attention of your colleagues and make this point. OA is about barrier-free sharing of research results with colleagues worldwide. This enlarges our audience and increases our impact. Anyone who takes half an hour to email an updated bibliography to the department chair or to snail-mail offprints to colleagues on other campuses should take five minutes to deposit a new article in an open-access archive or institutional repository. Enlighten your colleagues.

(2) Help authors provide OA to their work

Even when scholars see the connection between OA and research impact, they have to set priorities. It's not surprising that they give new research priority over enhancing the dissemination of old research, or that they give work with near deadlines priority over work with no deadlines. Here is where concrete help comes in.

Librarians can help faculty members deposit their work in an open-access, OAI-compliant archive, such as the university's institutional repository. It doesn't matter whether authors need help because they are too busy, because they are intimidated by metadata, or because their past work is voluminous or pre-digital. Librarians can help them digitize and deposit it. In most cases, student library workers can help in the same way.

Universities can help by providing the funds to pay librarians or student workers to provide this kind of help. They can help by paying the processing fees charged by OA journals when funding agencies will not do so. They can help by offering workshops on how authors can retain the rights they need to authorize OA. They can help by suggesting model language for authors to use in copyright transfer agreements.

(3) Remove disincentives for authors to provide OA to their work

When Franz Ingelfinger was the editor of the *New England Journal of Medicine*, he adopted a policy not to accept any article that had previously been published or publicized elsewhere. As the policy spread to other journals, it became known as the Ingelfinger Rule. It seems to be in decline nowadays, but it's hard to tell because many journals do not say explicitly on their web sites whether or not they follow the rule. The rule, and the uncertainty about where it applies, deter authors from depositing their preprints in OA archives. Researchers who proudly disregard the risk that their work will offend church and state flee from the risk that preprint archiving will disqualify their work for later publication in a peer-reviewed journal.

The best way for journals to remove this disincentive is to abandon or modify the Ingelfinger Rule and to say so publicly. Journals only have to modify the rule enough to let authors take advantage of online preprint exchanges. They can still refuse to consider submissions that have been formally published elsewhere. The second best way for journals to remove this disincentive is to make their policies clear and explicit on their web sites so that authors can make informed decisions about the risks. Authors in fields where the rule is rare, or who have no plans to submit their work to journals where it is still in force, will then have the confidence to provide OA to their preprints.

Promotion and tenure committees (P&T committees) create a disincentive for submitting work to OA journals when they only reward work published in a certain set of high-impact journals. The problem is that most OA journals are new and don't yet have impact factors. When a committee makes impact factor a necessary condition for review, then it discriminates against new journals, even excellent new journals. It not only discriminates against new journals trying out a new business and distribution model, but against journals exploring a new research niche or methodology. The problem is not the committee's attempt to weed out the second-rate. The problem is doing it badly, with a crude criterion, so that the committee also rules out much that is first-rate.

Administrators who understand this problem can set policy for their P&T committees. Faculty who understand this problem can volunteer to serve on the committee.

Foundations that fund research are often as blinkered as P&T committees, even if the same foundations try to support OA through other policies. If they tend to award grants only to applicants who have published in the usual small set of high-impact journals, then they deter authors from publishing in OA journals, even while they show support by offering to pay the processing fees charged by OA journals.

(4) Create incentives for authors to provide OA to their work

Universities can create an incentive by requiring OA to all the research articles that faculty would like the P&T committee to consider. Because this can be done through OA archives, it is compatible with publishing the same articles in conventional, subscription-based journals. The policy needn't limit the freedom of authors to publish in any journal that will accept their work.

Funding agencies, public and private, can create an incentive for authors by requiring OA to the results of the funded research. They should let authors choose between OA archives and OA journals, and should make reasonable exceptions, e.g., for classified research and patentable discoveries.

Authors would not oppose these steps. A February 2004 study by JISC and OSI found (pp. 56–57) that when authors are asked "how they would feel if their employer or funding body required them to deposit copies of their published articles in one or more [open-access] repositories … [t]he vast majority, even of the non-OA author group, said they *would do so willingly*." (Italics in original.)

http://www.jisc.ac.uk/uploaded_documents/JISCOAreport1.pdf

Finally, we could provide a significant incentive for authors if we could make OA journals as prestigious as conventional journals of the same quality. Unfortunately, it's easier to control a journal's actual excellence than its reputed excellence, and prestige is all about reputed excellence. One way to boost prestige is to recruit eminent scholars to serve on the editorial board, a method used effectively by *PLoS Biology* and BMC's *Journal of Biology*. Another way is for eminent scholars who are beyond the reach of myopic P&T committees to submit new, excellent work to OA journals. This will tend to break the vicious circle by which new OA journals need excellent submissions to build prestige, and need prestige to attract excellent submissions.

Conclusion

[…] I make no claim that authors are the only ones to benefit from OA or that their reasons for wanting it are the only reasons for wanting it. Nor do I claim that it's more important for authors to solve their problems (in achieving visibility and impact) than for other stakeholders to solve their problems (libraries regaining control of their serials budgets, funders increasing the return on their investment in research, or taxpayers gaining access to the results of taxpayer-funded research). Nor do I claim that OA is more effective in helping authors advance their interests than it is in helping, say, libraries, foundations, or democratic governments advance theirs. Since OA will serve the interests of many groups in many ways, there is no need to rank or choose among these interests. Let's just work for OA and advance all their interests at the same time.

But thinking about how to achieve OA is different from thinking about who benefits or by how much. It's when we think about how to achieve OA that we must recognize the primacy of authors. Many groups suffer from dysfunctions in the current system of scholarly communication, but authors are at the frontline of control over the solution. Author decisions will affect the degree to which we achieve OA and the rate at which we achieve it.

It does not follow that we should only appeal to authors. Rather, we should focus first on authors and the institutions in a position to influence authors. If we limit our appeal to authors, then we will sacrifice the power of a wide partnership of stakeholders, not to mention powerful ways to influence authors themselves. If we overlook authors, or focus first on another group, like publishers, then we will miss precious opportunities to realize the benefits of OA for everyone.

A revised and abridged version of this article was published as "The Primacy of Authors in Achieving Open Access," *Nature*, June 10, 2004.

http://www.nature.com/nature/focus/accessdebate/24.html

The present version of the article borrows some, but not all, of the revisions from the *Nature* version.

Six Things That Researchers Need to Know about Open Access

From "Six things that researchers need to know about open access," *SPARC Open Access Newsletter*, February 2, 2006.

http://dash.harvard.edu/handle/1/4739013

When I was a graduate student, my elders never took me aside to pass on the secrets of academic publishing. I hope this failure isn't widespread, and simply reflects on my discipline, my school, my decade, or perhaps even my elders. Today's graduate students deserve a more effective rite of passage. But even if they're told all they need to know about in-journals and out-journals (at least by the standards of their elders), publishing contracts, submissions etiquette, turn-around time, referee behavior, citation politics, impact factors, and perishing, I know they're not told all they need to know about open access. Here's a brief attempt to remedy that. [...]

Readers of this newsletter shouldn't find anything new here. But if you want a short list of what your colleagues (junior and senior) need to know, I hope this will fit the bill. We'll know we're making progress if we can shorten this list every year until it disappears.

(1) What OA journals exist in your field?

When "presented with a list of reasons why they have not chosen to publish in an OA journal and asked to say which were important ... [t]he reason that scored highest (70%) was that authors were not familiar enough with OA journals in their field." Alma Swan and Sheridan Brown, "Authors and Open Access Publishing," *Learned Publishing*, July 2004, p. 220.

http://eprints.ecs.soton.ac.uk/11003/

There's no excuse not to know the OA journals in your field. Go to the DOAJ and browse by discipline.

http://www.doaj.org/

Some of the journals you find may not meet your standards for prestige or impact. But others might. According to the ISI's own studies, nearly every scientific discipline has an OA journal in the top cohort of impact factors.

http://www.isinet.com/media/presentrep/acropdf/impact-oa-journals.pdf (April 2004)

http://www.isinet.com/media/presentrep/essayspdf/openaccesscitations2.pdf (October 2004)

If you learn what OA journals exist in your field and decide against each of them, all right. At least you made an informed decision. But check the DOAJ again when you've written your next paper. Things are changing fast. Established OA journals are growing in prestige; some are getting impact factors; new OA journals are being launched; non-OA journals are converting to full OA or OA hybrid models; and non-OA journals are experimenting with different forms of OA.

If you don't publish in an OA journal, you can publish in a non-OA journal and self-archive the peer-reviewed version of your manuscript in an OA repository. About 70% of existing non-OA journals already permit this. More in #4 below.

(2) OA journals are not the whole story of OA. There are also OA archives or repositories.

When people hear about OA for the first time, they tend to take away that OA journals are the way to deliver it. Even when they hear a two-sided presentation that gives equal attention to OA journals and OA repositories, they tend to remember the part about OA journals and forget the part about OA repositories. Sometimes a policy proposal may be about nothing but OA repositories and some readers will still think it's about OA journals. Sometimes this happens even when the readers have with Ph.D.s.

This is puzzling and harmful. Part of the explanation is that we assimilate new ideas to older and more familiar ideas, and we already understand what journals are. But try to shake yourself loose from this assimilation—or shake your colleagues loose from it. There are two primary vehicles of OA, not just one. OA repositories don't perform peer review; they merely make their contents freely available to the world. But they can contain peer-reviewed postprints as easily unrefereed preprints. You can deposit a preprint at the time you submit it to a journal and then deposit the postprint after it's published. You can deposit your postprint in an OA repository even if you also publish it in a conventional or non-OA journal. Don't let the novelty of OA repositories make them invisible. Don't believe that if the concept is too good to be true then it can't be true.

The best places to look for OA repositories are the Registry of Open Access Repositories (ROAR) and OpenDOAR (Directory of Open Access Repositories).

http://roar.eprints.org/

http://www.opendoar.org/

Here's more detail on the distinction between OA journals and OA archives or repositories.

http://www.earlham.edu/~peters/fos/overview.htm#vehicles

(3) OA archiving only takes a few minutes.

"Authors have frequently expressed reluctance to self-archive because of the perceived time required and possible technical difficulties in carrying out this activity, yet findings here show that only 20% of authors found some degree of difficulty with the first act of depositing an article in a repository, and that this dropped to 9% for subsequent deposits." Alma Swan and Sheridan Brown, Open access self-archiving: An author study, JISC, May 2005.

http://cogprints.org/4385/

Les Carr and Stevan Harnad studied two months of log activity at a much-used repository and found that the time required for deposit averaged 10 minutes per paper. Taking into account the rate at which authors had their work archived for them by others (co-authors, librarians, students, or assistants), authors who published one paper per month would spend less than 40 minutes per year on their deposits.

http://eprints.ecs.soton.ac.uk/10688/

If you haven't deposited papers in a repository yourself and worry about adding one more task to your schedule, at least trust the Carr-Harnad evidence more than any anecdotes you might have heard from colleagues. If you've deposited once but not twice, trust the Swan-Brown evidence that the time requirement plummets. (Compare the first time you used endnotes in a word processor with the second time.) If you're worrying about adding a new task regardless of the time required, then think about the many more time-consuming jobs you already do to make your work known to the world, such as keeping your c.v. up to date, mailing offprints, and sending your bibliography to deans and department chairs. Self-archiving takes less time and has more impact than any of these.

(4) Most non-OA journals allow authors to deposit their postprints in an OA repository.

The best current estimate is that 70% of non-OA journals consent in advance to post-print archiving.

http://www.sherpa.ac.uk/romeo/statistics.php

When you publish in one of these journals, you don't need further permission for self-archiving, even if you've transferred the copyright to the journal. These journals have already given permission. For this significant majority of peer-reviewed journals, the obstacle to OA is author failure, not copyright complexity or publisher opposition. Journals have opened the door and authors have to walk through.

SHERPA and Eprints both maintain online databases where you can look up a journal and finds its policy on self-archiving.

http://www.sherpa.ac.uk/romeo/

http://web.archive.org/web/20060114082419/

http://romeo.eprints.org/

Three notes on the 70% figure. First, it represents surveyed journals. Among unsurveyed journals, there are likely to be journals that do, and journals that don't, permit postprint archiving. We don't know their proportions yet. Second, the number represents journals that consent in advance to postprint archiving without requiring case-by-case requests. Many that do not consent in advance will still consent if asked individually, however. Elsevier routinely granted individual requests until mid-2004 when it decided to offer blanket permission instead. Third, it represents the journals that consent to postprint archiving, not preprint archiving. If we count the journals that consent to preprint or postprint archiving (or both), the figure rises to 93%.

Note the all-important consequence of this kind of blanket permission. OA archiving is compatible with publishing in most conventional, subscription-based journals. If the top journals in your field (by impact or prestige) are not OA, you can go for impact or prestige and still have OA. It's rarely a trade-off.

(5) Journals using the Ingelfinger Rule are a shrinking minority.

Some authors are afraid that depositing a preprint in an OA repository will disqualify it for subsequent publication. It's true that some journals refuse to publish papers that have previously circulated as preprints or whose results have been publicized. This is called the Ingelfinger Rule, named after a former editor at the *New England Journal of Medicine*. The rule is rare outside the field of medicine and in decline.

There are some very rare journals, like the *California Law Review*, that allow postprint archiving but not preprint archiving. But essentially all the journals that don't allow preprint archiving (i.e., that follow the Ingelfinger Rule) also bar postprint archiving. Only 7% of surveyed journals fall into this category. Don't let groundless fears deter you from preprint archiving. If you worry about the Ingelfinger Rule, check out the policies of the journals where you intend to submit your work.

(6) OA enlarges your audience and citation impact.

This is the chief reason for authors to provide OA to their own work. OA increases the audience for a work far beyond the audience of any priced journal, even the most prestigious or popular journal. Studies in many fields show a correlation between OA and citation-count increases from 50% to 250%.

http://opcit.eprints.org/oacitation-biblio.html

There is almost certainly causation here as well as correlation, though this hasn't been nailed down yet. There are many hypotheses to explain the correlation. Some of it seems to arise from the fact that self-archived articles circulate sooner than journal-published articles (and have a head-start toward citations) and the fact that authors self-archive their best work (biasing the OA sample toward quality). But it's very likely that ongoing studies will show that much of the correlation is simply due to the larger audience and heightened visibility for the work among researchers who find the work useful, relevant, and worth citing in their own work.

These studies bring a welcome note of self-interest to the case for OA. Providing OA to your own work is not an act of charity that only benefits others, or a sacrifice justified only by the greater good. It's not a sacrifice at all. It increases your visibility, retrievability, audience, usage, and citations. It's about career-building. For publishing scholars, it would be a bargain even if it were costly, difficult, and time-consuming.

Trends Favoring Open Access

Originally published as "Trends favoring open access," *SPARC Open Access Newsletter*, May 2, 2007.

http://dash.harvard.edu/handle/1/4552060

This article began with a simple attempt to identify trends that were changing scholarly communication. I expected to find trends that were supporting the progress of OA and trends that were opposing it or slowing it down. The resulting welter of conflicting trends might not give comfort to friends or foes of OA, or to anyone trying to forecast the future, but at least it would describe this period of dynamic flux. It might even explain why OA wasn't moving faster or slower than it was.

But with few exceptions I only found trends that favored OA. Maybe I have a large blind spot; I'll leave that for you to decide. I'm certainly conscious of many obstacles and objections to OA, and I address them every day. The question is which of them represent trends that are gaining ground.

While it's clear that OA is here to stay, it's just as clear that long-term success is a long-term project. The campaign consists of innumerable individual proposals, policies, projects, and people. If you're reading this, you're probably caught up in it, just as I am. If you're caught up in it, you're probably anxious about how individual initiatives or institutional deliberations will turn out. That's good; anxiety fuels effort. But for a moment, stop making and answering arguments and look at the trends that will help or hurt us, and would continue to help or hurt us even if everyone stopped arguing. For a moment step back from the foreground skirmishes and look at the larger background trends that are likely to continue and likely to change the landscape of scholarly communication.

I've found so many that I've had to be brief in describing them and limit the list to those that most affect OA.

(1) First there are the many trends created by OA proponents themselves: the growing number of OA repositories, OA journals, OA policies at universities, OA policies at

public and private funding agencies, and public endorsements of OA from notable researchers and university presidents and provosts. Each new OA repository, journal, policy, and endorsement contributes to a growing worldwide momentum and inspires kindred projects elsewhere. Funding agencies are now considering OA policies in part because of their intrinsic advantages (for increasing return on investment by increasing the visibility, utility, and impact of research) and in part because other funding agencies have already adopted them. The laggards are being asked why the research they fund is less worth disseminating than the research funded elsewhere. The growing mass of OA literature is becoming critical in the sense that the growth is now a cause, and not just an effect, of progress. OA literature is the best advertisement for OA literature; the more we have, the more it educates new scholars about OA, demonstrates the benefits of OA, and stimulates others to provide or demand it.

(2) Although knowledge of OA among working researchers is still dismally low, every new survey shows it increasing, and every new survey shows increasing rates of deposits in OA repositories and submissions to OA journals. The absolute numbers may still be low, but the trajectories are clearly up.

(3) More scholars are posting their articles online even if they don't have their publisher's permission. As long ago as October 2005, Alma Swan found that seven out of eight articles published in the inaugural issue of *Nature Physics*, which had a six month embargo on self-archiving, were free online somewhere on the day of publication. Regardless of what this shows about copyright, it shows a healthy desire for OA. We don't know whether the volume of OA produced this way is large or small, but already (according to the April 2007 RIN study) readers routinely try Google and email requests to the author before interlibrary loan when they hit a pay-per-view screen at a journal Web site. Both trends—posting OA copies, with or without permission, and searching for OA copies—are growing.

(4) Subscription prices are still rising faster than inflation after more than three decades. A March 2006 study by the ALPSP found that high journal prices cause many more cancellations than OA archiving. Rapidly rising prices undermine the sustainability of the subscription model. They undermine publisher arguments that all who need access already have it. They undermine publisher arguments that we shouldn't fix what isn't broken. They undermine the credibility, and even the good faith, of publishers who argue that OA threatens peer review, by threatening their subscriptions, when their own hyperinflationary price increases are far more potent in the same cause. They strengthen the incentives for libraries, universities, funders, and governments to join the campaign for OA.

(5) The cost of facilitating peer review is coming down as journal management software improves, especially the free and open source packages like DPubS, E-Journal, ePublishing Toolkit, GAPworks, HyperJournal, OpenACS, SOPS, TOPAZ, and the

segment leader, Open Journal Systems. This reduces the cost of publishing a peer-reviewed journal, improves the financial stability of peer-reviewed OA journals, and multiplies the number of business models that can support them.

(6) More publishers are launching hybrid OA journals, which will make any of their articles OA if an author or author-sponsor pays a publication fee. I've been critical of many of these programs, in part for high prices and needless restrictions that reduce author uptake. But even with low uptake they will (slowly) increase the volume of OA literature, (slowly) spread the OA meme to more authors and readers, and (slowly) give publishers first-hand experience with the economics of one kind of OA publishing.

(7) More journals are willing to let authors retain key rights, especially the right of postprint archiving, and more are willing to negotiate the terms of their standard copyright transfer agreement. More authors are willing to ask to retain key rights and more institutions are willing to help them. More organizations are drafting "author addenda" (contract modifications to let authors retain key rights), and more universities are encouraging their faculty to use them. There are now major addenda from SPARC, Science Commons, OhioLINK, the Committee on Institutional Cooperation, and a handful of individual universities. The default in most journals and fields is still for authors to transfer nearly all rights to publishers, including the right to decide on OA for the peer-reviewed postprint. Corrections to this imbalance haven't gone nearly far enough, but the slope of the curve is definitely up.

(8) More and more toll-access (TA) journals are dropping their print editions and becoming online-only. Steven Hall of Wiley-Blackwell predicts that 50% of scholarly journals will become online-only within the next 10 years. As high-quality, high-prestige journals make this transition, scholars who still associate quality and prestige with print will (happily or unhappily) start to unlearn the association. At the same time, the rise of high-quality, high-prestige OA journals will confirm the new recognition that quality and medium are independent variables. TA publishers are joining OA advocates in creating an academic culture in which online publications can earn full credit for promotion and tenure. Online publications needn't be OA, of course, but changing the culture to accept online publications is more than half the battle for changing the culture to accept OA publications.

(9) More journals, both OA and TA, encourage or require OA to the data underlying published articles. Major publisher associations like ALPSP and STM, which lobby against national OA policies for literature, encourage OA for data. Even when these policies don't cover peer-reviewed articles, they accelerate research, demonstrate the benefits of unrestricted sharing, and build expectations and momentum for OA in other categories.

(10) More journals (OA and TA) are integrating text and data with links between text and data files, tools to go beyond viewing to querying data, dynamic charts and tables to support user-driven what-if analyses, and multimedia displays. Some types of integration can be done in-house at the journal and kept behind a price wall. But other types, especially those added retroactively by third parties, require OA for both the text and data. OA invites motivated developers to use their cleverness and creativity, and the existence of motivated developers invites authors and publishers to make their work OA.

(11) Thomson Scientific is selecting more OA journals for Impact Factors, and more OA journals are rising to the top cohort of citation impact in their fields. For scholars and institutions using Impact Factors as crude metrics of quality, this trend legitimates OA journals by showing that they can be as good as any others. There are other gains as well. Because OA increases citation impact (studies put the differential at 40–250%, depending on the field), high-quality OA journals can use citation impact to shorten the time needed to generate prestige and submissions commensurate with their quality. OA journals with rising impact are successfully breaking a vicious circle that plagues all new journals: needing prestige to attract high-quality submissions and needing high-quality submissions to generate prestige. OA journals high in impact, quality, and prestige are improving their own fortunes and changing expectations for other OA journals. But they are also making two little-known truths better known: first, that OA can help journals, not just readers and authors, and second, that a journal's impact, quality, and prestige do not depend on its medium or business model—except insofar as OA models actually amplify impact.

(12) New impact measurements are emerging that are more accurate and nuanced, more inclusive, more timely, and less expensive than Impact Factors. These include Eigenfactor, h-Index, Journal Influence and Paper Influence Index, Mesur, Usage Factor, Web Impact Factor, and Y Factor. What most of them have in common is the harnessing of new data on downloads, usage, and citations made possible by OA. In this sense, OA is improving the metrics and the metrics are improving the visibility and evaluation of the literature, especially the OA literature.

(13) Download counts are becoming almost as interesting as citation counts. Not only are they being incorporated into impact metrics, but a CIBER study (September 2005) discovered that senior researchers found them more credible than citations as signs of the usefulness of research. A Brody-Carr-Harnad study (March 2005) found that early download counts predict later citation counts. No one thinks download counts mean the same thing as citation counts, but they're easier to collect, they correlate with citation counts, and they're boosted by OA. In turn they boost OA; repository managers have learned that showing authors their download tallies will encourage other authors to deposit their work.

(14) The unit of search has long since shifted from the journal to the article. Now the unit of impact measurement is undergoing the same transition. Authors and readers still care about which journal published a given article, but they care less and less about which other articles appeared in the same issue. More and more, finding a relevant article in an OA repository, separated from its litter mates, gives searching scholars all they want.

(15) Big publishers are still getting bigger: merging with one another (most recently, Wiley and Blackwell), acquiring smaller publishers, and acquiring journals. Market consolidation is growing, monopoly power is growing, and bargaining power by subscribers is declining. This interests government anti-trust officials—who in the UK, for example, would already have acted if the OA movement hadn't give them a reason to watch and wait. It gives the players representing research rather than for-profit publishing (universities, libraries, funders, and governments) additional incentives to work for OA. It also gives the smaller, non-profit publishers, excluded from big deals and competing for limited subscription funds against the market titans, reasons to consider the big publishers more threatening than OA and reasons to consider OA a survival strategy.

(16) More for-profit companies are offering services that provide OA or add value to OA literature: repository services, search engines, archiving software, journal management software, indexing or citation tracking services, publishing platforms, print preservation. These services create or enhance OA literature, fill the cracks left by other services, create a market for OA add-ons, and show another set of business judgments that OA is on the rise. If you think, as I do, that one promising future for non-OA publishers is to shift from priced access to priced services for adding value to OA literature, then these projects can help opponents become proponents.

(17) More mainstream, non-academic search engines like Google, Yahoo, and Microsoft are indexing OA repositories and journals. This makes OA content easy to find for users unacquainted with more specialized tools. This in turn helps persuade even more publishing scholars that OA really does increase visibility and retrievability. Hence, it helps correct a particularly common and harmful misunderstanding among authors: that work on deposit in an institutional repository is only visible to people who visit that particular repository and run a local search.

(18) While OA journals and repositories continue to multiply, other vehicles for delivering OA are finding more and more serious scholarly applications: blogs, wikis, ebooks, podcasts, RSS feeds, and P2P networks. This is more than a geeky desire to play with cool new tools. It's a desire to find ways to bypass barriers to communication, collaboration, and sharing. Serious researchers are discovering that these tools are actually useful, not just cool, and are taking advantage of them. Like cell

phones, wifi, and the internet itself before them, these tools are overcoming the stigma of being trendy and moving from the periphery to the mainstream.

The direct benefit is that all these tools presuppose OA. Their widespread use enlarges the volume of OA research communication and spreads the conviction that research benefits from both the speed and the reach of OA. The indirect benefit is that they foster disintermediation (and hence reduce costs and delays) without sacrificing peer-mediated forms of quality control. Since the rise of peer-reviewed journals in the 17th century, most publicly disseminated works of scholarship have been vetted and distributed by publishers. Letters and lectures were exceptions. Today, the categories of exceptions, the volume of research-reporting they represent, and their integration into the workflow of ordinary research, are all growing.

(19) New and effective tools for collaboration are triggering adoption and excitement, e.g., social tagging, searching by tags, open peer commentary, searching by comments, social networking, community building, recruiting collaborators, facilitating work with collaborators you already have, following citation trails backward and forward, following usage-based "similar to" and "recommended" trails, open APIs, open standards, and mash-ups. Collaboration barriers are becoming almost as irritating and inimical to research as price and permission barriers. A new generation of digital scholars is deeply excited by the new collaboration services that presuppose and build on OA.

To focus on social tagging and folksonomy tools for a moment: when applied to research literature (Connotea, CiteULike) and combined with OA and search engines, they do more than OA alone, or OA plus search engines, to enhance the discoverability of OA literature. Because tags are added retroactively to open content by uncoordinated users, they stimulate the imagination of creative developers; once we have OA to literature and data, we can add layers of utility indefinitely.

(20) Interest in OA and projects to deliver on that interest are growing fast in the humanities. Humanists are exploring OA for books and journals, and exploring the universe of useful services that can be built on an OA foundation, from searching and annotation to text-mining, co-writing, and mash-ups. We already knew that OA was useful to scholars, as authors and readers, in every field. But the humanities are now showing that OA is not limited to fields with high journal prices (to serve as a goad) or high levels of research funding (to pay for it).

(21) Huge book-scanning projects, particularly those from Google, the Open Content Alliance, The European Library, the Kirtas-Amazon partnership, and Project Gutenberg, steadily increase the number of print books available in some free-to-read digital form. We'll soon reach a crossover point when more full-text, public-domain books are freely available online than on the shelves of the largest university library. Apart from lowering the access barriers to a large and uniquely

valuable body of literature, the book-scanning projects together create one more large real-time demonstration that useful literature is even more useful when it's OA.

(22) At the same time, the price of book scanning is dropping quickly. The usefulness of book literature and the absence of legal shackles on public domain texts are attracting large corporations, whose investments and competition are driving down the costs of digitization. The repercussions will be felt in every category of print literature, including the back runs of print journals.

(23) Steady decreases in the size and cost of hardware and memory are making possible steady increases in the volume of data people can carry in their palm or pocket. Free *offline* access to usefully large digital libraries is on the horizon. Every effort for free online access will free up content for portable offline access as well.

(24) Evidence is mounting that OA editions increase the net sales of print editions for some kinds of books, including scholarly monographs. This not only enlarges the corpus of OA literature, but chips away at the simplistic, reflexive fear that OA is incompatible with revenue and profit. Every month another university press explores this space by creating an imprint or division dedicated to dual-edition monographs (OA editions and priced/printed editions), OA-plus-POD monographs, or OA-only monographs.

On the other hand, OA books may only stimulate sales of print editions as long as most people dislike reading whole books on screen. This trend may be reversed by a counter-trend to improve ebook readers.

(25) A textbook pricing crisis is stimulating OA solutions just as the journal pricing crisis before it stimulated OA solutions. There are now major projects to produce OA textbooks from the following: Amedeo, Atomic Dog, BookPower, the California Open Source Textbook Project, CommonText, the Free Curricula Center, Free High School Science Texts, Freeload Press, FreeTechBooks, Global Text Project, Libertas Academica, Liberty Textbooks, Medical Approaches, MedRounds Publications, nexttext, the Open Textbook Project, the Potto Project, Science Classics, Textbook Revolution, and Wikibooks.

(26) More universities and independent non-profits are creating open courseware, OA teaching and learning materials, and other open educational resources (OERs). These help all teachers and students, even those at affluent schools. Like the kindred movement for OA to research literature, this one is demonstrating to a growing audience that useful content is more useful when OA. It also helps generalize a fact highlighted by researchers: that content creators who depend on salaries rather than royalties, or who write for impact and not for money, have everything to gain and nothing to lose by consenting to OA.

(27) There is a rising awareness of copyright issues in the general public, rising frustration with unbalanced copyright laws, and rising support for remedies by

governments (legislation) and individuals (Creative Commons licenses and their equivalents). Copyright laws are still grotesquely unbalanced, and powerful corporations who benefit from the imbalance are fighting to ensure that they are not revised in the right direction any time soon. But in more and more countries, an aroused public is ready to fight to ensure that they are not revised in the wrong direction either, something we haven't seen in the entire history of copyright law.

However, this only guarantees that the content industry will have a fight, not that users and consumers will win. Nearly every week the content industry scores another victory, either in court or in arm-twisting another developing country into harmonizing its copyright laws with the unbalanced North. There are victories for balance as well, but less often in courts and legislatures than in think tanks, conference declarations, government commissions, and newspaper editorials. The trend is only for awareness and opposition, but it's sharply up.

(28) The shock of the new is wearing off. OA is gradually emerging from the fog of misunderstanding. For this one, I won't be brief.

Scholars who grew up with the internet are steadily replacing those who grew up without it. Scholars who expect to put everything they write online, who expect to find everything they need online, and who expect unlocked content they may read, search, link, copy, cut/paste, crawl, print, and redistribute, are replacing those who never expected these boons and got used to them, if at all, looking over their shoulder for the copyright police. Scholars who expect to find the very best literature online, harmlessly cohabiting with crap, are replacing scholars who, despite themselves perhaps, still associate everything online with crap.

Some lazy scholars believe that if something is not free online, then it's not worth reading. This has never been true. However, it's gradually becoming true, and those who want it to become true can accelerate the process. Those who want to live in a world where all peer-reviewed journal literature is free online are themselves growing in numbers and will soon have the power in universities, libraries, learned societies, publishers, funding agencies, and governments to bring it about.

Moreover, as the OA percentage of research literature continues to grow, then more users will start to act (with or without justification) as if all research literature worth reading is already OA. As this practice spreads, it will function as one more incentive for authors and publishers to make their work OA.

In short, generational change is on the side of OA.

But even the passage of time without generational change is on the side of OA. Time itself has reduced panic and panic-induced misunderstandings of OA. Everyone is getting used to the idea that OA literature can be copyrighted, the idea that OA literature can be peer-reviewed, the idea that the expenses for producing OA literature can be recovered, and the idea that OA and TA literature can co-exist (even for the same work). Surprisingly, many of the early obstacles to OA can be traced to the fact that many seasoned academics just couldn't grasp these ideas. The problem was not incoherent ideas or stupid people—though both hypotheses circulated widely—but panic, unfamiliarity, and the violation of unquestioned assumptions. For some stakeholders, clear explanations, repetition, or experience with working examples solved the problem. But for others it just took time.

When *Nature* broke the story in January 2007 that the Association of American Publishers, American Chemical Society, Elsevier, and Wiley, had hired Eric Dezenhall, "the pit-bull of PR," to help their lobbying campaign against OA, the resulting controversy brought OA to the attention of many academics for the first time. Unlike earlier waves of newcomers, for example, after Congress asked the NIH to develop an OA policy in July 2004, this wave typically got it right the first time. "Of course OA is compatible with peer review." "Of course there are no copyright problems if the copyright-holder consents." "Of course the public deserves OA to publicly-funded research." "Of course the argument that OA is a kind of censorship is Orwellian doublespeak."

When newcomers got OA wrong in the past, sometimes they had been misled by an explicit error published somewhere, perhaps by another newcomer. But most of the time they just made unconscious assumptions based on incomplete information and old models. This is the shock of the new at work. If OA uses the internet, then it must bypass peer review. (Right?) If OA articles can be copied *ad lib*, then there must be copyright problems. (Right?) If OA is free of charge for end-users, then its proponents must be claiming that it costs nothing to produce and it must be impossible to recover the costs. (Right?) These conclusions, of course, were uninformed leaps. Many who understood the conventional model (priced, printed, peer-reviewed, copyright-protected) saw a proposal for something different and didn't know how many parameters of the old paradigm the new proposal wanted to tweak. Their hasty and incorrect surmise: all of them. It was a classic case of seeing black and white before seeing shades of gray.

Suddenly everything good about the present system had to be defended, as if it were under attack. A lot of energy was wasted defending peer review, when it was never under attack. A lot of energy was wasted defending copyright—or celebrating its demise—when it was never under attack. (More precisely, copyright was under attack from other directions, but OA was compatible with unrevised, unbalanced, unreconstructed copyright.) The debate about OA often drifted toward the larger debate about what was good and bad, or functional and dysfunctional, in the present system of scholarly communication overall. This was valuable, but mixing narrow OA issues with broader ones created false impressions about what OA really was, how compatible it was with good features of the present system, and how easy it was to implement.

The OA debates still waste a lot of energy talking about peer review and copyright. The shock of the new hasn't fully worn off; it's wearing off gradually. OA advocates, growing in numbers and effectiveness, can't keep the idea from being distorted or misunderstood. But they have kept it from being distorted or misunderstood as much as it would have been otherwise.

As time passes, we see a steady rise in the proportion of correct to incorrect formulations of OA in the widely-read discussions. When people encounter a fragmentary version of the idea for the first time today, their guesswork to flesh it out is guided by a much more reliable range of clues than just a few years ago. If they take the time to run an online search, the chances that they'll find good information before someone else's guesswork are nearly 100%.

It's tempting to focus on the elegance of OA as a solution to serious problems and overlook the need for the sheer passage of time to overcome the shock of the new. Even if we acknowledge the need for cultural change in the transition to OA—far more critical than technological change—it's easy to underestimate the cultural barriers and the time required to work through them. Yes, OA is compatible with peer review, copyright, profit, print, prestige, and preservation. But that doesn't quiet resistance when those facts about it are precisely the ones hidden by false assumptions caused by the shock of the new.

I'm not saying that all resistance to OA is, or was, based on a misunderstanding of the idea itself. But much past resistance was based on misunderstanding; that portion is in decline; and that decline is largely due to the passage of time and the rise in mere familiarity with a new idea.

The changes wrought by time point up a sad irony in the 15 year history of OA. Nobody is surprised when cultural inertia slows the adoption of radical ideas. But cultural inertia slowed the adoption of OA by leading many people to mistake it for a more radical idea than it actually is.

I know that this account of trends would not be complete without those that work *against* OA. But there aren't many. I've mentioned the improvement in ebook readers, which may interfere with the ways that OA books increase sales for print editions. Here are two more.

(29) Researchers themselves control the rate of progress toward OA, but after all these years most of them are still oblivious to its existence and benefits. As I've noted above, there is a trend toward greater familiarity and understanding. But there is also a longstanding counter-trend of impatience with anything that distracts attention from research. This preoccupation is generally admirable and makes researchers good at what they do. But even from the narrow perspective of what advances research, it is having perverse consequences and limiting the audience, impact, and utility of the research on which scholars are so single-mindedly focused.

(30) Some publishers opposed OA from the beginning, and sometimes their opposition was fierce. But some who opposed it apparently saw it as a utopian fantasy of naïve academics that would never be embraced by serious researchers, let alone by serious institutions like universities, libraries, foundations, and government agencies. Publishers in the second camp, who thought OA would be alarming if it caught on, but then hit the snooze button, are now hearing the alarm. While some publishers actively support OA, or experiment with it in good faith, those that oppose it are getting their act together and spending serious money to lobby against government OA policies. In money and person-power, their lobbying forces in Washington and Brussels vastly exceed our own. All we have going for us are good arguments and good trends.

This version draws upon some revisions I made for its republication in *CT Watch Quarterly*, August 2007.

http://www.ctwatch.org/quarterly/print.php%3Fp=81.html

Gratis and Libre Open Access

From "Gratis and libre open access," SPARC Open Access Newsletter, August 2, 2008.

http://dash.harvard.edu/handle/1/4322580

In February 2002, the Budapest Open Access Initiative called for a kind of online access to research literature that was free of charge and free of most usage restrictions. It offered a name ("open access") for the unified concept, but it didn't suggest names for the two component parts.

http://www.budapestopenaccessinitiative.org/read

In a February 2003 article, I distinguished those two parts and called them the "removal of price barriers" and the "removal of permission barriers." But those were negative terms, and I didn't think to offer matching positive ones describing kinds of access rather than kinds of access barriers.

http://www.earlham.edu/~peters/writing/acrl.htm

When the Bethesda and Berlin statements came out (June and October 2003) they followed the Budapest statement in calling for the removal of both price and permission barriers. As a result, all three components of the Budapest-Bethesda-Berlin (BBB) definition of OA now call for both sorts of free online access.

http://www.earlham.edu/~peters/fos/bethesda.htm

http://openaccess.mpg.de/Berlin-Declaration

But unfortunately we still don't have widely accepted terms for the two sorts of free online access: (1) the kind which removes price barriers alone and (2) the kind which removes price barriers and at least some permission barriers. This gap in our vocabulary has caused confusion and conflicts, not least because it created pressure to use the term "open access" for each.

In April 2008, Stevan Harnad and I proposed the terms "weak OA" and "strong OA" for these two species. I wrote a blog post to explain what we meant.

http://www.earlham.edu/~peters/fos/2008/04/strong-and-weak-oa.html

But we quickly realized that "weak OA" was needlessly pejorative and started looking for more neutral and descriptive language. Stevan launched a public discussion on the American Scientist Open Access Forum.

http://listserver.sigmaxi.org/sc/wa.exe?A2=ind08&L=american-scientist-open-access-forum&D=1&F=l&O=D&P=38999

Unfortunately, however, the discussion hasn't come up with clear winners. If the terms Stevan and I introduced in April had been better chosen, and widely supported, I'd have used them 100 times already in my blog and newsletter. I need them almost every day.

In the absence of terms that are neutral, accurate, and widely supported, I've decided to make a provisional decision as an individual writer while the larger discussion continues. For now, my choice is to use "gratis" and "libre." They are accurate, neutral, and descriptive. In the neighboring domain of free and open source software, they exactly express the distinction I have in mind.

http://en.wikipedia.org/wiki/Gratis_versus_Libre

The terms may be unfamiliar in the domain of OA or scholarly communication. But as far as I can see at the moment, that's their only drawback, and it's one I may be able to overcome by writing this article. Their relative unfamiliarity is even a kind of advantage. They're not common words with clouds of common connotations. "Weak/strong" were not objectionable because of their new definitions, but because of their preexisting connotations, and "gratis/libre" won't run into that problem.

This choice is personal in the sense that I'm making a decision for my own writing. It's provisional in the sense that I'll continue to look for better terms.

I've already used "gratis/libre" in a few blog posts. But I didn't want to use them frequently until I had time to write up this longer case for them.

http://www.earlham.edu/~peters/fos/2008/05/more-on-freeopen-and-textdata.html

http://www.earlham.edu/~peters/fos/2008/07/more-on-two-sidedness-of-oa.html

Here's the updated heart of my April 2008 blog post using "gratis/libre" in place of "weak/strong." But while my original post described a decision Stevan Harnad and I reached together, in this version I'll speak for myself.

http://www.earlham.edu/~peters/fos/2008/04/strong-and-weak-oa.html

The term "open access" is now widely used in at least two senses. For some, "OA" literature is digital, online, and free of charge. It removes price barriers but not permission barriers. For others, "OA" literature is digital, online, free of charge, and free of unnecessary copyright and licensing restrictions. It removes both price barriers and permission barriers. It allows reuse rights which exceed fair use.

There are two good reasons why our central term became ambiguous. Most of our success stories deliver OA in the first sense, while the major public statements from Budapest, Bethesda, and Berlin (together, the BBB definition of OA) describe OA in the second sense.

I've decided to use the term "gratis OA" for the removal of price barriers alone and "libre OA" for the removal of price and at least some permission barriers. The new terms allow us to speak unambiguously about these two species of free online access.

On this new terminology, the BBB definition describes one kind of libre OA. A typical funder or university mandate requires gratis OA. Many OA journals provide libre OA, but many others provide only gratis OA.

There is more than one kind of permission barrier to remove. Therefore, there is more than one kind or degree of libre OA.

I've often wanted short, clear terms for what I'm now calling gratis and libre OA. But I've also wanted a third term. In my blog and newsletter I often need a generic term which means "gratis or libre OA, we don't know which yet." For example, a press release may announce a new free online journal, digital library, or database, without making clear what kind of reuse rights it allows. Or a new journal will make its articles available online without charge but say nothing about its access policy or licensing terms. I will simply call them "OA." I'll specify that they are gratis or libre OA only when I learn enough to do so.

The two new terms will help us avoid ambiguity without resisting current usage, which would be futile, or revising the BBB definition, which would be undesirable.

I learned a lot from the emails leading up to the "weak/strong" announcement in April, and especially from the emails and blog posts afterwards. Here's a mini FAQ responding the sorts of questions I've heard.

- Why introduce new terms at all? Weren't we doing fine before?

We were not doing fine. Our central term was (and is) widely used to cover two non-equivalent sorts of free online access. As long as we don't have narrower terms for the two sorts, then we'll continue to use the broader term "OA" for each, aggravating the ambiguity rather than resolving it.

- Are you saying that we should stop using the term "OA" and only use the narrower terms?

Not at all. I'm only introducing terms for sub-species when we need to speak unambiguously about sub-species. When we don't need that level of precision, "OA" is the perfect term, indeed, the only term.

"Gratis OA" and "libre OA" will supplement "OA," not supplant it—roughly the way "simple carbohydrate" and "complex carbohydrate" supplement "carbohydrate" without supplanting it.

- Isn't the green/gold distinction the same as the gratis/libre distinction?

No. The green/gold distinction is about venues (repositories and journals), while the gratis/libre distinction is about user rights or freedoms. Green OA can be gratis or libre, but is usually gratis. Gold OA can be gratis or libre, but is also usually gratis.

It's easier for gold OA to be libre than for green OA to be libre. But both can be libre. It follows that the campaign to go beyond gratis OA to libre OA is not just about journals (gold OA), even if it is primarily about journals.

For more on how these two distinctions differ, see the table I posted to my blog this morning,

http://www.earlham.edu/~peters/fos/2008/08/greengold-oa-and-gratislibre-oa.html

- Are you trying to legislate usage?

No. I'm in no position to legislate usage. If I were, usage would never have become ambiguous!

http://www.earlham.edu/~peters/fos/newsletter/09-02-04.htm#progress

I am proposing these terms for others to use as well. But even if I were able to legislate usage, this choice would still be personal and provisional. I need terms to use in my own writing, and I'll use these until I find better ones. I don't want to preempt the search for better terms, by myself or others, and I don't want to tie my hands about using the fruits of that search.

- Are you trying to revise the BBB definition of OA?

No. It hasn't changed and I don't want to change it. Nor—slightly different thing—am I retreating from my endorsement of it. (I was the principal drafter of the Budapest statement and stand by it.)

I'm simply trying to clarify communication by introducing terms for different sorts of free online access. It's all about vocabulary, and not at all about policy.

There is a problem to solve. It's not that the BBB definition has changed, or needs to change, but that the term "open access" has changed, and is now widely used in both a BBB and non-BBB sense. As I've argued elsewhere, our term has spread faster and further than the BBB definition. That usage is a fact of life, and support for the BBB definition doesn't make it go away. There are roughly two ways to approach this problem. We could fight the tide of usage and try to make "OA" refer to nothing but BBB OA again. But that's unwinnable. (I deliberately say nothing about the advantages and disadvantages of winning it if it were winnable; that's a pointless exercise.) Or we could cure the ambiguity by using separate names, like "gratis OA" and "libre OA," for the two important things which have been going under the same name. That's more than winnable. It's easy. It will support unambiguous communication without fighting usage, without modifying the BBB definition, and without giving anyone a reason to diminish their support for it.

- Is "libre OA" synonymous with "BBB OA"?

No. Because there is more than one kind of permission barrier to remove, there is more than one kind or degree of libre OA. BBB OA is one kind or subset of libre OA. But there are others, and not all libre OA is BBB OA.

For example, permitting all uses except commercial use (the CC-NC license) and permitting all uses except derivative works (the CC-ND license) are not equivalent to one another and—ignoring certain subtleties—not compatible with the BBB definition. But they all remove price barriers, they all remove at least some permission barriers, and therefore they are all libre OA.

We shouldn't speak as if there were just one kind of libre OA. Gratis OA may be just one thing (freedom from price barriers), but libre OA is a *range* of things (freedom from price barriers and one or more permission barriers).

- What's the best way to refer to a specific type of libre OA?

With a license. We'll never have unambiguous, widely-understood technical terms for every useful variation on the theme. But we're very likely to have clear, named licenses for every useful variation on the theme, and we're already close. Licenses are more precise than single terms and not nearly as susceptible to misunderstanding or divergent usage.

- What's the borderline between gratis and libre OA?

Gratis OA removes no permission barriers and libre OA removes one or more permission barriers. (Both of them remove price barriers.)

http://wwmm.ch.cam.ac.uk/blogs/murrayrust/?p=1073#comment-189844

But what does it mean to remove a permission barrier? If copying a short excerpt is permitted by "fair use" (or "fair dealing" or the local equivalent), then users may do it without asking anyone's permission. Hence, there are no permission barriers in the way. If copying full text and redistributing it to others exceeds fair use, then users must ask permission, take the legal risk of proceeding without it, or err on the side of non-use. In general, when a use requires permission, users face a permission barrier. This doesn't mean that permission is denied, only that permission is not already given and must be sought if one wishes to proceed. When rightsholders grant permission in advance for uses that exceed fair use, then they remove permission barriers. As a practical matter, there are two ways to remove permission barriers: (1) with copyright holder consent, through a license or statement permitting uses that would otherwise be impermissible or doubtful, and (2) with the expiration of copyright and the transition of the work into the public domain.

http://www.earlham.edu/~peters/fos/2008/05/boundary-between-removing-no-permission.html

In short, gratis OA alone allows no uses beyond fair use, and libre OA allows one or more uses beyond fair use.

- What's wrong with "full OA" (instead of "libre OA")?

"Full OA" implies just one degree or kind of OA, in fact a maximum. But libre OA is a range of many positions, corresponding to the many permission barriers which we could remove.

Hence, "full" isn't a good word to contrast libre OA with gratis OA. But it's a perfectly good word to contrast OA journals with hybrid OA journals. For example, I see no problem with saying that "full OA" journals provide OA to all their articles, while "hybrid OA" journals provide OA to some and not others.

- What's wrong with "free" access?

The main problem is that some people already use "free" to mean gratis ("free as in beer") and some people already use it to mean libre ("free as in speech"). It would be very hard to give this widely used and versatile word a narrower meaning for some special purpose, and make it stick. Making "free" a technical term would increase ambiguity, not decrease it.

It's relevant that "gratis" and "libre" emerged to resolve an ambiguity endemic in the "free" software movement.

- Why was the original "weak/strong" announcement presented as a joint decision with Stevan Harnad?

Simply because Stevan and I came up with it together. (Not because we are a cabal.) The background is important. Stevan wanted to recognize the movement's many gratis OA success stories. But because gratis OA doesn't meet the terms of the BBB, he felt it necessary to revise the BBB. I wanted to join him in recognizing the many gratis OA success stories, but I didn't want to revise the BBB. Whether the BBB needed revision became a tactical disagreement of growing importance between us, showing up in many of our blog posts, taking more of our time, and perhaps even overshadowing our agreements on most issues of substance and strategy. As we talked it out, however, we realized that our disagreement on the BBB arose from an inadequate vocabulary for the varieties of free online access. Once we had that vocabulary we could agree in our speech as much as we agreed in substance, and we could take revision of the BBB off the table. It was a beautiful resolution—except that we settled too quickly on the wrong pair of words ("weak/strong").

To show the new terms in action, here's how they help clarify the major points of substance and strategy on which Stevan and I agree. We agree that gratis OA is a necessary but not sufficient condition of libre OA. We agree that gratis OA is often attainable in circumstances when libre OA is not attainable. We agree that gratis OA should not be delayed until we can achieve libre OA. We agree that libre OA is a desirable goal above and beyond gratis OA. We agree that the desirability of libre OA is a reason to keep working after attaining gratis OA, but not a reason to disparage the difficulties or the significance of gratis OA. We agree that the BBB definition of OA does not need to be revised.

- Why do we have to recognize this distinction at all?

Because there really is a difference between removing price barriers alone and removing both price and permission barriers, and because this difference really matters to users, strategies, and policies. The distinction by itself isn't new or even controversial. All that's new here is the proposal to use certain terms to name its two parts. But even if you don't like the terms I plan to use, and even if you don't plan to use any special terms yourself, understanding the distinction itself is necessary to understand the day-to-day progress and discussions of the OA movement.

More on the Case for Open Access

The Scaling Argument

From "The scaling argument," SPARC Open Access Newsletter, March 2, 2004.

http://dash.harvard.edu/handle/1/4723859

Open-access literature has four key properties: it's digital, it's online, it's free of charge, and it's free of most copyright and licensing restrictions. There are many arguments for OA, but these four properties support an important argument that's seldom heard: open access scales better than toll access.

The background here is the continuing explosion of knowledge. We suffered from information overload even in the age of print. It has accelerated since the birth of the internet, but it would have accelerated anyway. It seems to be accelerating now at an accelerating rate.

Will our methods of disseminating knowledge keep pace with the rate of discovery and publication? Or will they function as an artificial brake on the growth of knowledge itself and our ability to find and assimilate it?

Print literature is expensive to purchase, store, and search. All three problems are aggravated as the volume of literature grows. When the literature is digital but not online, then purchase, storage, and searching all become easier, and they become easier again when the digital literature moves online. Then we can store it in multiple sites around the world, distribute the costs and labor of maintenance, reach the distributed sites as if they were sectors of our own hard drives, and search across them as if they were one. When the literature is digital and online but priced, then it's locked away behind passwords, which excludes non-paying users and most search engines. Even when it's searchable, it's no longer affordable. However, when it's digital, online, and free of price and permission barriers, then finally it scales. We can search it, store it, and afford it, and growth in its volume no longer raises insuperable financial or ergonomic hurdles.

Most universities already have trouble storing their print literature. But all have trouble paying for journals, whether print or electronic. None can buy access to all the priced journals their faculty need to keep up in their fields. If affluent universities like the University of California, the University of Connecticut, Cornell, Duke, Harvard, MIT, the University of Maryland, the University of North Carolina at Chapel Hill, and Stanford cannot afford the current array of journals, then the current system does not scale. It would not scale even if knowledge grew at a slower rate. But knowledge will continue to grow, probably at an exponential rate. If we do not find a dissemination and access paradigm that scales up more efficiently, and soon, then researchers will be publishing more and more for fewer and fewer.

But we have such a paradigm. OA scales. It greatly reduces the costs of production, distribution, and storage, and of course access and usage are free of charge. OA accommodates growth on a gigantic scale and, best of all, supports more effective tools for searching, sorting, indexing, filtering, mining, and alerting—the tools for coping with information overload.

Using these tools to find what we need when we need it is the only solution to information overload compatible with the growth of knowledge. In a toll-access future, we'll have to cope by doing without access to a growing percentage of the published literature, curtailing the publication of otherwise worthy research, or simply shutting our eyes.

One lesson: don't ask merely how bad the serials crisis is or how bad information overload is. Ask how bad both will become, as knowledge continues its explosive growth, if we don't fundamentally change our methods of funding, distribution, and access. There will be scaling problems even with OA, but there's no doubt that OA scales better, on every parameter, than the current toll-access system. [...]

Problems and Opportunities (Blizzards and Beauty)

From "Problems and opportunities (blizzards and beauty)," *SPARC Open Access Newsletter*, July 2, 2007.

http://dash.harvard.edu/handle/1/4727450

What makes you interrupt important work? We all have our provocations and temptations. For me, two recurring excuses are very bad weather and very good weather. A blizzard will make me drop everything and shovel snow. A beautiful moment of late-afternoon sunlight will make me drop everything and take pictures. Your answers may fall into roughly the same two categories, which we could call solving problems and seizing opportunities.

I think about OA in the same terms, perhaps because it's interrupting my work in philosophy. There are two deep reasons to pursue OA, even to interrupt important work to pursue it: to solve problems and to seize opportunities. They're not the same thing. One is duress and one is pleasure. One is a push from behind and the other a pull from the front. We work on problems with dutiful determination and on opportunities with creative unconstraint. Even when they stress us, there's a difference between worry that a nagging problem will persist and worry that a beautiful opportunity will slip through our fingers.

I'd like to think that we'd pursue OA even if historical circumstances gave us only one of these motivations rather than both at once—that is, if we suffered from access problems and had no new technology to exploit, or if we had a spectacular new technology to exploit but no particular problem to solve.

But we have both and we should acknowledge it more often. Too much of our conversation is problem-oriented. Let's complement it with a conversation that is opportunity-oriented.

Yes, OA solves problems. There's the access-to-authors or knowledge problem for readers. There's the access-to-readers or impact problem for authors. There's the affordability problem for libraries. There's the unfairness problem of making taxpayers pay a second time for access to research they funded. There's the inefficiency problem of funding useful research that isn't accessible to everyone who can make use of it. There's the perversity problem of making a public commitment to use public money to expand knowledge and then hand control over the results to businesses who believe, correctly or incorrectly, that their revenue and survival depend on limiting access to that knowledge.

Then there are the problems arising from the subscription business model itself. The chief problem is not that subscriptions cost money, because the alternatives also cost money. It's not even that subscriptions in the sciences cost a *lot* of money. The subscription model has problems even if we assume that the OA alternative will cost exactly the same (which I don't think is true). The subscription model makes a publisher's method of cost recovery function as an access barrier. It requires artificial scarcity for information when digital technologies can abolish information scarcity altogether. It makes publishers insist on controlling access to research they didn't perform, write up, or fund. It makes them act (to use the wonderful PLoS analogy) like midwives who insist on keeping the baby rather than midwives who deliver the baby, hand it back to its parents, and take payment for services rendered. It means that after publishers add value through peer review and copy editing, they feel financial pressure to subtract value by imposing password barriers, locking files to prevent copying or cutting/pasting, freezing data into images, cutting good articles solely for length, and turning gifts into commodities which may not be further shared. Because journals don't publish the same articles, they don't compete for readers or subscribers (even if they compete for authors), removing market pressures for publishers to keep subscription prices low or even correlated with their size, costs, impact, or quality.

The subscription model doesn't scale with the explosive growth in the volume of published research, and it wouldn't scale even if prices were low. It entails that as the volume of published research grows, the accessible percentage of it for the average library shrinks, and that the faster the literature grows, the faster the accessible percentage shrinks. It means that despite their growing access gaps, libraries end up paying for bundles of journals when local patrons only use a subset, and whole journals when they only use certain articles. It means that when they pay for electronic journals, which are increasingly replacing print journals, they license rather than own copies and suffer under licensing terms and software locks that limit usage much more than they were ever limited in using paper journals. It means that subscribers pay for more than they need and get less than they need, a problem severely aggravated by hyperinflationary price increases. Finally, it means that different universities pay redundantly for access to the same literature, instead of sharing the costs so that each pays for part and together all pay for all.

There's a lot of snow to shovel here. But …

There are also beautiful opportunities to seize. There's the fact that the internet emerged just as journal subscription prices were reaching unbearable levels. There's the fact that the internet widens distribution and reduces costs at the same time. There's the fact that digital computers connected to a global network let us make perfect copies of arbitrary files and distribute them to a worldwide audience at virtually no cost. There's the fact that unrestricted access to digital files supports forms of discovery and processing impossible for paper texts and DRM-clamped digital files. There's the fact that for 350 years, scholars have willingly (even eagerly) published journal articles without payment, a custom that frees them to consent to OA without losing revenue. There's the fact that OA is already lawful and doesn't require copyright reform, even if it would benefit from reforms of the right kind. There's the fact that OA is within the reach of authors acting alone and needn't wait for publishers, legislation, or markets. There's the fact that, for researchers acting on their own, the goal of OA is even easier to accomplish than the goal of affordable journals.

Let me elaborate on one of these opportunities a bit. The Budapest Open Access Initiative said that "[a]n old tradition and a new technology have converged to make possible an unprecedented public good. The old tradition is the willingness of scientists and scholars to publish the fruits of their research in scholarly journals without payment ... The new technology is the internet." OA is the name of the beautiful opportunity created by this convergence of the willingness of scholars to give away their work and the existence of a medium for delivering that work at vanishing marginal cost to a worldwide audience. If you have the willingness of authors but not the medium, then you have scholarship in the age of print. If you have the medium but not the willingness, then you have music and movies in the age of the internet (so far). The beautiful opportunity for researchers is that we now have both.

Here's a less obvious but even more fundamental opportunity. Knowledge is "non-rivalrous" (to use a term from the economics of property). That means we can share it without dividing it, and consume it without diminishing it. My possession and use of some knowledge doesn't exclude your possession and use of the same knowledge. By contrast, familiar physical goods like land, food, and machines are all rivalrous. To share them, we must take turns or settle for portions.

We're very fortunate that knowledge is non-rivalrous. We can all know the same facts or ideas without my knowledge blocking yours or yours blocking mine. We're even more fortunate that speech is non-rivalrous, since this allows us to articulate and share our knowledge without reducing it to a rivalrous commodity. We can all hear the same spoken words without my listening blocking yours or yours blocking mine.

But for all of human history before the digital age, writing has been rivalrous. Written or recorded knowledge became a material object like stone, clay, skin, or paper, which was necessarily rivalrous. Even when we had the printing press and photocopying machine, and could make many copies at comparatively low cost, each copy was a rivalrous material object. Despite its revolutionary impact, writing was hobbled from birth by this tragic limitation. We could only record non-rivalrous knowledge in a rivalrous form, much as we could only translate one poem into a different poem.

Digital texts, however, are non-rivalrous. If we all have the equipment to support them, then we can all have copies of the same digital text without excluding one another, without multiplying our costs, and without depleting our resources. Digital writing is the first kind of writing that does not reduce recorded knowledge to a rivalrous object.

I've heard physicists refer to the prospect of room-temperature superconductivity as a "gift of nature." Unfortunately, it's not quite within reach. But the non-rivalrous property of digital information is a gift of nature that we've already grasped and put to work. We only have to stand back a moment to appreciate it. To our ancestors, the prospect of recording knowledge in precise language, symbols, sounds, or images without reducing the record to a rivalrous object would have been magical or miraculous. But we do it every day now and it's losing its magic.

The danger is not that we already take it for granted but that we might stop short and fail to take full advantage of it. The point is not to marvel at its potential but to seize the opportunities it creates. It can transform knowledge-sharing if we let it.

We take advantage of this gift when we post information online and permit free access and unrestricted use for every user with an internet connection. But if we charge for access, enforce exclusion, create artificial scarcity, or prohibit essential uses, then we treat the non-rivalrous digital file like a rivalrous physical object, dismiss the opportunity, and spurn the gift.

I don't want to create an artificial distinction between solving problems and seizing opportunities, which are intimately connected. In our case, we're solving access problems by seizing the opportunities created by digital computers connected by digital networks exchanging non-rivalrous digital information. So if you're working on solving a problem, don't stop. But if you find yourself thinking that the task of promoting OA is just a battle against problems, take a step back. It's a lot more than that. It's also the creative and open-ended process of seizing a beautiful opportunity.

This dual perspective matters for morale. It also matters for strategy, since it affects our conception of the goal and our conception of who our natural allies are in the larger cause of taking advantage of the opportunities created by digital information and digital technology. It affects our horizons.

When publishers argue that there are no access problems, and that we shouldn't fix what isn't broken, there are two answers. First, that's mistaken; there are deep and serious access problems. Publishers who really don't know this should talk more to the libraries who subscribe to their journals, and even more to the libraries who don't. But second, leaving that quarrel entirely to one side, there are good reasons to pursue OA anyway, even reasons urgent enough to interrupt important work.

Open Access and the Self-Correction of Knowledge

From "Open access and the self-correction of knowledge," *SPARC Open Access Newsletter*, June 2, 2008.

http://dash.harvard.edu/handle/1/4391168

Here's an epistemological argument for OA. It's not particularly new or novel. In fact, I trace it back to some arguments by John Stuart Mill in 1859. Nor is it very subtle or complicated. But it's important in its own right and it's importantly different from the moral and pragmatic arguments for OA we see more often.

The thesis in a nutshell is that OA facilitates the testing and validation of knowledge claims. OA enhances the process by which science is self-correcting. OA improves the reliability of inquiry.

Science is fallible, but clearly that's not what makes it special. Science is special because it's self-correcting. It isn't self-correcting because individual scientists acknowledge their mistakes, accept correction, and change their minds. Sometimes they do and sometimes they don't. Science is self-correcting because scientists eventually correct the errors of other scientists, and find the evidence to persuade their colleagues to accept the correction, even if the new professional consensus takes more than a generation. In fact, it's precisely because individuals find it difficult to correct themselves, or precisely because they benefit from the perspectives of others, that we should employ means of correction that harness public scrutiny and open access.

I draw on two propositions from John Stuart Mill. It may seem odd that they don't come from his philosophy of science, but his short treatise on the freedom of expression, *On Liberty* (1859). Mill made a powerful argument that freedom of expression is essential to truth-seeking, and in elaborating it pointed out the essential role of opening discussion as widely as possible. Here's how the two propositions look in their natural habitat:

Mill, *On Liberty* (Hackett Pub. Co., 1978) at p. 19:

[T]he source of everything respectable in man either as an intellectual or as a moral being ... [is] that his errors are corrigible. He is capable of rectifying his mistakes by discussion and experience. ... The whole strength and value, then, of human judgment depending on the one property, that it can be set right when it is wrong, reliance can be placed on it only when the means of setting it right are kept constantly at hand.

Mill at p. 20:

The beliefs which we have most warrant for, have no safeguard to rest on, but a standing invitation to the whole world to prove them unfounded. If the challenge is not accepted, or is accepted and the attempt fails, we are far enough from certainty still; but we have done the best that the existing state of human reason admits of; we have neglected nothing that could give the truth a chance of reaching us: if the lists are kept open, we may hope that if there be a better truth, it will be found when the human mind is capable of receiving it; and in the meantime we may rely on having attained such approach to truth, as is possible in our own day. This is the amount of certainty attainable by a fallible being, and this the sole way of attaining it.

Here's a quick paraphrase: To err is human, but we can always correct our errors. We needn't distrust human judgment just because it errs. But to trust human judgment, we must keep the means for correcting it "constantly at hand." The most important means of correction is "a standing invitation to the whole world" to find defects in our theories. The only kind of certainty possible for human judgment is to face and survive that kind of public scrutiny.

Let's look more closely at the process.

Mill argues at length that self-correction only works when people who think a theory is false or incomplete are allowed to say so. If church, state, tenure committees, or department heads punish deviations from orthodoxy, they will silence many voices, including—for all we know—the voices that could identify and correct its deficiencies. In short, scientific self-correction depends on the freedom of expression and works best in a free society.

Mill at pp. 20–21:

To call any proposition certain, while there is any one who would deny its certainty if permitted, but who is not permitted, is to assume that we ourselves, and those who agree with us, are the judges of certainty, and judges without hearing the other side.

Of course scientific self-correction depends on the usual ingredients of good science: observation, evidence, experiment, reasoning, and imagination. What is usually overlooked, and what Mill is adding to the list, is that it also depends on institutions, like legislatures, courts, and universities, in a position to protect the freedom of expression.

It's not enough to free up large numbers of people. We also need to free up all kinds of people. The reason is simply that there is such a thing as perspective, partiality, or prejudice. In fact, these are among the usual suspects for causing errors in human judgment, including errors in science. If the only people free to speak their minds are people like the author, or people with a shared belief in current orthodoxy, then we'd rarely hear from people in a position to recognize deficiencies in need of correction.

In short, we must issue "a standing invitation to the whole world" to find fault with our knowledge claims. This requires disseminating our claims as widely as possible. We don't have to compel everyone to read our work and comment on it. (It's an invitation, not an obligation.) But we do have to make our claims available to everyone who might care to read and comment on them.

That's OA in a nutshell, or OA from the perspective of authors and publishers. We can see the same point from the perspective of readers. Before we can identify the weaknesses in a theory, or hope to correct them, we must know what the theory says. Before we can decide whether an alleged error is an actual error, or whether a proposed correction is justified, we must know what the proponents and opponents of the theory have to say about it. Hence, another condition of scientific self-correction is access to the literature and discussion, the flip side of the worldwide invitation to scrutinize. Authors must provide access, and readers must have access. For the purposes of scientific progress, a society in which access to research is limited, because it's written in Latin, because authors are secretive, or because access requires travel or wealth, is like a society in which freedom of expression is limited. In both cases, we shrink the set of people who are in a position to notice and correct the deficiencies of a deficient theory. We add friction to the process of scientific self-correction.

Mark Twain said that the person who doesn't read has no advantage over the person who can't read. Similarly, at least for the purpose of scientific self-correction, scientists who are free to speak their minds but lack access to the literature have no advantage over scientists who lack the freedom to speak their minds.

Yes, this is the many-eyeballs theory, as it looked in the mid-19th century. Opening new theories to many eyeballs for scrutiny, especially when those eyeballs belong to people who are free to speak their minds, releases a torrent of many voices from many perspectives. The resulting disagreements make life difficult, and the standing invitation to the whole world makes it even more difficult. But working through those difficulties, or evaluating the evidence and arguments that can be brought to bear against a new claim, are exactly what scientists must do to inch asymptotically toward certainty. To short-circuit this process in the name of convenience is to compromise the possibility of correction.

Mill at pp. 19–20:

[T]he only way in which a human being can make some approach to knowing the whole of a subject, is by hearing what can be said about it by persons of every variety of opinion, and studying all modes in which it can be looked at by every character of mind. ... The steady habit of correcting and completing his own opinion by collating it with those of others, so far from causing doubt and hesitation in carrying it into practice, is the only stable foundation for a just reliance on it: for, being cognizant of all that can, at least obviously, be said against him, and having taken up his position against all gainsayers knowing that he has sought for objections and difficulties, instead of avoiding them, and has shut out no light which can be thrown upon the subject from any quarter—he has a right to think his judgment better than that of any person, or any multitude, who have not gone through a similar process.

Mill at p. 36:

So essential is this discipline to ... real understanding ..., that if opponents of [an idea] do not exist, it is indispensable to imagine them and supply them with the strongest arguments which the most skilful devil's advocate can conjure up.

Scientific self-correction depends on public scrutiny for two different purposes: first for noticing any errors in a theory and then for correcting them. OA advances both purposes, by exposing the theory to more readers, just as political liberty advances both purposes, by freeing readers to register their dissent and argue for other points of view. But the two steps don't always occur together. When a theory is false or incomplete, we make progress by noticing its weaknesses, even if we don't immediately know how to correct them. We make progress on both fronts by enlisting as much help as we possibly can.

We may discover new ideas in private and shape them into plausible hypotheses in private. But we validate knowledge claims in public. By embracing the method of public scrutiny, we aim for the kind of certainty that can answer criticism, not the kind of private certitude that excludes it. But once we acknowledge that the process is intrinsically public, and designed to move beyond the private feeling of confidence to the public examination of evidence, we must protect the process that makes it work. We may have to accept access restrictions, when we can't remove them ourselves, but we shouldn't forget the principle and believe that the process works as well with access restrictions as it would without. In a similar way, patriots may put their country ahead of individuals, on the ground that the whole is greater than the parts, but shouldn't forget the principle and put their country ahead of the world.

Mill at p. 17:

All silencing of discussion is an assumption of infallibility. ... [W]hile every one well knows himself to be fallible, few think it necessary to take any precautions against their own fallibility. ...

Maximizing access to our ideas, and inviting the whole world to scrutinize them, is one precaution against our fallibility which we can keep constantly at hand with very little effort. Print works better than letters to friends and colleagues; online access to paying customers, at least when many pay, can work better than print; OA works best of all.

The method of public scrutiny doesn't produce mathematical certainty in empirical sciences where the most we can expect is a high degree of confirmation. On the contrary, it introduces a very different standard: not proof, but longevity in a free society. The longer a theory survives the open challenge to expose its flaws, when everyone who cares has access to the literature and the freedom to speak their minds, the lower the odds that the theory has flaws to expose.

If a scientific result gains credibility the longer it lasts in a free society without falsification, then it gains an even greater measure of credibility the longer it lasts in free society *with OA* and without falsification. You might say that surviving n years with OA is equivalent to surviving mn years without OA, when m is a coefficient representing the friction in a non-OA system, or the inefficiency and delay caused by the lack of OA. Just don't start looking for m as if it were a constant of nature. Toll access varies widely in its extent, from work to work, place to place, and time to time, making m another variable, not a constant.

For scientific self-correction, OA is lubricant, not a precondition. Science made extraordinary progress during the age of print, when OA was physically and economically impossible. Indeed, much of the scientific progress in the 16th and 17th centuries was due to the spread of print itself and the wider access it allowed for new results. Widening access further through OA harnesses the same process for the same purpose. Limits on access (like limits on liberty) are not deal-breakers, just friction in the system. But we owe it to ourselves and our planet to take the friction out of the system as far as we can.

Postscript

Here are a few minor points I'd include in footnotes, if I had footnotes.

In my opening paragraph I distinguished moral, pragmatic, and epistemological arguments for OA. But clearly they overlap. In particular, pragmatic arguments (for example, that OA accelerates research) are components of moral arguments (accelerating research is good). Likewise, the epistemological argument I just sketched (OA facilitates scientific self-correction) can easily become a component of a moral argument (facilitating self-correction is good). So I'm less interested in drawing sharp lines to separate the types from one another than in pointing out that there *are* epistemological arguments for OA. OA can affect knowledge itself, or the process by which knowledge claims become knowledge.

Here are some examples of what I mean by moral arguments: OA frees authors and readers from needless access barriers; it returns the control of scholarship to scholars; by increasing the author's impact, it advances the author's purpose in writing journal articles for impact rather than money; it counteracts the deliberate creation of artificial scarcity; it counteracts the deliberate and accidental maldistribution of knowledge; it de-encloses a commons; it serves the under-served; and for the special subset of publicly-funded research, it is part of fundamental fairness to taxpayers.

Here are some examples of what I mean by pragmatic arguments: OA accelerates research and increases the productivity of researchers; it makes research more useful and increases the research funder's return on investment; it helps authors find readers and readers find authors; it reaches a wider audience at lower cost than toll-access forms of distribution; it saves money at both the author and reader sides of the distribution process; it widens dialog, builds community, and supports cooperation; it enhances preservation by freeing downstream users to make copies and migrate content to new media and formats; and it makes research literature and data available for crunching by new generations of sophisticated software (indexing, mining, summarizing, translating, linking, recommending, alerting, mash-ups, and other forms of processing).

The Millian argument for OA is not the "wisdom of crowds," at least not in the way in which this term was used and made popular by James Surowiecki. It's not about averaging or taking the vector of many disparate judgments. In an important way, it's the contrary. It's not about synthesizing plural judgments, but eliciting plural judgments without attempting to synthesize them. The precious correction we need is at least as likely to be found in an eccentric loner or statistical outlier as in a popular proposal or artificial synthesis.

All correctness, confirmation, and certainty under this theory coexist with the fallibility of human judgment and the possibility of challenge from unexpected directions. We needn't say that perfect certainty and objectivity are attainable, or that we've attained them; and if we did, our claim would be subject to criticism and correction like any other human judgment.

I didn't try to give an exhaustive account of the conditions that make scientific self-correction possible, and wouldn't trust myself to do so. I only wanted to go far enough to show the role of OA. If I were to extend the analysis to other conditions, I'd start with peer review and the kind of empirical content that underlies what Karl Popper called falsifiability.

Finally, by chance, there was a beautiful illustration of the Millian thesis in the news during May [May 2008, the month before this piece was published]. Jeffrey Young reported in the *Chronicle of Higher Education* that journal editors are noticing an "alarming" level of image-tampering in submitted articles. But journals needn't depend on the small number of in-house experts to detect the tampering. Quoting Young:

http://chronicle.com/free/2008/05/3028n.htm

http://www.earlham.edu/~peters/fos/2008/05/oa-enhances-error-correction.html

> One new check on science images, though, is the blogosphere. As more papers are published in open-access journals, an informal group of watchdogs has emerged online.
>
> "There's a lot of folks who in their idle moments just take a good look at some figures randomly," says John E. Dahlberg, director of the division of investigative oversight at the Office of Research Integrity [at the US Department of Health and Human Services, which includes the NIH]. "We get allegations almost weekly involving people picking up problems with figures in grant applications or papers."
>
> Such online watchdogs were among those who first identified problems with images and other data in a cloning paper published in *Science* by Woo Suk Hwang, a South Korean researcher. The research was eventually found to be fraudulent, and the journal retracted the paper. …

Open Access and the Last-Mile Problem for Knowledge

From "Open access and the last-mile problem for knowledge," SPARC Open Access Newsletter, July 2, 2008.

http://dash.harvard.edu/handle/1/4322587

After Hurricane Katrina hit the US gulf coast in August 2005, the Federal Emergency Management Agency (FEMA) bought 11,000 mobile homes for $431 million and shipped them to Arkansas for the evacuees. Six months later the homes were still sitting unused in an Arkansas cow pasture because federal rules—ironically, FEMA rules—prohibited the use of mobile homes in a flood plain.

http://tinyurl.com/4rks8t

In September 2005, Britain donated $5.3 worth of military rations to Americans displaced by Katrina. A month later the food was still sitting on a tarmac at Little Rock Air Force Base while officials tried to figure out whether US rules banning British beef allowed them to distribute the food to the needy. Meantime, the US was paying $16,000/month to store the food, and its expiration date was approaching fast.

http://www.washingtonpost.com/wp-dyn/content/article/2005/10/13/AR2005101 302084.html

When Cyclone Nargis hit the cost of Burma in May 2008, dozens of governments around the world shipped relief supplies to the country. At first the Burmese junta refused to accept the aid; then it accepted the aid but not aid workers; then it accepted aid and air workers but not ships or helicopters. Even after allowing aid into the country, much of it was stolen by the Burmese military and much was delayed on airport tarmacs or offshore until it was unusable. On June 5, more than a month after the disaster, a carrier group of four US ships returned to the US after being denied permission to unload its relief supplies.

http://en.wikipedia.org/wiki/Cyclone_Nargis#Military_junta.27s_blockade_of_aid

You could call this the "tarmac problem" for disaster relief. Or you could use a telecom analogy and call it a disastrous version of the last-mile problem.

In telecommunications the "last-mile problem" is the problem of connecting individual homes and businesses to the fat pipes connecting cities. Because individual homes and businesses are in different locations, hooking up each one individually is expensive and difficult. The term is now used in just about every industry in which reaching actual customers is more difficult than reaching some location, like a store or warehouse, close to customers.

We're facing a last-mile problem for knowledge. We're pretty good at doing research, writing it up, vetting it, publishing it, and getting it to locations (physical libraries and web sites) close to users. We could be better at all those things, but any problems we encounter along the way are early- or mid-course problems. The last-mile problem is the one at the end of the process: making individualized connections to all the individual users who need to read that research.

The last-mile problem for knowledge is not new. Indeed, for all of human history until recently it has been inseparable from knowledge itself and all our technologies for sharing it. It's only of interest today because the internet and OA give us unprecedented means for solving it, or at least for closing the gap significantly.

The problem is not that librarians "warehouse" knowledge in the pejorative sense of that term. On the contrary, they go out of their way to help users find and retrieve what the library has to offer, and often do the same for much beyond the library as well. The problem is to make individualized connections between knowledge, wherever it lies, and users, wherever they are. Even a well-stocked and well-organized library staffed by well-trained librarians can only solve a subset of that problem and connect a subset of users with a subset of knowledge.

A journal is many things, for example a collection, a periodical, a brand, and a peer-review filter. But it's also a tarmac. It's not the final destination for new research, just a landing place close to the final destination. If the articles inside only reach the journal and not the readers beyond, or if they only reach some but not all of the readers who need to read them, then every player up and down the chain of scholarly communication is frustrated: authors, author funders, author employers, editors, referees, publishers, librarians, and readers.

It helps to distinguish two reader-side stages of the last-mile problem for knowledge. Stage One is getting access to texts or data, and Stage Two is getting answers to questions. The first treats scholarly communication as a delivery system. When there's a problem, it's the failure to complete the delivery. The second treats scholarly communication as a knowledge system. When there's a problem, it's the failure to convey understanding.

Consider the difference between a conference lecture and the question period afterwards. The lecture is accessible to the people in the room, even unavoidable to them. There's no Stage One problem. But not even a good speaker can customize the talk for every member of the audience. For some listeners, the talk may be in the wrong language, at the wrong speed, at the wrong level of abstraction, or on the wrong subtopics. It may presuppose too much background or too little. It can still leave an unclosed gap between the speaker's knowledge and a given listener's understanding. The Q&A period can close that gap, at least when people with questions actually ask them and people with answers, perhaps the speaker, actually answer them.

Unfortunately, most existing knowledge isn't even as close to us as the conference lecture, let alone the individualized answer to our question. That's one reason, by the way, why Plato preferred speech to writing. Speakers are interactive and can close knowledge gaps in real-time Q&A, while writers are generally unavailable for interrogation about their writings, sometimes for the good reason that they are dead. Plato had a point: speech usually surpasses writing at solving the Stage Two problem. But the reverse is true for the Stage One problem. If we had to depend on live speakers for transmitting knowledge, when knowledgeable speakers were few and far between, then Stage One of the last-mile problem would be much more difficult than it already is.

First Things First: Stage One

You solve the last-mile problem for a published journal article when you put your hands on a hardcopy or display a digital copy on a screen in front of your face. This requires open access (OA) or money to pay for toll access (TA).

Acknowledging that money solves the problem, at least for some researchers, is just as important as acknowledging its limitations as a solution. It works for lucky individuals who have the money or who work at institutions that have the money. The snag, of course, is that all of us are unlucky for some priced literature, and most of us are unlucky for most of it.

The fact that the money solution doesn't work for everyone is the chief reason why the last-mile problem is a problem. Paying to make individualized connections for *some* individuals is clearly feasible and clearly affordable. But the problem is to make individualized connections for all individuals, or all those who need connections. Money just doesn't scale to the size of this problem. If the supply of published knowledge were fixed, money might have a chance to catch up with the demand. But the supply is growing exponentially and money to buy access to it is not. Inevitably, then, as the volume of TA literature grows, the percentage of it accessible to the average researcher declines, and the faster the volume of TA literature grows, the faster the accessible percentage declines. If all literature put a price on access, or if money were the only solution to the last-mile problem, the problem would worsen every year.

OA is the only solution that scales to the full size of the problem and keeps pace with the growth of published knowledge. No matter how fast the OA literature grows, you'll only need an internet connection to have access to all of it.

http://www.earlham.edu/~peters/fos/newsletter/03-02-04.htm#scaling

Until the 19th century, mailed letters were like scholarly journals: the costs were paid by readers or recipients. Senders could send mail without charge, but recipients had to pay to pick up their mail from the post office. If they couldn't pay, they had to do without. They often had to do without, creating a last-mile problem begging for a solution. Rowland Hill introduced the postage stamp in 1837 precisely to shift costs from recipients to senders. The sender-pays model made the system scale for the first time, triggered an explosion in the use of mail, and solved the last-mile problem.

http://www.earlham.edu/~peters/fos/newsletter/03-11-02.htm#analogies

When I say that the money solution doesn't scale, I mean money to pay for access to published literature, not money to do the research or publish the literature in the first place. That is, I mean money to solve the last-mile problem, not money to solve one of the early- or mid-course problems. Hence, the conclusion that the OA solution works better than the money solution doesn't imply that publishing can be made costless, any more than mail delivery can be made costless. The question raised by OA is not whether the production costs can be reduced to zero, but whether there are better ways to pay the bills than by charging readers, creating access barriers, and aggravating the last-mile problem.

Non-OA publishers, even those who lobby hard against OA policies, want to solve the last-mile problem as much as anyone. Non-profit or for-profit, green or gray, they have nothing to gain by leaving end-users disconnected from the knowledge they publish. The difference is that they want to steer stakeholders toward the money solution, not the OA solution. That's why Elsevier's Crispin Davis used to argue "that the government needs to lay down guidelines on the proportion of university funds that should be set aside for the acquisition of books and journals, or even increase funding to ensure that universities can buy all the material they need. ..."

http://www.theguardian.com/business/2005/feb/19/science.comment

http://www.earlham.edu/~peters/fos/2005/02/more-from-elsevier-ceo-on-university.html

If the telecom version of the last-mile problem had to be solved with copper wire or optic fiber, it would be much more difficult and expensive than it need be. Wireless connectivity solves the last-mile problem at a stroke for everyone with the right equip-ment. OA is the analog of wireless in the last-mile problem for knowledge. OA solves the Stage One problem at a stroke for everyone with an internet connection. Wireless and OA are revolutionary shortcuts that make connections to individual users without the need for individualized labor and expense.

If OA doesn't solve the problem for literally everyone, it's only because we haven't finished solving the telecom version of the last-mile problem. If both the money and OA solutions leave some people out, at least the OA solution will leave out fewer and fewer people as the digital divide continues to shrink, and the money solution will leave out more and more people as the volume of TA literature continues to grow.

Stage Two

Suppose you have a question. You're lucky if some careful, curious researchers have already asked the same question and done some of the needed research. You're luckier if some of them have taken the research far enough to answer the question, write up their answers, win the approval of peer reviewers, and publish them. You're even luckier if there's a scientific consensus on the right answer to your question and that among the published papers on it, at least one is up to date, written in your language, and written at your level of understanding. You're even luckier if the Stage One prob-lem has been solved and, thanks to OA or money, you have access to at least one of the enlightening papers which meets all your conditions.

It may look like this scenario goes about as far as it can to close the gap between you and existing knowledge. But it leaves some nagging parts of what I'm calling Stage Two of the last-mile problem. How do you go beyond access to answers? We grant that you're darned lucky, and that if you could find one of the enlightening papers, then you could retrieve it, and if you could read it, then you could understand it. But not all published papers meet your conditions for an enlightening paper. In fact, nearly all of them don't. How do you know that an enlightening paper even exists? When you go looking, how can you find one that meets your conditions, and distinguish it from other papers which happen to use the same keywords or even address the same question?

Without solutions to these problems, you might as well be trapped in a maze knee-deep in conflicting maps thrown over the wall by people trying their utmost to be helpful.

For people with less luck, Stage Two problems are more numerous and more dif-ficult. How do you do find a good answer when there's no consensus? When there *is* a consensus answer, how do you learn what it is when papers describing it are mixed together in your search results with papers describing discredited answers? How do you learn the consensus answer when there isn't a good paper in your language or at your level of understanding, or when the best papers use terms you'd never think to use in your search query? How do you get answers when nobody has yet posed the question exactly as you have posed it, and when partial answers lie scattered in dozens or hundreds of different papers in different journals in different languages and even different fields?

To solve these problems, access to the papers is necessary but not sufficient. But while OA is only part of the solution to the Stage Two problem, it's a precondition to most other parts of the solution. No tools yet suffice to solve the Stage Two problem, and maybe no tools ever will. But the tools that help us inch toward a solution presuppose OA literature and data the way telescopes presuppose open access to the sky. In fact, one of the primary benefits of OA is to provide the inputs to a new generation of sophisticated tools to facilitate research, discovery, and analysis. Whatever methods we use to attack Stage Two problems, OA will streamline our solutions and lack of OA will limit their scope and slow us down.

We already have some means to help us solve the Stage Two problem. Some are fairly mature and some are very rudimentary, but in every case talented people are working hard to improve them. I'm thinking of means to learn about the existence of relevant new work (alert systems), find the texts and the passages we need (search engines), find work already found by colleagues (tagging and social networking systems), find articles similar to ones we know to be relevant (recommendation systems), find articles in our own language (machine translation), navigate to cited sources (reference linking), navigate to different versions of cited sources or other relevant destinations (multiple-resolution hyperlinks), convert a text to speech when we can't read the screen (voice readers), paraphrase articles we don't have time to read (text summarizers), digest larger volumes of literature than we could ever read (text mining), combine independent resources to create new synergies and utility (mash-ups), find information relevant to our questions even when we don't know the relevant keywords (semantic web), distill uncopyrightable facts from natural-language texts and enter them into queryable OA databases (knowledge extraction), pose our search queries in our own words and sometimes even get back direct answers rather than mere pointers to literature that may contain answers (natural language search engines).

Most Stage Two problems can only be solved with human judgment. But that doesn't rule out the possibility of technologies to lend us a hand. The reason is simply that we are building technologies that harness human judgments, at least when those judgments are digital, online, and accessible to the tools. Stage Two solutions don't require machine-generated answers to our questions or magical forms of artificial intelligence. They only require barrier-free access to human-generated answers, human evaluations of those answers, and human evaluations of the evaluations. Tools to do these jobs are multiplying, they are improving, and they are interconnecting so that the output of one is the input to another. We don't have to predict the future in order to know that this kind of incremental, recursive progress can continue indefinitely, just as the compounding of mathematical functions can continue indefinitely.

As long as the last-mile problem remains unsolved, rapidly growing human knowledge will coexist with rapidly growing unmet demand for that knowledge. As long as the problem remains unsolved, the uses we make of recorded knowledge will fall far short of its usefulness.

It's staggering to think about what could happen if the knowledge we have painstakingly discovered, articulated, tested, refined, validated, gathered, and delivered to the tarmac were systematically distributed to all who need it. Imagine if what was known became more widely known, especially among those who could put it to use. Imagine if we became even 10% more effective at using what we know.

Delivering Open Access

The Case for OAI in the Age of Google

From "The case for OAI in the age of Google," SPARC Open Access Newsletter, May 4, 2004.

http://dash.harvard.edu/handle/1/4455494

Why don't more faculty deposit their eprints in open-access, OAI-compliant (OA-OAI) archives? This is a mystery. Two explanations we can rule out right away are opposition to open access and opposition to OAI [Open Archives Initiative, short for OAI-PMH or Open Archives Initiative Protocol for Metadata Harvesting] metadata sharing. These never come up when faculty are asked about their archiving inertia, which only makes the mystery even more puzzling.

When asked about archiving inertia, some faculty say that putting an eprint on a personal web site is just as good as putting it in an OAI-compliant archive. Google will find an eprint on a personal web site and make it visible to those who might need it for their research. Let's look at this one more closely. *Is* Google just as good? How strong is the case for OAI archiving in the age of Google?

For this purpose, let me use the name "Google" to represent not only Google itself but any Google rival or future iteration of Google that improves on Google's famously effective relevancy algorithm and wide scope. In short, let "Google" be our name for the state of the art in indexing by mainstream search engines.

So, is Google good enough? If not, why not?

(1) If we only care about open access itself, then it's true that putting an eprint on a personal or institutional web site is good enough. It's open access. [...]

(2) The OA-OAI proponent might concede that eprints on personal web sites can be OA. "But OA-OAI archiving enhances visibility more than Google indexing does."

The Google reply: This may have been true once, but it's less true or untrue today. There are two reasons why: Google is very good and getting better, and many more people turn to Google before they turn to OAI search tools. The second reason is peculiar. [...] Even if OAI tools would do a better job than Google, if they were as popular as Google, Google's surpassing popularity gives it a self-nourishing advantage. [...]

(3) This actually answers another argument that might be made for OAI archiving, but let's make the argument explicit anyway. "Scholars doing serious scholarly research look in specialized scholarly tools and resources before they look in Google."

The Google reply: Again, this might have been true once, and perhaps it ought to be true now, but either it's becoming untrue or it's already untrue.

Working researchers certainly do use Google even if they also use specialized scholarly tools. Moreover, unfortunately, in the period before scholars used Google for serious research, they weren't using OAI tools instead. Google and OAI tools are both rising in usage.

Two years ago (April 2002) a study by DK Associates showed that professional analytic and organic chemists turned first to ChemWeb and second to Google. It's impressive that Google occupied such an exalted position among such serious researchers that early in its evolution. The same study showed that chemists in management and development positions used Google first and ChemWeb second.

http://web.freepint.com/go/newsletter/109#feature

Since then, Google has improved its algorithms, its index size, and its popularity—and Elsevier has decided to discontinue ChemWeb. I haven't seen a more recent study, but I wouldn't be surprised if Google was #1 among working chemists today.

In his February 2004 keynote at the NFAIS annual meeting (p. 8), John Regazzi reported, "In a survey for this lecture, librarians and scientists were asked to name the top scientific and medical search resources that they use or are aware of. The difference is startling. Librarians named Science Direct, ISI Web of Science, and Medline, while scientists named Google, Yahoo, and PubMed (librarians also named PubMed)." Regazzi is Elsevier's Managing Director of Market Development.

http://www.nfais.org/RegazziFinalMilesConrad2004.pdf

[...]

(4) "Archiving will give an eprint a permanent or persistent URL." Compared to eprints on personal web sites, eprints in OAI archives rarely move. When scholars change institutions or retire, they usually change web sites, with the effect of breaking links that point to their work e.g., in search engines, bibliographies, footnotes, and other indices around the world. This is a reason to favor archives over personal web sites.

Google reply: True, but Google has a large and useful cache that greatly mitigates the damage of link rot.

Archiving will give an eprint other kinds of longevity, not just URL longevity. Those who maintain OAI-compliant repositories take steps to assure long-term access and preservation. [...]

(5) "OAI-compliant searching tools refresh their indices faster than Google."

Google reply: But this is not quite true. Google refreshes its index for different kinds of content at different rates, and assigns a slow rate to most scholarly pages. But eprints at sites that Google already rates highly are refreshed at a much faster rate. On the other side, the refresh rate at OAI-compliant data services is up to the service providers. At least this means that when we want to refresh the index often, we can do so, and we needn't hire expensive experts in "search engine optimization" in order to scam the Google index in a way that might not work next week.

(6) "OAI tools rest on a standardized metadata schema and therefore support field searching (e.g. on 'author' or 'title')."

Google reply: True, but the Google syntax does a lot of this and over time will do a lot more.

Here's a variation on the OAI argument: if users search for articles by their citations, rather than by content-based keywords, then OAI tools will help them more than Google will. I owe this argument to the EPrints Handbook.

http://software.eprints.org/incoming/lac/overview.php

The Google reply: It's true that OAI tools will provide better visibility to those who search by citations. But talented Google searchers will prefer to search by content-based keywords, not by citations. If they do, then they will likely find the same articles by a different route, though they will be combined with all the other articles that also satisfy the keywords. Insofar as the size of the hit list is a problem, see the next OAI argument.

(7) "OAI archiving reduces information overload." When you search across OAI-compliant archives for research literature, you find only research literature. But when you search in Google, you get commodities with the same names, popular literature on scientific topics, scientific name-dropping, crackpot hallucinations, and much more that you definitely don't want.

Google reply: This is true, but it overlooks the Google relevancy algorithm. In Google, you may get more hits than you could ever scan, and many of them will be worse than useless, but Google's PageRank algorithm does a pretty good job of putting the ones you want near the top. Just as it doesn't matter how deep the ocean is, as long as you can swim, it doesn't matter how many hits your search returns, as long as the ones you want float to the top. Moreover, skillful users know how to tweak their search strings to narrow the results and improve their relevancy. Finally, remember, the Google algorithm (in fact and ex hypothesi) is improving all the time. We don't have to say that the Google algorithm is perfect, merely that a good algorithm can neutralize much of the advantage of a smaller or more focused index and that this one is good and getting better.

Judge for yourself. Here are some terms from different academic fields and their Google hit tallies as of April 18, 2004. Run some of them and see whether any non-academic sites make it near the top of the list. Then tweak the search to refine the list. "Poincare conjecture" (2.8 thousand), "third-wave feminism" (3.9 thousand), "proto Indo-European" (12 thousand), "categorical imperative" (25.4 thousand), "valence electron" (27.2 thousand), "battle of Hastings" (39.7 thousand), "collateral estoppel" (46.9 thousand), "obsessive compulsive" (304 thousand), "black hole" (2.7 million), "inflation" (4.9 million), and "protein" (26.8 million). The general terms toward the end of the list get the most hits. But it's easy to conjoin them with other terms in order to reduce the hit list and improve relevancy. For example, try "black hole" plus "event horizon" (41.8 thousand), "inflation" plus "junk bond" (6.6 thousand), or "protein" plus "chirality" (47.8 thousand).

On the other side, any improvements that come to the Google algorithm could also in principle come to the OAI search tools. That would give the OAI tools a twofold strategy for reducing information overload—intelligent sorting and smaller or more focused indices. But even then, Google could claim a twofold strategy for finding what you want—the same intelligent sorting but yoked to a larger and more wide-ranging index. In short, the same small OAI indices that some cite as an advantage in reducing overload can always be seen as limitations on the search for what you want.

Here's a variation on the same OAI argument: "If you're searching for an unusual author name or term in Google, you'll probably find what you want. But if you're searching for a common term or name, then OAI searches will probably shorten your search."

I owe this argument to a participant in David Prosser's workshop on filling OAI archives at the CERN OAI meeting in February—a participant whose name unfortunately I do not know. If you are searching for "John Anderson," "piano," or "chess," Google will be less useful than if you are searching for "Spiro Agnew," "sackbut" or "43-man squamish".

(8) I'm out of OAI virtues that might surpass Google virtues. Are there any Google virtues that might surpass OAI virtues? Here's one: a gigantic index. But as we just saw, this advantage competes with the advantage of the smaller and more focused OAI indices. For some searches, a wide scope (plus a good relevancy algorithm) is more useful than a manageable hit list (plus a good inclusion policy), while for other searches the reverse is true.

Another place where Google has the advantage is full-text indexing. So far, OAI tools only search metadata. The very welcome OAI reply is that full-text indexing is coming. For one approach to it, see the work on the OA-X protocol.

http://web.archive.org/web/20040411030821/http://eepi.ubib.eur.nl/iliit/archives/ 000471.html

Sub-total

For every OAI virtue, there is some Google counterpart. This doesn't mean that the Google counterparts are superior or even equivalent. That will depend on variables such as your search skill, your search goal, and the year (remember, what we're calling Google is always improving).

I know you want me to choose between them but I'm not going to do it. If their merits really depend on your needs and circumstances, however, then this is already a kind of victory for Google, at least insofar as it means that putting an eprint on your personal web site won't *always* be worse, or won't be *much* worse, than depositing it in an OA-OAI archive. (If you're sorry that I'm not choosing between them, then here's a clue to my personal position: It was very difficult to bring myself to write out the previous sentence.)

Note how we have confirmed the wisdom of a general practice within the OA movement. If we provide OA to our eprints, then services to index and preserve them will come along after the fact. Depositing eprints in OAI-compliant archives makes those eprints fodder for all future OAI-compliant data services. Depositing eprints on a personal web site makes them fodder for all future iterations and rivals of Google. We don't have to wait for these services to emerge, or to reach a certain level of adequacy, before we provide OA to our eprints. On the contrary, we should provide OA to our work right now and let evolving data services compete to improve upon the visibility and longevity of our work for the rest of time. [...]

But this is key: OA-OAI archiving and Google indexing are completely compatible. We can do both, and we should. That's the main reason why I'm not going to choose between them. [...]

Good Facts, Bad Predictions

From "Good facts, bad predictions," SPARC Open Access Newsletter, June 2, 2006.

http://dash.harvard.edu/handle/1/4391309

Last year, the Kaufman-Wills Group sent a detailed questionnaire to a large number of journals, and received 248 responses from OA journals listed in the DOAJ, the largest number of OA journals ever surveyed. The responses turned up details on the business models of OA journals that are not visible from their web sites.

Among the Kaufman-Wills discoveries were two that I found especially striking:

(1) The majority of OA journals charge no author-side fees at all.
(2) The majority of non-OA journals do charge author-side fees (in addition to reader-side subscription fees).

Table 30 of the Kaufman-Wills report shows that 52.8% of DOAJ journals charge no author-side fees at all. The percentage for subscription journals was much lower: ALPSP journals overall (23.4), ALPSP for-profit journals (44.9), ALPSP non-profit journals (10.1), AAMC journals (14.7), Highwire subset (17.6). The Highwire subset consists (p. 3) of "those making their original articles freely available at some point after publication; that is Delayed Open Access journals."

As Sally Morris put it in her introduction to the report (p. 1), "On the financial side, we were very surprised to find just how few of the Open Access journals raise any author-side charges at all; in fact, author charges are considerably more common (in the form of page charges, colour charges, reprint charges, etc) among subscription journals." As Kaufman and Wills put it in the body of the report (p. 44), "Contrary to general belief, more than half of DOAJ journals did not charge author-side fees of any type, whereas more than 75% of ALPSP, AAMC, and HW subset journals did charge author-side fees."

See Cara Kaufman and Alma Wills, The Facts About Open Access, October 11, 2005. Their study was sponsored by the Association of Learned and Professional Society

Publishers (ALPSP), the American Association for the Advancement of Science (AAAS), and HighWire Press (HW), with additional data from the Association of American Medical Colleges (AAMC).

http://web.archive.org/web/20051103010701/http://www.alpsp.org/publications/pub 11.htm

For convenience, let me call these the "two facts" or "two discoveries."

The two discoveries were not only unexpected, but strikingly favorable to OA. They should recast much of the debate about OA journals. (Kaufman and Wills made other discoveries that are more critical of OA journals.)

The report came out in October 2005, and in the next three months I saw no signs of the debate-recasting that I expected. Nevertheless in January 2006 I made this prediction:

"It will start to sink in that fewer than half of OA journals charge author-side fees and that many more subscription-based journals do so than OA journals. ... What will this mean in practice? People will stop talking about "the OA business model" for journals as if there were just one. People will talk less about how OA journals might exclude indigent authors and compromise on peer review and talk more about how toll-access journals do so. We'll start to document the range of models actually in use for OA journals and learn as much about them as we now know about the model that charges author-side processing fees. We'll get more creative in finding models that suit the range of niches, which differ significantly by discipline and by nation. We'll see OA journals use multiple sources of revenue or subsidies, allowing even those that charge author-side fees to lower their fees."

http://www.earlham.edu/~peters/fos/newsletter/01-02-06.htm#predictions

This is the worst prediction I've ever made. The Kaufman-Wills figures have not been questioned, but their significance is not sinking in.

Significant for Five Reasons

The two facts should have implications for at least five aspects of the debate about OA journals.

(1) They should put an end to the false but widespread assumption that there is just one business model for OA journals (the one misnamed the "author pays" model). Some OA journals charge author-side fees and some don't—in fact, most don't. That's at least two models. There are undoubtedly many different models among the no-fee journals, but we'll have to do a lot more digging to find out what they

are. Opponents of OA like to say that "one size doesn't fit all" but in fact OA journals have embodied this truth from the beginning.

(2) The two facts should put an end to publisher objections that OA journals are more likely than non-OA journals to exclude indigent authors. The only basis for this charge was the hasty generalization that OA journals charged author-side fees and the ignorance that non-OA journals did so more often. Now we know that insofar as charging fees excludes indigent authors, many more subscription journals are guilty than OA journals. We know this even before we take into account that, when OA journals do charge fees, funding agencies are often willing to pay them and journals often waive them in cases of economic hardship.

http://www.earlham.edu/~peters/fos/newsletter/11-02-03.htm#objreply

(3) The two facts should put an end to publisher objections that OA journals are more likely than non-OA journals to compromise on peer review. This charge is based on the hasty generalization that OA journals charge a fee for every accepted paper, and the presumption that charging such a fee creates a financial incentive to lower standards. Now we know that insofar as charging fees for accepted papers is an incentive to lower standards, many more subscription journals are guilty than OA journals. We know this even before we take into account that OA journals with many excellent submissions can often accept more papers without lowering standards (because they have no size limits) and OA journals with a dearth of excellent submissions can accept fewer papers without shortchanging subscribers (because they have no subscribers). We know it before we take into account that OA journal fees are much closer to "subsistence-level" compensation than typical subscription fees. We know it before we take into account that subscription journals justify price increases by pointing to the growing volume of published articles. We know it before we take into account that fee-charging OA journals have firewalls between their financial and editorial sides. We know it before we take into account that subscription journals with lower standards and lower rejection rates have higher profit margins (because they perform peer review fewer times per published paper).

http://www.earlham.edu/~peters/fos/newsletter/03-02-04.htm#objreply

(4) The two facts should put an end to studies of author attitudes toward OA journals that misinform the interview subjects before interviewing them. I've been a referee for two studies that told authors that OA journals (per se, without qualification) charged "author fees" and then asked authors about their willingness to pay. The results were described as author attitudes toward OA journals (per se, without qualification) rather than author attitudes toward fee-charging OA journals.

(5) Finally, the two facts should put an end to the myth that if all journals converted to OA, then universities would pay more in author-side fees than they pay now in subscriptions. I want to say a lot more about this one, so let me start a new section.

Would Universities Pay More?

Last month, two new calculations appeared purporting to show that high-output research universities would pay more in author-side fees for OA journals than they pay now in subscriptions for non-OA journals:

William Walters, Institutional Journal Costs in an Open Access Environment, a preprint forthcoming from the *Journal of the American Society for Information Science and Technology*. (The preprint was released c. April 24, 2006.)

http://web.archive.org/web/20060514153639/http://www.library.millersville.edu/public_html/walters/journal_costs.pdf

http://legacy.earlham.edu/~peters/fos/2006/04/what-will-oa-journals-cost-universities.html

Magaly Báscones Dominguez, Economics of open access publishing, *Serials*, March 2006.

http://serials.uksg.org/ (no deep link)

http://legacy.earlham.edu/~peters/fos/2006/05/economics-of-oa-publishing.html

Before these two studies, Phil Davis and his colleagues did a similar calculation for Cornell University, August 2004.

https://dspace.library.cornell.edu/handle/1813/193

http://dspace.library.cornell.edu/handle/1813/236

When the Walters study came out, Phil Davis started a discussion thread on it at LibLicense, April 24, 2006.

http://web.archive.org/web/20060515181758/http://www.library.yale.edu/~llicense/ListArchives/0604/msg00106.html

All three studies calculate the difference between present university costs for subscriptions and the costs for author-side fees in a hypothetical world in which all journals converted to OA. In doing the calculation, all three assume that 100% of OA journals charge author-side fees. That is, none takes into account the Kaufman-Wills finding that only a minority of OA journals do so. (The Davis study came out in August 2004 and could not have taken this into account.)

Moreover, all three assume that 100% of the fees would be paid by universities, none by funding agencies. Yet today, I don't know of a single university that has started to pay these fees, but I know more than a dozen funding agencies willing to do so (some overtly, some quietly). The assumption in the calculation not only reverses the current reality, and has universities pay more fees than funding agencies, it utterly zeroes out the contribution from funding agencies.

It's not surprising that under these unrealistic assumptions, high-output research universities would pay more in author-side fees than in subscriptions. But there are two ways to regard that conclusion. We can take it as a glimpse of our likely future under OA journals, or we can take it merely as the unfolding of the consequences of certain assumptions, likely or not. The first picture aims to be true to the world, while the second only aims to be true to the premises. But this means that it's either false or useless. As a picture of our likely future, it depends on the truth or likelihood of its assumptions, and so fails. But I assume that it is a true picture of its premises even if it's a false picture of the world. That is, I assume that the authors did the math accurately. So now we know what would happen if a couple of very unlikely things happened. Does this help us? Only to the extent that the scenario it describes is plausible, realistic, or likely.

The authors of these studies don't say that their assumptions are true so much as convenient. But OA opponents have seized upon their calculations as if they depicted our likely future under OA journals. This is a mistake. Anyone who wants to use the calculations as credible pointers to a likely future must go beyond what the three authors have done and argue that the assumptions are true or likely to become true. So far nobody has done that (with the two key assumptions on which I'm focusing here) and I don't see that anybody can.

It's not regrettable that the authors undertook to the show the consequences of an unrealistic what-if scenario. What's regrettable is the way the conclusion is easily misinterpreted—and widely taken—as a picture of our future. It's equally regrettable that we don't yet have an equally careful picture of the consequences of more realistic what-if scenarios.

Let's continue to explore the hypothetical world in which all journals convert to OA. But instead of the very unlikely scenario in which 100% of OA journals charge fees, let's explore the scenario in which about half do and half don't—the scenario closest to a clean extrapolation from present patterns. Since present patterns may not hold, let's also explore the scenarios in which 0%, 10%, 20% … 100% of OA journals charge fees. Let's use a wider range of assumptions, including some that are true today, and debate later about which are more likely or realistic for our future.

Let's also explore the scenario in which some considerable percentage of fees is paid by funding agencies. I've never seen a good estimate of what that percentage is today, so we can't extrapolate from the present. To be fair to all possibilities, then, let's explore the scenarios in which 0%, 10%, 20% … 100% of author-side fees are paid by funders. Again, let's use a range of assumptions and debate later about which are more likely.

The results could be reported in a matrix showing when universities would pay more than they do now and when they wouldn't, and (for example) whether they'd pay more if 60% of OA journals charged fees and 30% of those fees were paid by funders.

Seeing the range of assumptions and their outcomes will not only help us discuss intelligently which scenarios are most likely, but also which are most desirable. We'll draw a map of hypothetical futures enabling us to steer toward the future we want.

It's somewhere between absurd and dishonest to assume that the one scenario already studied is the most likely, especially when it's so far from the present reality and when nobody is arguing that it's a likely evolution from the present reality. Let's stop citing the result as a picture of our future and start citing it as a picture of convenient but implausible assumptions that ought be refined and replaced by more accurate assumptions in follow-on calculations.

When we re-do the calculations with refined assumptions closer to today's reality, I'm convinced they will show that universities will pay *less* for OA journals than they pay today for subscription journals, even the universities with the highest research output. I'll bet a public apology on it.

Refining the calculations and publicizing the results is important and not just to set the record straight. Let me quickly put it in context. No serious OA advocate has ever said that OA literature is free to produce or publish. It can only be made free of charge for readers if people other than readers pay the bills. Producing broadcast television is not free of cost either; in fact, it's very expensive. But it's distributed to viewers without charge because others have agreed to pay the bills—for commercial TV, advertisers, and for public TV, donors of good will. That's the general model that will pay for OA journals, though the money can come from many sources other than advertisers and donors. So far, a good number of private foundations and public funding agencies have agreed to pay the bills (article processing fees) on behalf of their grantees. This helps researchers with grant funds, but unfortunately most researchers in most fields are not funded. We can close the funding gap for all academic researchers by persuading universities to start paying the fees on behalf of their faculty— or the subset of the fees not already covered by funding agencies. This will happen sooner rather than later if universities realize that paying these fees for OA journals will *cost them less* (and benefit everyone more) than paying subscription fees for toll-access journals.

Strengths of the Three Studies

I've criticized the two false assumptions used in all three studies, but I don't want to give the impression that the studies are not valuable in other ways. Nor do I want to give the impression that they are all the same.

Davis is very good at sketching some of the turf battles and political difficulties that are likely to arise once universities start to pay OA journal processing fees. These problems, though very ugly, aren't enough to make me stop calling on universities to start paying these fees—today as an investment in a superior scholarly communication system, tomorrow from the savings on canceled subscriptions—, but they are good reasons to start thinking about these problems now, before they arise.

Davis has helpfully made his data OA in an online spreadsheet. I'd have re-done his calculation myself but his spreadsheet isn't set up to make altering the two key assumptions easy. I haven't had time to figure out how to alter these two assumptions without an extensive rewrite of the sheet's structure and formulas. (Maybe a SOAN reader can with this.)

http://dspace.library.cornell.edu/handle/1813/236

Walters treats two scenarios separately. Under the first, OA journals charge the same author-side fee that PLoS journals charge ($1,500). Under the second, they charge whatever fee they need to generate the same revenue (including profit or surplus) that they receive today from subscriptions. Under the first scenario, all universities, even those with the greatest research output, would pay less for OA journals than they pay now for subscriptions. In fact, the savings would be significant. Top tier research universities, like the University of Michigan, would save about half their current serials budgets and low-output universities would save up to 97%. Only under the second scenario would the top tier research universities pay more. This distinction mitigates the harm of the two large false assumptions still present on his second scenario (that 100% of OA journals charge fees and that 100% of the fees are paid by universities), especially if we agree that subscription journals converting to OA will not maintain revenues at their old levels and will not need to.

BTW, Ray English shows in a LibLicense posting (April 27, 2006) that if the average fee per article was $3,363 or less, then even under Walters' second scenario all institutions would benefit from the conversion of subscription journals to fee-charging OA journals, *even if* we continued to assume that 100% of OA journals charge fees and that 100% of the fees are paid by universities. Walters showed what fee would be needed to preserve journal revenues at current levels, which came to over $6k/article, but not the fee needed to trigger savings for all universities, including those with the largest research output, which is what English computed.

http://web.archive.org/web/20060524070558/http://www.library.yale.edu/~llicense/ListArchives/0604/msg00125.html

Dominguez recognizes that some OA journals charge no author-side fees, but oddly, in her calculation, focuses on those that do charge fees, in effect assuming that all OA journals, or all the ones that matter, charge fees. She also understands that a good percentage of these fees is paid by funding agencies, though again, in her calculation she assumes that the research institution on which she focuses (CERN) would pay all of the fees incurred by its researchers.

A Few Qualifications

(1) There are two senses in which "universities will pay more" in a hypothetical future in which all journals are OA. First, high-output research universities may pay more *than low-output universities* to support OA journals. Second, high-output research universities may pay more for OA journals *than they pay now* for subscription journals. (The same distinction applies to the senses in which high-output *nations* will pay more.) The first is almost certainly true and I've never contested it. Nor do I think that it's a reason to resist OA journals—it's the flip side of the unobjectionable fact that high-output research universities pay more than low-output universities for journal *subscriptions* and would *save* more when these journals convert to OA. But that's a subject for another day.

(2) I'm not saying that present patterns will hold in the future. Today most OA journals charge no author-side fees. Today there are far more non-OA journals than OA journals, both in percentages and absolute numbers, that charge author-side fees. Today universities pay virtually no OA journal fees and foundations pay a hefty percentage (though we don't know the percentage). All three patterns are in flux. My argument is that we should look at a range of likely futures, not just the one very unlikely future.

(3) I have no idea whether the fee-based OA journals are higher in quality, lower in quality, or on average equal in quality to the no-fee OA journals. As far as I know, no one has studied this question. It only comes up here because someone might reply to my argument as follows: "Yes, most OA journals don't charge fees today. But most of the OA journals in which elite researchers are most likely to publish do or will charge fees." This is plausible, but the opposite guess is also plausible. Until we know more than we know now about the range of OA business models, their stability, and their relationship to editorial quality, let's enlarge our calculation to include different scenarios.

In the meantime, we shouldn't treat guesswork about quality as evidence of quality, and shouldn't make assumptions about quality unless we make plural assumptions in order to investigate this space without bias. Studies that limit themselves to fee-based journals on the assumption that they the only ones that matter must not draw sweeping conclusions about "OA journals" as such, but speak carefully about "OA journals that we assume are high in quality"—just as the studies to date should have spoken carefully about "OA journals that charge fees."

If you want a few quick examples of high-quality no-fee OA journals, then I can point to BMC's Beilstein Journal of Organic Chemistry and the Max Planck Institute's three Living Reviews on solar physics, relativity, and European governance. Like the Beilstein Journal, many other high-quality, high-prestige, and high-impact journals may prefer to arrange institutional subsidies than to charge author-side fees.

A Few Calls to Action

I'd like to revise my prediction, but it's safer to make the future than to predict it. So let me issue a few calls to action instead.

(1) Spread the word about the two facts unearthed by the Kaufman-Wills study. When you see someone assume that there's only one business model for OA journals (namely, author-side fees), or that OA journals are more likely than non-OA journals to exclude indigent authors, or that OA journals are more susceptible than non-OA journals to lowering their standards in order to generate revenue, then correct them. We know they're wrong. When you see someone assume that universities will pay more in author-side fees than they now pay in subscriptions, correct them. We know they're not relying on a fact but on a what-if scenario with false assumptions. If enough people cite the two facts, maybe in a year or so, they really will start to sink in.

(2) Over time, especially as high prices and OA competition cause more cancellations of subscription journals, universities will enter the game of paying processing fees at the subset of OA journals that charge fees. When that happens, not only will we have to face and work out the ugly political scenarios sketched by Phil Davis, but we will have to investigate the many no-fee business models and their relationship to journal quality. We need to know how many different ways there are to pay the bills of a peer-reviewed journal and how well they work in different niches. Let's start now.

(3) As more institutions become willing to pay the processing fees charged by the subset of OA journals that charge fees (public funding agencies, private foundations, universities, sponsors), the terms "author fees" and "author pays" will be even more deceptive than they are today. Let's kill them once and for all. They're false when applied to the majority of OA journals that charge no fees. They're misleading when applied to journals whose fees are frequently waived or paid by sponsors on the author's behalf. And they're harmful for raising groundless or exaggerated fears among authors. They're much better for anti-OA FUD than accurate communication.

No-Fee Open-Access Journals

From "No-fee open-access journals," SPARC Open Access Newsletter, November 2, 2006.

http://dash.harvard.edu/handle/1/4552050

A year ago last month, Cara Kaufman and Alma Wills found that only 47% of surveyed OA journals charged author-side fees (see pp. 1, 44, and Table 30).

http://www.alpsp.org/Ebusiness/ProductCatalog/Product.aspx?ID=47

To me, this was a little like the first human sighting of the Antarctic land mass in 1820: proof that a huge terra incognita existed just over the horizon, awaiting exploration.

Only a minority of existing OA journals actually used the most-studied and most-discussed business model for OA journals—charging author-side fees. (Let's call these "fee-based" OA journals.) The majority of OA journals turned out to use business models that had rarely been acknowledged, let alone studied. (Let's call these "no-fee" OA journals.) We thought we understood OA journals but we only understood a subset, and the greater part of the whole was still largely unknown.

I wish I could tell you how many different ways the no-fee journals have found to pay their bills, and which methods work best in which disciplines and countries. But I can't. No one has done the studies yet. A few ships have approached the coastline of this land mass but we haven't come close to penetrating the interior or producing a map.

Some no-fee OA journals have direct or indirect subsidies from institutions like universities, laboratories, research centers, libraries, hospitals, museums, learned societies, foundations, or government agencies. Some have revenue from a separate line of non-OA publications. Some have revenue from advertising, auxiliary services, membership dues, endowments, reprints, or a print or premium edition. Some rely, more than other journals, on volunteerism. Some undoubtedly use a combination of these means. But we don't know how many other sources of revenue might be missing from this short list. We don't know how many no-fee journals use which method, and we don't know how the methods compare with one another for financial sustainability.

We have a lot to learn from the no-fee journals. Whatever their business models, and whatever their adequacy, they have found ways to generate revenue or subsidies that other journals (both OA and non-OA) could use or try. Exposing their models to scholarly attention and community-wide discussion might even uncover ways to refine and enhance them. Understanding how no-fee journals make ends meet will not only open up new ways to support OA journals, but also new ways to help TA journals convert to OA. And beyond financial support, no-fee journals have some clear advantages over fee-based OA journals, even if fee-based journals have their own set of advantages. The more we know about them, the more editors and publishers can make intelligent decisions that fit their research niches and special circumstances.

For about five years, the discussion of OA journals has been harmed by a family of false assumptions: that all OA journals are fee-based; that all good OA journals must be fee-based; that author-side fees are "author fees" to be paid by authors out of pocket. Learning about no-fee OA journals will correct at least the first two of these. Correcting them will lower the temperature of some debates and save time we now waste correcting errors, interviewing misinformed interview subjects, or dragging discussions back on topic. It will also help us overcome a collective blindspot. When we do, we'll see many beautiful opportunities that we have been too blind to pursue.

And beyond all these good utilitarian reasons to outfit some ships and start exploring, there's this simpler reason: the majority of OA journals are no-fee. We should know our own world.

But while we're waiting to hear back from the explorers, there's a lot that we can already say about the characteristics and advantages of no-fee OA journals. Here's a start.

*

I've often argued that fee-based OA journals don't exclude indigent authors. But that's only if they offer fee waivers or if sponsors are available to pay the fees on behalf of authors. These safety nets must be arranged and, no doubt, cannot always be arranged. No-fee OA journals cut through the difficulties and put well-funded and unfunded authors on the same footing, without further ado.

*

Likewise I've often argued that fee-based OA journals don't corrupt peer review. But that requires good firewalls between the editorial and business sides of the journal, and it's hard to know exactly what firewalls are in place at a given journal and easy to take cheap shots. No-fee OA journals disarm the objection without the need for further explanation or proof.

In both cases (excluding indigent authors and corrupting peer review), no-fee OA journals eliminate both the problem, to whatever extent it actually exists, and the appearance of the problem. Hence, they make it unnecessary to take other steps to avoid the problems, saving time and money, and they put common objections to bed, changing the rhetoric and direction of the debate.

*

The no-fee sources of revenue can help a journal make ends meet even if they don't suffice. One important consequence is that they can help a fee-based journal keep its fees low, perhaps low enough to attract authors who don't have sponsors and improve author uptake.

For semantic reasons, we can't say that fee-based and no-fee models can coexist in the same journal, since even a small author-side fee is a fee. But the different forms of generating revenue can not only coexist, but complement each other in very helpful ways.

The coexistence might be contingent. For example, an institution, like a university, might agree to cover a journal's expenses provided the journal charged author-side fees to authors whose research was funded by a grant. Because funders would pay first, universities would save money (compared to paying all a journal's expenses). Because universities would play back-up, scholars wouldn't be bereft or out of pocket in fields where funding is scattered or uncommon.

Even non-OA journals could strike such arrangements with institutions. If some percentage of their costs were covered by an institutional subsidy, then they could lower their subscription prices accordingly. If the non-subscription income grew to a certain size, they could convert from subscription journals to low-fee journals and perhaps later to no-fee journals.

*

The fee-based model works best in fields, like medicine, where most research is funded and most funders are willing to pay the fees. It's hard to know without study where the no-fee model will work best. It will work in fields where there are already institutions willing to subsidize an OA journal. But it will also work in fields where scholarly entrepreneurs, who are highly motivated and know the terrain, could *find* an institution to support a journal, even if the institution never thought about it before.

Conversely, the fee-based model is not well-suited to fields, like social sciences and humanities, where little research is funded. And again, it's hard to know where the no-fee model might not be suited; we may not know until scholarly entrepreneurs try hard and fail to find subsidies.

Because both models have their place, I don't want to say that the advantages of no-fee journals mean that fee-based journals should give way to no-fee journals. Not at all. I just want to point out the advantages of the no-fee model so that it will be fully explored by journals that can't make the fee model work for them.

For example, we should remember that the Hindawi OA journal collection is already profitable, and that all the journals in the collection depend on author-side fees. This means that author-side fees can not only generate enough revenue to pay the bills, but can also generate more. This is a signal success that we shouldn't try to undo. Instead, we should pursue no-fee journals alongside successful fee-based journals.

On the profitability of the Hindawi OA journals, see Paul Peters' comment on the Nature Newsblog, June 21, 2006.

http://blogs.nature.com/news/blog/2006/06/openaccess_journal_hits_rocky.html# comment-17436

*

Rick Johnson once argued that university libraries should "adopt" journals in order to digitize their backfiles for OA and preservation.

http://eprints.rclis.org/archive/00007465/01/Open_Past.pdf

http://legacy.earlham.edu/~peters/fos/2006/10/digitizing-journal-backfiles-for-oa .html

That's an excellent idea. Likewise, universities should adopt OA journals in order to pay their expenses. One of my favorite examples is Philosophers' Imprint, whose expenses are covered by the University of Michigan. Its motto is "Edited by philosophers, published by librarians." The editors in the philosophy department and the "publishers" in the library are already on the university payroll and allowed to spend some of their time putting out the journal. As a result, the journal doesn't charge subscriptions on the reader-side or fees on the author-side.

http://www.philosophersimprint.org/

*

I'm glad to see so many traditional publishers experiment with hybrid OA journals. But so far all of them are fee-based. I'd like to see publishers start experimenting with institutional subsidies as well. If a journal can't secure a permanent or renewable subsidy, it should try a temporary one. If it can't secure a full subsidy, it should try a partial one or several partial subsidies from several institutions.

The experiments could also run the other way. Universities, labs, libraries, societies, museums, foundations, learned societies, and government agencies should consider offering full or partial subsidies or forming consortia to offer subsidies.

There could even be hybrid OA journals that depend on subsidies rather than author-side fees. If a journal can arrange subsidies to allow (say) 20% of its research articles to be OA, then it could provide OA for that 20% and TA for the rest. Or it could provide no-fee OA to 20%, fee-based OA to another 20% (or whatever uptake it could generate), and TA for the rest. It could use any number of criteria or methods to pick the lucky no-fee OA articles—author preference, editor preference, length, use of multimedia, likelihood of citations, likelihood of interest from policy-makers or the media, or relevance for solving important scientific or social problems.

One more thing we don't know: how much experimentation has been stymied by the false belief that OA journals must use author-side fees.

*

An institution can subsidize a journal without publishing it, for example, the way the Beilstein-Institut covers the costs of the Beilstein Journal of Organic Chemistry (allowing the journal to charge no author-side fees) while the publishing is left to BioMed Central. Conversely, an institution can publish a journal without subsidizing it, something we see at any OA journal published by a university press and using a fee-based model rather than a subsidy model. Or an institution can do both, for example, the way the University of Michigan both subsidizes and publishes Philosophers' Imprint.

*

In an August 2004 report, librarians at Cornell envisioned that universities would trigger difficult political tensions on campus as they started to pay author-side fees and set faculty into competition for support from a limited fund. While I reject one of the main conclusions of the report (see SOAN for June 2006), its recognition of potential turf battles in the allocation of author-side fees is astute and needs wider discussion.

http://dash.harvard.edu/handle/1/4391309

> Cornell Task Force on Open Access Publishing, August 2004 (see esp. pp. 10–11)
>
> http://web.archive.org/web/20041220211746/http://dspace.library.cornell.edu/handle/1813/193
>
> In a later LibLicense posting, Phil Davis elaborated on these scenarios, April 2006.
>
> http://web.archive.org/web/20060524070725/http://www.library.yale.edu/~llicense/ListArchives/0604/msg00132.html

I concede that these scenarios are ugly, but I still want universities to join foundations in their willingness to pay author-side fees, and to start thinking about allocation procedures that faculty will accept as fair. But part of our thinking should be that no-fee OA journals will make *this* problem disappear. To the extent that no-fee journals spread, universities will not have to pay author-side fees or adjudicate disputes between rival professors applying for limited funds.

On the other hand, tensions might merely shift from individual faculty seeking subsidies for articles to departments or research centers seeking subsidies for journals. The problems may be tractable: after all, libraries currently pay more (much more) for journals in some disciplines than others without triggering campus wars. Or they might be as difficult and ugly as Cornell predicted for author-side fees. Whether support for one kind of OA journal will be easier—financially or administratively—than support for the other is one more thing we still have to learn. And there's some urgency about it because the money now spent on subscriptions will be needed, long-term, to pay for the OA alternative, and the transition is already under way.

Apart from fairness issues, supporting some number of no-fee journals should be less bumpy than paying the author-side fees incurred by individual faculty. The expenses will be more predictable. Hence, at least in this respect, universities should find it easier to put journal subsidies into the budget than author-side fees—though I hope they will do both, as money is freed up from subscriptions.

*

One silly criticism of author-side fees is that they're just subscriptions under a new name, especially if the money to pay them comes from the library's serials budget. It's silly because it overlooks the role of *open access*, the whole point of the new model. Author-side fees may be payments that help cover journal expenses, like subscription fees, but they pay for open access, not private use and consumption. Hence, they make a journal's contents freely available to everyone, including those who don't pay fees.

As no-fee OA journals spread, including the kind supported by institutional subsidies, we should expect to hear a new version of the same silly criticism: institutional subsidies are just subscriptions under a new name. The answer is the same: yes, these are payments that help cover journal expenses, but they pay for open access, not private consumption. For example, if a no-fee journal uses an institutional-subsidy business model, then only one institution has to make the payments for everyone else to have access.

*

I'm not committed to the term "fee-based" OA journal and would welcome a better one. But in the meantime, it's infinitely better than the term "author pays." First, it's not false or misleading. "Author pays" is false for the majority of OA journals that charge no author-side fees, and false or misleading for most of the remaining OA journals whose fees are often waived or paid by sponsors on the author's behalf. Second, it's not as frightening to authors or as helpful to the anti-OA FUD campaign. Third, it pairs up nicely with the "no-fee" OA journal, helping us communicate the true diversity of the OA journal landscape.

*

It used to be very hard to tell whether an OA journal was fee-based or no-fee and impossible to search for one type or the other in a given field. But just last month the Directory of Open Access Journals (DOAJ) added features to help on both fronts.

http://www.doaj.org/

[...] The announcement (October 14, 2006) of the new service, and most of the blog and listserv discussion, have focused on the new visibility of hybrid journals in the directory. But in my view the new visibility of no-fee journals is at least as useful. With the help of the DOAJ's new service and some old notes, here are some representative no-fee, peer-reviewed OA journals from 22 different fields.—My apologies to good no-fee journals not on this list; I had to keep it short. This is a glimpse of the continent we need to explore. [Here omitting the list of journals from the original article.]

[Note added in 2009:] Since this article appeared in November 2006, newer studies have confirmed and extended the finding that most OA journals charge no publication fees. In November 2007, Caroline Sutton and I found that 83% of society OA journals charged no publication fees. In December 2007, Bill Hooker's survey of all full-OA journals in the DOAJ found that 67% charged no publication fees. In March 2008, Heather Morrison found that 90% of the psychology journals listed in the DOAJ charged no publication fees. In May 2009, Stuart Shieber found that 70.3% of all full-OA journals in the DOAJ charged no publication fees.

http://dash.harvard.edu/bitstream/handle/1/3746501/suber_news115.html#list

http://legacy.earlham.edu/~peters/fos/2007/12/new-data-showing-that-most-oa-journals.html

http://poeticeconomics.blogspot.com/2008/03/less-than-10-of-open-access-journals-in.html

http://blogs.law.harvard.edu/pamphlet/2009/05/29/what-percentage-of-open-access-journals-charge-publication-fees/

Balancing Author and Publisher Rights

From "Balancing author and publisher rights," SPARC Open Access Newsletter, June 2, 2007.

http://dash.harvard.edu/handle/1/4391158

In order for authors to provide OA to their own work, they don't need to retain full copyright, and in order for publishers to publish, they don't need to acquire full copyright. This raises the hope that we might find a balance giving each side all it needs. But even with good will on both sides, this win-win compromise may be out of reach; each side might give and receive significant concessions and still not have all it needs.

There were two developments in May [2007] that could affect the balance between author and publisher rights. First, a group of universities adopted an "author addendum" to modify standard publisher copyright contracts and a pair of non-profits enhanced their own author addenda. Second, a group of publishers adopted a position statement on where the balance lies. Not surprisingly, the two groups strike the balance in different places. I'll look at them in order.

(1) Author addenda

[...]

(2) Publishers describe how they'd balance author/publisher rights

Meantime on May 9 [2007], three publisher associations released a position paper titled, "Author and Publisher Rights For Academic Use: An Appropriate Balance." The three groups were the ALPSP (Association of Learned and Professional Society Publishers), AAP/PSP (Association of American Publishers / Professional/Scholarly Publishing), and STM (International Association of Scientific, Technical & Medical Publishers).

For convenience I'll call the authors of this document "the publishers." But everyone should understand that not all publishers share the views set forth in this document, perhaps not even all publishers who belong to the ALPSP, AAP/PSP, or STM.

The heart of the document lies in two assertions, one on author rights and one on publisher rights:

[1] Academic research authors and their institutions should be able to use and post the content that such authors and institutions themselves provide ... for internal institutional[,] noncommercial research and education purposes; and

[2] Publishers should be able to determine when and how the official publication record occurs, and to derive the revenue benefit from the publication and open posting of the official record (the final published article), and its further distribution and access in recognition of the value of the services they provide.

*

The first statement, on author rights, seems to say that free online access should be limited to the author's own institution.

But I'm not sure. Does the adjective "internal" apply only the word immediately following it or to all the words following it to the semi-colon? If the former, then the statement would allow OA postprints to be used for non-commercial research whether or not it was internal to the author's institution. That's good; authors need at least that much, and OA archiving provides it. If the latter, then the statement would restrict the use of archived articles to the author's institution. That would mean the end of OA archiving, which by design makes content accessible to all users everywhere. If the publishers meant to limit free access to the author's institutions, then their position is one-sided, insufficient, and a retreat from the permissions most publishers already give to post to an institutional repository.

The sentence in the press release slightly supports the first reading by inserting a comma after "institutional," while the sentence in the body of the paper slightly supports the second reading by omitting the comma.

Several contributors on several discussion lists interpreted the statement in the second way and publishers on the same lists did not contradict them. So it appears that publishers did mean to limit free access to the author's institution.

But what does it mean for publishers to have meant that? The question arises because most of the same publishers permit OA archiving without delay, fee, special requests, or scope restrictions. The publishers' position paper is at odds with their own copyright transfer agreements.

In explaining this disparity, one possibility is that publishers permitted self-archiving in the first place without quite understanding what they were getting in for, and are now testing the waters for a retraction. (That is, they underestimated the power of OAI interoperability and didn't anticipate crawling by Google, Yahoo, Microsoft, and Scirus, let alone archiving mandates from funding agencies and universities.) They may see the position paper as the first step toward creating a "new normal" in which permission for self-archiving is limited to permission to make a work accessible to the author's own institution. Or, they may have no plans for a retraction, but feel the need to push back against the rising talk of author rights, for example, represented by the proliferating author addenda. They may eventually revise their copyright agreements to match the position paper, which would obstruct research, alienate authors, and deter submissions. Or they may revise the position paper to match their copyright agreements, which they would probably cast as a concession to authors. But as long as they do neither, it's hard to know their real position.

The publishers don't even acknowledge the disparity between the position paper and the widely-granted permission for unrestricted postprint archiving. In one section of the position paper, alluding to the permission to self-archive, they write that, "[g]iven the scholar-friendly nature of most academic journal publishers' copyright policies, a further question may be raised as to whether anything more is needed from publishers in order to accommodate the needs of academics and academic institutions." If publishers do grant permission for unrestricted self-archiving, then indeed authors may not need more. But if publishers are cutting the heart out of that permission, then authors need a lot more.

What matters for authors is that about 93% of surveyed non-OA journals currently allow preprint archiving without institutional or geographic limits, and about 70% allow equally unrestricted postprint archiving. Our job is to make sure that authors understand that self-archiving is easy, lawful, beneficial, and an opportunity that only they can seize.

Note that the position paper also limits free access to non-commercial use. While I've often argued that researchers should permit commercial re-use of their work, publishers needn't permit commercial re-use of theirs. On the other hand, publishers only need to restrict the commercial distribution of their publications, not the use of their publications by researchers with commercial plans or motivations.

*

For the rest of the reason why the publisher position is unbalanced we have to look at the next statement, on publisher rights. Unfortunately it's even more difficult to parse.

"Publishers should be able to determine when and how the official publication record occurs. ..." If the occurrence of a record is the publication of an article, then determining "how" it occurs is the whole question. Giving this entirely to publishers is to give up the quest for balance.

"Publishers should be able to ... derive the revenue benefit from the publication. ..." Is the "revenue benefit" more than just "the revenue"? Publishers do have the right to sell their publications, of course. That's non-controversial. But are publishers also claiming the right to all the revenue that anyone can make from it? What if I'm offered an honorarium to speak at a conference on the strength of my publication? What if Google indexes the repository copy and puts ads on the page of search returns? What if I link to a copy, even the publisher's copy, from a page hosting ads? What if a team of industrial scientists pays for access but uses the resulting knowledge to make a product which their company sells for a profit? I'm not saying that the publishers are claiming all this revenue, merely that the statement needs clarification.

"… and open posting of the official record (the final published article) …" What's the open posting of the official record? What's the revenue benefit of the open posting of the official record? If this is about open access to the publication, then what revenue are the publishers talking about?

"… and its further distribution and access in recognition of the value of the services they provide." I understand that publishers want the revenue from the paper's "further distribution and access." But is this "further distribution" more than the publication already mentioned? If so, what does it include? Self-archiving? If so, again, what revenue are they talking about?

More importantly, are the publishers saying they deserve the revenue because of the value of the services they provide? It seems so. But there are three problems here. First, authors, referees, and funders provider valuable services that enhance the same final product, competing with the publishers' claim to exclusive rights. I'll say more about this one below. Second, a significant fraction of publisher revenue doesn't come from the value they add but from price increases made possible by monopoly power and market dysfunction. Reducing their prices to the value they add would be a nice change. And third, in order to keep the revenue stream flowing, publishers take many steps that actually subtract value from the final product, such as password protection, packaging in locked PDFs, cutting good articles solely for length, turning processable data into unprocessable images, and turning gifts into commodities which may not be further shared.

Let's look more closely at the first of these. The publishers are arguing that because they add value to the publication, they deserve exclusive rights in it, in effect letting them control access beyond the author's own institution. This is neither balanced nor good for research. Publishers do add value, primarily the organization of expert volunteers who provide peer review. But no matter how many other forms of publisher-added value we recognize, and no matter how we estimate their overall benefits, there's no doubt that publishers add *less* value to the final product than authors, who do the research and writing, and funders, who pay for the original research. When there are funders in the picture at all, their support is usually at a level greater than the cost of publication and sometimes at a level thousands of times greater. But in current practice authors and funders don't get the right to control access to the final product, and in this document publishers want to perpetuate the arrangement in which the right to control access ends up in their hands, not those of contributors who add greater value.

There are two main reasons why we find ourselves in the odd situation in which publishers get to control access even though they add less value than authors or funders.

The first is that publishers demand compensation for their services, while authors and funders do not. The second is that publishers believe the only way to be compensated is to control access and charge for it. This is their business model from the age of print, when it was physically impossible to make perfect copies for a worldwide audience at zero marginal cost. Their business model depends on scarcity, which for digital texts in a networked world is always artificial scarcity.

Publishers are not appealing to the principle that adding value carries the right to control access. If they were, then all contributors who added value would have to share control. Nor are they appealing to the principle that the right to control access belongs to the contributor who adds the greatest value. If they were, they'd have to make a serious argument that their contribution is more valuable than the author's or funder's. They are demanding the right to control access because they need compensation for their services and choose a business model that depends on access barriers and artificial scarcity.

Even if we don't think this situation is perverse and cries out for change, at least we should notice that their position is not about balance. It's about what publishers need or want, regardless of what authors need or want.

Am I saying that publishers should join authors and funders in working without direct monetary compensation? Not at all. Publishers deserve to be paid for the value they add. But it doesn't follow that they deserve to control access or that they deserve a package of exclusive rights that bars author-initiated OA. These extra demands don't arise from the value they add but from an access-limiting business model that is optional, obstructive, and obsolete.

Instead of starting from the proposition that publishers add value, and deserve whatever they think it takes to compensate them for it, including artificial limits on access to knowledge, I suggest that it's more balanced to start from the proposition that many contributors add value, that they all deserve suitable compensation, and that letting publishers limit access prevents this equitable division of rewards, harms the other contributors, and harms research.

The position paper makes several other, lesser assertions.

"Exclusive rights also provide a legal basis for publishers to ... enforce copyright claims with respect to plagiarism. ..."

*

It's inaccurate and disingenuous to argue that publishers need exclusive rights to prosecute plagiarists. First, the rights are rarely used this way. Plagiarism is typically punished by the plagiarist's institution, not by courts—that is, by social norms, not by law. Second, if it's ever desirable to pursue a plagiarist in court and authors don't give publishers the right to do so on their own, then authors retain that right to use as they see fit. Third, many authors would rather have a larger audience and impact than give their publisher the seldom-used legal tools to prosecute plagiarists. Authors should make this decision, not publishers. Finally, if an author discovers a plagiarist and the publisher really wants to get involved, the author can always delegate the publisher to act as his/her agent. For this purpose, publishers don't need rights from the time of publication, nor do they need exclusive rights, let alone a policy to limit access to the author's work.

Behind this argument there's a confusion of plagiarism and copyright infringement. Someone can commit plagiarism without infringing copyright (by copying a fair-use excerpt and claiming it as one's own) and infringe copyright without committing plagiarism (by copying a larger excerpt but with attribution). One can also commit both together (by copying a large excerpt and claiming it as one's own), but that doesn't collapse the distinction. One can commit just about any two offenses together.

*

Publishers "are concerned about the potential to waste monies with unnecessary duplicate systems" (when public funding agencies mandate OA archiving for publicly-funded research).

It's also disingenuous for publishers to argue that OA mandates at public funding agencies will lead to wasteful duplication. Some publishers do provide OA to some content when it's sufficiently old. But this is a far cry from providing OA to virtually all publicly-funded research within six months of publication. If ALPSP, AAP/PSP, and STM are saying that the voluntary efforts of their members will approach what FRPAA [Federal Research Public Access Act] (for example) would mandate, then the duplication argument starts to make sense. But in that case they have to stop arguing that OA to publicly-funded research would kill their revenues, kill their journals, and kill peer review. They can't have it both ways.

*

"[F]unding agencies, search engines, and other third parties who wish to use or distribute the publisher versions of journal articles should only do so upon consultation and under an agreement with the publisher. ..."

It's vast over-reaching to say "use or distribute" here. Third parties like readers may lawfully "use" publisher versions in countless ways without consultation or permission.

If we limit the statement to "distribute," it's fair enough but not really responsive to funder mandates for OA archiving. These funder mandates do not apply to the published version of an article, but only to the final version of the author's peer-reviewed manuscript.

*

Finally, publishers argue that fair use is limited to print: "there are exceptions and limitations to copyright laws that may in certain limited circumstances permit the copying of journal articles for certain purposes, but ... these exceptions are thus far limited to traditional photocopying and do not permit the exploitation of such materials over the Internet."

This is simply untrue. For example, the US District Court of Nevada ruled that it was fair use for Google to index and cache a copyrighted online news story by Blake Field (Field v. Google, 2 F. Supp. 2d 1106 (D. Nev. 2006)). The Ninth Circuit Court of Appeals ruled that it was fair use for Arriba to display thumbnails of Kelly's copyrighted online photographs even if it might not be fair use to display full-sized copies (Kelly v. Arriba Soft, 280 F.3d 934 (CA9 2002)).

Even if publishers could subtract fair use from the online freedoms of researchers, they would simply have to add even more to the authors' pan of the scale if they really want to achieve a balance.

*

I haven't answered the big question whether a win-win balance can be struck that gives both authors and publishers all that they need. I'm not ready yet. I know the publishers' position statement is not that balance, and they may say that no author addendum they've yet seen is that balance either. Universities adopting author addenda are at least trying to approach such a balance by correcting the imbalance that currently favors publishers. The publisher position statement is trying to tilt it further toward publishers.

If publishers really need the rights this position paper says they need, then no win-win balance is possible. The closest we could come is a set of mutual concessions that at least one side will find insufficient. But if some of the positions the publishers are taking here, like limiting free online access to the author's institution, are just trial balloons, then we can still hold out hope of a win-win balance. Much constructive work remains to be done. I expect it from individual publishers who grant authors more rights than this position paper would allow and then demonstrate that they can still survive and prosper, perhaps even increasing their submissions.

[...]

Author and Publisher Rights For Academic Use: An Appropriate Balance, May 2007. A joint position paper by ALPSP, AAP/PSP, and STM.

http://legacy.earlham.edu/~peters/fos/2007/05/publisher-view-of-how-to-balance-rights.html

—The ALPSP announcement

http://web.archive.org/web/20070612031904/http://www.alpsp.org/ngen_public/article.asp?id=1&did=47&aid=992&st=&oaid=-1

—The ALPSP text

http://web.archive.org/web/20070612031852/http://www.alpsp.org/ForceDownload.asp?id=39

—The STM announcement

http://web.archive.org/web/20070515023111/http://www.stm-assoc.org/home/stm
-aappsp-alpsp-issue-white-paper-on-academic-use-of-journal-content.html

—The STM text

http://web.archive.org/web/20070515023111/http://www.stm-assoc.org/documents
-statements-public-co/2007%20-%2005%20Author%20Publisher%20Rights%20for
%20Academic%20Uses--%20an%20Appropriate%20Balance.pdf

—Les Carr, PSP and ALPSP: j'accuse! American Scientist Open Access Forum, May 11, 2007.

http://listserver.sigmaxi.org/sc/wa.exe?A2=ind07&L=american-scientist-open-access
-forum&D=1&F=l&P=57722

—Discussion thread based on Carr's message.

http://listserver.sigmaxi.org/sc/wa.exe?A2=ind07&L=american-scientist-open-access
-forum&D=1&F=l&P=57722

Les Carr, Starting a community response to ALPSP/PSP? American Scientist Open Access
Forum, May 12, 2007.

http://listserver.sigmaxi.org/sc/wa.exe?A2=ind07&L=american-scientist-open-access
-forum&D=1&O=D&F=l&S=&P=58723

—Kevin Smith, Publisher position on author rights, Duke Scholarly Communications,
May 20, 2007.

http://library.duke.edu/blogs/scholcomm/2007/05/20/position-paper/

Flipping a Journal to Open Access

From "Flipping a journal to open access," SPARC Open Access Newsletter, October 2, 2007.

http://dash.harvard.edu/handle/1/4322572

Mark Rowse was the CEO of Ingenta when Paula Hane interviewed him for *Information Today* in December 2003. During the interview he sketched an elegant idea:

> Imagine a publisher that has already licensed content to all the library consortia in the U.S. The publisher could, at a stroke, say that the license will now confer rights for the academics in those institutions to submit content rather than to access content. The publisher would have successfully flipped its business model completely, to being an open access business. So I think it's possible to see a transition from where we are now to a completely open access world without fundamentally destroying the existing scholarly publishing business.

See Paula Hane, Stable and Poised for Growth, Information Today, December 2003.

http://www.infotoday.com/it/nov03/hane2.shtml

http://www.earlham.edu/~peters/fos/2003/11/interview-with-mark-rowse.html

Rowse didn't elaborate on the idea in the interview. But I was so intrigued when I reread it recently, that I started to elaborate it on my own. Then I had the even better idea to call Rowse and hear how he would put flesh on these bones himself.

I interviewed him by phone on September 6 [2007] and followed up by email when finishing my draft. This is his idea in my words.

Let's start with Rowse's assumption that a journal is selling subscriptions (licensing content) to all library consortia in the US. It's hard to imagine this happening, and we'll make the assumption more realistic in a minute. But let's assume it for now in order introduce complexity slowly rather than quickly. In fact, let's assume the journal currently sells subscriptions to all libraries (not just library consortia) in the world (not just in the US).

Let's also assume that all researchers are affiliated with a subscribing institution. But again, since this is false, we'll have to make the assumption more realistic later.

And let's make one semi-realistic assumption: that the journal charges no color or page fees. All the journal revenue is from reader-side subscription fees, and none from author-side fees.

Now what does it mean for a journal to "flip its business model"? There are four primary elements:

(1) The journal converts from toll-access (TA) to open-access (OA). All the articles it publishes after that point are OA from birth.

(2) It pays its bills by charging a publication fee on accepted articles. The fee is sometimes paid by authors, sometimes by the author's funder or employer, and sometimes waived.

The most straightforward version of Rowse's idea applies only to fee-based OA journals, but in a minute I'll consider some ways to adapt it to no-fee OA journals.

(3) The journal waives the publication fee for authors affiliated with an institution that pays what used to be called a subscription.

(4) The same institutions that formerly paid subscriptions pay the same amounts to the same journal, at least at first. But both the journal and the paying institutions put a new interpretation on the payments: they are now OA publication fees for a group of authors rather than TA subscription fees for a group of readers.

Under our simplifying assumptions, all researchers already have pre-paid access as readers, because they are all affiliated with institutions that pay subscriptions. After the journal flips its business model, they all have open access. From the standpoint of reader access, nothing changes except perhaps the number of clicks or keystrokes required for access. We shift from pre-paid access (access is priced but someone is paying on our behalf) to open access (access is not priced), but end users don't notice the difference except in the freedom from the hassle of authentication.

Likewise, all authors already have a no-fee route to publication, since the journal doesn't levy page or color charges. After the journal flips its business model, they all still have a no-fee route to publication, but for a different reason: the journal now charges author-side publication fees but waives them for authors from paying institutions, and we're supposing that all authors are affiliated with paying institutions. In effect, the journal adopts a fee-based model, but waives the fee for everyone. Hence, from the standpoint of author access, nothing changes either.

Nor has anything changed from the standpoint of journal revenue. The same institutions that formerly paid subscriptions are still sending the same amounts to the same accounts. We're just changing the name of the payments from subscription fees to publication fees. If the journal was breaking even, running at a loss, or making a profit before, then it's doing the same now.

(For now let's also assume that OA and TA publishing cost the same. However, if OA publishing costs less, which I believe, then the difference makes flipping even more attractive. The savings could show up in reduced fees for institutions, more frequent waivers for unsubsidized authors, or both.)

Flipping the business model is a simple act because, under our assumptions, it changes almost nothing. It's like changing the way we interpret an optical illusion. Suddenly the drawing that looked concave looks convex. Nothing has changed but our interpretation of what's going on.

But now let's move to a more realistic assumption in which pre-flip subscriptions cover only 70% (rather than 100%) of the world's researchers. Under the new assumption, 100% of researchers have no-fee access to the pre-flip journal as authors, but only 70% have pre-paid or no-fee access as readers. In this world, flipping the business model will change nothing for the lucky 70% affiliated with fee-paying institutions: they will still have no-fee access as readers and will still be able to publish in the journal without facing a publication fee. But the flip will significantly change things for the 30%: they will gain no-fee access as readers, for the first time, and they will face publication fees as authors, also for the first time. As readers they will see access barriers fall, and as authors they will see them rise. The percentage of readers with no-fee access will rise from 70% to 100%, but the percentage of authors with no-fee access will drop from 100% to 70%.

I picked the numbers 70 and 30 out of a hat. For a journal with much lower circulation, say, reaching only 5% of the world's researchers, then the flip would cause much larger disparities. The flip would remove access barriers for 95% of readers and add publication fees for 95% of authors.

Even under realistic circulation numbers, nothing will change for the journal, at least at first. If the revenue it had before was adequate (or inadequate), it will still be adequate (or inadequate). But after the flip, the journal may notice some drift. Some institutions that formerly paid subscription fees may not want to pay publication fees. They may decide that their faculty don't publish in the journal often enough to justify the expense. And conversely, some institutions that formerly didn't subscribe may want to start paying publication fees. These losses and gains may not cancel each other out.

What kinds of journals are best situated to flip their business models without losing revenue? If a journal has roughly as many authors as readers at subscribing institutions, then those institutions will be most likely to continue their payments after the journal flips, and therefore to keep the journal revenue at pre-flip levels.

To see the logic of this, imagine an extreme version of the opposite situation. If all a journal's readers are at Harvard and all its authors at Stanford, then flipping would be attractive to Harvard (it could stop paying and still have free access for its readers) but unattractive to Stanford (it would have to shoulder the whole burden alone). However, if an institution has roughly as many authors as readers, then it's likely to see the value in paying for author uploads instead of reader downloads.

The basic idea remains simple even if we make the math more complicated and realistic. For example, if there are fewer authors than readers overall, and hence fewer authors than readers at the average paying institution, but if the publication fee per author is higher than the subscription fee per reader, then it still follows that the more that reading and writing institutions overlap, the more likely it is that the paying institutions will think it worthwhile to keep paying after the flip.

For most well-established, high-quality journals there's already a good match between the institutions where readers are located and the institutions where authors are located. For them, the flip can promote research and protect revenue at the same time.

If the number of authors or readers at an institution grows, that will not break the match. Only if the number of authors declines will that undermine the match and make the institution less willing to pay. But Rowse points out that the same is true today. If a university closes down a department (reducing both authors and readers in that field), then it's less likely to keep paying for journals in that field.

It's easy for a journal to measure the extent of the match between its reading and writing institutions. Simply calculate the percentage of published authors who are affiliated with subscribing institutions. Even journals that are quite sure they would never flip their business model should do the calculation. The door may be open, and that's a fact worth knowing.

Society journals with a good match between their reading and writing institutions may worry that flipping their business model would eliminate one incentive for individual scholars to join up. Rowse points out that they could replace the old incentive (a free or discounted journal subscription) with a new one, such as fast-track review. I can add another possibility, inspired by the American Society of Plant Biology: waive the publication fee for society members who are not affiliated with paying institutions.

On the other hand, the smaller the overlap between the reading and writing institutions, or the closer the journal gets to the Harvard/Stanford (read-only / write-only) model, the more it is likely to lose paying institutions after the flip.

Here's where we see the advantages for a publisher to flip many journals at once, which we could call a bundled flip. If a publisher flips many journals at once, and waives the publication fees at all the flipped journals for all authors at all paying institutions, then more institutions would have an incentive to pay. The more journals in the bundled flip, the more the reading and writing institutions will overlap, and hence the more the reading/subscribing institutions will have an incentive to keep paying. Likewise, the more journals in the bundled flip, the more nonpaying institutions will have an incentive to start paying. For publishers of many journals, the more they are willing to flip at once, the more likely it is that post-flip business would be better than pre-flip business.

The door may be open for most successful TA journals. If there's already a good match between a journal's reading and writing institutions, then it can flip on its own. If not, it can flip as part of a suite of journals from the same publisher.

Rowse points out that the benefits of flipping are reserved for the bold. One advantage of a flip is to give up the overhead of TA publishing—print, subscription management, user authentication, licensing, and perhaps even marketing. If a publisher went halfway by flipping some titles and not others, or if a single journal flipped but kept its TA overhead in readiness to flip back, then it would not realize all the possible savings.

Finally, Rowse argues that bold journals or publishers willing to make the flip may be rewarded by a virtuous circle. Flipping will create OA, which will increase readership, which will usually increase submissions (from spreading exposure, rising impact factor, or both). If submissions increase, then more institutions will have an incentive to pay publication fees, which would increase journal revenue, permit more fee waivers, and/or allow the journal to reduce fees for everyone.

That's the idea in a nutshell. Here are some thoughts of my own.

*

Flipping is attractive because it produces full OA in a way that can be safe for publishers. Even if you think that publisher safety doesn't matter, or that safe business models are already common, this is still a welcome new option.

Hybrid OA journals are also safe for publishers, since the publisher continues to receive subscription revenue while testing the market for fee-based OA. But hybrid OA journals generally have low uptake and produce little OA. Flipping could be at least as safe for publishers and more beneficial, since it would provide OA for every article in a journal. Moreover, some percentage of authors (namely, those affiliated with paying institutions) would face no publication fees.

Flipping also gives institutions an incentive to pay. Hybrid OA journals create no such incentive and leave most authors to pay publication fees out of pocket or plead for case-by-case subventions. That's clearly part of the reason why hybrid OA journals have such low uptake.

*

Flipping also enjoys the general advantage that journal conversions have over brand new launches. When successful TA journals convert to OA, they bring their readership, reputation, impact factors, and prestige with them. They don't get caught in the vicious circle of needing good submissions to generate prestige and needing prestige to attract good submissions.

*

It's possible to imagine an inverted hybrid journal: one that is OA by default but willing to publish TA articles for authors who couldn't pay publication fees. Flipping, however, doesn't lend itself to these inverted hybrids. If a flipped journal wanted to publish some TA articles for authors who couldn't pay publication fees, it would have to support all the publishing overhead required for TA publication, cutting into the financial advantages of the flip.

A flipped journal with a good surplus could afford to offer an inverted hybrid option. But if it had a good surplus, then it could lower its publication fees or waive them more often. That would eliminate publication barriers for authors, make the inverted hybrid option unnecessary, and still assure that all its articles would be OA.

*

The virtuous circle Rowse sketches is very likely. If journals find revenues going up after a flip, and use them to reduce fees or increase fee waivers, then they will continue to stimulate submissions and keep the circle turning.

Here's another side effect. Because different journals publish different papers, they compete much less for readers than they do for authors. If you need to read a certain paper, then it doesn't matter that another journal in the same research niche is less expensive or even OA. In a subscription world, this makes every journal a mini-monopoly shielded from the market forces that would normally make prices competitive and affordable. But in a world in which payments represent authors rather than readers, we can have a healthy market that keeps prices competitive. If a journal charges much higher publication fees than a journal of comparable quality and prestige in the same field, then submissions and money will go elsewhere, at least more readily than they do today for journals charging higher subscription prices than their peers. Flipping payments from reader-sponsors to author-sponsors will expose journals to price competition, for nearly the first time, and do so without making journals any more fungible or less distinctive than they are today.

*

The CERN plan to convert TA journals in particle physics to OA is the closest thing I've seen to a Rowsean flip. In brief, the CERN plan is to get TA journals in the field to agree to convert to OA at the same time that the subscribing institutions agree to replace their subscription fees with publication fees, which CERN expects to be lower than the earlier subscription fees. Because CERN dominates particle physics the way no other institution dominates any other field, it was able to use its unmatched convening power to bring all the players together, make the case for the win-win logic of flipping, and create a consortium, SCOAP3 (Sponsoring Consortium for Open Access Publishing in Particle Physics), which is currently working out the details. The pre-flip planning assures participating journals that the institutions now paying will continue to pay after the flip. The lesson is to enhance the flip planning for a journal or publisher with this kind of wider disciplinary planning whenever possible. It will not only reduce risk for the journals, but improve the economics in the same way that a bundled flip creates more incentives for paying institutions than a single journal flip.

CERN

http://www.cern.ch/

CERN's OA plan

http://open-access.web.cern.ch/Open-Access/

My discussions of the CERN plan in earlier issues of SOAN

http://www.earlham.edu/~peters/fos/newsletter/09-02-06.htm#cern

http://www.earlham.edu/~peters/fos/newsletter/12-02-06.htm#cern

http://www.earlham.edu/~peters/fos/newsletter/01-02-07.htm#2006

It doesn't matter whether we see Rowse's idea and the CERN plan as the same or merely variations on a theme. Insofar as they differ, they show that there's more than one way convert TA journals to OA and keep revenue flowing from the institutions that formerly paid subscriptions. There may be an even larger family of solutions here awaiting exploration.

*

Universities might act together to persuade publishers to flip their journals. If a consortium of universities now paying subscription fees would be willing to continue paying publication fees, they could approach a publisher and ask it to flip its journals. The lure for the publisher would be the assurance of large-scale participation. In return for this assurance, the universities could sweeten the deal for themselves by offering to pay (say) 75% of what they now pay, rather than 100%. This reflects the fact that increased participation increases publisher revenue and allows it to lower publication fees. Universities could make the deal even more appealing to publishers if they could recruit some non-subscribing institutions to join the consortium.

*

There are a couple of ways in which a flipped journal could become a no-fee OA journal. This matters to me because the chief drawback to the flipping model, for real-world journals that don't already reach all researchers, is that it introduces publication fees for some percentage of authors (namely, those not affiliated with paying institutions), and many of those authors will not have funders or employers willing to pay the fees on their behalf.

One way to flip toward a no-fee journal is to start with a standard flip and rely at first on publication fees. But the journal could then solicit subsidies from institutions with more authors than readers or from institutions wanting the prestige of hosting the journal. If the subsidies sufficed to cover its expenses, then it could drop publication fees and become a no-fee OA journal.

This is advantageous even if the subsidies don't suffice to replace publication fees. Any level of subsidy would let the journal reduce its publication fees, waive them more often, or both. The more it reduced its fees, the more institutions it could find who would be willing to pay them. This could in turn create in a net increase in revenue, which would allow it to lower the fees even further.

If a journal looks for subsidies before rather than after the flip, and if it finds enough, then it could convert directly to OA without a flip. If it doesn't find enough, then it could flip, supplement its subsidies with publication fees, and keep its fees low while looking for additional subsidies.

Another variation is a double flip: first flip subscription fees to publication fees (download payments become upload payments), and then, sooner or later, flip publication fees to institutional subsidies (payments for specific articles or authors become payments to support general operating expenses). The second flip in this process is not as novel as it may appear. The Stanford Encyclopedia of Philosophy is in the middle of something very similar right now. To build an endowment to cover its expenses, it's asking institutions to make payments that resemble "flipped subscriptions": institutions make annual payments, as they would for subscription or publication fees, but when SEP has raised enough money, the payments stop and the encyclopedia is OA, no-fee, and self-sustaining.

Stanford Encyclopedia of Philosophy (SEP)

http://plato.stanford.edu/

SEP's fund-raising strategy

http://plato.stanford.edu/fundraising/

*

For real-world TA journals that don't already reach all researchers, flipping will remove fee barriers for all readers and add fee barriers for some authors. It will always be a net gain for researchers qua readers. Whether it's a net gain for researchers qua authors will depend on at least five variables: (1) the number of authors not affiliated with paying institutions, (2) the size of the publication fee facing those authors, (3) the willingness of funding agencies to pay those fees for grantees, (4) the willingness of universities not paying institution-wide fees to pay fees for individual faculty on a case-by-case basis, and (5) the willingness of flipped journals to waive their fees in cases of economic hardship. Depending on the values of these variables, some flips will impose fees on a majority of authors and some will impose fees on a minority. In principle, both kinds of flip could be safe for the publisher.

When high-circulation journals flip, they mitigate this problem by reducing the number of authors in category #1 (authors not affiliated with paying institutions). When low-circulation journals flip, they aggravate this problem by increasing the number of such authors.

This problem is the only drawback I can see to a flip. But publication fees needn't be higher at flipped journals than at born-OA journals and OA converts using the publication fee business model. In fact, the Rowsean virtuous circle may allow flipped journals to set their publication fees even lower. In addition, flipped journals would waive their publication fee for all authors from paying institutions, and the number of authors receiving waivers should be well above average for the class of fee-based OA journals, equalled only by the few with successful institutional membership programs. In any case, it would be inconsistent to welcome the launch of new fee-based OA journals and not welcome flipped journals.

*

In short, flipping has many attractions, and its only drawback is shared by other fee-based OA journals (which comprise about 47% of all OA journals) and may be less burdensome than at most other fee-based OA journals. I definitely like the idea enough to hope that some journals and publishers will try it out. We could all learn more from those who did, and while we were learning, the journal would be OA.

Where are the journals and publishers curious enough to do the math and bold enough to take the first steps?

Postscript

Mark Rowse left Ingenta in October 2005, though he is still on the board. The company has been called Publishing Technologies since February 2007 when it merged with Vista. In addition to serving on the board, he's involved in various publishing startups and thinking about how to bring Web 2.0 thinking to academic publishing. I interviewed him once before (August 8, 2002), on OA topics but not on flipping business models.

http://www.earlham.edu/~peters/fos/newsletter/08-08-02.htm#rowse

In the next issue of SOAN [November 2, 2007], I published the following update:

http://www.earlham.edu/~peters/fos/newsletter/11-02-07.htm#followup

In my article last month on flipping subscription journals to open access, I gave two partial examples: CERN's SCOAP3 project and the Stanford Encyclopedia of Philosophy. This month I've got two follow-ups.

(1) I missed a good one and thank Jan Velterop for reminding me. In June 2007, Springer struck a deal with the Dutch library consortium, Universiteitsbibliotheken en de Koninklijke Bibliotheek (UKB), allowing the UKB's subscription payments to count as publication fees on behalf of faculty affiliated with UKB member institutions. It's only a partial example because the journals don't become OA. But the new articles by authors at UKB member institutions do become OA. For details and links, see my blog post for October 3 [2007],

http://www.earlham.edu/~peters/fos/2007/10/more-on-flipping-journals.html

BTW, since the UKB deal, Springer has struck a similar deal with the University of Göttingen.

http://www.earlham.edu/~peters/fos/2007/10/springer-deal-with-u-of-gttingen.html

(2) I described the funding model of the Stanford Encyclopedia of Philosophy only enough to show its similarity to (ahem) the second half of a two-flip conversion. As a result, I left out many details and probably left a false impression for many readers. SEP's Principal Editor Ed Zalta and Senior Editor Uri Nodelman wrote a good note to clarify the model. For details and links, see my blog post for October 4 [2007],

http://www.earlham.edu/~peters/fos/2007/10/more-on-stanford-encyclopedia-of.html

Society Publishers with Open Access Journals

From "Society publishers with open access journals," SPARC Open Access Newsletter, November 2, 2007, co-authored with Caroline Sutton.

http://dash.harvard.edu/handle/1/4387568

PS note: This is the first time I've co-authored an article in SOAN. I'm drawing special attention to it in order to make sure that no one overlooks the contribution of my co-author, Caroline Sutton of Co-Action Publishing.

We are pleased to announce the first results of an ongoing research project.

The overall project has two phases. Phase One is to make a comprehensive list of scholarly societies worldwide that support gold OA for their own journals. The journals might be full OA or hybrid OA, and the society's relationship to its journals might be that of owner, publisher, or partner with the publisher. (For convenience, when we say below that a society "publishes" an OA journal, we'll mean that it has at least one of these relationships to it.) The list includes the journals themselves, and associated data, as well as the societies.

If we can find funding, Phase Two will survey the societies turned up in Phase One in order to learn details about their turn to OA, their business models, and the financial and academic consequences of their OA policies.

The idea was to test the widespread impression that learned societies as such feel threatened by OA. The impression isn't just a side-effect of hearing some society publishers publicly oppose OA; it's often deliberately cultivated by associations representing society publishers such as the ALPSP and the DC Principles Coalition. A related goal was to learn business-level details from the OA-friendly societies in order to help other societies make the transition.

Today we're releasing the provisional results of Phase One. We've found 425 societies publishing 450 full OA journals, and 21 societies publishing 73 hybrid OA journals. (Three societies publish both types of journal and are counted in each total; the list covers 468 societies altogether.)

The full list is OA in an Excel spreadsheet under a Creative Commons Attribution license.

http://www.co-action.net/projects/OAsocieties

If you have additions or corrections, please send them to Caroline Sutton at <projects@co-action.net>.

The full OA journals are associated with societies in 57 countries and regions. The top three countries are the US (with 93), Japan (84), and India (62). One sign that there's a long tail is that the number drops off quickly between number three, India, and number four, Canada (with 18). By contrast, the hybrid OA society journals are largely concentrated in the US (49) and the UK (19).

The society with the most OA journals is the World Academy of Science, Engineering and Technology (formerly the World Enformatika Society), with 22. One society publishes seven, one society publishes six, two publish three each, and 11 publish two each. Most societies publishing OA journals publish just one.

The society with the most hybrid OA journals is the American Chemical Society, with 33. The Royal Society has 11, the American Physical Society has seven, the Linnean Society of London has three, and three societies have two each. Only five societies publish just one hybrid journal.

Just as some societies publish more than one journal, some journals are published by more than one society. Seven journals on our list are joint projects of more than one society. One journal, *Informatika*, involves seven cooperating societies. Another, *Contemporary Issues in Technology & Teacher Education*, involves five. Three journals involve two societies, and two journals involve three societies.

When societies want to outsource the publication of their full OA journals, or partner with others in their publication, most pick for-profit publishers. Medknow publishes 44 society journals. In fact, all but one of Medknow's journals are society journals. Most of the societies choosing Medknow are Indian, but a few are Saudi Arabian. MedKnow, by the way, is not only for-profit but also profitable. Hindawi, also for-profit and profitable, co-operates with nine societies to publish 11 journals. BioMed Central publishes three, and Springer and Lippincott each cooperate on one. Of the non-profit publishers, Highwire Press co-operates on 7, the Royal Society of Chemistry publishes 1, and seven university presses publish one each. Co-Action Publishing itself will publish one starting in 2008.

Of hybrid journals, 12 are published by for-profit publishers, and the rest by societies.

Most full OA society journals (234) ask authors to transfer copyright. 148 don't describe their copyright policies on their web sites. Only 51 allow authors to retain copyright in some form. Only 15 say they use Creative Commons licenses, although some may do so without mentioning it and some mention using equivalent licenses.

Two journals ask authors to agree to joint ownership of the copyright with the society. One lets authors choose whether to transfer or retain copyright, and one allows the author to retain copyright but imposes a one-year embargo on the author's own posting of the article elsewhere.

Of hybrid OA society journals, 33 allow authors to retain copyright and 39 require them to transfer copyright. 13 use CC licenses. Only one copyright policy was too unclear for us to summarize. Clearly hybrid OA journals pay more attention to copyright issues than full OA journals do.

Most society OA journals (356) are in the STM fields. 51 are in the social sciences, 32 in the humanities, five in the arts, and the rest multidisciplinary.

Of hybrid OA journals, two are in the social sciences and all the rest in the STM fields. Hybrid journals are clearly most common in the fields in which most authors have research grants from which they might be able to pay the journal's publication fee.

Compared to full OA society journals, hybrid OA society journals are (1) rarer; (2) published in fewer countries; (3) more likely to be part of a suite of similar journals from the same society, as opposed to the society's only journal; (4) more likely to be published by for-profit publishers; (5) more likely to have a clear and publicly-available copyright policy; (6) more likely to let authors retain copyright; (7) more likely to use CC licenses; and (8) more likely to be in the STM fields.

Of the full OA journals, 75 charge author-side publication fees. In some cases, however, a journal may provide society members (or even others) with anywhere from 2 to 8 pages free of charge. 12 journals charge submission, as opposed to publication, fees; and of these 12, eight also charge publication fees. Two journals invite authors to make voluntary contributions to cover the cost of publication.

In an October 2005 study sponsored by the ALPSP, Cara Kaufman and Alma Wills found that a majority of OA journals (52.8%) charged no publication fees. Our list shows that a much larger majority (83.3%) of society OA journals charge no publication fees.

Why bother?

As we mentioned, two goals of the project are to test the widespread impression that learned societies as such feel threatened by OA and to learn business details from the societies with gold OA experience that might help those without it. A third goal was to help societies find similarly situated, OA-friendly societies in the hopes that conversations with fellow society publishers might be more productive than conversations with OA advocates who are neither society officers nor publishers.

This summer Peter was talking to a society publisher who voiced the common argument that society publishers can't move to gold OA because they need subscription revenue to support their journal's quality as well as other society operations. Peter mentioned that the Optical Society of America publishes an OA journal (*Optics Express*) which makes a surplus and has the highest impact factor in its field.

The publisher's response was essentially, "Yes, but our society is not like the OSA."

It's a fair answer, and it would have been just as fair if Peter had cited a different society publisher of a different OA journal. There's a very wide variation among learned societies. No matter which OA-friendly society you cite as a model, and no matter which OA-averse society you might be talking to, the odds are that your dialog partner could truthfully respond, "Yes, but our society is not like that one. Ours is larger or smaller. It's in a different field. Our journal has a higher or lower circulation. It has a higher or lower price. It has a higher or lower impact factor. It has a higher or lower rejection rate. It competes with a, b, and c, rather than x, y, and z. It comes out more often or less often. It does more or less copy editing. It depends more or less on advertising and reprints. It provides a higher or lower percentage of society revenue. It has a higher or lower percentage of individual subscribers. It publishes a higher or lower percentage of articles based on publicly-funded research."

One purpose of our list is to move conversation and debate past the "yes, but" response, which is justified as a statement of fact but not as a conversation-stopper. In one-on-one comparisons between societies, the odds are that we will find more relevant differences than similarities. But the list reduces or reverses the probabilities. The societies on our list are very diverse, nearly as diverse as the larger population of society publishers overall. The odds are that there is at least one society on our list with which any given society will have more relevant similarities than differences.

These similarities may be as unexpected to the societies themselves as they are to OA advocates. Societies that just don't see how to make gold OA work in their own case may be surprised to find similarly situated societies who are making it work or giving it a serious try.

We're not saying that all the OA society publishers are doing as well as the Optical Society of America. We won't know until we do Phase Two. But we hope that society officers who haven't seen a promising way to convert their own journals to OA will find encouragement in this list, look for similarly situated societies, and explore new OA possibilities in constructive conversations with their counterparts from other societies. We hope that rank and file society members will do the same.

We realize that the motivations to publish full OA journals differ significantly from the motivations to publish hybrid OA journals, and therefore we treat them separately in our list.

There may still be good reasons for a given society publisher to conclude that it cannot convert its journal to OA. In that case, we hope the society can at least support green OA and not lobby against government OA policies. On the question of gold OA, the length of our list changes the question from what makes the OA society publishers rare and special to what makes the OA holdouts hold out. How many of the objections or fears will turn out to be myths that can be answered by the publishers with actual OA experience?

When the DC Principles Coalition issued a press release in February 2007, opposing government OA mandates, it claimed that 75 society publishers supported its position, though it didn't list them.

http://www.dcprinciples.org/press/2.htm

http://www.earlham.edu/~peters/fos/2007/02/dc-principles-coalition-still-opposes.html

Our list of 425 societies is six times larger than that set of 75 societies.

When the Association of American Publishers sent a letter to members of Congress in June 2007, opposing efforts to strengthen the NIH policy, it solicited signatures from as many like-minded publishers as it could find. It found 46, of which 34 were society publishers.

http://www.pspcentral.org/publications/LHHS_appropriations_bills.pdf

http://www.earlham.edu/~peters/fos/2007/07/publishers-oppose-strengthening-nih.html

Our list of 425 societies is 12.5 times larger than that list of 34 societies.

These comparisons are admittedly rough, if only because lobbying against OA mandates is not the opposite of publishing OA journals. Some societies do both, and some societies do neither. But even as a very rough comparison, it seems that the society publishers supporting gold OA far outnumber those opposed to government OA policies—and the disparity would only widen if we threw in the society publishers supporting green OA.

We know that our list raises more questions than it answers, and hope to be able to provide some of those answers in Phase Two. When societies convert their journals to OA, or hybrid OA, do they lose money? Do their impact factors reflect the OA impact advantage? Do submissions go up or down? If they charge a publication fee, how do they set its level? If they don't charge publication fees, how do they cover their publication expenses? How did they make their decision to convert to OA?

In short, are there lessons here for other societies considering a turn to gold OA?

Method

Our list has two sources. First, Peter had been maintaining an informal database of the OA and hybrid OA society journals he encountered in his daily research. Second, Caroline systematically completed Peter's list from the DOAJ (Directory of Open Access Journals) and research on individual society and journal web sites.

(PS note: My contribution was to do small amounts of work over a long period of time, while Caroline's was to do a very large amount of work over a short period of time.)

In DOAJ, we conducted searches based on the following key words: "society," "association," "federation," and "organization/organisation." The database searches were conducted first in the general DOAJ and then in the "for Authors" section in order to capture information on the hybrid OA journals. We used these words in English for our preliminary results and hope to supplement those results as we go forward.

We're likely to have overlooked societies if they never crossed Peter's radar and do not use any of the keywords above in their journal title. That's one reason we regard the list as unfinished and ask for your additions and corrections.

There were several kinds of borderline case that we omitted from our list. For example, we excluded journals associated with university departments or research institutes rather than learned societies. If a journal used one of our keywords in its title but was not associated with a scholarly society, we excluded it. We also excluded journals no longer accepting submissions, and journals only offering OA for an introductory trial period.

We didn't require that the societies on our list own the journals associated with them. They might own and publish them; or they might own them and outsource the publishing to a separate company or organization; or they might regard the journal as the official journal of the society even if owned and published by a separate organization. What we required was an official endorsement and a significant form of cooperation with the journal.

Most regrettably, the list is limited to journals with enough editorial matter in English to enable us to identify them as OA or OA hybrid journals significantly associated with a learned society. We're sure we've omitted many eligible journals and welcome word of them from people in a position to know their status.

A number of new OA journals will start publishing in January 2008, and a number of older journals will convert to OA in January 2008. We included these on the list.

All the journals on the list are peer reviewed or conduct some other form of professional quality control. The vast majority of the journals listed are research journals containing original research articles and reviews. Some of the titles listed are newsletters and contain administrative information in addition to scholarly contributions.

If we can secure funding for Phase Two, we hope to work with a considerably larger and more comprehensive list of societies and journals.

Note from May 2015: Caroline and I published a second edition of the catalog in December 2011, for which I wrote an accompanying article.

http://dash.harvard.edu/handle/1/8592165

With a new third co-author, Amanda Page, we published a third edition of the catalog in September 2014. The project now has a name, Societies and Open Access Research (SOAR), and a home page.

http://cyber.law.harvard.edu/hoap/Societies_and_Open_Access_Research

The second and third editions of the catalog are in a Google spreadsheet under a Creative Commons Attribution license, and no longer include hybrid journals. We update the spreadsheet regularly.

https://docs.google.com/spreadsheet/ccc?key=0AgBYTDKmesh7dDZ6UnBfcnpOdVpn
d3ptSnVpQ0xrenc#gid=15

As of May 2015, the catalog lists 967 societies publishing 923 full (non-hybrid) OA journals.

Ten Challenges for Open-Access Journals

From "Ten challenges for open-access journals," SPARC Open Access Newsletter, October 2, 2009.

http://dash.harvard.edu/handle/1/4316131

The launch of the Open Access Scholarly Publishers Association (OASPA) is a mark of movement maturity and a promise of mutual support, wisdom-sharing, and self-regulation for OA journals and OA publishers.

http://www.oaspa.org/

I want to celebrate the progress of OA journals and the launch of the OASPA by setting out what I see as the 10 greatest challenges facing OA journals. I want to do this without pretending to set the association agenda and without presupposing that association members don't already know these challenges very well. I'm not a member of the association or even a publisher. I merely want to see OA journals succeed.

(In what follows, when I say "you," I'm talking to those who edit or publish OA journals.)

I start with three disparities: the gap between journal performance and what prevailing metrics say about journal performance (#1); the gap between the vision of OA embodied in the Budapest, Bethesda, and Berlin statements and the access policies at 85% of OA journals (#2); and the gap between a journal's quality and its prestige, even when the quality is high (#3). Then I move on to seven kinds of doubt: doubts about quality (#4), preservation (#5), honesty (#6), publication fees (#7), sustainability (#8), redirection (#9), and strategy (#10).

(1) Measuring up

Even when OA journals are strong, the most widely-used measurement doesn't always show them to be strong. Impact Factors (IFs) discriminate against new journals and most OA journals are new.

This is not a conspiracy. Journals are not even eligible for IFs until they are two years old, and after that Thomson Scientific only computes IFs for a select subset of journals. The need to wait two years applies equally to OA and TA journals, and the eligibility for IFs after that extends, as far as I can tell, about equally to OA and TA journals.

There are many problems with IFs, but here I want to focus on the discrimination against new journals. For my full critique, see Section 8 of this article from September 2008.

http://www.earlham.edu/~peters/fos/newsletter/09-02-08.htm#prestige

Alternative impact metrics could solve the problems left by IFs, including the discrimination against new journals. The challenge is to find metrics that are truly better for the many purposes of the many stakeholders. There's a lot of work being done in this area. For example, these are the alternative impact metrics I know about. Very likely there are even more:

- Age-weighted citation rate (Bihui Jin)
- Batting Average (Jon Kleinberg et al.)
- Distributed Open Access Reference Citation project (University of Oldenburg)
- Eigenfactor (Carl Bergstrom)
- g-index (Leo Egghe)
- h-index (J.E. Hirsch)
- Contemporary h-index (Antonis Sidiropoulos et al.)
- Individual h-index (Pablo D. Batista et al.)
- Journal Influence Index and the Paper Influence Index (Center for Journal Ranking)
- MeSUR (MEtrics from Scholarly Usage of Resources) (LANL)
- SCImago Journal Rank and SJR Indicator (University of Granada)
- Strike Rate Index (William Barendse)
- Usage Factor (UKSG)
- Web Impact Factor (Peter Ingwersen)
- y-factor (Herbert van de Sompel et al.)

I'm happy to leave the development and evaluation of these metrics to experts, and hope that some of you will be among the experts. What matters here is that we have an interest in the success of this work in progress, and that the dominance of IFs is an impediment to the growth and acceptance of OA journals.

The IF doesn't harm new journals on its own. It only harms new journals because its heavy use by promotion and tenure (P&T) committees creates a disincentive for faculty to submit work to new journals. The challenge is to monitor the alternative metrics in progress, to be ready to recognize and support superior metrics when they emerge, and to be prepared to argue their superiority to our local P&T committees. We should have allies in all the new research fields and methodologies, whose journals, even if TA, are also overwhelmingly new. Superior metrics are only half the solution; the rest is making use of them to remove disincentives to submit work to new journals.

A related challenge is to make clear that we're not looking for new metrics biased in favor of OA journals. We're looking for less biased or unbiased metrics. Only unbiased metrics can help the cause of OA journals and get the buy-in from other stakeholders needed to make them fly.

IFs may be biased against new journals, and this fact may harm more OA journals than TA journals. But IFs are not biased against OA journals that make it out of adolescence. On the contrary, because OA articles are cited more often than TA articles, OA journals can play the IF game to win.

http://opcit.eprints.org/oacitation-biblio.html

For example, in the 2008 Journal Citation Reports, Thomson Reuters reports that five OA journals had the highest IFs in their fields:

http://web.archive.org/web/20090629065224/http://thomsonreuters.com/content/press_room/sci/448197

- PLoS Neglected Tropical Diseases = first in Tropical Medicine (out of 15)
- PLoS Pathogens = first in Parasitology (out of 25)
- PLoS Computational Biology = first in Mathematical & Computational Biology (out of 28)
- PLoS Biology = first in Biology (out of 71)
- Journal of Medical Internet Research = first in Medical Informatics (out of 20)

(Thanks to Paul Peters for the alert and details.)

Optics Express, from the Optical Society of America, was formerly first in optics but dropped to third in 2008.

http://www.osa.org/en-us/about_osa/newsroom/

Even in 2004 when there were many fewer OA journals, and the oldest ones were younger than today's, Thomson Scientific's own studies showed that there was at least one OA journal in the top cohort of IFs in nearly every scientific discipline.

http://web.archive.org/web/20040715031442/http://www.isinet.com/media/presentrep/acropdf/impact-oa-journals.pdf

http://ip-science.thomsonreuters.com/m/pdfs/openaccesscitations2.pdf

In 2007, Molecular Diversity Preservation International (MDPI) converted four hybrid OA journals to full OA. In 2009 it presented evidence that the conversion boosted the IFs for all four journals.

http://www.mdpi.com/1420-3049/14/6/2254/pdf

These successes are important, but they are not reasons to stick with IFs. When OA journals have high IFs, it's because they have high impact, not because they benefit from a bias built into the metric. OA journals would do as well or better under superior metrics. Even the OA journals most successful under IFs have everything to gain and nothing to lose by developing impact metrics which are more accurate, more nuanced, more timely, more automated, more fair to the variety of scholarly resources, more welcoming to the variety of data which illuminate impact, and more welcoming to new journals.

The Public Library of Science understands this well. Four of its journals have the highest IF in their fields, and yet it is pioneering the distribution of article-level impact data in order to support article-level impact metrics to displace simplistic IFs. All seven PLoS journals now share their "usage data, page views, citations, social networking links, press coverage, comments, and user ratings."

http://www.earlham.edu/~peters/fos/2009/01/plos-one-will-offer-more-impact-related.html

http://article-level-metrics.plos.org/

Other OA journals should do the same. So should TA journals interested in more nuanced and accurate impact metrics.

I'm not saying that if your journals do well under IFs, you shouldn't boast about it. You should. As your journals grow in impact, you should collect the evidence and boast about it. But at the same time you should work for superior metrics. Playing the IF game without working on alternatives will only encourage others to play it as well, entrenching the discrimination against new journals (as well as the other IF problems not covered here). To stop playing the IF game, you don't have to give up on impact as a goal or on impact measurements as ways of marking progress. Play for real impact accurately measured, without bias against any journals on account of their age, field, language, reputation, or business model.

(2) Opening up

How many OA journals listed in the DOAJ use some kind of CC license? Answer = 637 out of 4,362 = 14.6% (as of October 2, 2009)

The challenge is to get more OA journals to be more open.

Let me review some terminology to help us talk about this issue. Gratis OA removes price barriers but not permission barriers. It makes content free of charge but not free of copyright or licensing restrictions. It gives users no-fee access for reading but no more reuse rights than they already had through fair use or the local equivalent. It's free as in beer, not also free as in speech. By contrast, libre OA removes price barriers and at least some permission barriers. It lifts at least some copyright and licensing restrictions and permits at least some uses beyond fair use. It's free in beer and free as in speech.

http://www.earlham.edu/~peters/fos/newsletter/08-02-08.htm#gratis-libre

In most countries in the world today, new writings fall under all-rights-reserved copyrights from the moment of birth. As a result, authors can only provide libre OA to their work by affirmatively waiving some of their rights. If you're not sure how to waive some rights without losing your ability to enforce others that you retain, don't worry. Creative Commons licenses are designed for just this job. There's more than one CC license because there's more right in the copyright bundle that you might want to waive. For the same reason, libre OA is a range of things, and the range of CC licenses correspond to the most commonly adopted positions within that range. Apart from assignment to the public domain (waiving all rights), the most open CC license is CC-BY, which waives all rights except the right of attribution. The CC-BY-NC, by contrast, waives all rights except the right of attribution and the right to block or control commercial reuse.

OASPA recommends the CC-BY license or equivalent for all its members. It accepts some less open licenses, such as the CC-BY-NC, but it does not recommend them. In any case, both provide libre OA. OASPA also *requires* that members who want to impose any restrictions on reuse must make the restrictions explicit, for example through a license. (See the OASPA bylaws, Appendix II.)

http://oaspa.org/about/by-laws/

The SPARC Europe Seal program requires the CC-BY license and libre OA.

http://web.archive.org/web/20080501171956/http://www.doaj.org/doaj?func=loadTe
mpl&templ=080423

SURF recommends the "the most liberal Creative Commons licence" for articles, which is CC-BY. For data it recommends the more liberal assignment to the public domain, as required by the Science Commons Protocol for Implementing Open Access Data. On both fronts it recommends libre OA.

http://www.earlham.edu/~peters/fos/2009/08/licensing-normative-and-actual.html

The Budapest, Bethesda, and Berlin statements all call for libre OA, without naming specific licenses.

http://www.earlham.edu/~peters/fos/overview.htm#definition

The challenge is that more than 85% OA journals now in the DOAJ don't use any kind of CC license. Some of these might use equivalent non-CC licenses and some may use homegrown language with a similar legal effect. But these exceptions are rare. No matter how you slice it, most OA journals are not using open licenses. Most are operating under all-rights-reserved copyrights and leaving their users with no more than what they already had under fair use. Most are not offering libre OA.[1]

If 14.6% of the journals in the DOAJ use some kind of CC license, how many use the CC-BY license recommended by OASPA, SPARC Europe, and SURF? Answer = 416 out of 4,362 = 9.5% (as of October 2, 2009)

How many use CC licenses other than CC-BY? Answer = 221 out of 4,362 = 5.1%[2]

I know that many OA journals want to restrict commercial reuse and resist the recommendations to use CC-BY. I don't want to enter that debate here. If you want to restrict commercial reuse, then use a CC-BY-NC license or equivalent rather than no open license at all. Join the 5% of DOAJ journals which have adopted that solution.

I once talked to an OA journal publisher who feared that open licenses would deter submissions. It turned out he feared that allowing commercial use would deter submissions and assumed that all open licenses allowed commercial use. Moreover, he only had a few anecdotes to support his theory about the effect on submissions. But whether or not his fear was groundless, there's a simple way to use an open license and restrict commercial use. Just use a CC-BY-NC or equivalent. Let's agree to move beyond an all-rights-reserved copyright to libre OA, and argue later about whether to move beyond CC-BY-NC to CC-BY.

If a journal is already free of charge, then why use any open license at all? Why move beyond gratis OA to libre OA?

The short answer is to spare users the delay and expense of seeking permission whenever they want to exceed fair use.

Why would users want to exceed fair use? Here are some of the answers I gave to Richard Poynder in October 2007 (p. 37):

http://poynder.blogspot.com/2007/10/basement-interviews-peter-suber.html

[T]here are good reasons to exceed fair use, for example, to quote long excerpts, print full-text copies, email copies to students or colleagues, burn copies on CDs for bandwidth-poor parts of the world, distribute semantically-tagged or otherwise enhanced versions of a text, migrate copies to new formats or media to keep a text readable as technologies change, archive copies for preservation, include the work in a database or mashup, copy the text for indexing [or] text-mining ..., make an audio recording of the text, or translate it into another language.

Fortunately it's easy for OA journals to adopt open licenses and permit these uses in advance. It's easy free their users. It's easy to provide libre OA. In fact, it's easier for OA journals than OA repositories (or easier for gold OA than green OA). OA repositories generally stick to gratis OA because they can't generate the needed permissions for libre OA on their own. But OA journals can generate the permissions on their own.

Some OA journals know that CC licenses are free of charge and easy to use. Their reservations are less straightforward. I once talked to an OA journal editor-publisher who said: "Our journal is already free of charge. What else would anyone want? If users want to copy and redistribute the files, they are free to do so. We don't care. We allow that."

How would users know that the journal allows them to copy and redistribute the files? Fair use does *not* allow that, and conscientious users will limit themselves to fair use. When they don't have permission to exceed fair use, they will either slow down to ask permission or err on the side of non-use. These are impediments to research that OA was designed to remove.

Some people believe that, for better or worse, conscientiousness about copyright is a scruple fading into quaintness, like sexual prudery. But it remains the formal policy of every university and library in the world. Even when individuals are not conscientious, their institutions are, and they require their affiliated users to be. Even if you can wink at individuals to let them know that they may do what they want with your files, institutions are not allowed to take the hint. They can exercise their rights under libre OA, when they know they have them. But they can't act on a wink alone. And if you really are willing to provide libre OA, then there's no reason whatsoever not to say so in an explicit statement or license.

Even when users want to do something allowed by fair use, they have to deal with the fact that fair use itself is vague and contestable. For example, informed people disagree about whether it covers text-mining. Another reason to use an open license, then, is to free users from the fear of liability and from self-imposed restrictions arising from that fear. This will benefit not just the users who need libre OA, but also benefits the users who want to do something lawful, though not widely known to be lawful, under fair use.

Don't make conscientious users choose between the delay of seeking permission and the risk of proceeding without it. Don't make them ask permission. Don't make them pay for permission. Don't make them err on the side of non-use. Don't increase the pressure to make them less conscientious. Don't free your users to exceed fair use without telling them that they are free to exceed fair use. If you think you're providing libre OA but don't use an open license or equivalent language, then you're not providing libre OA. You're using an all-rights-reserved copyright, perhaps yoked with a private resolve not to enforce it, forcing conscientious users to seek permission. Your private resolve not to enforce your legal rights doesn't free anyone from the need to learn what their own rights are. But your public resolve through an open license will do so simply and elegantly.

(3) Closing up

Here I mean closing the gap between a journal's quality and prestige. New journals can be excellent from birth, but even the best cannot be prestigious from birth. This annoyance rises to the level of a serious challenge when we understand that submissions follow journal prestige more than journal quality, when the two differ.

This is another dimension of the burden facing new journals, aggravated by the fact that new journals don't have IFs. Promotion and tenure committees tend to treat journal IFs as a major component of journal prestige, and to use both IFs and prestige as surrogates for article quality and author quality.

I used to think it was just a matter of time before high-quality OA journals earned prestige in proportion to their quality. I'm less sure now. As I argued in an article last year, limited library budgets (for "must-have" journals) and limited human attention (for journal brands) mean that journal prestige is closer to a zero-sum game than journal quality. Incumbents with a headstart have a powerful advantage.

http://www.earlham.edu/~peters/fos/newsletter/09-02-08.htm#prestige

New journals trying to close the prestige-quality gap already know the basic strategies. Recruit eminent authors. Recruit eminent editors. Earn high impact (and boast about the evidence). Reach out to the media with the newsworthy discoveries or analyses you publish. Wait, endure, and persist. Unfortunately, even if time is not sufficient, it is still necessary. Even if you're doing all you can, this one remains a continuing challenge.

The only effective shortcut I know is not available to existing OA journals, namely, to convert existing high-prestige TA journals to OA. When a journal converts, it carries its prestige with it, along with its reputation, IF, quality, standards, editors, and readers.

The prestige-quality gap affects new OA and new TA journals equally. If there's a difference, it's that a larger percentage of OA journals are new and face the challenge of closing the gap. Conversely, a larger percentage of TA journals have already closed the gap and earned prestige commensurate with their quality. Because this has been the case since long before the emergence of OA journals, institutions sensitive to journal prestige, such as university promotion and tenure committees and funding agency award committees, tend to focus on TA journals.

When we can, we should try to make quality count for more and prestige count for less. But we can omit those strategies here because, at best, they wouldn't close the prestige-quality gap. They would merely prevent it from harming authors and journals. For some elaboration, however, see Section 8 of my 2008 essay above.

Likewise, when there is no high-prestige OA journal in a field, authors who can publish in high-prestige TA journals can usually deposit copies of their peer-reviewed manuscripts in OA repositories. In that sense, green OA means that authors rarely have to choose between journal prestige and OA. But this does not close the gap for gold OA, or prevent it from harming OA journals; it merely prevents it from harming authors.

(4) Doubts about quality

Even though peer-reviewed OA journals have been around now for more than 20 years, some academics believe that OA journals bypass peer review. Some believe that OA journals skimp on peer review. Some believe that publication fees corrupt peer review. Some confuse lack of prestige with lack of quality. ("If I haven't heard of it, how good could it be?") Some generalize too quickly from weak journals. ("I'm skeptical about these new OA journals. I saw one the other day that was second-rate.")

All these judgments are hasty. The most common question I ask myself as I sift through the daily debates is this: "Can this Ph.D. be as careless in his research as he is in this comment?" But even if false and hasty, the judgments exist. That's the challenge.

One solution is to point to high-quality OA journals. You don't have to argue that they are more numerous than they are. The fact that they do exist proves that they can exist. If some OA journals are strong and some are weak, then we must be a bit more empirical. We have to look and see and see before we judge, just as we do for TA journals. We must move beyond prejudice, impressionism, rumor, and stereotype to discrimination.

It helps to point out that the range of OA journals is just like the range of TA journals: some are gems and some are clunkers. It may sound obvious, but in defending OA journal quality, only defend the quality journals. If you defend weak journals on the ground that they are OA, you give the impression that you will forgive a journal any lapses provided it is OA. You may even be able to defend your forgiveness, but you will only feed doubts about quality. The best way to defend OA journals as a class is not to defend them all.

Another strategy is to distinguish quality from prestige, or real excellence from reputed excellence. We all understand this distinction once it's pointed out. But all too often we're accustomed to use prestige as a surrogate for quality and need to be reminded of the differences.

http://www.earlham.edu/~peters/fos/newsletter/09-02-08.htm#prestige

Similarly, distinguish quality from IFs. The differences are just as real and just as generally unacknowledged as those between quality and prestige.

Point out that the primary factors affecting journal quality are independent of the journal's access policy: the quality of its authors, editors, and referees. Point out that some factors favor OA journals. For example, when an OA journal has many excellent submissions, then it needn't reject any for reasons of space. When an OA journal has few excellent submissions, then it can publish a short issue rather than lower standards to fill out an issue. By contrast, TA journals can't publish short issues without short-changing subscribers, pointing up one of the hidden blessings of having no subscribers.

Unfortunately these strategies all require conversation with the doubters. The challenge is not that these conversations go badly when they take place, but that they don't take place often enough.

BTW, it would be a mistake to underestimate the challenge of these doubts on the ground that careful and informed people do not make hasty generalizations. Many people are careless or uninformed, including many careful people who are too busy to inform themselves.

(5) Doubts about preservation

"Digital documents last forever—or five years, whichever comes first."
—Jeff Rothenberg, 2001

http://www.amibusiness.com/dps/rothenberg-arma.pdf

The more important the work you publish, the more important it is to preserve it.

Fortunately, serious preservation options are neither expensive nor difficult, at least for the journals being preserved, as opposed to the services preserving them. Several of the best are free of charge, both for the journals and for users who want to access the content.

If you held off on making a preservation plan, fearing the expense and complexity, it's not too late to adopt one now. I almost said "it's never too late," but that is exactly what we cannot say.

E-only TA journals face the same challenge. The difference is that TA journals have more options because they needn't insist on preservation methods that provide OA to the preserved content.

I recommend LOCKSS (OA at least for the hosting institutions) and the DOAJ preservation system (OA for all). Both are free of charge for the journals.

http://www.lockss.org/

http://web.archive.org/web/20090827065335/http://www.doaj.org/doaj?func=loadTempl&templ=longTermArchiving

Another free and stable option is to deposit your digital content with a trusted, financially secure, and well-equipped meatspace library. For example, BioMed Central has been depositing its digital output since 2003 in the National Library of the Netherlands, just as the DOAJ preservation program does today.

http://web.archive.org/web/20100430124914/http://www.biomedcentral.com/info/presscenter/pressreleases?pr=20030917

Many other publishers deposit their digital contents in the British Library.

http://web.archive.org/web/20070731021130/http://www.bl.uk/aboutus/stratpolprog/ccare/introduction/digital/

National libraries and university libraries with digital preservation programs could render a great service by opening their vaults to peer-reviewed ejournals (OA and TA).

BioMed Central and the Public Library of Science routinely deposit their articles in PubMed Central. This greatly increases the likelihood that users will be able to find them again, and find them OA, if the publishers went out of business. This is smart and easy. I recommend routine deposits in a suitable repository for all OA journal publishers.

(Similarly, I recommend that authors avoid hybrid OA journals which do not allow deposits in a repository independent of the publisher.)

http://www.earlham.edu/~peters/fos/newsletter/09-02-06.htm#3

However, repository deposit should not be a journal's only preservation plan. Peter Hirtle has shown why.

http://www.earlham.edu/~peters/fos/2007/04/are-oa-repositories-adequate-for-long.html

But repository deposit can still provide an extra layer of security for ejournals, both before they work out long-term solutions and then later alongside long-term solutions. Among other benefits, this can free new OA projects from the delay of making ironclad preservation a precondition of launch.

A decisive way to answer doubts about digital preservation is to make printouts and preserve the paper. As I argued in 2002:

http://jbiol.com/content/1/1/3

So far, paper is the only commonly used medium that we know can preserve texts for hundreds of years. There are many creative methods emerging for storing digital texts electronically with at least the security of paper. ... The only problem is that it will take hundreds of years to monitor the outcome of present-day experiments. But we don't have to choose between insecure storage and retreat from the digital revolution: the shortcut to preservation is to print digital texts on paper. ... Preservation in the digital era [can] be as good as paper, just as it was before the digital era.

Microtome is one company that offers paper-based preservation to OA journals.

http://www.mtome.com/Services/printarchiving.html

Finally, let me repeat the point from #2 that libre OA facilitates preservation by granting permission in advance for migrating digital files to new formats and media to keep them readable as technology changes, and for copying files for multiple deposits. In fact, the built-in reasons why repositories (as opposed to journals) find it difficult for to offer libre OA lie at the basis of Hirtle's argument that repositories are inadequate for preservation.

In some countries, like the US, copying for preservation is allowed by a special provision of copyright law. But this sort of copying is not allowed in all countries, and not part of fair use. Without this permission from the statute or an open license, we could only preserve a mass of content by hunting down each individual copyright holders to ask permission. The expense and delay can be deal-breakers. If you're concerned enough about the future of your content to *want* to preserve it, then you should be concerned enough to facilitate that preservation with an open license.

Some friends of OA object that preservation is not intrinsically part of providing OA. That's true. But the same could be said of peer review and grammatical sentences. "Separate" doesn't mean "unimportant" or "incompatible." Think of preservation as a separate essential, like truth, clarity, and punctuation. You can provide OA without it, but you shouldn't want to.

(6) Doubts about honesty

Are OA journals a scam? Are *fee-based* OA journals a scam? Are *some* fee-based OA journals scams? Do *some observers believe* that some fee-based OA journals are scams? Does this *belief* harm OA journals as a class?

Although you edit or publish OA journals yourself, you probably gave one, two, or three "yes" answers to these five questions. That's the challenge.

Here are some of the suspicious practices which give rise to doubts about a journal's honesty:

- Providing little or no evidence of peer review
- Spamming researchers
- Claiming vaporware titles to be published journals
- Hiding the names of editors
- Hiding the names of owners
- Hiding the journal's business address

For this purpose the problem with spam is not the annoyance of unsolicited email. The problem is carelessness on one of the points where we'd expect serious, peer-reviewed journals to be careful. When a journal asks you to submit work or join an editorial board, you're flattered because you respect its discriminating judgment. It doesn't make this invitation to just anyone. But when a journal tries to flatter you in this way and gets your field comically wrong, you know it knows nothing about you. You know it's making this invitation to just about everyone. If it knows nothing about you, why does it want you to join its editorial board? Did it fail to do its homework on something this basic, or did it not really care? Which would be worse?

The problem with vaporware is not premature announcement, but confusion about the purpose of an announcement. All new journals go through stages when they haven't yet named their editors or published any articles. It's hard to know when along this continuum to say that the journal "exists" or has "launched," or when to list the title on the publisher's web site. Honest journals can draw the line at different places. But in my experience, journals with other suspicious practices tend to draw the line unusually early in the process and tend to do it for dozens or hundreds of titles at once, as if they thought it more important to impress the reader with the ambition of the list than the working operation of any individual journal.

The challenge behind this challenge is that we rarely have more than grounds for suspicion. We'll often have doubts about our doubts about a journal's honesty. In my own mind, it's important to leave space to distinguish a scam from a clumsy start-up. An entirely honest but clumsy start-up might announce titles far in advance of their content and forget to disclose the editors or owners. My recommendation is two-sided. On the one hand, don't be the last to criticize dishonest practices and low standards. The longer you hesitate, the more it appears that you will overlook a journal's vices as long as it is OA. (Think about Republicans who hesitate to criticize a dishonest fellow Republican and Democrats who hesitate to criticize a dishonest fellow Democrat.) On the other hand, don't create a hostile or unwelcoming environment for new start-ups.

These two recommendations are compatible. But while one says "don't be the last to criticize," the other doesn't quite say "don't be the first." Your experience as an editor or publisher may help you know sooner than others that a certain new initiative is engaged in deception. Just don't pounce until you're confident that you're dealing with deceptive practices rather than clumsiness and inexperience. Or pounce differently in the two cases. Even clumsy but honest start-ups need a reminder about professional standards, even if they don't deserve condemnation for ethical lapses. Don't let ours become a revolution that eats its own children.

The OASPA code of conduct is a beacon here. Not only does it say the right things: disclose your peer review process, your contact info, your fees, and don't spam. It is the voice of OA publishers themselves, not critics of OA publishers. It shows that OA publishers are willing to articulate these norms and willing to enforce them. It's public self-regulation. It's available for supporters, critics, and start-ups to consult it as an emerging standard.

http://oaspa.org/membership/code-of-conduct/

Remember the Davis/Anderson hoax from June 2009. Phil Davis and Kent Anderson submitted five pages of computer-generated nonsense to The Open Information Science Journal (TOISCIJ), published by Bentham Open. The journal accepted the paper and sent the authors a bill for $800.

http://scholarlykitchen.sspnet.org/2009/06/10/nonsense-for-dollars/

http://www.earlham.edu/~peters/fos/2009/06/hoax-exposes-incompetence-or-worse -at.html

The incident hurt OA journals in one respect and helped in another. It hurt by feeding hasty generalizations about OA journals and the business model of charging author-side publication fees, though Davis and Anderson themselves did not draw these hasty generalizations. (More on doubts about publication fees in #7 below.)

The hoax made all OA journals look bad. You might quarrel with the word "all." Not all OA journals charge publication fees. Not all OA journals that do charge fees take the money and fail to deliver honest peer review, or even a cursory human glance. True and true. The actual number of journals like TOISCIJ is very small. But most people who hear about the Davis/Anderson hoax don't understand the distinctions among OA journals, just as most people who heard about the 1996 Sokal hoax didn't understand the distinctions among cultural studies journals or even among humanities journals. Jumping to the conclusion that the problem lies with OA as such or publication fees as such is not justified and not fair. But that's the challenge.

By contrast, TA journal scams –like the nine fake journals published by Elsevier– seldom trigger generalizations about the faults of TA journals as such. From long familiarity, most academics have learned to discriminate among TA journals. But most are still learning to discriminate among OA journals.

On the other side, the Davis/Anderson hoax helped OA journals by drawing humiliating attention to embarrassing behavior. It should deter similar behavior. Whether you consider the TOISCIJ to have been guilty of dishonesty or incompetence, other journals dishonest or incompetent in the same way will have to worry that they could be next. We can't know how widely the deterrent effect will operate or for how long. It won't drive all dishonest journals from the field, even if we wish it would. But it does help.

(7) Doubts about publication fees

Some critics believe that author-side publication fees corrupt peer review, an idea which puts honest journals under a cloud. Some believe that the fees must be paid by authors out of pocket, an idea which scares authors in nearly every field and every country.

We can respond to the corruption charge by pointing to the financial firewalls in place at fee-based OA journals. Outsiders can't be expected to know about them, and journals have to take the initiative to explain the systems they have in place.

http://www.earlham.edu/~peters/fos/newsletter/11-02-03.htm#objreply

http://www.earlham.edu/~peters/fos/newsletter/10-02-06.htm#quality

We can respond to the author fear by educating authors about sources and sponsors willing to pay publication fees on their behalf. In March 2009 the Research Information Network urged universities and funding agencies willing to pay these fees to make their willingness clear to authors. If they don't, too many authors will continue to assume that "author fees" are to be paid by authors out of pocket.

http://www.rin.ac.uk/system/files/attachments/Paying-open-access-charges-guidance.pdf

http://www.earlham.edu/~peters/fos/2009/03/guidance-on-paying-publication-fees.htm006C

For universities willing to pay fees on behalf of faculty, see the list at the Open Access Directory (a wiki you can update).

http://oad.simmons.edu/oadwiki/OA_journal_funds

For funding agencies willing to pay fees on behalf of grantees, see the (short) list at BioMed Central and its (longer) table of policies.

http://www.biomedcentral.com/about/apcfaq/grants

http://www.biomedcentral.com/funding/funderpolicies

But clarity about the availability of funds is a step best taken by universities and funders themselves. One thing you can do as journals and publishers is to be more careful with your language. "Author pays" and "author fees" are deeply misleading terms. They are false for the majority of OA journals which charge no fees at all, and false in all cases when fees will be paid by the author's funder or employer or waived on grounds of economic hardship. "Publication fees" and "processing fees" are both less frightening and more accurate. If you want to mention authors, for symmetry with reader-side subscription fees, then "author-side fees" is less frightening and more accurate than "author fees." Terminology matters, especially when so many people have only a tenuous grasp of what OA is and how it's funded.

http://www.earlham.edu/~peters/fos/2006/09/against-term-author-pays.html

Clearly I'm not recommending that you look for a euphemism to hide or disguise the existence of fees when you charge fees. Everyone can tell that a "publication fee" is a fee. (Moreover, hiding your fees would violate the OASPA code of conduct!) But don't mislead in the other direction either. It's misleading to leave the impression that fees must be paid by authors when they *need not be paid by authors*.

If author-side fees intrinsically corrupt peer review, then then corruption is more widespread at TA journals than OA journals. The reason is simply that many more TA journals charge author-side fees than OA journals, both in percentages and absolute numbers. The Kaufman-Wills report in October 2005 found that 75% of TA journals charged author-side fees, compared to only 47% of OA journals. Stuart Shieber's study in May 2009 lowered the number for OA journals to 29.7%. But as far as I know, no new study has updated the number for TA journals.

Kaufman-Wills study, October 2005

http://www.alpsp.org/Ebusiness/ProductCatalog/Product.aspx?ID=47

Shieber study, May 2009

http://blogs.law.harvard.edu/pamphlet/2009/05/29/what-percentage-of-open-access-journals-charge-publication-fees/

Used properly this argument is not a "tu quoque" (deflecting criticism on the ground that "you too" are doing the same thing). It's a consciousness raiser and a goad to be more empirical. It doesn't ask critics to forgive a practice at OA journals just because it also takes place at TA journals. The practice might cause problems at both. Instead the argument asks, "Do you really think that author-side fees *intrinsically* corrupt peer review? Or, realizing that this affects 75% of subscription-based journals, do you want to acknowledge that sometimes fees corrupt and sometimes they don't, back down from the flat generalization, put on your empiricist glasses, and look for individual signs and symptoms of corruption and evolving best practices about safeguards?"

Likewise, if the incentive to generate more revenue leads journals to publish more articles and lower their standards, then the problem is worse at TA journals than OA journals. The reason in this case is that TA subscription fees contain high profit margins much more often than OA publication fees. Most OA publication fees are subsistence-level. When a TA journal increases its volume to justify a price increase, it will typically clear much more than an OA journal which increases its volume in order to bring in more publication fees.

http://www.earlham.edu/~peters/fos/newsletter/10-02-06.htm#quality

(8) Doubts about sustainability

Unfamiliarity with OA journals leads many academics to frame an unconscious dilemma: "OA journals couldn't possibly pay their bills. They won't last long. But if they can pay their bills, they must not be doing much work. Their quality must be low."

As usual, one strategy is education. Point out the OA journals and publishers making profits or surpluses—for example, BioMed Central, Hindawi, Medknow, Optics Express, PLoS ONE.

Distinguish the long-term outlook from the present transition period. Long-term the money needed to support peer-reviewed OA journals in every research niche is locked up supporting peer-reviewed TA journals. The money is already in the system. If comparatively little is spent today on OA journals, that says much more about the history of journals (in which TA journals arrived long before OA journals) than about the sustainability of OA journals.

Monopolistic profit margins above 25–30% at the largest publishers show that the amount we currently pay for peer-reviewed journals is significantly more than the cost of producing peer-reviewed journals. That gap should reassure us about the long-term sustainability of OA journals, even if it says nothing about navigating the transition period.

The sustainability of *subscription* journals is far from clear after nearly four decades of raising average prices faster than inflation. When the University of California studied the question, its concluded that "[t]he economics of [subscription-based] scholarly journal publishing are incontrovertibly unsustainable."

http://web.archive.org/web/20050405224414/http://libraries.universityofcalifornia.edu/news/facmemoscholcomm_010704.pdf

With care this argument needn't be a "tu quoque" either. (We can't deflect doubts about the sustainability of OA journals by raising doubts about the sustainability of TA journals; perhaps both are unsustainable.) It's a goad to put questions about the sustainability of OA journals into a larger context. What is our standard of sustainability? Do we need a guarantee before we support a promising new idea? Are we more interested in whether the average OA journal can meet a given standard, per se, or whether the average OA journal can meet a given standard as well as the average TA journal?

The situation is much like the two hikers in the mountains who came around a bend and encountered a bear. One dropped to the ground, pulled off his hiking boots, and began putting on a pair of running shoes. "What are you doing?" the second hiker asked. "You can't outrun a bear." The first replied, "I don't have to outrun the bear. I only have to outrun you."

If a journal must survive a certain number of years to prove its sustainability, then no new journals can supply the proof, OA or TA, just as we can't know that digital files can be preserved for 100 years until 100 years have passed. But if a new journal uses a model that other journals have used successfully to pay their bills, perhaps with some surplus thrown in, then new OA journals can meet the standard as well as new TA journals.

If your OA journals are breaking even or making a surplus, consider sharing your business data. It would answer doubts about sustainability. More important, it would help other OA journals learn from your experience. Let's be more intentional about sharing hard-won tips, warnings, and best practices.

I'd like to see the OASPA coordinate a kind of journal buddy system in which experienced journals help inexperienced journals work out sustainable business models and answer the kinds of rubber-on-the-road questions that come up in the daily management of a journal. If there are many basic models and variations, and if the landscape differs from field to field and country to country (and decade to decade), then experienced journals can help guide newer journals through the landscape. Even if journals are not willing to share their business data with the public, they should be willing to share them in confidence with OASPA-buddies.

At the Open Access Directory, I've been trying to document the OA journal business models actually in use. The idea is to show that there is more than one, and to show which ones are in use where. The variety should help critics avoid generalization, help new journals find models to suit their niche, and stimulate everyone's imagination to conceive other models and other variations on the existing themes. But so far I've been working almost alone on the list. If you can help, please do. It's a wiki.

http://oad.simmons.edu/oadwiki/OA_journal_business_models

Finally, don't dismiss questions about sustainability. They are not code for opposition, any more than questions about preservation are code for opposition. Like preservation, the importance of sustainability rises in direct proportion to the importance of the work you are publishing.

(9) Doubts about redirection

Suppose you're persuaded that most of the money needed to support OA journals is tied up supporting TA journals and that redirecting funds would suffice. You may well wonder: Will it happen? If so, how? What can we do to nudge it along?[2]

Redirection is already happening on a small scale. Whenever a TA journal converts to OA, we're seeing small-scale redirection.

OA journal funds at universities are potential examples. Most of the current funds are adding new money to the system. But if they last long enough and grow large enough to face the replenishment problem, and if universities make them a priority for any funds saved from the cancellation or conversion of TA journals, then the funds will become redirection devices.

Redirection is also taking place on a large scale, primarily through CERN's SCOAP3 project (Sponsoring Consortium for Open Access Publishing in Particle Physics). SCOAP3 is an ambitious plan to convert all the major TA journals in particle physics to OA, and redirect the money formerly spent on reader-side subscription fees to author-side publication fees. It's being worked out in a large-scale negotiation with all the stakeholders, including publishers.

http://www.scoap3.org/

First let's help SCOAP3 work in particle physics. Then when it's working, let's study why it works, with an eye on transferring the model to other fields. Some factors in its success will be physics-specific, such as the small number of targeted journals, the green OA arXiv culture embraced even by TA publishers in the field, and the dominance of CERN. Other factors will not be physics-specific, such as the win-win logic which appeals, or could appeal, to research institutions, libraries, funders, and publishers. It's the win-win logic which makes me think that other fields might pull this off without a CERN. If other fields can do this, they won't need CERN-like money or dominance so much as CERN-like convening power. If they can bring the stakeholders together to discuss the idea, then the win-win logic has a chance to take over from there.

SCOAP3 is the not only most ambitious redirection project now under way. It's also the furthest along and the most refined by reality-tests. (There's nothing like asking an institution to commit money to bring out its latent doubts and test your ability to answer them.) If it's not the best model for some other fields, then let's figure that out and think hard about other large-scale redirection strategies alongside SCOAP3. But if it could work in other fields, we'd lose a precious opportunity if we didn't apply the lessons of SCOAP3 everywhere they are applicable.

We can't underestimate rising levels of green OA as another impetus to large-scale redirection. This is one more reason for OA journals and publishers to support green OA mandates at universities and funding agencies, and oppose publisher trade associations who lobby against them. But we should also realize that rising green OA levels may have no effect on redirection. In physics, the highest levels and longest history of OA archiving have not triggered TA journal cancellations or freed up money which could be redirected to OA journals; but they have led indirectly to SCOAP3.

If rising levels of green OA do force redirection in fields outside physics, it will only be after a period of antagonism and polarization like nothing we've seen to date. Hence, while we continue to work unabated for green OA, let's also try to understand whether a faster and more frictionless method like SCOAP3 could work in fields outside physics.

Mark Rowse, former CEO of Ingenta, sketched another strategy for large-scale redirection in December 2003. A publisher could "flip" its TA journals to OA at one stroke by reinterpreting the payments it receives from university libraries as OA publication fees for a group of authors rather than TA subscription fees for a group of readers. One advantage over SCOAP3 is that the Rowsean flip can be tried one journal or one publisher at a time, and doesn't require discipline-wide coordination. But at the same time, it can scale up to the largest publishers or the largest coalitions of publishers. If the Rowsean flip hasn't been tried in its pure form by any publisher, several ongoing projects have Rowsean characteristics, such as SCOAP3 itself, the Stanford Encyclopedia of Philosophy, and the Springer deals with some universities and libraries to include OA publication fees in the price of subscriptions.

For more detail on the Rowsean flip, see my elaboration of the idea from October 2007.

http://www.earlham.edu/~peters/fos/newsletter/10-02-07.htm#flip

We have to be imaginative but we don't have to improvise. There are some principles we can try to follow. Money freed up by the cancellation or conversion of peer-reviewed TA journals should be spent first on peer-reviewed OA journals. Large-scale redirection is more efficient than small-scale redirection. Peaceful revolution through negotiation and self-interest is more amicable and potentially more productive than adaptation forced by falling asteroids.

(For more on the need to redirect savings from the cancellation and conversion of TA journals to OA journals, see my article from September 2007, esp. Section 13.)

http://www.earlham.edu/~peters/fos/newsletter/09-02-07.htm#peerreview

For the record, in case it doesn't go without saying, I advocate redirecting money freed up by cancellations or conversions, not canceling journals in order to free up the money. This may look like hair-splitting, but the difference is neither small nor subtle. It's roughly the difference between having great expectations and planning to kill your parents.

(10) Doubts about strategy

Here I mean doubts about strategies for addressing the other challenges to OA journals. These are doubts you might have yourself, not the doubts of others.

You're keenly aware of the challenges facing OA journals and deal with them every day. The strategies for doing so seem to fall into into two large families.

The first is to cultivate your own garden. Prove that OA journals can publish good work by publishing good work. Prove that OA journals can survive by surviving. Prove that OA journals can operate with rigor and integrity by operating with rigor and integrity. Silence doubts and disarm criticism by succeeding.

The second is activism. Engage in the debate and converse with doubters. Answer objections and misunderstandings. Share your data and experience, offer direct assistance to buddy-journals, and work for more fee-paying funds, better metrics, and redirection.

If you can't do both, then choose gardening. If you have to withdraw from public discussion and keep your head down in order to make your journal succeed, then do that. We need your success. But if you don't have to withdraw from public discussion in order to make your journal succeed, then I hope you'll take part in it. When the TA publishing lobby makes its blanket assertions that threats to TA journals are threats to peer review itself, that journal publishers require exclusive rights, or that everyone who needs access already has access, your response as a journal publisher or journal editor will have more authority than the same responses from other players. Journal insiders have a unique opportunity in this debate and should seize it more often.

For example, see the editors of The Lancet disavowing the tactics used by the Association of American Publishers in opposing the NIH policy, October 2004,

http://www.thelancet.com/journals/lancet/article/PIIS0140673604172322/fulltext

http://www.earlham.edu/~peters/fos/2004/10/lancet-supports-nih-plan-with.html

Or see Cambridge University Press, Cold Spring Harbor Laboratory Press, Columbia University Press, MIT Press, Nature Publishing Group, Oxford University Press, Pennsylvania State University Press, Rockefeller University Press, and the University of Chicago Press disavowing or distancing themselves from the deceptive PRISM campaign, October 2007.

http://www.earlham.edu/~peters/fos/2007/10/mit-press-dissociates-itself-from-prism.html

Or see Mike Rossner and the Rockefeller University Press disavowing the American Association of University Presses support for the Conyers bill, September 2008.

http://www.earlham.edu/~peters/fos/2008/09/rockefeller-up-disavows-aaup-support.html

But I don't want to draw too sharp a distinction between gardening and activism.

Even if you want to focus on cultivating your own garden, you will recognize that misunderstandings about OA will limit your submissions and that the failures of other OA journals (ethical and financial) will harm your reputation. Helping to spread the truth about OA journals as a class will help your OA journals individually. Debunking myths about OA journals will help you recruit submissions and gain the support of promotion and tenure committees. Even the narrow goal to publish good work and survive might require some activism.

Conversely, reputable OA journals can lift the reputations of other OA journals. If you publish good work and survive, your success will directly support other OA journals and advance the debate. Examples are more persuasive than arguments. The most harmful objections to OA journals allege that something intrinsic to OA limits their quality, their integrity, or their financial viability. When you succeed, you prove that is false.

Postscript

This is an expanded, full-prose version of my keynote address last month at the 1st Conference on Open Access Scholarly Publishing (Lund, September 14–16, 2009).

http://web.archive.org/web/20090405223351/http://www.oaspa.org/coasp/

Notes

1. Just to clarify some points often misunderstood: All CC licenses provide libre OA, although some are more open than others. But no CC licenses are required for libre OA. You can provide libre OA through an equivalent non-CC license or homegrown language instead, if you like. But libre OA requires some kind of open license. When a copyrighted text doesn't use any sort of open license, then it falls under an all-rights-reserved copyright, which shrinks user rights down to fair use and rules out libre OA.

2. The DOAJ doesn't actually count journals with CC-BY licenses [in 2009]. It counts journals with the SPARC Europe Seal, which requires CC-BY licenses. But the Seal also requires journals to share metadata in a certain way. Hence, it's possible for many journals to use CC-BY and fail to earn the Seal because they don't share their metadata appropriately. In that case the SPARC Seal tally would undercount the journals using CC-BY. But in fact, many more DOAJ journals share their metadata than use CC-BY, making the Seal tally a good approximation to a CC-BY tally. Thanks to Lars Björnshauge for this detail.

3. Why say that "most" rather than "all" the money needed to support OA journals is tied up in TA journals? Because some of the money needed to support OA journals is *not* tied up in TA journals and already flows to OA journals. Also note, however, that even if we reach a world in which most journals are OA, and all are adequately funded, some TA journals will almost certainly coexist with OA journals and attract some money to themselves.

Funder and University Policies

The Final Version of the NIH Public-Access Policy

From "The final version of the NIH public-access policy," SPARC Open Access Newsletter, March 2, 2005.

http://dash.harvard.edu/handle/1/4552041

The day after I mailed last month's issue of SOAN [February 2005], the NIH released the final version of its public-access policy. My comments in the February issue focused on new concessions to publishers that weakened the policy. I was hoping that by the time the final version of the policy was announced, these concessions would be rolled back, but it was not to be. Hence, I stand by the assessment I wrote last month.

However, many aspects of the policy and its public roll-out deserve some public attention.

The policy was published in three parts: Background (Section I), Public Comments and NIH Responses (Section II), and Text of Final Policy Statement (Section III). While the third section is the most important for NIH-funded authors and their publishers, Section II is definitely worth a close read. It's the longest section of the document and carefully answers the major objections raised against the policy during the comment period.

*

The policy will take effect on May 2 [2005]. (Section III.) It will apparently apply to all outstanding NIH grants as of May 2, not just to new grants made on or after May 2. That means that we can expect to see some articles based on NIH-funded research show up in PubMed Central (PMC) fairly soon after May 2, even if the rate of deposit is initially slow. If the policy only applied to new grants, then we'd have to wait for newly funded research to be completed, written up, published, and deposited.

*

The policy has three official purposes. "The policy is intended to: 1) create a stable archive of peer-reviewed research publications resulting from NIH-funded research to ensure the permanent preservation of these vital published research findings; 2) secure a searchable compendium of these peer-reviewed research publications that NIH and its awardees can use to manage more efficiently and to understand better their research portfolios, monitor scientific productivity, and ultimately, help set research priorities; and 3) make published results of NIH-funded research more readily accessible to the public, health care providers, educators, and scientists." (Section I.)

Later in the document, NIH elaborates on the third purpose. "We believe that improved access through PMC to peer-reviewed, final manuscripts of NIH-supported investigators will facilitate scientific progress because it will enable NIH to manage better its research portfolio and funding choices. The NIH encourages the sharing of ideas, data, and research findings to help accomplish its important public mission to uncover new knowledge that will lead to better health for everyone." (Section II.E.)

From the standpoint of research and researchers, the third purpose is the most important. The overriding benefit of free online access to research literature is the way it accelerates research, shares knowledge, and enhances the productivity of everyone using the literature. By advancing research, it advances all the benefits of research, from economic prosperity to public health.

*

NIH is asking authors to deposit "an electronic version of the author's final manuscript upon acceptance for publication, resulting from research supported, in whole or in part, with direct costs from NIH. The author's final manuscript is defined as the final version accepted for journal publication, and includes all modifications from the publishing peer review process." (Section III.) It's not clear whether authors may enhance this edition with changes introduced by a journal's copy editing process. But at least PMC will accept "corrections and other necessary revisions of the author's final manuscripts" (Section II.D.)

*

The recent good news and bad news are closely yoked together. The bad: the permissible delay after publication has been extended beyond six months. The good: NIH will exhort authors to choose the shortest possible delay. Here's how the policy phrases this key provision: "At the time of submission, the author will specify the timing of the posting of his or her final manuscript for public accessibility through PMC. Posting for public accessibility through PMC is requested and strongly encouraged as soon as possible (and within twelve months of the publisher's official date of final publication)." (Section III.)

In the new FAQ on the policy, the NIH goes beyond exhorting grantees to authorize early release by suggesting language for authors to include in their copyright transfer agreements with publishers (Question 26): "Journal acknowledges that Author retains the right to provide a copy of the final manuscript to NIH upon acceptance for Journal publication or thereafter, for public archiving in PubMed Central as soon as possible after publication by Journal."

http://web.archive.org/web/20050331181102/http://www.nih.gov/about/publica
ccess/022405QA.pdf

If taxpayers can't simply mandate deposit as a condition of public funding, then
"strong encouragement" and suggested contract language are just about second best.
We'll see how well it works in practice, especially if some publishers refuse to sign the
new contract language and strongly encourage authors to take the opposite course and
either deposit as late as possible or never deposit at all.

*

Is publisher permission needed for author deposits in PMC? This simple question
is harder than it looks. First note that the suggested contract language (above) asks
journals to acknowledge that authors have permission to deposit their work in PMC. But
is this strictly necessary or simply a prudent way to guarantee what is already
permissible?

The NIH says that it has two independent and separately sufficient legal grounds to
disseminate the research articles of its grantees: one is copyright-holder consent and
the other is a government-purpose license long since codified in the Code of Federal
Regulations (45 C.F.R. 74.36). The NIH has decided to rely on the former and to hold
the latter in readiness in case it is ever needed. (Section II.P.2.)

So the answer to the question seems to be: no, publisher permission is not needed
but NIH has decided to seek it anyway. One day we may hear the story on why it is
taking this position.

*

In the teleconference announcing the new policy, Elias Zerhouni made a good point
that is often obscured in the press. The policy has not replaced a firm six month maximum embargo with a firm 12 month maximum embargo. It has replaced a firm six
month maximum embargo with a flexible period whose duration depends on the
author's discretion.

We could say that the new embargo is "zero to 12 months" but that does not reflect
the reality that deposit is "voluntary" (Section III) and needn't occur at all. The policy
encourages authors to deposit as soon as possible within 12 months. But we have to
understand that 12 months is not a deadline but just another part of the NIH
encouragement.

If there's a contradiction in suggesting a deadline (with the "12 month" language)
and suggesting that there is no deadline (with the "voluntary" language), then the final
version of the policy and the accompanying commentary do nothing to dispel it.

*

There will be no penalties for non-deposit. (Section II.O.) It's not clear whether this is
new. When the "requirement" was reduced to a "request" in the September 3 draft
released for public comment, there were vague but ominous suggestions that

non-compliance might jeopardize a grantee's future funding. Now it's clear that it won't. But perhaps it never would have; we'll never know.

Publishers who dislike the policy are saying that any "request" from a funding agency, especially one accompanied by "strong encouragement," is intrinsically coercive even without formal penalties. Perhaps. But I wonder whether it's any more coercive than a request from a journal, especially one accompanied by strong encouragement, to delay PMC deposit. The two requests seem roughly equal in power to me, whether we call them both coercive or neither coercive. And that is what worries me: there is dangerous potential in this policy to create painful and career-jeopardizing dilemmas for researchers who will have to choose between snubbing their funder and snubbing their publisher. A simple mandate would not only deliver more OA content to the public, but spare authors this dilemma.

Some publishers are already on record as willing to accommodate any decision made by their NIH-funded authors. That's excellent and I hope that others follow suit.

*

The good news is that authors can take steps to avoid the painful funder-publisher dilemma. One simple way is to submit their work to an OA journal. Another is to submit their work to one of the non-OA journals that has publicly stated its willingness to accommodate any author decision on PMC timing. But the simplest way of all may be for authors to self-archive their work, and to do so as soon as possible after publication.

Authors who experience the funder-publisher dilemma once needn't experience it twice by taking any one of these three remedies. Conversely, journals that refuse permission for postprint archiving and play tug of war with the NIH, using authors as rope, will only hurt themselves in the long run by deterring submissions.

*

The NIH explains that extending the six month delay up to 12 months or even beyond will provide greater "flexibility" (II.A, II.F, II.J) and therefore should assure greater "participation" (II.J). But if you look closely, NIH is clear that this is flexibility for publishers, not authors. For example: "NIH has made modifications to the proposed policy to provide greater flexibility to accommodate the range of business models represented by large commercial publishing houses through the smaller specialized journals of learned societies." (Section II.F)

It's true that this extension will give publishers greater flexibility and it's true that publishers were asking for greater flexibility. But the central request in the policy is directed to authors, not publishers. Greater flexibility for publishers would only assure different decisions by authors if author decisions are controlled or influenced by publishers. Are they? We don't know yet. But if they are, then publisher influence is more likely to pull against author participation and early release than in favor of them.

In the teleconference announcing the policy, Elias Zerhouni succinctly justified the new concession to publishers on the ground that it provides "maximum flexibility for maximum participation." But if the NIH really wanted maximum participation, then it should require participation.

The kind of flexibility now built into the policy doesn't ensure full participation. It makes participation discretionary and ensures that some authors will participate and some won't. The NIH can't have it both ways. If public access through PMC is voluntary, there won't be maximum participation. If it wants maximum participation, then it should ignore publisher preferences and bind authors with an OA condition on their research grants.

Maximum participation is the right goal—for the NIH, for taxpayers, for health care, and for science. Hence, NIH should adopt the most effective means to that goal (a participation requirement), not endanger the goal in order to fit the most politically expedient means (request plus discretion plus exhortation). If it's true that NIH's government-purpose license is a sufficient legal basis for the public-access policy, and that publisher permission is unnecessary, then compromises designed to give publishers flexibility and solicit their permission are also unnecessary.

*

While the request for PMC deposit is directed at authors, consenting publishers may improve upon the author's decision in two ways. "The publisher may choose to furnish PMC with the publisher's final version, which will supersede the author's final version. Also, if the publisher agrees, public access to the publisher's final version in PMC can occur sooner than the timing originally specified by the author for the author's final version." (Section III.)

Publishers who worry about the version control problem (one version on PMC and another version at their own site) should take advantage of the first option. It will not only address their worry. It will make their branding visible in their own chosen way and provide exactly the links they want back to their own site. As long as authors are complying with the NIH request, publishers have everything to gain and nothing to lose by replacing the authors' versions with their own.

*

Note that there are now *three* publication-related requests in the overall NIH grants process. (1) Grantees are "expected" to publish the results of their research rather than not to publish them. (2) Grantees are "required" to turn in copies of any publications based on funded research at end of grant period as part of their review. These copies will not necessarily be deposited in PMC for public access. (3) Grantees are "requested" but not required to deposit their publications in PMC as soon as possible within 12 months after publication. Acceding to this third request will also satisfy the second, which is another incentive for authors to deposit their work.

*

NIH continues to allow OA journal processing fees, as well as color and page charges at TA journals, to be "allowable charges" to NIH research grants. (Section II.H.)

In fact, NIH spends about $30 million/year on "direct costs for publication expenses, including page and color charges and reprints." (Sections II.F, II.L.) Compare that with the estimated $2 to $4 million/year that the public-access program will cost. (Section II.L.) The public-access budget is a pittance of the journal-subsidy budget for subscription-based journals. Publishers of subscription journals who object the NIH program is diverting money from research on cures should relinquish their taxpayer-funded subsidies if they want to make the argument with clean hands.

*

The NIH will create an "NIH Public Access Advisory Working Group of the NLM Board of Regents" to advise it "on implementation and assess progress in meeting the goals" of the policy. (Section II.F.) This sounds like a good idea, but I worry. If the advisory group is not balanced, it will be criticized. If it is balanced, it could be paralyzed.

*

The "final" version of the policy is not really final. "Once the system is operational, modifications and enhancements will be made as needed with the Working Group, or a permanent subcommittee of the Board, providing ongoing advice on improvements." (Section II.F.) "This Policy is subject to periodic review based upon lessons learned in the course of its implementation. Issuance of this Policy is the beginning of a process that will include refinement as experience develops, outcomes are evaluated, and public dialogue among all the stakeholders is continued." (Section II.O).

*

Dr. Zerhouni told the Chronicle of Higher Education on January 7 that public comments on the six-month version of the policy were "overwhelmingly supportive."

http://web.archive.org/web/20070405232406/http://chronicle.com/prm/weekly/v51/i18/18a02801.htm

http://legacy.earlham.edu/~peters/fos/2005/01/more-on-nih-plan.html

So has the NIH left its moorings by changing a central element of the policy after the public comment period closed? All it says about this in the new document is that the "final Policy reflects consideration of public comments received. ... " (Section I.)

*

One of the only obscure sentences in the new NIH document raises intriguing possibilities: "Finally, authors can indicate what copyright restrictions, if any, apply to their manuscripts when submitting them to PMC and can choose an appropriate PMC submission agreement that recognizes those rights." (Section II.P.2.) Does this simply accommodate the difference between government-funded scientists, whose work is copyrightable, and government-employed scientists, whose work is is not? Or does it accommodate authors who are copyright holders at the time of deposit and wish to waive some of their rights and allow PMC users to exceed fair use in copying and sharing their work? Is NIH offering flexibility similar to the Creative Commons?

*

Free online PMC content will be free to everyone with an Internet connection, not just to U.S. taxpayers. During the comment period, some critics not only observed that this goes beyond the taxpayer argument for open access, but somehow "disadvantages American scientists." It's hard to decide which would be more commendable in a responsible public agency, ignoring absurd objections like this or answering them. NIH decided to answer this one and did it well: "We believe that American scientists and global health will benefit from greater access to research publications leading to increased collaborative efforts worldwide. In an increasingly interdependent world, the United States and nations around the globe not only share the risk of diseases, but also the challenge to respond. This can best be accomplished in an environment in which rapid communication is possible, wherein scientific knowledge is readily available to all, and where research is conducted based on partnership." (Section II.N.)

If you're curious just how far the taxpayer argument alone can go in answering this objection, then see my discussion of Canada's attempt to offer some publicly funded research free online only to Canadians (from SOAN for 9/03),

http://legacy.earlham.edu/~peters/fos/newsletter/09-04-03.htm#taxpayer
(Scroll to Section 4.)

*

In January, Dr. Zerhouni told the Washington Fax that "[t]he fundamental break-through of this policy is … not the timing, it's the fact that we're creating for the first time the precedent and the right for a federal agency to have a venue or pathway for its scientists to publish and give access to the public."

http://legacy.earlham.edu/~peters/fos/2005/01/why-nih-weakened-its-policy.html

This is a good point. I don't want to shift attention away from the unjustified weakening of the policy. But I do want to acknowledge that, despite the weakening, the policy does establish a significant new precedent. U.S. federal funding agencies can provide free online access to the results of publicly-funded research, even when the research was not performed by government employees.

The trick will be to get other funding agencies to take the right lesson from this precedent. Which leads to the final question:

Where do we go from here? Here are the main steps:

(1) Let's strengthen the NIH policy. First, make the request a requirement. Taxpayer access to publicly-funded medical research should be guaranteed. Second, reduce the permissible delay to six months.

The House of Representatives originally recommended both of these provisions and it hasn't forgotten. I've been visiting the offices of members of both parties in both Houses of Congress and detect bipartisan support for strengthening the policy. Revising the policy won't be easy or quick, since there are also members who side with publishers or don't care. But there are real grounds for hope.

U.S. citizens, and U.S. institutions like universities and libraries, can write to their members of Congress to let them know how they feel.

http://www.congressmerge.com/onlinedb/powersearch.htm

U.S.-based institutions and organizations can join the Alliance for Taxpayer Access, which is very active and effective in this cause.

http://www.taxpayeraccess.org

Stakeholders can also write directly to the NIH.

PublicAccess@nih.gov

(2) Get Congress to monitor compliance. What percentage of NIH grantees deposit their work in PMC within 12 months? Of those that do, what is the average delay after publication authorized by the author? If the compliance rate is low, or if the average delay is long, then the urgency of revising the policy will increase.

(3) Get other funding agencies—inside and outside the U.S.—to adopt the best parts of the NIH policy and avoid worst. Do provide free online access to publicly-funded research, but don't make it discretionary and don't delay the public release more than six months.

(4) Encourage NIH-funded researchers to deposit all their eligible publications and to authorize public release immediately upon publication.

At the same time, encourage them to self-archive all their research articles, including those based on NIH-funded research. If they do, they'll get—and give—the benefits of OA for all their work. If they do it for their NIH-funded work, then the compromises in the new policy will not matter at all. The NIH welcomes its grantees to deposit their articles in other, fully OA repositories in addition to PMC.

(5) Encourage all biomedical journals to let their NIH-funded authors follow the NIH's "strong encouragement" to authorize immediate public release. Don't make authors choose between their funder and their publisher. If you belong to a scientific society that publishes journals in biomedicine, then let the society know that this is how you feel. If you edit or referee for a journal in biomedicine, then let the journal know that this is how you feel.

I'd like to hear about any journals that pressure their authors not to comply with the NIH request or that refuse to accept articles by NIH-funded authors. If you write to me in confidence, I will respect your confidence. If you authorize me to do so, I will post your message to the SPARC Open Access Forum.

Policy on Enhancing Public Access to Archived Publications Resulting from NIH-Funded Research (the text of the new policy, February 3, 2005)

http://grants.nih.gov/grants/guide/notice-files/NOT-OD-05-022.html

http://legacy.earlham.edu/~peters/fos/2005/02/nih-public-access-policy-finally.html

NIH press release on the final version of the policy, February 3, 2005

http://www.nih.gov/news/pr/feb2005/od-03.htm

NIH policy implementation plan

http://www.nih.gov/about/publicaccess/publicaccess_imp.pdf

http://legacy.earlham.edu/~peters/fos/2005/02/nih-policy-implementation-plan.html

NIH public-access policy home page (many related documents)

http://web.archive.org/web/20050211033606/http://www.nih.gov/about/publicac-cess/index.htm

NIH policy FAQ (enlarged, updated, and improved)

http://web.archive.org/web/20050331181102/http://www.nih.gov/about/publicaccess/022405QA.pdf

My comments from last month on the weakening of the NIH policy

http://legacy.earlham.edu/~peters/fos/newsletter/02-02-05.htm#nih

[...] [Here omitting some news stories and press releases on the NIH policy from the previous month.]

Another OA Mandate: The Federal Research Public Access Act of 2006

From "Another OA mandate: The Federal Research Public Access Act of 2006," SPARC Open Access Newsletter, May 2, 2006.

http://dash.harvard.edu/handle/1/4391159

Earlier today, Senators John Cornyn (R-TX) and Joe Lieberman (D-CT) introduced the Federal Research Public Access Act of 2006 (FRPAA) in the US Senate. This is giant step forward for OA, even bigger than the CURES Act that Senator Lieberman introduced in December 2005.

Like CURES, FRPAA will mandate OA and limit embargoes to six months. Unlike CURES, it will not be limited to medical research and will not mandate deposit in a central repository. It will apply to all federal funding agencies above a certain size. It instructs each agency to develop its own policy, under certain guidelines laid down in the bill. Some of those agencies might choose to launch central repositories but others might choose to mandate deposit (for example) in the author's institutional repository. Finally, while CURES was mostly about translating fundamental medical research into therapies, with a small but important provision on OA, FRPAA is all about OA. Here are some details, citing the bill by section number in parentheses.

*

FRPAA applies to all federal funding agencies that spend more than $100 million/year on research grants to non-employees ("extramural" research) (Section 4.a). At the moment, 11 agencies fall into this category: the Environmental Protection Agency (EPA), National Aeronautics and Space Administration (NASA), National Science Foundation (NSF), and the cabinet-level Departments of Agriculture, Commerce, Defense, Education, Energy, Health and Human Services, Homeland Security, and Transportation.

While the breadth of disciplines doesn't extend to the humanities or social sciences (beyond economics), it's much wider than medicine alone. Also note that by covering the Department of Health and Human Services, FRPAA covers the NIH.

Remember that in George Bush's state of the union address on January 31, 2006, he proposed spending an additional $146 billion on science over the next 10 years, including $50 billion to double the budgets of the NSF, the Department of Energy's Office of Science, and the Department of Commerce's National Institute of Standards and Technology. If Congress adopts these budget increases, they will directly expand the size of the federal commitment to OA—assuming that Congress also adopts the FRPAA.

*

Agencies will have one year from the adoption of the bill to develop their OA policies (4.a).

*

Agencies may host their own OA repositories (4.b.6.A), the way NIH hosts PMC, or they may ask grantees to deposit their work in any OA repository meeting the agency's conditions of open access, interoperability, and long-term preservation (4.b.6.B).

*

FRPAA applies to the final version of the author's peer-reviewed manuscript (4.b.1), which must incorporate all changes introduced by the peer-review process (4.b.2). Publishers will have the option to replace the author's manuscript with the final published version (4.b.3.A), at least when the agency decides that the published version advances the agency's "goals … for functionality and interoperability" (4.b.3.B).

*

FRPAA applies to manuscripts arising from "research supported, in whole or in part from funding by the Federal Government" (4.b.1). Hence it applies to projects with multiple sources of funding, provided that at least one is covered by FRPAA. It applies to manuscripts with multiple authors, provided that at least one is covered by FRPAA.

*

Agencies must insure free online access to these manuscripts "as soon as practicable, but not later than 6 months after publication in peer-reviewed journals" (4.b.4).

*

Agency policies must apply to agency employees as well as agency grantees (4.c.1). In the former case, the resulting articles will be in the public domain from birth, labeled as such, and released to the public immediately upon publication (4.c.2).

*

The OA mandate does not apply to lab notes, preliminary data analyses, personal notes, phone logs (4.d.1), classified research, revenue-producing publications like books, patentable discoveries (4.d.2), or work not submitted to journals or not accepted for publication (4.d.3).

*

Agencies will maintain OA bibliographies of publications resulting from their funded research, with active links from citations to OA editions (4.b.5).

*

Nothing in the bill modifies patent or copyright law (4.e).

*

Instead of (or perhaps simply before) relying on copyright-holder consent as the legal basis for disseminating copies of the articles, the agencies must "make effective use of any law or guidance relating to the creation and reservation of a Government license that provides for the reproduction, publication, release, or other uses of a final manuscript for Federal purposes" (4.c.3).

This section does not give agencies a license but asks them to use existing statutory or regulatory licenses as fully as possible. It's relevant, then, that there are two such licenses on which agencies may rely: 2 CFR 215.36(a) and 45 CFR 74.36(a).

Don't let the technical detail of this section disguise its importance. The NIH recognized the existence of a government license to provide OA to NIH-funded research, but deliberately decided not to use it. Instead, it relied on publisher consent, with the effect that it accommodated, if not invited, publisher resistance. By relying on government licenses instead, FRPAA makes publisher dissent irrelevant.

The 2 CFR 215.36(a) government license.

https://www.law.cornell.edu/cfr/text/2/215.36

The 45 CFR 74.36(a) government license.

https://www.law.cornell.edu/cfr/text/45/74.36

[...]

*

Here's how the bill describes its rationale: "Congress finds that the Federal Government funds basic and applied research with the expectation that new ideas and discoveries that result from the research, if shared and effectively disseminated, will advance science and improve the lives and welfare of people of the United States and around the world" (2.1). Moreover, "the Internet makes it possible for this information to be promptly available to every scientist, physician, educator, and citizen at home, in school, or in a library" (2.2).

The FRPAA is certainly the strongest OA policy proposed to date in the US. It's comparable in strength to the draft RCUK policy (June 2005), though different in several details. I'd be delighted if it passed. But for completeness, let me point out three ways in which it could be even stronger.

(1) FRPAA contains no provision to let grantees use grant money to pay processing fees charged by OA journals. This is regrettable. Funders should support OA journals as well as OA archiving. Long-term, we will need both, especially if subscription-based journals decline. The CURES bill has the same regrettable omission.

(2) FRPAA is silent on the timing of deposit, as opposed to the timing of OA release. By contrast, CURES requires deposit at the time an article is accepted by a journal. CURES has the advantage on this score, and we can hope that FRPAA will adopt its approach before much longer. If authors deposit their articles upon acceptance, then repositories can release the metadata immediately (to jumpstart awareness,

discoverability, and impact), and release the full text after the author-requested embargo, or six months, whichever comes first.

(3) FRPAA is silent on the consequences of non-compliance. The CURES bill, by contrast, explicitly says that non-compliance may be a ground for the funding agency to refuse future funding. Again, CURES has the advantage here.

However, the fact that FRPAA doesn't address these issues doesn't mean that the resulting OA policies won't address them. The covered agencies are free under the guidelines to let grantees use grant funds to pay OA journal processing fees, to require deposit at the time of publication, and to impose a sanction on non-compliance. But because the agencies are also free to go the other way, we'll have to lobby each agency separately and probably settle for a mix in which some policies are better than others.

*

While the FRPAA covers many agencies, if we focus on its consequences for the NIH, then we have to see it as the *fifth* recent sign that the NIH's weak request may become a strong requirement. On November 15, 2005, the agency's own Public Access Working Group (PAWG) recommended that the request for public access be upgraded to a requirement and that the permissible delay be shortened from 12 months to 6 months. On December 7, 2005, Senator Lieberman introduced the CURES Act, which would have the same effect. On February 8, 2006, the NLM Board of Regents endorsed the November 2005 PAWG recommendations in a letter to NIH Director Elias Zerhouni. On April 4, 2006, Zerhouni told the Subcommittee on Labor, Health and Human Services, Education, and Related Agencies that "it seems the voluntary policy is just not enough" to achieve the agency's goals [...]. And now FRPAA.

[...]

This is a superb bill. It's informed by the arguments for OA and the shortcomings of the NIH policy. It's one more sign that legislators, in the US and abroad, are not treating the NIH policy as a precedent but taking every opportunity to improve upon it: going beyond a request to a requirement, beyond long or indefinite embargoes to firm deadlines, beyond biomedicine to all disciplines, beyond publisher consent to a federal purpose license that does not accommodate publisher resistance, and at least possibly, beyond central to distributed archiving. FRPAA strengthens the NIH policy and extends the strong new policy to all the major research-funding agencies in the federal government. [...] It will give taxpayers access to the non-classified research they fund with their taxes. It will make a very large and useful body of research even more useful than it already is by sharing it with all who can apply or build upon it. In both respects it will increase the return on the taxpayers' enormous investment in this research.

[...]

Twelve Reminders about FRPAA

From SPARC Open Access Newsletter, May 2010.

http://dash.harvard.edu/handle/1/4725200

Past experience suggests that these are the 12 points that opponents are most likely to distort or fail to mention.

(1) FRPAA [Federal Research Public Access Act] mandates deposit in OA repositories, not submission to OA journals. It focuses on green OA and ignores gold OA.

(2) It does not mandate that subscription-based journals convert to OA. It does not tell any kind of journals what their access policies or business models ought to be. It regulates grantees, not publishers.

(3) It only applies to articles that have already been published in peer-reviewed journals.

This point has three important consequences. First, it means that FRPAA doesn't apply to unpublished articles or research notes. Therefore, it doesn't force premature disclosure from researchers who make patentable discoveries. The policy kicks in only after researchers voluntarily decide to publish.

Second, the policy does not bypass peer review. On the contrary, it demands peer review and merely widens access to peer-reviewed research.

Third, it's about archiving copies, not manipulating originals. Hence, the possibility of government censorship doesn't come up. The originals will be in libraries and independent web sites around the world, wherever the publisher's market reach and preservation back-ups have managed to place them. If some of the published originals are not in fact copied for OA archiving, or if some copies are removed after deposit, that would be regrettable (and violate the policy). But it would not affect the originals at all. It would not delete them from libraries and independent web sites around the world, shrink the range of their distribution, change their access policies, or reduce their visibility. To use the word "censorship" to describe the incomplete copying of literature already published, distributed, stored, curated, and preserved in independent locations is incoherent newspeak. Or (to play along), if occasional non-archiving really is a kind of censorship, then publishers who want to defeat an OA archiving mandate like FRPAA want systematic non-archiving and mass censorship.

Historical note: Hard as it is to believe, in the wake of the 2006 version of FRPAA a PR consultant advised the Association of American Publishers (AAP), Elsevier, and Wiley to argue that "Public access equals government censorship," and a short-lived organization created by the Association of American Publishers, called PRISM (Partnership for Research Integrity in Science & Medicine), actually tried it.

http://www.earlham.edu/~peters/fos/2007/01/siege-mentality-at-aap.html

http://www.earlham.edu/~peters/fos/2007/08/publishers-launch-anti-oa-lobbying.html

(4) Under FRPAA, the government will not tell journals what to publish. The government will not conduct peer review or tell journals how to conduct peer review. It will not become a publisher where it wasn't already a publisher. It will not "nationalize science" (whatever that means).

Government funding agencies will continue to decide what research they will fund. Because they control significant funds, that's a significant power. But FRPAA didn't create it and defeating FRPAA won't repeal it.

(5) FRPAA mandates deposit in an OA repository, but it does not limit deposits to a single repository.

This is true in two senses. First, FRPAA lets federal funding agencies host their own repositories or point grantees to suitable external repositories. Second, even after agencies make their choice, and authors deposit their work in the designated repository, authors are not limited to that repository and may deposit their work in any other repositories as well. The first point means that the designated repositories won't always be controlled by the government. The second point means that, even when they are, authors may deposit in independent repositories without restraint. The policy opens new access doors without closing any old ones.

(6) FRPAA does not mandate OA to the published edition of an article. It applies only to the final version of the author's peer-reviewed manuscript—basically, the version approved by peer review but not yet copy-edited. This is a concession to publishers to preserve library incentives to subscribe.

(7) FRPAA gives publishers the option to replace the author's manuscript in the designated repository with the final published version. This is a solution for publishers who worry about the circulation of multiple versions.

(8) FRPAA does not mandate OA immediately upon publication, but permits embargoes up to six months. This is a concession to publishers and a compromise with the public interest in immediate public access.

For the first six months after publication, publishers will have exclusive distribution rights to both the published edition and (at their choice) the final version of the author's peer-reviewed manuscript. After six months, publishers will still have exclusive distribution rights to the published edition, and the only time limit on that exclusivity is the duration of copyright itself (the life of the author plus 70 years). Of course, publishers may voluntarily waive some of these exclusive rights by permitting authors to self-archive their postprints, and today more than 60% of surveyed publishers do just that.

The NIH policy allows an embargo of up to 12 months. But the NIH is the outlier here, not FRPAA. Even if the NIH's own field of medicine, the NIH is the only OA-mandating medical research funder in the world allowing embargoes longer than six months. Every other one without exception limits embargoes to six months: the Arthritis Research Campaign (UK), British Heart Foundation, Canadian Breast Cancer Research Alliance, Canadian Health Services Research Foundation, Canadian Institutes of Health Research, European Research Council, Cancer Research UK, Chief Scientist Office of the Scottish Executive Health Department, Department of Health (UK), Fonds de la recherche en santé du Québec (Canada), Fund to Promote Scientific Research (Austria), Genome Canada, Howard Hughes Medical Institute, Joint Information Systems Committee (UK), Michael Smith Foundation for Health Research (Canada), National Cancer Institute of Canada, National Institute for Health Research (UK), Vetenskapsrådet (Swedish Research Council, Sweden), and the Wellcome Trust (UK).

(9) FRPAA does not provide funds for publication fees at fee-based OA journals.

There's a healthy ongoing debate about whether funding agencies should offer to pay these fees. Are they an unaffordable diversion of funds from research or a needed investment in unembargoed OA and peer-reviewed OA journals? (There are publishers and OA proponents on each side of this question.) The debate should continue, but don't let it confuse the issues. Objections to the practice are not objections to FRPAA.

(10) FRPAA does not depend on publisher consent or cooperation. It will rely—most likely—on a special license, already provided by federal law, authorizing federal funding agencies to disseminate the results of the research they fund. However, FRPAA-covered agencies could also rely on the NIH rights-retention method or other methods still to be devised.

The federal-purpose license and the NIH rights-retention method both give the government a non-exclusive right to disseminate OA copies of the articles. Both methods prevent publishers from acquiring the full bundle of exclusive rights they might have desired and might otherwise have acquired. Both methods require divided ownership. Publishers know this well, but they have track record of misrepresenting it in their public protests. They frame their complaint as if they were "the copyright holders" to these articles, without qualification. They often speak as if the government were expropriating their property or preventing them from enforcing rights they possess, as opposed to preventing them from acquiring rights they wish to possess.

http://www.earlham.edu/~peters/fos/newsletter/10-02-08.htm#nih

(11) FRPAA does not amend copyright law. It does not seize or invalidate copyrights, prevent government-funded researchers from holding copyrights on their work, prevent them from transferring rights to publishers, or prevent publishers from enforcing the rights they acquire from authors.

(12) Finally, FRPAA makes no assumptions about how many members of the lay public are interested in reading peer-reviewed scientific research articles. It doesn't matter that some members of the lay public won't care to read the articles that will become OA, or won't understand them, just as it doesn't matter that some drivers won't care to drive on a given stretch of publicly-funded road. If you don't care to have access to NIH-funded research yourself, you still benefit because doctors and researchers have access. Likewise, FRPAA will benefit everyone who cares to read this research, and benefit everyone else indirectly by benefiting researchers directly. The purpose is not to widen access for professionals alone, or lay readers alone, but to widen access for everyone who can make use of publicly-funded research.

I wrote the first version of these 12 reminders for the SPARC Open Access Newsletter, February 2, 2007.

http://www.earlham.edu/~peters/fos/newsletter/02-02-07.htm#frpaa

When FRPAA was re-introduced in the Senate in June 2009, I revised them in SOAN for August 2, 2009.

http://www.earlham.edu/~peters/fos/newsletter/08-02-09.htm#frpaa

When FRPAA was introduced in the House of Representatives in April 2010, I revised them again in SOAN for May 2, 2010.

http://www.earlham.edu/~peters/fos/newsletter/05-02-10.htm

The version here is the latest one, from May 2010.

An Open Access Mandate for the NIH

From "An open access mandate for the NIH," SPARC Open Access Newsletter, January 2, 2008.

http://dash.harvard.edu/handle/1/4322583

The day after Christmas, President Bush signed an omnibus spending bill containing a provision requiring the US National Institutes of Health (NIH) to mandate open access for NIH-funded research.

Here's the language that just became law:

> The Director of the National Institutes of Health shall require that all investigators funded by the NIH submit or have submitted for them to the National Library of Medicine's PubMed Central an electronic version of their final, peer-reviewed manuscripts upon acceptance for publication to be made publicly available no later than 12 months after the official date of publication: Provided, That the NIH shall implement the public access policy in a manner consistent with copyright law.

This is a momentous victory, despite the 12 month embargo. Measured by the ferocity of opposition overcome and the volume of literature liberated, it's the largest victory in the history of the OA movement. It's only a plateau, not a summit, but it's an immense success. Researchers, OA advocates, and everyone concerned to advance medical knowledge, are justified in feeling joy and relief.

It's big for at least five reasons:

(1) It's the first OA mandate for a major public funding agency in the US. It's also the first OA mandate for any government funding agency worldwide adopted by the national legislature rather than directly by the agency. (This explains, BTW, why publishing lobbyists have been able to delay it for three years.)

(2) It comes after a long struggle. Congress asked for an OA mandate at NIH in 2004 but in 2005 the agency adopted a policy to request rather than require OA. OA proponents have worked tirelessly to persuade Congress to strengthen it ever since. OA opponents

have worked just as hard on their side, first to keep the policy weak and then to make the weak policy succeed in order to head off momentum for a mandate.

For a timeline of the saga, with links, see SOAN for August 2007.

http://www.earlham.edu/~peters/fos/newsletter/08-02-07.htm#nih

But for a one-paragraph encapsulation, see SOAN for November 2007:

http://www.earlham.edu/~peters/fos/newsletter/11-02-07.htm#nih

> In September 2004, the House of Representatives appropriations report demanded an OA mandate at the NIH. The report language was not binding, and the NIH drafted a weaker policy requesting OA but not requiring it. The Senate appropriations bill remained silent on the issue, and the conference committee reconciling the House and Senate appropriations bills adopted the NIH's watered down version of the policy. In May 2005, the NIH policy took effect as a request. In November 2005, the NIH's own Public Access Working Group recommended that the policy be strengthened to a requirement. In February 2006, the National Library of Medicine Board of Regents affirmed the recommendation that the policy be strengthened to a requirement. The same month, the NIH released data showing that grantee compliance with its request was below 4%. In April 2006, NIH Director Elias Zerhouni told a House subcommittee that "the voluntary policy is just not enough" to achieve the agency's goals. In June 2006, the House Appropriations Committee again demanded an OA mandate at the NIH, this time as part of the binding appropriations bill. Again, the Senate was silent on the issue. But this time, before the conference committee could reconcile the bills, the Democrats took control of both the House and the Senate. Party bickering and budgetary delays forced Congress to turn to a continuing resolution to fund the government, dropping the House appropriations bill, canceling the vote on the Senate counterpart, and forcing us to start all over again the following year. In March 2007, Dr. Zerhouni testified again that the agency needed an OA mandate. In July 2007, once again, the House of Representatives adopted an appropriations bill demanding an OA mandate at the NIH. This time, in October 2007, finally, the Senate adopted the same language.

If NIH had adopted an OA mandate in 2004 when Congress originally asked it to do so, it would have been the first anywhere. Now it will be the 21st.

(3) It sets a precedent, breaks the ice, or cuts the shackles—pick your metaphor. Other US agencies no longer have to worry that a strong OA policy would antagonize Congress or the White House. This is a green light for agencies that have been waiting for a green light. Some agencies will act on their own and some will wait to see how the NIH policy fares in court.

(4) It's big because the NIH is big. The NIH is the world's largest funder of scientific research (not counting classified military research). Its budget last year, $28 billion, was larger than the gross domestic product of 142 nations. As my colleague Ray English points out, it's more than five times larger than all seven of the Research Councils UK combined. NIH-funded research results in 65,000 peer-reviewed articles every year or 178

every day. The NIH is the one funder that could do the most for OA. Its OA mandate will not only free up an unprecedented quantity of high-quality medical research. It will also make a giant step toward cultivating new expectations—among researchers, funders, governments, and voters—that publicly-funded research should be OA.

(5) Finally, the policy is strong. (Or: The policy is strong, finally!) The mandatory deposit policy will drive compliance toward 100%. The bill requires deposit immediately upon acceptance in a peer reviewed journal. That's much better than requiring deposit during or after the 12-month embargo period. Immediate deposit allows immediate release of metadata, enhancing the article's visibility, and allows the NIH to switch the article from closed to open access, automatically, as soon as the embargo runs. Agency staffers won't have to hunt down the author and beg for a copy of an old manuscript. In short, Congress is instructing the NIH to implement what I call the dual deposit/ release strategy or what Stevan Harnad calls immediate deposit / optional access.

The policy does permit a 12 month embargo, which I think is too long. But here's what I said about that in August [2007]:

> I wish the bill had shortened the embargo. Any embargo is a compromise with the public interest, and longer embargoes are more harmful in medicine than in other fields. But I'd much rather have a mandate than a shortened embargo, if we had to choose. The reason is simply that a short embargo without a mandate isn't really short, since there would be no enforceable deadline for ending the embargo and providing OA. Moreover, we don't have to choose. Shortening the embargo can be our next goal. ... The bill is ... a significant, unmistakable gain on the most important front—the mandate—and [since the current embargo is 12 months] it's not a loss or retreat on any front. ...

[...]

Last month I predicted a publisher lawsuit to prevent the NIH from implementing an OA mandate or at least to delay it as long as possible.

http://www.earlham.edu/~peters/fos/newsletter/12-02-07.htm#predictions

If publishers do sue, the NIH will defend vigorously—and of course will only benefit from the fact that Congress and the President ordered it to adopt an OA mandate. Since the bill itself requires the NIH to implement the mandate "in a manner consistent with copyright law," it would be premature for publishers to sue on copyright grounds before they see the final shape of the policy. In SOAN for August 2007, I outlined three ways in which NIH could implement an OA mandate without infringing copyrights.

http://www.earlham.edu/~peters/fos/newsletter/08-02-07.htm#nih

[...]

In the short time since President Bush signed the omnibus spending bill, I've seen journalists and bloggers make a range of mistakes in understanding what has taken place.

Among the misunderstandings: that the NIH now has a mandate in place (rather than instructions to adopt one); that the mandate is to publish in OA journals (rather than to deposit in OA repositories); that the mandate is to bypass journals and peer review (rather than provide OA to articles already published in peer-reviewed journals); that the mandate applies to the published versions of articles (rather than the final versions of the authors' peer-reviewed manuscripts); that the mandate will direct deposits to PubMed (rather than PubMed Central); that the new NIH budget is $29 million (rather than $29 billion); that the mandate will only last for one year (rather than indefinitely); that the OA mandate requires violation of copyright law (rather than compliance with it). The misunderstandings no longer function as impediments to legislation, but they could well function as impediments to implementation. As you see them crop up, please do what you can to correct them.

Many individuals and organizations deserve our thanks for this long-awaited and hard-won victory. Thanks to all supporters of OA in Congress, members and staffers alike. Thanks to all supporters of OA in the Executive branch, including the NIH itself. Thanks to SPARC and the Alliance for Taxpayer Access for their energetic and effective work with policy-makers. Thanks to Heather Joseph for her masterful and untiring leadership of both organizations. Thanks to all of you who wrote to your Representatives and Senators to support public access for publicly-funded research. And thanks to Santa!

The Consolidated Appropriations Act of 2008, containing the provision mandating OA at the NIH

http://thomas.loc.gov/cgi-bin/bdquery/z?d110:h.r.02764:

(The final colon is part of the URL.)

For more detail on the 2007 progress toward this victory, and my evaluation of the bill that is now law, see my newsletter articles from August, November, and December.

http://www.earlham.edu/~peters/fos/newsletter/08-02-07.htm#nih

http://www.earlham.edu/~peters/fos/newsletter/11-02-07.htm#nih

http://www.earlham.edu/~peters/fos/newsletter/12-02-07.htm#nih

[...]

The Open Access Mandate at Harvard

From "The open access mandate at Harvard," SPARC Open Access Newsletter, March 2, 2008.

http://dash.harvard.edu/handle/1/4322574

Harvard's new OA policy is not the first university-level OA mandate, but it's the first in the US, the first to be adopted by faculty rather than administrators, the first adopted policy to focus on permissions rather than deposits, and the first to catch the world-wide attention of the press and blogosphere.

Here's the heart of it:

Each Faculty member grants to the President and Fellows of Harvard College permission to make available his or her scholarly articles and to exercise the copyright in those articles. In legal terms, the permission granted by each Faculty member is a nonexclusive, irrevocable, paid-up, worldwide license to exercise any and all rights under copyright relating to each of his or her scholarly articles, in any medium, and to authorize others to do the same, provided that the articles are not sold for a profit. The policy will apply to all scholarly articles written while the person is a member of the Faculty except for any articles completed before the adoption of this policy and any articles for which the Faculty member entered into an incompatible licensing or assignment agreement before the adoption of this policy. The Dean or the Dean's designate will waive application of the policy for a particular article upon written request by a Faculty member explaining the need.

To assist the University in distributing the articles, each Faculty member will provide an electronic copy of the final version of the article at no charge to the appropriate representative of the Provost's Office in an appropriate format (such as PDF) specified by the Provost's Office. The Provost's Office may make the article available to the public in an open-access repository.

The Office of the Dean will be responsible for interpreting this policy, resolving disputes concerning its interpretation and application, and recommending changes to the Faculty from time to time.

Text of the resolution adopted by the Harvard Faculty of Arts and Sciences, February 12, 2008

http://web.archive.org/web/20080510121009/http://www.fas.harvard.edu/~secfas/February_2008_Agenda.pdf

http://www.earlham.edu/~peters/fos/2008/02/text-of-harvard-policy.html

[...]
(Disclosure: I consulted informally with proponents of the Harvard policy several times over the past few years.)

Here are some notes and reflections:
[...]

So far, it applies only to Harvard's Faculty of Arts and Sciences (FAS), not to the business school, law school, medical school, or other schools within the university. However, the Harvard library is actively taking the policy to the rest of the institution. As Robert Darnton told Library Journal Academic Newswire: "My position is to spread the FAS motion ... throughout the whole university. That is going to be one of my top priorities in the weeks and months ahead. I will be discussing this with the law school, medical school and business schools." Stay tuned.

http://www.libraryjournal.com/info/CA6535580.html?nid=2673#news1

http://www.earlham.edu/~peters/fos/2008/02/more-background-on-harvard-oa-mandate.html

If the Harvard policy is not the first university-level OA mandate, then what was?

Preceding the Harvard mandate are at least 12 other institutional mandates and three departmental mandates in nine countries: Australia, Belgium, France, India, Portugal, Russia, Swizterland, Turkey, and the UK.

http://www.eprints.org/openaccess/policysignup/

The pioneers on this frontier are Queensland University of Technology in Australia, whose mandate took effect on January 1, 2004, and the University of Minho in Portugal, whose mandate took effect one year later on January 1, 2005.

http://www.mopp.qut.edu.au/F/F_01_03.jsp

http://users.ecs.soton.ac.uk/harnad/Hypermail/Amsci/4277.html

If a dozen earlier university mandates came first, why was Harvard's was the first to grab the attention of the press and blogosphere? The answer is pretty clear: because it's Harvard and because this policy was adopted by the faculty itself.

Did I mention that the Harvard policy was adopted by the faculty itself? Did I say that the vote was unanimous?

The policy has critical support beyond the faculty, for example from Provost Steven Hyman and University Librarian Robert Darnton. But Professor of Computer Science Stuart Shieber, the policy's chief strategist and advocate, deserves special kudos for choosing to make the policy rest on faculty support and for his patient campaign of information and persuasion, which culminated in the unanimous faculty vote.

This is strong: Imagine any faculty voting unanimously for any interesting policy.

The publishing lobby has often argued that the call for OA mandates is a sign that researchers oppose OA and must be coerced. This argument always flew in the face of the evidence, but the unanimous Harvard vote should be the last nail in the coffin in which we bury the idea. For the same reason, the Harvard vote decisively confirms Alma Swan's finding that the overwhelming majority of researchers do not resent OA mandates and would *willingly* comply with one from their funder or university.

http://cogprints.org/4385/

But even OA supporters can learn something from this vote. We knew that faculty didn't oppose OA or need to be coerced. We knew that sluggish faculty support for OA initiatives was due more to lack of familiarity than informed opposition. While an administrative mandate is an effective shortcut to a good outcome, and one with which most researchers would willingly comply, Stuart Shieber and the Harvard Faculty of Arts and Sciences have shown that there's another route to the same goal. It may take longer, but it directly addresses the problems of faculty unfamiliarity and misunderstanding, and brings informed consent with it.

I've said many times that I only support OA mandates that are conditions on voluntary contracts. And while I believe that even administrative mandates fit this description, the voluntariness of the Harvard policy is conspicuous and unparalleled.

(For the fullest version of my argument that mandates should be conditions on voluntary contracts, and that administrative mandates at funding agencies and universities qualify, see my July 2006 article on mandating OA for electronic theses and dissertations.)

http://www.earlham.edu/~peters/fos/newsletter/07-02-06.htm#etds

The policy requires two things of FAS faculty: (1) that they give Harvard non-exclusive permission "to exercise any and all rights under copyright" over their scholarly articles, which includes permission to disseminate OA copies through the institutional repository, and (2) that they send digital copies of their articles to the Provost's Office.

I call these requirements, but the resolution approved by the faculty avoids words like "requirement," "mandate," and "must." Instead, it says that "[e]ach Faculty member grants ... permission ...," "[t]he policy will apply to all scholarly articles written while ...," and "each Faculty member will provide. ..." These are direct statements of what is and will be the case, much as statutes describe legal obligations with the word "shall." If there's any give in the policy, and there is, it lies in the fact that the policy allows opt-outs.

Faculty may opt out of both requirements. From the resolution: "The Dean or the Dean's designate will waive application of the policy for a particular article upon written request by a Faculty member explaining the need." [...]

Will it be easy or hard to get a waiver? In one sense, it will be very easy. Stuart Shieber elaborated for Nature News: "If the author requests a waiver, the dean will provide a waiver."

http://www.nature.com/news/2008/080215/full/news.2008.605.html

http://www.earlham.edu/~peters/fos/2008/02/more-on-harvard-mandate.html

But the request and explanation must be in writing. Moreover, faculty members may not ask for one waiver to cover all their articles, but must submit separate requests for separate articles.

This mix of ease and difficulty is clearly deliberate. On the one hand, FAS faculty wanted the freedom to make exceptions. Either they could foresee cases in which they would want exceptions for themselves or they foresaw the vote without that freedom built in. On the other hand, they wanted to give themselves an additional incentive to push back against the publishers who will ask faculty to ask for waivers.

Does the existence of an automatic opt-out, even with a small administrative hurdle, vitiate the policy? Not at all. Think of a classroom in which teachers require students to sign out before leaving the room. The "waiver" is automatic and students use it. But it's the exception and most students are in their seats most of the time. The policy sends the signal about what is expected, and the expectation alone, perhaps with a small administrative hurdle, makes the scene very different from one with no policy at all.

Is a policy with an automatic opt-out on request still a mandate? This is an unfruitful question which devolves quickly into a verbal dispute. A better question is whether opt-outs will be rare or common.

The opt-out will certainly reduce compliance from 100% to something less. But if opt-outs are rare and the compliance only drops to 95%, give or take, then the policy will still be a huge success. Moreover, even if the initial gap is large, it will very likely shrink over time. For example, if some faculty are inclined to opt out today because they believe that OA archiving will bypass peer review or violate copyright, then they'll drop that objection when they understand the facts. If they are inclined to opt out because they want to publish in a certain journal, which asks them to opt out, then over time they may be more willing to ask the journal to accommodate Harvard, rather than the other way around, and over time the journal itself may be willing to do so.

In December 2006, the Australian Research Council (ARC) adopted a policy requesting—not requiring—its grantees to self-archive, but requiring non-complying grantees to justify their non-compliance. You could call that a mandate or not. But as I pointed out at the time, it's the functional equivalent of a mandate. "It creates a strategic consideration that is not a sanction but more consequential than anything to be found in some of the policies that use mandatory language."

http://www.earlham.edu/~peters/fos/2006/12/australias-arc-expects-oa-for-arc.html

The Harvard policy is stronger than the ARC policy for going beyond the language of mere requests, but weaker for granting exemptions automatically. And on top of this mix of strengths and weaknesses, the Harvard policy uses a strategy similar to the ARC's for shrinking the exemption loophole and creating the functional equivalent of a mandate. Nevertheless, I'm the first to admit that English has a limited vocabulary for the shades and hues of regulatory strength. If we had a better word than "mandate" for this particular shade, I would use it.

(For more on the regrettable and sometimes misleading connotations of the word "mandate" in this context, see this dialog between Jan Velterop and me a year ago this month.)

http://theparachute.blogspot.com/2007/03/mandate-debate.html#902509335709
9085662

Pat Schroeder, President of the Association of American Publishers (AAP), told Science Magazine that Harvard's willingness to grant opt-outs means that the policy is not a mandate. OK. But even Pat Schroeder knows that shifting the default and requiring dissenters to opt out can be a game-changer. Otherwise she wouldn't object to Google's opt-out Library Project or make her organization the lead plaintiff in a lawsuit to stop it.

Even at schools with more mandatory mandates, or no opt-outs, successful implementation depends (as I've often argued) on expectations, education, assistance, and incentives, not coercion. For example, I don't know of any university that exacts a punishment for failure to comply with an OA "mandate." Universities with mandates achieve their objectives, as Harvard plans to, by communicating a firm expectation, discussing the benefits, offering assistance, and creating incentives, even while they allow exceptions and avoid sanctions.

The Harvard policy shifts the default from non-archiving to archiving, and shifts the burden from OA cooperators to OA dissenters. That's much more than a mere request or encouragement. Before the Harvard vote, the default for faculty was non-archiving and the problem was to persuade them to do something they were not already doing (even if it takes very little time and brings a documented boost in citation impact). The new policy makes archiving the default, mediated by the Provost's Office, and faculty who want to do anything else must bear the burden of explaining their desire to the Dean.

It's not a heavy burden, but then neither is OA archiving. As we well know from long experience on the other side of this line, even a light burden can change behavior on a large scale. This is even more likely when we understand that the new default amplifies faculty research impact, rather than curtailing it, and that the Harvard policy nudges faculty toward their interests rather than away from them.

Daniel Pollock understood the policy well in Outsell Insights: "The faculty is using researchers' inertia to its advantage. ..."

http://www.outsellinc.com/services/insights_about

Before anyone puts too cynical an interpretation on this shrewd strategy, remember that it has unanimous faculty support. Harvard faculty now understand that faculty inertia works against self-archiving and have agreed to shift the default and let inertia work against publisher exclusivity instead.

Was the opt-out provision necessary to pass the resolution? Apparently yes. As Shieber told Robin Peek, "There was legitimate concern that there could be particular cases in which the license granted by the motion could work against the interest of a particular faculty member. The provision was certainly important in assuaging some faculty members' worries that they could be held hostage by the policy in cases where it wasn't serving their best interests."

http://www.earlham.edu/~peters/fos/2008/02/more-background-on-harvard-oa-mandate_27.html

When Harvard authors refuse to request waivers, how many journals will refuse to publish their work? Let's tighten the question even further. Journals will know from the submission cover letter that an author is affiliated with Harvard, but they will not know whether the author is requesting an opt-out from Harvard until after the peer review process is over, the article has been accepted, and the journal asks the author to sign the standard copyright transfer agreement. How many journals will refuse to publish works by Harvard authors when those works have already been approved by their peer review process?

The number must be very small today and will shrink steadily over time as journals consider their options and other universities adopt similar policies. Journals don't want to throw away the sunk costs of completed peer review; they don't want to turn away work they've already decided is good; and they don't want to become known as journals that reject good work because of the author's institutional affiliation.

But in the short term, journals can demand that their Harvard authors request waivers and many Harvard authors may comply with these requests. I won't regard that as a failure of the policy. To me the question is what happens over time, not what happens in the early stages.

If it's true that few journals will refuse to publish peer-reviewed work by Harvard authors, or that the number will decline over time, or both, then Harvard faculty have much to gain by refusing to request waivers. This remains the case even if it's also true that a waiver will sometimes be the only way to be published in a certain prestigious journal. The question is not how many journals want faculty to request waivers, but how many will refuse to publish an approved work in the absence of a waiver.

Because faculty have their own reasons for refusing to request waivers (the request process is a nuisance and OA will enlarge their audience and impact), and because journals have their own reasons for publishing already-accepted work by Harvard authors, Robert Darnton was right to say that faculty "will have the collective weight of Harvard behind them if they resist a journal's demand for exclusive rights." Harvard's collective weight will help faculty get published when they refuse to opt out, and (for that reason) it will also help them refuse to opt out.

Most schools don't have Harvard's weight, of course. But as more universities adopt similar policies, they will increase their collective weight and increase the likelihood that publishers will have to accommodate them. In that sense, the Harvard policy, and the earlier university-level OA mandates, are standing invitations to other universities to gain strength through common purpose and create a critical mass that will change journal policies for all authors. Think of the current university mandates as the first wave of a consumer movement in a journal marketplace distorted by monopolists.

Universities trying to estimate the benefits of an OA mandate should take into account that the benefits will be amplified by synergy with other institutions. Universities that wanted an OA mandate but didn't want to be at the front of the pack, fearing that publishers could refuse to publish work by their faculty, will now find it safer to act. Harvard has increased the bargaining weight of authors demanding the rights to self-archive, and every institution that now adopts an OA mandate will increase it even further, for themselves and for those still to follow.

Under the policy, Harvard faculty will still own the copyrights to their research articles. Harvard is not acquiring ownership, just a non-exclusive license. However, once faculty grant that non-exclusive license to the university, they will not be able to transfer the usual package of exclusive rights to a publisher. Under the new policy, then, faculty still own their own work "subject to" the Harvard license (as the Harvard press release puts it), and may still transfer their rights to publishers, subject to the same condition.

This has two important legal consequences when faculty do not request opt-outs. First, Harvard will have an express license from the copyright holder to host and disseminate OA copies of these works. Second, publishers will never acquire the rights which would allow them to forbid OA archiving at Harvard or to claim that it infringes their copyright.

This elegantly solves every copyright-based objection to OA archiving. The strategy was pioneered among funding agencies by the Wellcome Trust and among universities by the University of California (see the Postscript below). The idea is for authors to reserve the right to self-archive, even if they transfer everything else to a publisher. The less elegant and less effective alternative adopted at some funding agencies and universities is to require OA archiving except when publisher policies don't allow it, thereby giving the opt-out to publishers rather than authors.

If publishers dislike the Harvard policy, they must either ask the Harvard author to request a waiver, and hope the author will agree, or refuse to publish the work. It won't be enough to adopt an in-house policy against OA archiving, as it would have been in the old days when authors gave publishers the full package of exclusive rights.

This may be obvious, but let me elaborate for one more second. Publishers have two very different legal grounds to deny author preferences for OA: (1) the rights transferred to them by the author and (2) their own background right to refuse to publish any work for any reason. The first is based on copyright—the public statute and the private contract transferring rights from author to publisher. The second is utterly independent of copyright. When Harvard authors follow the new OA default, rather than request an opt-out, publishers have no copyright-based grounds on which to protest or prohibit the resulting OA. All they have left is the right to refuse to publish. There's no doubt that this power counts for much, especially at high-prestige journals. But there's also no doubt that authors have their own power in this game, from their ability to submit their work to other journals and from the growing number of authors who will demand the right to self-archive. At some journals, publishers will have the upper hand, but at others authors will have the upper hand. For Harvard authors who follow the new OA default, it's a power game now, not a rights game. And the balance of power just tipped toward authors because Harvard decided to throw its weight on that side. It will tip further toward authors every time another university adopts a similar policy.

The dozen pre-Harvard university mandates require faculty to deposit their eprints in the institution's OA repository. By contrast, Harvard requires faculty to give permission for OA archiving but not to make the deposits itself. That's why I call it a permission mandate rather than a deposit mandate.

Instead of making the actual deposits, Harvard faculty must send copies of their work to the Provost's Office, which will then deposit them. This approach raises at least three questions.

First, what will the Provost's Office actually do with the eprints? The resolution says only that "[t]he Provost's Office *may* make the article available to the public in an open-access repository" (emphasis added). I wish it had said "will" rather than "may" here. Will the Provost's Office be selective, depositing some but not others?

Second, how quickly will the Provost's Office make the deposits? If it works quickly, it could provide OA at or before the moment the article is published. If it works slowly, it will miss a beautiful opportunity to use the permissions it already has in hand. If it delays 6–12 months, then it may as well defer to publisher embargoes.

Third, if the faculty was willing to self-impose the expectation that they should send their eprints to the Provost's Office, why not self-impose the expectation that they should deposit them directly in the IR?

I don't know. But I suspect the answer is that the faculty wanted to lower the barrier to compliance, or reduce the burden on faculty, and understood that it's easier to email an eprint than to deposit one in a repository, even if the difference is small. For example, St. Andrews University takes this difference into account and boosts the deposit rate in its IR by asking faculty email their eprints to a librarian, who then makes the deposits.

http://eprints.st-andrews.ac.uk/proxy_archive.html

Les Carr and Stevan Harnad have shown that repository deposits are less time-consuming than faculty fear, averaging about 10 minutes per paper.

http://eprints.ecs.soton.ac.uk/10688/

Similarly, Alma Swan and Sheridan Brown have shown that the process is simpler than faculty fear, and that even the few who face difficulties the first time face fewer difficulties the second time.

http://cogprints.org/4385/

However, if faculty fear that self-archiving is difficult and time-consuming, even if their fears are groundless, then they aren't likely to vote to mandate self-archiving. If this is why the Harvard resolution didn't include a direct deposit requirement (and it may not be), then it's possible that further faculty education will reduce the anxiety level and allow a revision that ensures direct deposits in the IR. But it's also possible that no revision is needed. It's possible that the slightly reduced burden for authors will actually boost compliance, and it's possible that the Provost's Office will make the deposits at least as quickly and surely as faculty would under a direct deposit mandate.

Here's how I described the advantages of a permission mandate in SOAN for December 2007:

http://www.earlham.edu/~peters/fos/newsletter/12-02-07.htm#predictions

> This model reduces the demands on faculty and increases the certainty about permissions. As long as the university is willing to pay people … to make the actual deposits, it could be a faster and more frictionless way to move the deposit rate toward 100%.

The two key variables in implementing the Harvard policy are the rate of opt-outs and the speed of deposits. If the opt-out rate is low and the deposit speed is high, then it's hard to imagine a better university-level OA policy. But if the opt-out rate is high, or the speed is low, or both, then the policy won't meet its own objectives and Harvard faculty should consider revisions to fine-tune it.

Stevan Harnad is already calling for revisions. In particular, he'd like to see a deposit requirement (without an opt-out) alongside the existing permission requirement (with an opt-out). The particular deposit policy he'd like to see is what he calls immediate deposit / optional access (ID/OA), or what I call the dual deposit/release strategy: all articles are deposited immediately upon publication, but only the metadata are made OA at the same time; the texts become OA only when the university acquires permission or publisher embargo runs. Stevan and I both support the dual deposit/release strategy. But he argues that it is needed now to strengthen the Harvard policy, and I argue that it is not needed now and may never be needed. See our two blog posts encapsulating this debate,

http://www.earlham.edu/~peters/fos/2008/02/stevan-harnad-replies-to-mike-carroll.html

http://openaccess.eprints.org/index.php?/archives/366-The-Hybrid-Copyright-Retention-and-Deposit-Mandate.html

My argument in a nutshell is that the policy won't need revision if the rate of opt-outs is low and the speed of deposits is high. Harvard has adopted the world's first permission mandate and it deserves time to work out implementation procedures that will deliver on its own objectives. If the implementation doesn't deliver, then I'm confident that Harvard insiders will be at least as concerned as outsiders like me and will already be thinking about fine-tuning.

Harvard's permission mandate will assure that Harvard has the right to make every faculty eprint OA (except when faculty request opt-outs). Is this unnecessary in light of the fact that about two-thirds of surveyed TA journals already allow OA archiving?

http://web.archive.org/web/20080223085545/http://www.sherpa.ac.uk/romeo.php?stats=yes

No; it's still necessary and desirable. At most green journals, the Harvard [license] will be accepted as a matter of course. But it will clearly be necessary for the ungreen third of TA journals. It will even be necessary for some of the green two-thirds, as insurance against later changes to the journal's access policy. It will also be necessary for greenish journals that aren't green enough, for example, because they prohibit deposit in certain repositories, impose fees or embargoes on self-archiving, or limit re-use rights.

If you had to drive across a friendly border every day to get to work, and knew that two-thirds of the time you would be waved through, it would still make good sense to carry your passport. Likewise, Harvard's permission mandate makes good sense precisely because Harvard wants OA for all of its research output, not just for the fraction for which publishers are already granting permission.

[...]

I've already seen a rash of misunderstandings in the press and blogosphere about the Harvard policy. Here are the seven most common:

- "This is the first OA mandate at a university." Nope.
- "Harvard faculty may only submit articles to green journals (those that permit OA archiving)." Harvard faculty may submit to any journal. When they submit to a journal that does not ordinarily permit OA archiving, then either the author will ask it to do so in this case (through an author addendum) or the publisher will ask the author to request a waiver from Harvard. No journals will be off-limits to Harvard authors unless the journals themselves refuse to publish work by Harvard authors. This misunderstanding is closely related to the next:
- "The Harvard policy conflicts with policies at journals that do not allow OA archiving." First, either Harvard authors will request opt-outs or they won't. If they do, there's no conflict. If they don't, then either a journal will accept a particular paper (with the author's request to retain key rights) or it won't. If it does, then there's no conflict. If it doesn't, then the author will look for another publisher. Either the author and journal end up agreeing on terms, or the Harvard author is in the same position as a non-Harvard author with a rejected manuscript.
- "Harvard will own faculty writings." Faculty will continue to own the rights to their own work, until or unless they transfer those rights to a publisher. Harvard is a getting non-exclusive license, not ownership.
- "Harvard faculty will have to pay a fee to comply with this policy (either to publishers or to Harvard)." This is deeply confused. First, it falsely assumes that the Harvard policy is about publication in OA journals (gold OA), when it's really about distribution through an OA repository (green OA). Second, it falsely assumes that all or most OA journals charge publication fees, when only a minority do so.
- "The purpose of the policy is to bypass peer review." Half the sources making this mistake then express horror and half say "good riddance." But both the horror and joy are misplaced. We may not know all the versions to which the policy applies, but

it clearly applies to the "final version of the article" and therefore to some version of the peer-reviewed postprint. Hence, the purpose of the policy is not to bypass peer review, but to provide OA to peer-reviewed articles.

- "The policy will undermine peer review." If this one is based on a sloppy reading of the policy, concluding that its purpose is to bypass peer review, then it collapses into the previous misunderstanding. But otherwise it's based on a hasty prediction of doom for subscription-based journals, heedless of the counter-evidence, and a careless conflation of peer review with peer review at subscription-based journals. For a full answer to the objection that OA will undermine peer review, see my article in SOAN for September 2007.

  http://www.earlham.edu/~peters/fos/newsletter/09-02-07.htm#peerreview

Harvard's example will spread. Some universities will feel a competitive urge: "This policy will help Harvard and we have to keep up." Some will feel a cooperative urge: "The more universities adopt OA mandates, the more we will accelerate research and guarantee that publishers will adapt." Some will feel both.
[...]
At Open Access News, Gavin Baker and I put together five collections of comments on the Harvard policy:

February 13, 2008

http://www.earlham.edu/~peters/fos/2008/02/roundup-of-commentary-on-harvard-oa.html

February 14, 2008

http://www.earlham.edu/~peters/fos/2008/02/more-on-harvard-oa-mandate.html

February 15, 2008

http://www.earlham.edu/~peters/fos/2008/02/more-comments-on-harvard-oa-mandate.html

February 17, 2008

http://www.earlham.edu/~peters/fos/2008/02/more-comments-on-harvard-oa-mandate_17.html

February 22, 2008

http://www.earlham.edu/~peters/fos/2008/02/more-comments-on-harvard-oa-policy.html

Postscript

While Harvard is the first university to adopt a permission mandate, the University of California was the first to draft one.

California approved its first draft policy in December 2005 and distributed it in January 2006. It approved a revised draft in January 2007 and sent it to the 10 UC campuses for review in May 2007.

The California draft policy says that faculty "shall routinely grant" to the university a non-exclusive license to provide OA to their works through the institutional repository. When faculty sign copyright transfer agreements with publishers, they "must retain" the right to comply with the university policy. The draft policy also allows faculty to opt out, one work at a time.

According to the Chronicle of Higher Education for February 21, 2008, "Comments on [the California] draft last year reflected 'almost universal support for the concept,' says Gary S. Lawrence, director of systemwide library planning, 'but a great deal of concern about the implementation details.' Harvard's success in creating an arrangement that faculty members agreed on, he says, 'provides us a lot of encouragement.'"

http://chronicle.com/daily/2008/02/1738n.htm

http://www.earlham.edu/~peters/fos/2008/02/more-on-harvard-policy.html

University of California OA policy home page (updated as new steps are taken)

http://osc.universityofcalifornia.edu/openaccesspolicy/

The latest draft of the policy, January 29, 2007

http://osc.universityofcalifornia.edu/openaccesspolicy/OpenAccess-Policy-DRAFT1-29-2007.pdf

Policy FAQ, February 2007

http://osc.universityofcalifornia.edu/openaccesspolicy/oa_policy_faq.html

Faculty Senate review of the draft policy, July 9, 2007

http://www.universityofcalifornia.edu/senate/reports/ac.open.access.07.07.pdf

Administrative and other non-Senate reviews of draft policy, July 26, 2007

http://osc.universityofcalifornia.edu/openaccesspolicy/OApolicy-admin-responses-packageb.pdf

A study showing little faculty familiarity with OA or with the California draft policy: Faculty Attitudes and Behaviors Regarding Scholarly Communication: Survey Findings from the University of California, August 2007

http://osc.universityofcalifornia.edu/responses/materials/OSC-survey-summaries-20070828.pdf

http://www.earlham.edu/~peters/fos/2007/08/california-survey-of-faculty-attitudes.html

This article focuses on the OA policy at Harvard's Faculty of Arts and Sciences, the university's first. But today all Harvard schools have OA policies: Faculty of Arts and Sciences (February 2008), Law School (May 2008), Kennedy School of Government (March 2009), Graduate School of Education, Business School (June 2009), Divinity School (November 2010), Graduate School of Design (March 2011), School of Public Health (November 2012), and the Medical School (June 2014).

Subsequent policies refined the FAS policy in three major respects. First, the waiver does not require a written justification, just a check in a web form. Second, the waiver only applies to the license, or permission for OA, not to the deposit requirement. Third, the policy introduced an embargo option alongside the waiver option.

I've been a Faculty Fellow at Harvard's Berkman Center for Internet & Society since June 2009, and Director of the Harvard Office for Scholarly Communication since July 2013. But I wrote this piece before I had a Harvard connection and before any Harvard connection was on the horizon.

A Bill to Overturn the NIH Policy

From "A bill to overturn the NIH policy," SPARC Open Access Newsletter, October 2, 2008.

http://dash.harvard.edu/handle/1/4322592

Six months after the new, strengthened version of the NIH OA policy took effect, it faces a bill in Congress to overturn it.

Rep. John Conyers (D-MI) introduced the Fair Copyright in Research Works Act (H.R. 6845) on September 9 [2008]. Conyers is the chairman of the powerful House Judiciary Committee, which is the House committee most responsible for copyright legislation, especially through its Subcommittee on Courts, the Internet, and Intellectual Property. The subcommittee held a hearing on the Conyers bill on September 11. (For links to the bill and hearing, see the bibliography below.)

The gist of the bill is to prohibit federal funding agencies from requiring grantees to transfer any rights or licenses to the government as a condition of funding, for any works (1) even partially funded by a source other than a US federal agency and (2) even partially reflecting the "meaningful added value" of any other party.

Because peer review undoubtedly counts as "meaningful added value," because it is organized by private-sector journals at some expense to themselves, and because the NIH policy applies to peer-reviewed manuscripts, the bill clearly covers the NIH policy. The bill would not only overturn the NIH policy, but block similar policies at every other federal agency.

In December 2007, when Congress directed the NIH to adopt an OA mandate, it did not amend the US copyright statute. It merely asked the NIH to change its funding contract with grantees. But to overturn the NIH mandate, the Conyers bill would actually amend the copyright statute.

I won't do a section-by-section analysis of the bill. This has been done well by Mike Carroll and the Alliance for Taxpayer Access.

http://carrollogos.blogspot.com/2008/09/politics-and-popular-music.html

http://www.earlham.edu/~peters/fos/2008/09/unintended-consequences-of-publishers
.html

http://www.taxpayeraccess.org/action/call-to-action-ask-your-representative-to-opp
.shtml

http://www.earlham.edu/~peters/fos/2008/09/keep-pressure-on-congress-to-support
.html

Mike's analysis is particularly good at showing how crude and unsurgical the bill is, and how it would inadvertently repeal a good deal of federal procurement law. Federal agencies which procure copyrighted works routinely make their purchase or funding conditional upon a license to use the work. But here I'll focus on the intended damage rather than the collateral damage.

The bill isn't called the "Stop Open Access Act" or the "Put Publishers First Act." It's called the "Fair Copyright in Research Works Act." The name suggests that the purpose of the bill is to right some copyright wrong. Wrong.

Public statements from the publishing lobby are explicit in suggesting some kind of copyright problem, even if they are not specific about what it is:

A joint statement by the DC Principles Coalition (DCPC) and the Professional/Society Publishers division of the Association of American Publishers (AAP/PSP) asserted that "the mandate is being implemented in a manner that is inconsistent with U.S. copyright law. ..."

http://www.pspcentral.org/commPublicAffairs/attachComm/Joint%20Publisher%20
Letter%209-10-08.pdf

http://www.earlham.edu/~peters/fos/2008/09/two-public-statements-from-anti-oa.html

In a separate press release the AAP/PSP asserted that the mandate "undermin[es] copyright protection," "diminishes copyright protections," and "compromises copyright protections" for research articles.

http://web.archive.org/web/20080929032335/

http://www.publishers.org/FairCopyrightinResearchWorksAct.htm

The American Association of University Presses (AAUP) likewise asserted that the NIH policy would "weaken" and "diminish ... copyright protection."

http://aaupnet.org/aboutup/issues/letterFCRWA.pdf

http://www.earlham.edu/~peters/fos/2008/09/aaup-also-wants-to-overturn-nih-policy
.html

The Copyright Alliance asserted that after the embargo runs on articles deposited in PubMed Central, the US government treats them as "public domain work[s]."

http://www.copyrightalliance.org/news.php?id=46&print=1

http://www.earlham.edu/~peters/fos/2008/09/two-public-statements-from-anti-oa.html

The American Chemical Society asserted that research articles covered by the new bill "would be protected by copyright laws" as if they were not already protected.

http://pubs.acs.org/cen/news/86/i37/8637notw2.html

http://www.earlham.edu/~peters/fos/2008/09/acs-supports-bill-to-overturn-nih.html

In his statement introducing the bill, Rep. Conyers said that it would "preserve the intellectual property rights of our Nation's researchers" and "restore intellectual property protections for scientists, researchers and publishers. ..." (Not online.)

In an earlier joint statement (April 2008), before the Conyers bill was introduced, the AAP/PSP and DCPC asserted that the NIH policy denied "authors and publishers the benefits of their copyrights. ..."

http://www.pspcentral.org/publications/Letter%20to%20Zerhouni%20NIH%20-%20 AAP-DC%20Principles%204-16-08.pdf

The DCPC, the AAP/PSP, and the Copyright Alliance all say that the NIH policy "forces publishers to surrender their copyrighted scientific journal articles. ..." The Copyright Alliance goes a step further and says that a public research grant is no reason to "commandeer the resulting research paper and treat it as a public domain work." BTW, the word "surrender" was first introduced into this context by the press release announcing the launch of PRISM in August 2007.

https://mx2.arl.org/Lists/SPARC-OAForum/Message/3934.html

http://www.earlham.edu/~peters/fos/2007/08/publishers-launch-anti-oa-lobbying .html

Note that not one of these statements says that NIH policy *infringes* copyrights.

If the publishers could claim infringement, they would. They would have a remedy at law and would not need to amend the law to get it. But a specific charge like infringement is too easy to evaluate and dismiss. Hence, we face nebulous charges like "inconsistency with copyright law" or "diminished copyright protections."

The NIH uses a simple and elegant method to avoid infringement. When researchers publish an article based on NIH-funded research, they must retain the right to grant PubMed Central a non-exclusive license to disseminate a copy of their peer-reviewed manuscript. They may transfer all the remaining rights to publishers, if they wish, and they usually do.

There many ways to describe the result. OA through PubMed Central is expressly authorized by the copyright holders. Publishers no longer acquire full copyright to articles by NIH-funded authors, at least when those authors comply with the policy. Publishers don't acquire the rights they would need to negate the NIH's non-exclusive license or claim infringement. When researchers sign their funding contracts with the NIH, they are not committing any publisher to anything, let alone taking any intellectual property from anyone; they are only committing themselves to demand certain terms when they later write up and try to publish articles based on their funded research. The NIH is taking advantage of two important facts: (1) that authors are the copyright holders until they decide to transfer one or more of their rights to someone else, and (2) that researchers sign funding contracts before they sign publishing contracts. When NIH-funded authors do sign publishing contracts, they may only sign them subject to the terms of their prior funding contract.

The NIH succinctly describes this aspect of the policy in its policy FAQ: "Authors ... may assign ... rights to journals (as is the current practice), subject to the limited right that must be retained by the funding recipient to post the works in accordance with the Policy. ..."

http://publicaccess.nih.gov/FAQ.htm#813

When I refer to this later, I'll just call it "retaining the key right." It's what gives PMC permission to host OA copies of the author manuscripts. It's what prevents publishers from acquiring the full bundle of rights. It's what prevents the NIH policy from infringing the rights that authors may decide to transfer to publishers.

Let me digress on this point for a moment. There are two basic ways for funder OA mandates to avoid copyright infringement or secure permissions for OA. First, they may make an exception for publishers who won't allow OA on the funder's terms. Second, they may close that loophole and require grantees to retain the key right and use it to authorize the funder's OA, even if grantees may transfer all other rights to publishers. The first depends on permission from the publisher and the second depends on permission from the author prior to transferring rights to a publisher.

When publishers don't want to allow OA on the funder's terms, the first approach allows them to opt out. The second approach requires the author to find another publisher. In the first case, publishers may choose between accommodating the policy and resisting it. In the second case, they must choose between accommodating the policy and refusing to publish work by the agency's grantees.

The Conyers bill would block the stronger second path for US federal agencies, and allow the weaker first one. The NIH would have to retreat from assured author permission to contingent publisher permission, which is where it stood with the earlier, non-mandatory version of its policy, under which fewer than 10% of manuscripts based on NIH-funded research ever made it to OA from PubMed Central.

The strong second approach is taken by at least these eight funding agencies: the Arthritis Research Campaign (ARC, UK), Cancer Research UK (CR-UK), Department of Health (UK), Howard Hughes Medical Institute (HHMI, US), Joint Information Systems Committee (JISC, UK), Wellcome Trust (WT, UK), Medical Research Council (MRC, UK), and—for now—by the National Institutes of Health (NIH, US).

The weaker, first approach is taken by at least these seven: the Arts & Humanities Research Council (AHRC, UK), Canadian Institutes of Health Research (CIHR, Canada), National Cancer Institute of Canada (NCIC, Canada), Consejo Superior de Investigaciones Científicas (CSIC, Spain), Economic & Social Research Council (ESRC, UK), Higher Education Authority (HEA, Ireland), and Istituto Superiore di Sanità (ISS, Italy).

If the NIH policy doesn't infringe copyrights, or violate the federal copyright statute, then perhaps it violates our international IP treaties. Publishers have complained in the past that it violated US obligations under Article 13 of TRIPS (Agreement on Trade Related Aspects of Intellectual Property Rights) and the Article 9 of the Berne Convention. For example, see the AAP's 19 page letter to the NIH in May 2008,

http://publicaccess.nih.gov/comments2/files/AAP_NIH_Submission_05_30_08.pdf

But these objections would only apply if Congress had amended the Copyright Act in order to implement the NIH policy, which it did not do, or if it modified US law on copyright exceptions and limitations, which it did not do. On the contrary, it left copyright law unmodified and only modified the contract between the NIH and its grantees.

For detail, see the SPARC legal memorandum from July 2008, NIH Public Access Policy Does Not Affect U.S. Copyright Law.

http://www.arl.org/sparc/bm~doc/nihpolicy_copyright_july2008.pdf

http://www.earlham.edu/~peters/fos/2008/07/sparc-arl-response-to-aap-re-nih-policy
.html

The issue is also addressed in detail in the letter from 46 law professors to the Judiciary Committee, in response to the Conyers bill: "[T]he NIH Policy governs the terms of contracts, not exceptions to copyright law. As such, the Policy in no way implicates Article 13 of TRIPS or Article 9 of the Berne Convention, which address permissible copyright exceptions. These treaty provisions are completely silent on the issue of the terms a licensee can require of a copyright owner in exchange for valuable consideration."

https://mx2.arl.org/Lists/SPARC-OAForum/Message/4592.html

http://www.earlham.edu/~peters/fos/2008/09/law-professors-defend-nih-policy.html

In his opening statement, Rep. Conyers didn't say the NIH policy violates US treaties, but he did say that it "could severely impact important negotiations with our international trading partners. Already we are hearing reports, in conversations at the World Health Organization and in other international forums, [that] the new [NIH] policy to limit the exercise of copyright by authors and owners is being taken as a sign that the United States is shifting its position away from being a strong proponent of intellectual property rights and enforcement." (Not online.)

This appeal to trade issues conceals several problems. (1) The NIH policy doesn't violate the US copyright statute or treaties, and is completely compatible with intellectual property rights and their enforcement. If any of our trading partners think otherwise, they misunderstand the policy. Perhaps they only know what the publishing lobby has told them, which seems to be the case with several members of the Judiciary Committee. (Details below.) (2) The NIH OA mandate reflects US policy. In December 2007, it was approved by both houses of Congress and signed by the President. (3) A growing number of our trading partners are countries, or located in countries, with similar or even stronger policies. Worldwide, 29 funding agencies in 14 countries now have OA mandates: Austria, Belgium, Canada, the EU, France, Germany, Ireland, Italy, the Netherlands, South Africa, Switzerland, the UK, Ukraine, and the US. Without exception, all the medical research funders limit the embargo to six months, while the NIH allows 12 months. (4) If the NIH policy advances medical research without violating copyright, should we sacrifice it merely to ingratiate trading partners? What if their objections could be erased with a little accurate information? If this turns out to be a hard question of national priorities, do we really want to settle it in a committee devoted to copyright law? (5) If our trade partners understand that the policy doesn't violate copyright law, but still see it as a worrisome sign of national trends, and if the Judiciary Committee intervenes to act on their worries, then the Judiciary Committee is no longer defending the law of copyright, with its balance of competing interests, but the ideology of copyright maximalism.

But if the NIH policy doesn't infringe copyrights or violate our IP treaties, then in what sense is it "inconsistent" with copyright law? I don't see any non-cynical answers to that question. Perhaps publishers are deliberately blowing smoke, hoping that journalists and policy-makers will think infringement even where there isn't infringement. Perhaps they are dressing up a business setback as a copyright problem in order to get the attention of the Judiciary Committee. Perhaps publishers actually believe that their business setback, even without infringement, violates the "spirit" of the Copyright Act, as if the spirit of the act were to favor publishers over all other stakeholders, even for decisions made by authors at a time when authors, not publishers, are the copyright holders. Some of these theories are supported by the evidence that the Judiciary Committee is willing to credit the bogus copyright arguments, whether from misreading the NIH policy or a predisposition to help publishers.

In their rhetoric, publishers speak as if they are the copyright holders for these articles, and as if the NIH is blocking their full exercise of these rights or even expropriating them. But that is uninformed or deceptive. Because the NIH requires grantees to retain a key right, NIH-funded authors now transfer less than the full bundle of rights to publishers. Publishers don't like that, and it may be a problem for them, but it's not a legal problem. Despite their pose, publishers are not the copyright holders in these articles, without qualification, even after authors sign copyright transfer agreements. The NIH method of avoiding infringement means that there are plural rightsholders and divided rights in these articles: the authors have retained at least one and publishers have the rest. Publishers don't acquire the key right which would allow them to deny permission for OA or claim infringement or expropriation. As for the rights publishers do acquire, the NIH policy does nothing to diminish publisher freedom to hold and exercise them.

Have publishers forgotten this central feature of the NIH policy? Have its legal consequences still not sunk in? I find that theory hard to believe. It would entail that they haven't read, haven't remembered, or haven't understood the policy on which they have focused so much animus and lawyer time. And it doesn't square with their justified reluctance to claim actual infringement. But if they do understand this aspect of the policy, then we're only left with another cynical theory: that publishers deliberately stretch the truth by speaking without qualification as if they were the copyright holders for these articles. But strong or weak, the theory would explain a lot. If publishers did receive full copyright from authors, or if they believed they did, or if they had some reason to say they did, then their public rhetoric would make start to make sense. In that world, it would make sense to say that OA through PMC, against their wishes, would violate, diminish, or nullify one of their rights.

The snag, of course, is that the rhetoric is false, no matter what explains it. NIH-funded authors retain the key right and don't transfer full copyright to publishers. This is what I meant when I said (in SOAN for February 2008) that "publishers cannot complain that [the NIH policy] infringes a right they possess, only that it would infringe a right they wished they possessed."

http://www.earlham.edu/~peters/fos/newsletter/02-02-08.htm#mandates

In the DC Principles Coalition press release on the Conyers bill, Martin Frank puts the publisher complaint this way: "NIH has undermined our publishing activities by diminishing a basic principle under copyright— the right to control the distribution of the works we publish." (DCPC 9/12/08.)

http://www.pspcentral.org/commPublicAffairs/attachComm/Joint%20Publisher%20Letter%209-10-08.pdf

http://www.earlham.edu/~peters/fos/2008/09/two-public-statements-from-anti-oa
.html

It's true that if a publisher owns full copyright in a work, then it should have the
right to control its distribution. But publishers of NIH-funded work do *not* own full
copyright to those works. That's the point the publisher rhetoric keeps missing. The
principle Frank thinks is diminished is intact. Instead, authors are retaining a right that
publishers covet, something that authors are entitled to do under another basic principle of copyright.

Publishers can complain that under the NIH policy they don't acquire all the rights
they want to acquire or all the rights they formerly acquired. They can complain that
this creates problems for them. But they can't complain that the rights they do acquire
are infringed, diminished, nullified, or made unenforceable by the NIH policy. Nor can
they complain that authors don't have the right to transfer less than the full bundle to
publishers. If the "benefit of copyright" is the power to enforce the rights you actually
hold, then publishers enjoy the full benefit of copyright.

One version of the publisher complaint is that the NIH hosts and distributes peer-
reviewed manuscripts without compensating publishers for their expenses in supervis-
ing peer review. At least this argument has a basis in fact and doesn't depend on distorted
appeals to copyright law. Before we look at its flaws, we should recognize the truths on
which it is built. It's true that publishers organize peer review. It's true that that costs
them money, even when referees work without pay. It's true that the NIH policy applies
to peer-reviewed manuscripts, as opposed to unrefereed preprints. And it's true that the
NIH does not routinely compensate publishers for the service of organizing peer review.
To assess the argument in its strongest form, I'll ignore the $100 million/year the NIH
pays to journals to defray the costs of publishing NIH-funded research.

http://arstechnica.com/articles/culture/open-access-science.ars

http://www.earlham.edu/~peters/fos/2008/09/more-comments-on-conyers-bill.html

Why isn't that a slam-dunk?

It forgets or suppresses a critical fact. The NIH policy does not apply retroactively to
published articles on which publishers hold full copyright. It applies to future articles
published in conformity with the policy. The policy tells grantees, "When you publish
future articles based on your NIH-funded research, you must demand the following
terms from a publisher." When NIH-funded authors approach publishers, they ask publishers not only "will you publish my article?" but also "will you publish under these
terms?" It's a business proposition, and publishers are free to take it or leave it. But
either way, they have no complaint. If they accept the proposition, they have no

complaint: They have agreed to accommodate the policy. They have agreed to allow PMC to provide OA to the peer-reviewed manuscript after some embargo period. If they reject the proposition, they have no complaint: The authors go elsewhere and the publisher never invests in peer review for that manuscript.

Publishers may accept the business proposition only with reluctance. They may want a return to the days when they put terms to authors ("will you transfer full copyright?") and when authors' bargaining power was not buttressed by their funders or employers. Publishers may want to sweeten the deal, but they don't have a right to sweeten the deal. By contrast, however, authors do have the right to transfer all, some, or none of their rights to a publisher.

The expropriation argument hides the timeline of events and the role of publisher consent. It's not the case that publishers invest in peer review and then learn after the fact, helplessly, that the NIH will host copies of the peer-reviewed manuscripts. NIH-funded authors ask publishers in advance whether they are willing to publish under the terms required by the NIH. The decision is up to the publisher.

The current version of the NIH policy does not directly depend on publisher consent. But whether an article subject to the NIH policy appears in a certain journal does depend on publisher consent. The absence of publisher consent from the first step is what makes the NIH policy a mandate. Publishers cannot opt out except by refusing to publish NIH-funded authors or by charging a fee to do so, as the American Psychological Association once tried to do. The presence of publisher consent in the second step is what undercuts the publisher complaint about taking, surrender, expropriation, or lack of compensation. The NIH never disseminates the fruits of a publisher's investment in peer review without that publisher's knowing consent and cooperation.

One member of the subcommittee at the September 11 hearing, Bob Goodlatte (R-VA), suggested that we could moot the compensation question if the NIH policy applied to unrefereed preprints rather than to peer-reviewed postprints. But everyone else around the table rejected the idea, even Martin Frank representing the publishers. Frank said it would be "disastrous" to provide OA to unrefereed preprints in medicine, even with a disclaimer, since 90% of them are rejected by journals. (Piper 9/12/08.) This may be the first time that the Ingelfinger rule removed, rather than erected, an obstacle to OA.

http://www.warren-news.com/internetservices.htm

http://www.earlham.edu/~peters/fos/2008/09/more-on-hearing-on-bill-to-overturn-nih.html

The unsound compensation argument becomes dishonest when publishers disguise it as a copyright argument and introduce a hint of entitlement. There is nothing in copyright law requiring authors to transfer all rather than some of their rights to publishers, and there is nothing in copyright law protecting publishers from the risks of their own business decisions. It's dishonest to suggest that the letter or the spirit of copyright law should assure publishers of undiminished revenue or save them from hard bargaining. Publishers can complain that authors and funding agencies are waking up to the bad contracts authors have been signing with publishers, and waking up to their interest in retaining the right to authorize OA. But that's life in a changing world. Publishers can complain about the end of easy pickings, but they can't pretend that the easy pickings were ever an entitlement or that the end of easy pickings is inconsistent with law, any law.

The dishonesty is doubled when publishers pretend that they are protecting authors rather than themselves—for example, when the AAP/PSP says that the NIH policy denies authors the benefits of their copyrights, or when Rep. Conyers says that his bill would restore copyright protections for scientists. (More on this in the next section.)

Publishers sometimes put the compensation argument this way: supporters of funder OA policies want something for nothing. But on the contrary, supporters of funder OA policies want something for something. They want OA in exchange for the taxpayer investment in research. The "something for nothing" argument not only forgets that taxpayers pay for the underlying research, but also that publishers pay nothing to receive the written results. If publishers and taxpayers both make a contribution to the value of peer-reviewed articles arising from publicly-funded research, then what's the best way to split this baby? The NIH solution is a reasonable compromise: a period of exclusivity for the publisher followed by free online access for the public. The compromise is tilted further toward publishers by providing OA only to the peer-reviewed but unedited manuscript, not the published edition. If publishers want to block OA mandates per se, as the Conyers bill does, rather than just negotiate the embargo period, then they are saying that they want no compromise, that the public should get nothing for its investment, and that publishers should control access to research conducted by others, written up by others, and funded by taxpayers. That would be getting something for nothing.

The NIH policy is a compromise of mutual compensation: in consideration for publishing articles whose unedited manuscripts will become OA 12 months after publication, publishers get high-quality submissions, free of charge, reporting the results of expensive, quality-controlled research. In exchange for funding the research, at hundreds or thousands of times the cost of publishing the resulting articles, taxpayers get OA to a certain version after a certain delay. If the precise balance needs to be tweaked, then let's tweak it. But OA has to be part of the balance in order to give taxpayers something for something. And before we decide that a tweak favoring publishers is necessary, consider the evidence that it isn't: some publishers may be complaining, but with no tweaks at all they are almost unanimous in accepting the business proposition from NIH-funded authors.

William Patry, former Copyright Counsel to the House Judiciary Committee, puts it this way, with the accent less on publisher consent than balanced accounting:

http://williampatry.blogspot.com/2008/07/open-access-and-nih.html

http://www.earlham.edu/~peters/fos/2008/07/william-patry-on-nih-policy-and.html

> [W]hy do you disregard the money that NIH has sunk in? Why shouldn't you flip the analysis and require the publisher, as a condition of publishing the article and charging for the journal, to reimburse NIH for some of NIH's expenses? STM publishers seem quite exercised over articles they pay nothing for being made available to the public, but apparently have no qualms about making money off of research funded by the public. Their moral outrage and accounting seems curiously unidirectional.

Finally, I shouldn't leave the compensation argument without noting a deeper problem. The publishers who oppose the NIH policy have adopted a business model which depends on access barriers. Their method for generating revenue is to block access by default, or create artificial scarcity, and then open it up for paying customers. OA publishers need compensation too, but their business models do not depend on access barriers or artificial scarcity. Toll access (TA) publishers believe that the OA business models are inadequate. We can debate that, for example, in light of the evidence that more than 3,000 peer-reviewed OA journals are finding ways to pay their bills, the fact that several for-profit OA publishers are already showing profits, and the fact that most of the money to support OA journals is currently tied up supporting TA journals. But in the end it doesn't matter whether the TA publishers are right or wrong to believe that their compensation depends on access barriers. The deeper problem, as I argued in July 2007, is "making a public commitment to use public money to expand knowledge and then handing control over the results to businesses who believe, correctly or incorrectly, that their revenue and survival depend on limiting access to that knowledge."

http://www.earlham.edu/~peters/fos/newsletter/07-02-07.htm#problems

If the TA publishers are right that they must erect access barriers to reimburse themselves, then we'd be foolish to let them be the only outlets for publicly-funded research. If the TA publishers are wrong, then we'd be foolish to overturn the NIH policy, and erect access barriers to publicly-funded research, just to satisfy their wrong belief.

Another version of the publisher complaint appears to concede that authors have a right to transfer all, some, or none of their rights to a publisher, but points out that the NIH policy is a "mandate" which interferes with author freedom.

Of course publishers are not mounting an expensive lobbying campaign in order to enhance author freedom. They are acting for themselves. Far more publishers than authors complain about the supposed restrictions of NIH-style funding contracts. Alma

Swan's empirical studies have shown that "the vast majority (81%)" of researchers would "willingly" comply with an OA mandate from their funder or employer, and that 95% would comply willingly or reluctantly.

http://eprints.ecs.soton.ac.uk/12428/

But what about the "mandate" problem? Does this limit author freedom in a way that should alarm legislators or in a way that is "inconsistent" with copyright law?

Let's not forget the sense in which the NIH policy is mandatory. The NIH is putting an OA condition on a voluntary contract. It doesn't require OA unconditionally, and couldn't possibly do so. The NIH is saying, in effect, that in exchange for a grant of public money, we ask you to retain one of your rights as copyright holder and use it to authorize OA. This is a contract that researchers are free to decline. Researchers who don't like the terms (and I haven't heard of any), don't have to accept public money for their research. Just as publishers are free to accept or reject papers by NIH-funded authors, authors are free to seek or avoid seeking NIH grants.

As the 46 law professors put it:

> [T]he Policy does not create an involuntary transfer, a compulsory license, or a taking of the publishers' or investigators' copyright. ... [I]f the investigator chooses not to receive NIH funding, the investigator has no obligation to provide the article to PMC or a copyright license to NIH. But if the investigator elects to receive NIH funding, he or she accepts the terms of the grant agreement, which include the requirement to deposit the article with PMC so that the article can be made publicly accessible within one year after publication. Because the investigator has this basic choice, the policy does not constitute an involuntary transfer.

The relevant author freedom here isn't the freedom to deposit in PMC, which existed under the previous (non-mandatory) version of the NIH policy, but the freedom to accept a research grant which requires deposit in PMC. But all contracts contain terms that require something or another. The NIH funding contract requires authors to turn in a report at the end of the grant period, to spend the money only on approved research-related expenses, and many other things. Now it also requires them to demand certain terms when publishing articles based on the funded research. Publishers don't object to the other mandatory contract terms, and couldn't. But if they object to this one on the ground that it's mandatory, then they must object to them all. More, they must object to their own publishing contracts, which also require authors to transfer certain rights.

The publisher argument here skirts hypocrisy, and the only way to avoid it is with breathtaking one-sidedness: authors should be free to sign publishing contracts with mandatory terms but not funding contracts with mandatory terms. If publishers are serious, they are calling on Congress to tilt an unbalanced copyright system further toward themselves.

As I was going to press, I just read about H.R. 286, which would put another mandatory condition on federal funding contracts: the grantees must use the metric system.

Will the publishing lobby object that this limits researcher freedom? Or because it doesn't affect their own business model, will they let it go?

http://www.opencongress.org/bill/110-h286/show

Let's take the money complaint seriously for a minute. Perhaps the publishing lobby understands that NIH-funded authors retain a key right, that copyright law allows them to do so, and that publishers acquire less than the full bundle. Perhaps the complaint is that the missing right prevents publishers from making money from the remaining rights. Publishers may be able to exercise their rights in full but they can't make as much money as before.

That may be their complaint, and it may even be true. The answer is a variation of my earlier answers. First, nothing in copyright law says they must always make the same amount of money they previously made. It's not an entitlement. Second, NIH-funded authors are still putting forward a business proposition ("will you publish this article under these terms?") and publishers are still free to take it or leave it.

Moreover, if that is the complaint, why aren't publishers more candid in stating it? Why disguise their grievance as a copyright problem? Why speak as if they are the full copyright holders, somehow denied the rights of copyright holders? Why hide the fact that NIH-funded authors retain a key right and transfer only what's left? Why call the NIH policy "inconsistent with copyright law"? Why say that the NIH policy forces them to "surrender" their articles? Perhaps those are just exaggerations to get a hearing before the Judiciary Committee. But serious question: Why should publishers exaggerate about copyright violations to a Congressional committee which specializes in copyright law? Serious question: Why should we entrust the management of peer review to serial exaggerators?

If publishers admit that they have full legal authority to exercise the rights they acquire from authors, and merely want to acquire more rights from authors in order to make more money, then they'd have to admit that they are not suffering a legal injury. They'd have to admit that they are only facing a more difficult business climate because one source of their raw material is starting to offer it on less attractive terms, though still free of charge. They'd also have to admit that their preferred remedy would itself diminish copyright protection for authors, who are the original copyright holders here and who should be protected in their freedom to bargain away one of their rights in exchange for a large research grant.

Even if the NIH policy does lower the value of these works as investment opportunities for publishers, because publishers are no longer their exclusive distributors, it multiplies their value to authors and readers. I call this a step toward balancing the competing interests. But even if you wouldn't, it remains the case that publishers know when a submission comes from a NIH-funded author, know the terms, and accept it anyway.

For the record, by the way, it's far from clear that publishers *can't* make as much money as before. For the argument and evidence, see Sections 1–10 of this article from September 2007,

http://www.earlham.edu/~peters/fos/newsletter/09-02-07.htm#peerreview

In response to Elias Zerhouni's claim at the hearing that "there is no evidence that [the NIH policy] has been harmful" to publishers, Martin Frank told Science Magazine "that some journal editors believe the new policy is leading to 'fewer eyeballs coming to their sites.'" (Kaiser 9/11/08.) It's well-known and not surprising that OA archiving can reduce downloads from publisher web sites. But there's no evidence that these reduced downloads are reflected in reduced subscriptions. If there were, then publishers would cite the reduced subscriptions instead of the reduced downloads, to show that the policy is harming them.

Any systematic study of the harm question would also have to compare the few publishers who have publicly endorsed the Conyers bill with the hundreds who are voluntarily going beyond the terms required by NIH-funded authors:

Journals participating in PMC (many with embargo periods shorter than 12 months)

http://www.pubmedcentral.nih.gov/fprender.fcgi?cmd=full_view

Journals submitting the published editions of articles by NIH-funded authors to PMC (not just the unedited manuscripts)

http://publicaccess.nih.gov/submit_process_journals.htm

Journals depositing their articles in PMC, under open licenses, whether or not their authors are NIH-funded

http://www.pubmedcentral.nih.gov/about/openftlist.html

For more detail on various publisher positions, see the OAD list of publisher policies on NIH-funded authors

http://oad.simmons.edu/oadwiki/Publisher_policies_on_NIH-funded_authors

One more attempt at a non-cynical theory: Publishers know that they have a right to resist the NIH policy, but they are mistaking the legal basis for that right. They think it derives from copyright law when in fact it derives from their background right to refuse to publish any work for any reason.

I have more to say about this distinction in an article from October 2006.

http://www.earlham.edu/~peters/fos/newsletter/08-02-06.htm#lessons

The two rights are independent, and the second is not rooted in copyright law. Publishers have a right to refuse to publish any work, whether or not they possess any rights in the work. I support that right, strongly, and I hope we all do. It would be intolerable for a publisher to lose the right to reject a submission or for the government to dictate what a publisher must publish. My point here is not that it is in jeopardy but that it is unrelated to copyright.

When the OA policy at a funder like the AHRC or CIHR (see above) includes a loophole for publisher copyright policies, then publishers have a copyright-based right to escape the OA policy. But funders like the NIH and Wellcome Trust close that loophole, deny publishers the easy opt-out of changing their in-house rules, and leave only the hard opt-out of refusing to publish work based on research funded by those funders. It's time for publishers to choose the hard opt-out if they really dislike the NIH policy, or to admit that they have chosen not to.

At the very least, it's time to stop pretending that they are victims of a legal wrong with an entitlement to restore the previous arrangement. Authors and funders here are not violating copyright; they are making a canny and lawful use of copyright in order to advance their own interests. Publishers have the same right to resist that every business has in the face of hard bargaining: just say no.

Summary

Here are eight facts I'd like every member of Congress to understand, if they ever have to cast a vote on the Fair Copyright in Research Works Act. Or, here are eight corrections to eight false impressions created by the rhetoric of the publishing lobby.

(1) There is no copyright infringement here. OA through PMC under the NIH policy is expressly authorized by the copyright holders.

(2) There is no violation of our IP treaties here. The treaties would only come into play if Congress had amended the Copyright Act in order to enact the NIH policy, which it did not do. The NIH policy only changes the contract between the agency and its grantees. (However, the Conyers bill would amend the Copyright Act.)

(3) The NIH policy regulates grantees, not publishers. It doesn't require publishers to provide OA, to permit OA, to relinquish anything they possess or acquire, or to do anything they are unwilling to do. It merely requires grantees to ask certain terms from publishers.

(4) There is no surrender, commandeering, or expropriation of publisher property here. There's a business proposition which publishers can take or leave. The only taking here is that most publishers are taking it.

(5) NIH-funded authors who comply with the new policy do not transfer full copyright to publishers. Instead, they retain a non-exclusive right to authorize OA through

PMC. Consequently, publishers do not acquire full copyright in articles arising from NIH-funded research. Instead, at most, they acquire all but the right the author has retained. Publisher arguments that start with references to "their copyrighted articles" are already too sloppy deal justly with the actual policy.

(6) Publishers are failing to distinguish between (a) acquiring fewer rights from authors than they would like and (b) diminishing protection for the rights they do acquire. If they have a grievance, it's the former, not the latter. However, if one of these is inconsistent with copyright law, it's the latter, not the former.

(7) The NIH "mandate" is a mandatory condition in a voluntary funding contract, exactly as legitimate and consistent with copyright law as the mandatory conditions in publishing contracts.

(8) The mission of the NIH is to advance the public interest in medical research and health care, not the private interest of the publishing industry. Because the Judiciary Committee can set policy, its mission is not as clear-cut. But insofar as the committee sets policy on copyright, shouldn't its mission be less about creating artificial scarcity to publicly-funded research than promoting the progress of science and useful arts?

What's next?

Congress adjourned on September 26—not counting the special session to deal with the financial crisis—and isn't scheduled to reconvene until January 3, 2009. But it may come back during the break to deal further with the financial crisis, appropriations, or other hot issues. The Conyers bill is not one of those hot issues, and Howard Berman told Library Journal Academic Newswire that the subcommittee wouldn't take any action on the bill until at least January. However, Conyers or another proponent might attach the language to a bill that is moving toward a vote, during or after the recess.

When Congress reconvenes in January, we'll have a new Congress and soon after a new President as well. Whatever happens in the White House, Congress will have larger Democratic majorities than it has now. That won't necessarily help OA. John Conyers is a Democrat and John Cornyn (for example) is a Republican.

It helps us that the bill hasn't been endorsed by Howard Berman (D-CA) or Howard Coble (R-NC), the Chair and Ranking Minority Member of the Subcommittee on Courts, the Internet, and Intellectual Property. Richard Jones reports that Coble said the bill was "not your typical copyright issue" and that he "needed more time to learn and think about" it. According to Greg Piper, Coble hasn't endorsed the bill "because he had heard that some countries imposed similar requirements without violating IP treaty obligations."

http://www.aip.org/fyi/2008/091.html

http://www.earlham.edu/~peters/fos/2008/09/detailed-summary-of-hearing-on-conyers.html

http://www.warren-news.com/internetservices.htm

http://www.earlham.edu/~peters/fos/2008/09/more-on-hearing-on-bill-to-overturn-nih.html

Berman took a stronger stand, saying that the Conyers bill would "turn back the clock" by overturning the NIH policy.

http://www.the-scientist.com/blog/display/55009/

http://www.earlham.edu/~peters/fos/2008/09/turf-and-nothing-but-turf.html

It also helps us that the bill may reflect turf rivalries among House committees more than member opposition to the NIH policy. In introducing the bill, Conyers was more passionate in defending the "sacred jurisdiction" of his committee, and denouncing the Appropriations Committee for bypassing his committee last year, than in opposing the NIH policy.

http://www.govexec.com/story_page.cfm?articleid=40947&dcn=todaysnews

http://www.earlham.edu/~peters/fos/2008/09/turf-and-nothing-but-turf.html

http://www.libraryjournal.com/info/CA6596784.html?nid=2673#news1

http://www.earlham.edu/~peters/fos/2008/09/conyers-bill-on-ice-until-at-least-2009.html

On the turf question, by the way, it's relevant that William Patry, former Copyright Counsel to the House Judiciary Committee, believes it's "absurd" to think that the NIH policy raises copyright issues or that it had to be reviewed by the Judiciary Committee.

http://williampatry.blogspot.com/2008/07/open-access-and-nih.html

http://www.earlham.edu/~peters/fos/2008/07/william-patry-on-nih-policy-and.html

It helps that nobody seems to want ownership of the bill. Conyers also told the Library Journal Academic Newswire that the bill was coming out of Berman's office, while Berman said it was coming out of Conyers' office. (LJAN 9/16/08.)

http://www.libraryjournal.com/info/CA6596784.html?nid=2673#news1

Nevertheless, Conyers is a long-time opponent of the NIH policy and his opposition should not be doubted.

http://www.earlham.edu/~peters/fos/2007/08/more-on-prism_25.html

It helps that 46 law professors said there was no copyright problem with the NIH policy, and 33 Nobel laureates defended the NIH policy and charged that "the current move by the publishers is wrong." (Law profs 9/8/08 and Nobelists 9/9/08.)

https://mx2.arl.org/Lists/SPARC-OAForum/Message/4592.html

http://www.taxpayeraccess.org/supporters/scientists/an-open-letter-to-the-us-congress-signed-by-33-nob.shtml

It helps that the US Copyright Office does not endorse the bill. Ralph Oman is a former Register of Copyrights (from 1994), a supporter of the bill, and was a witness at the September 11 hearing. But that only made other witnesses wonder about the current Register of Copyrights, Mary Peters. According to Andrew Albanese in Library Journal, the Copyright Office confirmed that Peters was not asked to testify. Sources in the office told Albanese that "the Copyright Office is ... not ... persuaded by publishers' arguments regarding the NIH public access policy, and sees the recently introduced bill as unnecessary."

http://www.libraryjournal.com/article/CA6597446.html

It actually helps that subcommittee members were so uninformed about academic publishing and the NIH policy. It discredits the publisher lobbyists and suggests that a little more information in the right places could turn the tide. For example, some members didn't know that scholarly journals didn't pay authors or peer reviewers. Others didn't know that the NIH paid out $100 million/year to support the costs of publishing journal, which is about 30 times more than it spends implementing its public access policy.

http://arstechnica.com/articles/culture/open-access-science.ars

In the end, however, it doesn't matter whether the Conyers bill arises from turf rivalries among House committees or objections to the NIH policy, and it doesn't matter whether the objections to the NIH policy arise from copyright problems or an unabashed desire to protect a powerful private interest at the expense of the public interest. The bill could pass anyway. Nor do divisions within the committee matter if proponents of the bill can attach its language to another bill and bypass the committee. That's why we have to continue our efforts to defend the NIH policy and block any effort to overturn it, from any direction.

If you're an American citizen and you contacted your Congressional delegation before the recent recess, *thank you*. Be prepared to do so again in the new session.

It would help if sympathetic publishers would speak out even now, during the recess. The Association of American Publishers division of Professional/Scholarly Publishing

(AAP/PSP), the DC Principles Coalition (DCPC), and the American Association of University Presses (AAUP) have all endorsed the Conyers bill. In their letters to Congress, each group pretended to speak for its members. Rockefeller University Press has already spoken out, disavowing the AAUP statement and noting that the association did not consult its members before endorsing the bill.

https://mx2.arl.org/Lists/SPARC-OAForum/Message/4580.html

http://www.earlham.edu/~peters/fos/2008/09/rockefeller-up-disavows-aaup-support.html

University faculty, librarians, and administrators should ask their university presses to take a similar step. Publishers willing to do so should issue a public statement and send copies to their Representative, Senators, and the leadership of the House and Senate Judiciary Committees.

In August 2007, I made this assessment:

http://www.ctwatch.org/quarterly/print.php%3Fp=81.html

> There is a rising awareness of copyright issues in the general public, rising frustration with unbalanced copyright laws, and rising support for remedies by governments (legislation) and individuals (Creative Commons licenses and their equivalents). Copyright laws are still grotesquely unbalanced, and powerful corporations who benefit from the imbalance are fighting to ensure that [these laws] are not revised in the right direction any time soon. But in more and more countries, an aroused public is ready to fight to ensure that they are not revised in the wrong direction either, something we haven't seen in the entire history of copyright law. However, this only guarantees that the content industry will have a fight, not that users and consumers will win.

Already the opposition to the Conyers bill is proving this thesis, though the outcome is still up in the air. Even governments are acknowledging the change, which may be why those seeking the next ratchet-click of copyright maximalism have had to draft the Anti-Counterfeiting Trade Agreement in secret.

http://blog.wired.com/27bstroke6/2008/09/international-i.html

If the Conyers bill is defeated, or dies without a vote, we will not have mobilized for nothing. We will have saved a good policy from repeal. We will have made it harder for the publishing lobby to come back. It has now had its hearing, and won't be able to complain that it never got one. It got its shot at a copyright argument before the Judiciary Committee, and won't be able to complain that it never got one. It won't be out of options or give up, but it will be at least one step closer to adaptation.

Here are the basic links for the Conyers bill and the September 11 hearing on it:

Fair Copyright in Research Works Act (H.R. 6845) (Conyers bill)

http://thomas.loc.gov/cgi-bin/bdquery/z?d110:h6845:
(the final colon is part of the URL)

An image scan of the text of the bill

http://judiciary.house.gov/hearings/pdf/HR6845.pdf

Open Congress page on the H.R. 6845

http://www.opencongress.org/bill/110-h6845/show

The hearing on the bill conducted by the House Judiciary Committee, Subcommittee
    on Courts, the Internet, and Intellectual Property, September 11, 2008

http://judiciary.house.gov/hearings/hear_090911_1.html

The video webcast of the hearing

http://judiciary.edgeboss.net/real/judiciary/courts/courts09112008.smi

Transcript of the hearing (from a private company, not OA)

http://web.archive.org/web/20081012074709/

http://www.fednews.com/transcript.htm?id=20080911t6594

House Judiciary Committee

http://judiciary.house.gov/

Subcommittee on Courts the Internet and Intellectual Property

http://judiciary.house.gov/about/subcommittee.html

[...]

Also see the sequel to this article, "Re-introduction of the bill to kill the NIH policy,"
SPARC Open Access Newsletter, March 2, 2009.

http://www.earlham.edu/~peters/fos/newsletter/03-02-09.htm#conyers

Open Access Policy Options for Funding Agencies and Universities

From "Open access policy options for funding agencies and universities," SPARC Open Access Newsletter, February 2, 2009.

http://dash.harvard.edu/handle/1/4322589

Every research funding agency should have an OA policy, many already do, and most are probably thinking about it. Here's a guide to the major decisions which come up in framing a new policy, reviewing an older one, or thinking about policies elsewhere. I start with the choice-points facing funding agencies (1–12), and then look briefly at the choice-points which only arise for universities (13–18). I offer a recommendation for each.

(1) Request or require?

Will you require OA for the research you fund or merely request it? The original NIH policy, which took effect in May 2005, merely requested and encouraged OA. The agency strongly urged compliance, conducted many kinds of educational outreach for grantees, and was even joined, late in the game, by publishers who realized that their best hope of heading off an OA mandate was to make the voluntary policy succeed. But despite these efforts, the compliance rate barely broke double digits in two years. As soon as Congress ordered NIH to make the policy mandatory in December 2007, and even before NIH issued the new language in January 2008, compliance started to rise sharply. Three months after the mandatory version of the policy took effect the compliance rate was nearly five times greater than under the old policy, and is still climbing.

http://www.libraryjournal.com/info/CA6581624.html?nid=2673#news1

http://www.earlham.edu/~peters/fos/2008/07/more-evidence-that-mandates-work.html

Recommendation: If you're serious about achieving OA for the research you fund, you must require it.

The NIH experience proved the failure of requests and the success of mandates, for funding agencies. In a series of empirical studies Arthur Sale has offered the same dual proof, for universities.

http://fcms.its.utas.edu.au/scieng/comp/project.asp?lProjectId=1830

Institutions worried that mandates will face a barrier of resistance from researchers should look at the unanimous faculty votes for OA mandates (in #18 below). There's other evidence as well. Not only do the compliance rates steadily approach 100%, but even before the recent rise of mandates Alma Swan and Sheridan Brown found in surveys that 94% of researchers would comply with an OA mandate from their funder or employer, 81% of them willingly.

http://cogprints.org/4385/

Today there are 31 funder mandates in 14 countries, and 27 university mandates in 16 countries.

http://www.eprints.org/openaccess/policysignup/

(2) Green or gold?

Green OA is OA through repositories, and gold OA is OA through journals (regardless of the journal business models). If you want your research output to be OA, should you steer it toward OA repositories or OA journals?

Recommendation: If you decide to request and encourage OA, rather than a mandate it, then you can encourage submission to an OA journal and encourage deposit in an OA repository as well, especially when researchers publish in a toll access (TA) journal. But if you decide to mandate OA, then you should require deposit in an OA repository, and not require submission to an OA journal, even if you also encourage submission to an OA journal.

The green focus for OA mandates is supported by two independent considerations: preserving author freedom to submit work to the journals of their choice, and maximizing the chance of reaching OA for 100% of your research output.

Today only about 15% of peer-reviewed journals are OA. This fraction grows steadily, and one day there will be enough OA journals to justify a gold OA mandate (requiring submission to OA journals). But in the meantime, green OA mandates are compatible with author freedom to submit to the journals of their choice and gold OA mandates are not. Here's how I spelled out the argument in SOAN last April:

http://www.earlham.edu/~peters/fos/newsletter/04-02-08.htm#principles

> If it weren't for [faculty freedom], universities could require faculty to submit their articles to
> OA journals rather than deposit them in an OA repository (a gold OA mandate rather than a

green OA mandate). But there aren't yet enough OA journals; there aren't yet first-rate OA journals in every research niche; and even one day when there are, a ... policy to rule out submission to a journal based solely on its business model would needlessly limit faculty freedom. Not even the urgent need for OA justifies that kind of restriction, as long as we can achieve OA through OA repositories. That's why all university and funder OA mandates focus on green OA (through OA repositories) rather than gold OA (through OA journals).

OA repositories can accept deposits on any topic, in any field. But today OA journals are a small minority of peer-reviewed journals and most of them focus on just one field. Green OA can apply to 100% of the literature today; but until all or most journals are OA, gold OA cannot.

Green OA is compatible with publishing in either OA or TA journals. Today about 63% of TA journals give blanket permission for their authors to self-archive in OA repositories, and essentially all OA journals do. While we work to raise the percentage of TA journals permitting green OA, there are already battle-tested strategies for securing permission for green OA to 100% of new literature, regardless of where it is published (see #10).

(3) Which repository?

From here, I'll assume that your policy will mandate green OA. Next question: if you want to require deposit in an OA repository, then which repository?

The NIH hosts its own repository, PubMed Central (PMC) and requires deposit in it. Eight UK medical funders band together and host a consortial repository, UK PubMed Central (UKPMC), and require deposit in it. Three Irish funders either give grantees a choice between central and distributed (institutional) repositories or prefer them to use their institutional repository. University policies uniformly direct deposits into the institutional repository, even if they are compatible with deposits in disciplinary repositories as well.

OAI interoperability makes the question somewhat moot: what is deposited in one repository can have at least its metadata harvested by other repositories. Mutual harvesting between institutional and disciplinary repositories is not routine, but it could greatly lower the stakes in the question where an OA mandate should require initial deposit.

But even then it would not moot the question completely. There are great advantages in having authors deposit in their own institutional repository. It helps institutions share, analyze, and evaluate their own research output. It adds local incentives to funder mandates to prod and reward author participation. It adds robustness to preservation, on the LOCKSS principle, by distributing the literature around a large network. It ensures that the system will scale with the growth of published research, simply from the fact that distributed networks are more capacious than any individual node. Above all, it nurtures local cultures of self-archiving at every university, which will benefit non-funded research and research funded by non-mandating funders. Funders who mandate

OA will have one kind of impact; funders who mandate OA and direct deposits to institutional repositories (where they exist) will magnify that impact by spreading the culture of OA to other researchers. In the age of OAI interoperability and repository crawling by most major search engines, distributed local deposits do not detract from searching. In the age of SWORD-automated deposits, double deposits are not necessary to put the same articles into cooperating central or disciplinary repositories.

On the other side, there's some evidence that repositories which attract researchers in their capacity as readers or searchers also attract researchers in their capacity as authors or depositors. When researchers visit a repository like arXiv or PubMed Central to hunt for new literature, they quickly understand the point of depositing there. And of course, disciplinary repositories attract more readers or researchers than institutional repositories precisely because they organize the literature by field, which is relevant to most searchers, rather than by author affiliation, which is irrelevant to most searchers. Both the reader preference for disciplinary repositories and (therefore) the author preference for reader-preferred repositories should dwindle as cross-repository search tools become more comprehensive, more powerful, and more popular. But for now the behavioral difference is real, and it's bolstered by the tendency of researchers identify more with their field than with their university. If you want to get your compliance rate up, it makes sense to swim with this tide rather than against it.

Recommendation: Because there are advantages to each type of repository, and because each provides bona fide OA, the stakes are low in the choice between them. That is, you can't go seriously wrong by preferring one to the other. One path, then, is simply to make a choice. Another is to support both types in ranked order, for example, requiring deposit in an institutional repository, when the grantee's institution has one, and otherwise requiring deposit in the funder's repository or in a designated disciplinary or multi-disciplinary repository. Another path is to shift the choice to authors. The 2006 version of FRPAA (Federal Research Public Access Act) allowed grantees to satisfy the OA mandate by depositing in any repository which met certain conditions of open access, interoperability, and long-term preservation.

In any case, the repository destination you choose should not be exclusive. After authors deposit in the repository you designate, they should be free to deposit elsewhere as well.

Funders with their own repositories will naturally have a procedure to process submissions. Long-term, it would be very helpful if they also developed a procedure to harvest selected manuscripts on deposit in other repositories. That would allow distributed deposits to facilitate central deposits as well. And it will probably turn out that harvesting an already-deposited manuscript is less expensive than processing a raw submission. Likewise, it would help if institutional repositories developed the same capacity, so that central deposits could facilitate distributed deposits. We all have an interest in harnessing the full power of repository interoperability.

As we approach that point, however, we don't approach complete neutrality on the choice between central and distributed repositories. On the contrary, if deposits any-where could be harvested wherever they might also be desirable, that would strengthen the case for institutional deposits. Other things being equal, we should make the choice which will strengthen the culture of spontaneous self-archiving.

(4) Gratis or libre?

Gratis OA removes price barriers but not permission barriers. It makes content free of charge but not free of copyright or licensing restrictions. It gives users no more reuse rights than they already have through fair use or the local equivalent. Libre OA removes price barriers and at least some permission barriers. It loosens copyright and licensing restrictions and permits at least some uses beyond fair use.

http://www.earlham.edu/~peters/fos/newsletter/08-02-08.htm#gratis-libre

The BBB (Budapest-Bethesda-Berlin) definitions of OA all call for libre OA. But most of the research on deposit in OA repositories is merely gratis OA. While most TA journals permit OA archiving, nearly all of them limit their permission to gratis OA. If institutional policies required libre OA, they would increase the difficulty of publishing in nearly all TA journals, which would increase the difficulty of publishing in most peer-reviewed journals. They would even increase the difficulty of publishing in many OA journals, which still limit themselves to gratis OA. Hence, for now a libre OA mandate would hurt authors.

This will change as more TA journals convert to OA and as more OA journals them-selves move from gratis to libre OA. It will also change as the number of funder and university policies grows; when there is a critical mass, resistant publishers will find it easier to accommodate the policies than to refuse to publish the work of affected authors. But it won't change quickly. In SOAN for December 2008, I put "libre green OA" as the 12th out of 12 cross-over points to expect in the future of the OA movement.

http://www.earlham.edu/~peters/fos/newsletter/12-02-08.htm#predictions

The Wellcome Trust, the UK Medical Research Council, and other funders in the UKPMC Funders Group (some public, some private) require libre OA when they pay part of the cost of publishing an article. I recommend that practice (#11). However, that libre OA is gold, not green, and the question doesn't come up for funders who subsidize research but not publishing. But when a funder pays some publishing costs, then it can demand libre OA, and it can do it now without boosting the rejection rates for its grant-ees. When a publisher receives an acceptable publication fee for an article, then it needn't be concerned to protect a future revenue stream from that article.

http://www.earlham.edu/~peters/fos/2008/04/revision-to-oa-mandate-at-mrc.html

http://www.earlham.edu/~peters/fos/2007/10/funders-and-publishers-agree-to-remove
.html

Recommendation: For now, green OA mandates for funded research should require gratis OA. But when all or most journals provide libre OA, or when a libre OA mandate would elicit journal accommodation more often than refusals to publish, then funders can shift their demand from gratis to libre. Even now however, funders should demand libre OA when they pay for publication, not just for research.

If a funder does want to mandate libre OA—for example, because it pays some of an article's publication costs—, what flavor of libre OA, or what license, should it demand? I recommend the CC-BY (Attribution) license or the equivalent. It imposes the fewest restrictions on users while preserving the author's right of attribution, and it's fully compatible with the BBB definitions of OA. For these reasons, it's also the license recommended by the Open Access Scholarly Publishers Association and the SPARC Europe seal of approval program.

http://www.oaspa.org/

http://www.doaj.org/doaj?func=loadTempl&templ=080423

(5) Deposit what?

Most funder and university OA policies today don't ask authors to deposit the published edition of an article, but merely the final version of the author's peer-reviewed manuscript. That's the version approved by peer review but not yet refined by copy editing or final formatting.

This is a working compromise. It gives users the benefit of the peer-reviewed language, and it doesn't ask more than most publishers are willing to give. If an embargo is a compromise by time, this is a compromise by version. Like any compromise, it's not as good as getting everything you want. But if (today) requiring authors to deposit the published edition would lead more publishers to refuse to publish their work, then (today) the compromise is more desirable than a stronger policy.

But the funder policy can also require deposit of data files. Data are uncopyrightable facts. Even in countries with a quasi-copyright "database right," the right belongs to the compiler, who is the researcher more often than the publisher. Hence, publishers rarely oppose OA for author data. It doesn't interfere with anything they're selling. In fact, many publishers who oppose OA for articles actually recommend or require OA for data. It facilitates research and enhances the value of what they're selling.

Recommendation: Require the deposit of the final version of the author's peer-reviewed manuscript, not the published version. For publishers who worry about circulation of multiple versions of the peer-reviewed text, offer the option to replace the author's manuscript in the repository with the published edition. Require the deposit of data generated by the funded research project. In medicine and the social sciences, where privacy is an issue, OA data should be anonymized.

A peer-reviewed manuscript in an OA repository should include a citation and link to the published edition. This practice helps authors by offering proof and provenance of peer review; it helps readers by allowing them to identify peer-reviewed works; and it helps publishers by spreading their brand and recognizing their standard of peer review. Does this rule belong in a funder policy, or is it for authors and repository managers? Either way, I recommend it.

http://www.earlham.edu/~peters/fos/newsletter/05-02-05.htm#brand

As time passes, and OA becomes the default for more and more kinds of research literature, it may be possible to require green OA for the published versions of articles without harming authors. Institutions should watch for that moment.

Likewise, institutions should adapt their OA policy to the evolving forms of quality-controlled research publications, which needn't remain confined to what today are called journals. The purpose of these recommendations is to maximize OA for peer-reviewed research, not to entrench journals against change.

If you want to mandate open data, then what license should you demand? I recommend the public domain rather than an open license. For the supporting argument and a full analysis of the issues, see the Science Commons Protocol for Implementing Open Access Data.

http://sciencecommons.org/projects/publishing/open-access-data-protocol/

Some policies require OA for conference presentations. That can be a desirable option, but it's not as essential as OA for data or peer-reviewed articles. For research resulting in books, see #8 below.

(6) Scope of policy?

Should you apply your OA mandate only to research for which you are the sole funder? Or should you apply it even when the researcher has funding from other sources as well?

It can't be the first, or publishers who want to derail an OA mandate only have to give researchers a penny of supplementary funding. But if partial funding is enough to trigger the policy, should there be a threshold?

The Public Access to Science Act, introduced in the US House of Representatives in June 2003, tried to set a threshold. It applied an OA mandate to all works "substantially funded" by the federal government. (The bill was the first anywhere that would have mandated OA; it never came up for a vote.)

http://www.earlham.edu/~peters/fos/newsletter/07-04-03.htm#sabo

The problem is that the substantiality threshold is vague. It's not obvious to researchers, who would therefore not know whether they were bound to comply. Nor is it obvious to funding agencies, who would therefore not know whether to demand compliance. We could replace the vague threshold with a sharp one, for example, a specific percentage like 30%. But without a lot of complicated bookkeeping, researchers wouldn't know whether a particular grant exceeded 30% of their total funding, for example, if different grants kicked in at different times and covered different aspects of the project. Nor would funders know when their grant exceeded 30% of the grantee's total without examining the grantee's financial records.

Recommendation: For simplicity and enforceability, follow the example of most funding agencies: apply your OA policy to research you fund "in whole or in part."

This rule also has the benefit of making the policy clear when a research team has many members, or an article many co-authors, and only one of them is your grantee. Your interest in OA won't be held hostage by unfunded or differently-funded co-authors, whether they were good faith participants or added cynically to evade the policy. Grantees bear the responsibility of telling their co-authors that they are bound by the funder's OA policy.

What about the scope of the policy in time? I recommend following most agencies: make the policy prospective only, at least at first. It applies to all research funded on or after a certain date. Or use the NIH variation on this theme: the policy applies to all articles (based on funded research) accepted for publication on or after a certain date. I also recommend the second step pioneered by the Wellcome Trust: one year after mandating OA prospectively, mandate OA for the results of all previous grants still generating publications.

(7) What embargo?

All funder OA mandates allow delays between the publication of a work and its OA release to the public. The main reason is to give publishers a chance to recoup their expenses and relieve the pressure to refuse to publish works subject to OA policies.

The appropriate length of an embargo is a matter of dispute and experimentation. All medical funders with OA mandates use six month embargoes, except the NIH, which uses a 12 month embargo. The EU pilot project uses different embargo periods for different fields, ranging from 6 to 12 months. The European Research Council currently uses a six month embargo but says it is "keenly aware of the desirability to shorten" it. The publishing lobby generally wants longer embargoes than any of these, even though many individual publishers voluntarily provide OA to their publications after a 6–12 month delay, with no apparent harmful consequences.

The embargo periods built into OA mandates represent permissible delays, not mandatory delays. For example, the Wellcome Trust policy requires OA "as soon as possible and in any event within six months of the journal publisher's official date of final publication." No policy anywhere requires a mandatory delay.

An embargo in this sense is about when a work becomes OA, not when it is deposited (without OA) in a suitable repository. It's perfectly consistent, and even desirable, for OA policies to allow delays before deposits become OA, but not to allow delays for deposits themselves (see #9).

An OA mandate undercuts its own force if it allows an embargo but puts no upper limit on its duration. Without a deadline, grantees never need to make their work OA and there's no effective sense in which the policy is mandatory. For this purpose, vague deadlines ("within a reasonable time after publication") are equivalent to no deadlines.

Recommendation: Cap the permissible embargo at six months. Any embargo is a compromise with the public interest; even when they are justified compromises (and I've argued elsewhere that they are), the shorter they are, the better.

If publishers insist that a six month embargo will harm them, ask for evidence that the existing OA mandates with six month embargoes have harmed them. At least in your own mind, ask as well why an extra increment of revenue for publishers should justify an extra incursion on the public interest. If publishers insist that funders should not allow any embargoes shorter than those the publishers themselves allow, ask why you should put publisher interests ahead of your own interests. If publishers insist that a study is necessary before adopting the policy you have in mind, point out that many studies are already under way, including the natural experiment of monitoring the consequences of existing OA mandates. At most, offer to modify your embargo period in light of future evidence. But be clear that future evidence may show that shorter embargoes may achieve the same policy objectives as longer ones.

(8) What exceptions?

If your policy spells out the types of work to which it applies (see #5), then it usually needn't spell out the types to which it doesn't apply. The second is implied by the first. But you can reassure anxious researchers by enumerating some of the exceptions anyway. That's why the 2006 version of FRPAA explicitly exempted work not intended for publication (such as lab notes, phone records, preliminary data and analyses, drafts), work rejected by publishers, and work that is only published in royalty-producing forms like books. Enumerating the exceptions can also disarm lobbies ready to pounce, which is why FRPAA explicitly exempted patentable discoveries and classified research.

Recommendation: Exempt private notes and records not intended for publication. Exempt classified research. Either exempt patentable discoveries or allow an embargo long enough for the researcher to apply for a patent. (This could be a special embargo not allowed to other research.) And unless you fund research which often results in royalty-producing books, exempt royalty-producing books.

There's no need to make a permanent exemption for patentable research. Since your policy applies to work that grantees have chosen to publish, it does not force their hands or compel disclosures they are unwilling to make.

Books are hard cases for funder policies. One principle requires funded work to be OA, especially when the funds flow from taxpayers. But another principle limits OA to works, like journal articles, which authors publish without expectation of payment. Despite this tension, I've defended the possibility of OA mandates for books, even royalty-producing books.

http://www.earlham.edu/~peters/fos/2008/01/very-idea-of-funder-oa-mandate-for.html

http://www.earlham.edu/~peters/fos/2008/01/more-on-possibility-of-funder-oa.html

The critical condition is author consent. Researchers must know when applying for a grant that the funder's OA policy will apply to books based on the funded research, not just journal articles. While author consent suffices (under the principle, injuria non fit volenti), two other considerations support the justification and even facilitate author consent. First, for nearly all research monographs, the benefits of OA outweigh the value of royalties. Why? Because, for nearly all research monographs, royalties range from meager to zero, and the negligible royalties do not diminish the value of OA in an enlarged audience and increased impact. Second, a growing body of evidence shows that, for monographs, an OA edition boosts sales of the priced, print edition.

http://ur1.ca/14hz

(9) What timetable?

Most repository software now allows deposits to be open or closed, at the author's choice. Submissions are not OA just because they are on deposit; they are OA because they are on deposit and the author has chosen to make them OA. If a work is initially "dark," the author or repository manager may switch it to OA at a later date.

This feature allows us to distinguish the timing of deposit from the timing of OA release. Publisher objections to OA do not apply to dark deposits. So even when a publisher requires an embargo before OA, authors may deposit their postprints much earlier and switch them to OA when the embargo runs. The advantage of early deposit is that authors or repository managers don't have to hunt down the manuscript 6–12 months later, let alone scan or rekey it. Nor do authors have to interrupt a new research project to tie up a loose end on an old one.

At repositories like PubMed Central, which put submissions into a common format and add links and other features, immediate deposit gives the funder time to do the needed processing and still release the OA version at the end of the embargo period. If the deposit isn't made until the embargo period ends, then the processing delays the OA release even further.

Recommendation: Require deposit of the full text and metadata at the time an article is accepted for publication. Require OA for the metadata from the time of deposit, even if the full text must initially be dark. Require OA for the full text as soon as the publisher embargo runs, or as soon as your own deadline arrives, whichever comes first.

I call this the dual deposit/release strategy and Stevan Harnad calls it immediate deposit / optional access. It insures that the article is in the repository and ready to be switched to OA, that the metadata are making the article visible to search engines and potential users, and that the article is switched to OA, sometimes automatically, at the earliest possible moment.

http://www.earlham.edu/~peters/fos/newsletter/08-02-06.htm#dual

http://openaccess.eprints.org/index.php?/archives/71-guid.html

EPrints and DSpace repositories support an "email request button" allowing users to request an email copy of an article on dark deposit. The request is automatically routed to the author, who only needs to click "yes" to send the text on its way. As long as we have to live with embargoes, we can mitigate the damage with early deposits, OA metadata, and email circulation.

(10) Source of permission?

There are two basic ways for you to secure the needed permissions for OA and steer clear of copyright infringement.

First, you could get the permissions from publishers, after authors transfer their rights. In practice, mandates of this type require OA to a certain version on a certain timetable except when the grantee's publisher won't allow it. The funder policy defers to publisher policies. For example, the UK Economic & Social Research Council (ESRC) requires OA "where this is permitted by publishers' licensing or copyright arrangements." The Canadian Institutes of Health Research (CIHR) requires OA "where allowable and in accordance with publisher policies."

Second, you could close this loophole and get the permissions from authors before authors transfer any rights to publishers. Mandates of this type take advantage of the fact that funders are upstream from publishers and their funding contracts bind researchers long before those researchers sign copyright transfer agreements with publishers. Your funding contract can require grantees to retain the right to authorize OA on your terms. When a given publisher will not allow OA on your terms, you can require the grantee to look for another publisher. This approach was pioneered by the Wellcome Trust in 2004 and subsequently adopted by the Arthritis Research Campaign (ARC, UK), Cancer Research UK (CR-UK), Department of Health (UK), Howard Hughes Medical Institute (HHMI, US), Joint Information Systems Committee (JISC, UK), Medical Research Council (MRC, UK), and the National Institutes of Health (NIH, US).

The first method removes all the teeth from the mandate and puts publisher interests ahead of funder interests. It makes permission depend on publishers, who will often withhold it. The second method mandates OA to all the funder's research, not just a subset of it, and replaces contingent publisher permission with assured author permission. If the second method triggered more publisher refusals than accommodation, then it would hurt authors and limit their freedom to submit to the journals of their choice. But in fact publisher refusals are very rare, and publishers look for ways to accommodate these policies. It helps that this method is now adopted by some very large funders, including the NIH, the largest funder of non-classified research in the world.

Recommendation: If you're serious about wanting OA for the research you fund, close the loophole and adopt the second strategy. If you decided (back in #1) to require OA rather than request it, then this recommendation follows directly from your earlier decision. Policies with loopholes for unwilling publishers may use mandatory language, but they function like requests and cannot provide the needed permissions for 100% of your research until 100% of your grantees' publishers agree to play along. The second method shows that you don't have to leave this decision up to publishers.

In the US, two federal regulations give federal funding agencies "a royalty-free, non-exclusive and irrevocable right to reproduce, publish, or otherwise use the work for Federal purposes, and to authorize others to do so." One regulation, 45 CFR 74.36(a) (2003) applies to all agencies within the Department of Health and Human Services, including the NIH. The other, 2 CFR 215.36(a) (2005) applies to all federal agencies, not just to those within HHS.

https://www.law.cornell.edu/cfr/text/45/74.36

https://www.law.cornell.edu/cfr/text/2/215.36

In countries with such standing licenses, it should be unnecessary to rely on publisher consent and unnecessary to ask grantees to retain any rights. For example, the 2006 version of FRPAA relied on the second of these licenses. However, the method used by the NIH policy now has the advantage of being battle-tested. If it permitted any copyright infringement, publishers who bitterly oppose the policy would be in court suing to stop it. But because the policy doesn't allow any infringement, and has survived this kind of "hostile scrutiny," the publishing lobby must turn to Congress instead and ask it to amend US copyright law.

http://www.earlham.edu/~peters/fos/newsletter/10-02-08.htm#nih

(11) Pay publication fees?
When your grantees want to publish in a fee-based OA journal, will you help them pay the fees? You could allow them to use grant funds for this purpose, letting them decide its priority relative to other research needs. Or you could allow them to request

supplemental funding specifically for the fees. Some funders do one, some the other, and some don't offer to pay the fees at all.

The main reason to pay these fees, when you can, is to support gold OA alongside green OA. There are many reasons to do this, but the main one is to cultivate peer-reviewed OA journals in case the growing volume of green OA causes the decline or demise of TA peer-reviewed journals. (Note that paying these fees only supports the fee-based OA journals, and most OA journals charge no fees.) Will green OA actually cause the decline or demise of TA journals? Nobody knows yet; currently the evidence suggests not, but that may change as the volume of OA rises in many different fields.

http://www.earlham.edu/~peters/fos/newsletter/09-02-07.htm#peerreview

Recommendation: If you can afford it, offer to pay the fees. If you can, offer supplemental funds for the purpose. When journal publication fees must compete with equipment, assistants, and supplies, grantees may have a disincentive to publish in OA journals, which is the opposite of what's intended. But if you can't offer supplemental funds, allowing grantees to use grant funds is better than nothing. Whenever you pay publication fees, then demand that the journal provide libre OA (#4).

Do not offer to pay publication fees at hybrid OA journals using the "double-charge" business model: charging publication fees for OA articles without reducing subscription fees in proportion to the number of OA articles they publish. Paying their fees simply enriches cynical publishers at the expense of funders and libraries. Note that not all hybrid OA journals use the double-charge model, and there's no reason to shun those, like Oxford and Springer, which cut subscription prices roughly in proportion to author uptake of their OA option. Last November, ETH Zürich became the first institution otherwise willing to pay publication fees to draw the line at double-charging hybrid journals. Its rule should become the norm.

A willingness to pay publication fees will give one more answer to TA journals worried that green OA will force them to convert to OA. This policy tells them that if they do convert, funders will help pay the costs of publication. At some agencies, this is as important to the funder as it is to the publisher. Many funders who mandate green OA want to know that if green OA does undermine TA journal subscriptions, then a new generation of OA peer-review providers will be ready to take their place.

NIH is willing to pay the fees, but it does not allocate new funds for them, it puts a reasonableness condition on them, and offers to pay reasonable fees at both OA and TA journals (for example, publication fees at OA journals, page and color charges at TA journals).

http://publicaccess.nih.gov/FAQ.htm#810

I support the reasonableness condition. There's no need to pay whatever fee a journal chooses to charge. But while the parity between OA and TA journals seems even-handed and fair, I don't think it's justified. On the contrary, I believe that public funding agencies like the NIH have an obligation to put an OA condition on their largesse. If they pay page or color charges at a TA journal, they should demand that the article be OA (indeed, libre OA, #4).

(12) What sanctions?

What if your grantees don't comply with your policy? How will you nudge them toward compliance? If need be, how will you enforce the policy?

OA mandates put an OA condition on a research grant, which implies that if the condition is not met, the funding may be withheld. No funder policy anywhere imposes a penalty beyond that, such as forcing grantees to repay funds already disbursed. Most policies, including all of the RCUK policies and FRPAA, are silent on sanctions. The NIH doesn't even take past compliance into account when evaluating new applications, but it does say that "non-compliance will be addressed administratively, and may delay or prevent awarding of funds."

http://publicaccess.nih.gov/FAQ.htm#763

In September 2008, the NIH sent a letter to grantees, reminding them of their obligation under the funding agreement.

http://grants.nih.gov/grants/guide/notice-files/NOT-OD-08-119.html

http://www.earlham.edu/~peters/fos/2008/09/more-on-how-nih-encourages-and-monitors.html

The reminder was very effective in nudging non-compliant grantees toward compliance. Earlier in the year Science Magazine described what options the agency had up its sleeve. "Other possible ways of forcing scofflaws to comply range from having a program director call with a reminder to 'the most extreme: suspending funds,' says NIH Deputy Director for Extramural Research Norka Ruiz Bravo."

http://www.sciencemag.org/cgi/content/full/319/5861/266

http://www.earlham.edu/~peters/fos/2008/01/more-on-nih-oa-mandate.html

Just last month the Wellcome Trust took began issuing similar reminders in what it called a compliance audit.

http://www.earlham.edu/~peters/fos/2009/01/compliance-audit-for-wellcome-trust-oa.html

Both the NIH and the Wellcome Trust send their compliance reminders to a grantee's institution, not just the grantee. This is a gentle and effective way to give universities their own interest in grantee compliance. The NIH laid the groundwork for this step by making clear in its policy that "institutions and investigators are responsible for ensuring that any publishing or copyright agreements concerning submitted articles fully comply with this Policy."

http://grants.nih.gov/grants/guide/notice-files/NOT-OD-08-033.html

http://www.earlham.edu/~peters/fos/2008/01/nih-releases-its-new-oa-policy.html

The University of Minho has another way to spread around the interest in grantee compliance, although it's easier for universities to apply than funders. It provides a "financial supplement" to departmental budgets in proportion to the departmental compliance rate. This creates an incentive for departments to create their own incentives, and to help faculty understand the policy and deposit their articles.

https://mx2.arl.org/Lists/SPARC-OAForum/Message/2807.html

http://www.earlham.edu/~peters/fos/2006/03/encouraging-oa-archiving-at-minho.html

The NIH policy also requires grantees to use the "Manuscript Submission reference number" in any future progress reports or funding applications "when citing applicable articles that arise from their NIH funded research." Since grantees obtain the needed reference numbers only when they deposit their work in PMC, enforcement is seamlessly blended into the routine.

Recommendation: There's a lot of wisdom evolving on ways to ensure compliance without cracking the whip. Start gently with reminders. Involve the grantee's institution, and make clear that both parties are responsible for compliance. Be prepared to delay or withhold funds. Require proof of deposit in progress reports and future funding applications.

*

Additional questions for universities

In most respects universities should follow the recommendations for funding agencies, replacing "grantees" with "faculty" and "research you fund" with "research produced at your institution." But here are some areas where their different circumstances raise different policy questions.

(13) Where deposit?

Funders may be agnostic about the OA repositories in which grantees deposit their work (#3), but universities should require faculty to deposit their work in the institutional repository. All the advantages of depositing in their IR listed in #3 still apply of course. But when the policy-maker is the university itself, there are new advantages to take into account. In particular, universities should recognize their interest in showcasing the work done at the university and their interest in helping researchers elsewhere benefit from it.

Recommendation: Launch an institutional repository, staff it adequately, and require faculty to deposit their peer-reviewed postprints in it. Remember the lessons of #1 above: launching a repository and requesting and encouraging deposits are not enough. The hard part of achieving OA, and not just endorsing it, is the policy to fill the repository. When the repository is your own, you're in an especially good position to set policy, monitor compliance, educate users, and provide incentives and assistance. For more on one the most powerful incentives, see #16.

Of course, depositing in the IR does not prevent faculty from depositing in their disciplinary repository as well, if they like. If the IR is willing, it could even use SWORD to automate those deposits and save faculty the trouble of making double deposits.

http://www.ukoln.ac.uk/repositories/digirep/index/SWORD

(14) What may be deposited?

Apart from what must be deposited (#5), what may be deposited?

Even when funding agencies host their own repositories, they tend not to allow grantees to deposit work they are not required to deposit. But if a university requires the deposit of peer-reviewed postprints, it may allow, and even encourage, the deposit of much else.

Recommendation: Allow the deposit of unrefereed preprints, previous journal articles, conference presentations (slides, text, audio, video), book manuscripts, book metadata (especially when the author cannot or will not deposit the full-text), and the contents of journals edited or published on campus. The more categories you allow, the more you cultivate a culture of self-archiving.

I'm only listing the research-related types of work that authors might deposit. But the university itself could consider other categories as well, such as open courseware, administrative records, and digitization projects from the library. For theses and dissertations, see #17.

(15) Allow faculty to opt-out?

While you should not allow publisher opt-outs (#10), faculty opt-outs are quite different. If you require faculty to provide OA to their peer-reviewed manuscripts, without exception, they may sometimes be unable to publish an otherwise acceptable article in the journal of their choice.

If you allow opt-outs, then you allow faculty to publish in any journal where their work is accepted, an important kind of faculty freedom. If your opt-outs only apply to OA, not to deposits, then you continue to respect that freedom but still collect all the articles in the repository. If your opt-outs are always temporary, like embargo policies, then all peer-reviewed manuscript on dark deposit will eventually be switched to OA.

A mandate with this kind of opt-out is not a contradiction in terms. It still does the important work of shifting the default from non-OA to OA. Faculty who don't want their manuscripts to be OA on the usual timetable must go to the trouble of requesting a waiver. That's not a heavy burden. In fact, it's about as light as self-archiving itself. But we know that the light burden of self-archiving has deterred many faculty from doing it, and it's likely that the light burden of requesting a waiver will deter many faculty from doing so. Changing the default can change behavior on a large scale.

Recommendation: Allow faculty to opt-out. But make the opt-outs apply only to OA, not to deposits—that is, require deposit of all faculty peer-reviewed postprints, even if some deposits are initially dark. And make the opt-outs temporary, so that all dark deposits can eventually be switched to OA. Harvard adds a nice touch: don't allow faculty to request opt-outs for all their works at once; require separate requests for separate articles.

As more TA journals convert to OA, and more accommodate university OA mandates, and as more universities adopt OA mandates, then universities may safely strengthen the policy by phasing out opt-outs or increasing the difficulty of obtaining them. If publishers accommodate university OA mandates, then opt-outs will not be necessary in order to protect faculty freedom to publish in the journals of their choice. When enough universities adopt OA mandates, we'll be there. But until then opt-outs preserve faculty freedom without reducing repository deposits or OA.

(16) Internal use?

You might think that an OA mandate has nothing to gain from incentives. But all OA mandates use some combination of mandatory language, clear expectations, encouragement, education, assistance, and incentives. Your OA mandate will cause compliance to edge toward 100%. But incentives can accelerate the process and remove some friction from the system.

Recommendation: Whenever the institution reviews faculty publications for promotion, tenure, funding, or any other internal purpose, limit the review of journal publications to those on deposit in the IR. This powerful incentive was adopted last year at Napier University and the University of Liege. Use your repository for internal evaluations of research, not just for external showcasing of research. Review the articles faculty want you to review, as before, but require that they be on deposit in the repository. Stop circulating stacks of paper to promotion and tenure committees and start circulating URLs to OA editions of the same work.

This recommendation will not lower standards for promotion and tenure—a common worry when anyone proposes a tweak to the process. It's not about P&T standards at all. It's about what faculty do with the articles on which they wish to be judged, not how they select those articles or how the committee evaluates them.

This a policy that will get faculty attention without lowering institutional standards, limiting faculty freedom, or increasing their rejection rate at journals. It's a way of saying: "Yes, we will evaluate your work on its merits, looking for quality. But we also care about access. The point of doing good research is to make it available to others who can build on it. This isn't an irrelevant bureaucratic requirement. It's a guarantee that your work will be as useful as possible. Our mission is not merely to encourage good work, but to make good work available to the world."

(17) Apply to ETDs?

Should your OA mandate also apply to electronic theses and dissertations (ETDs)? These are not peer-reviewed publications, or even preprints in the usual sense of the term. But they are careful works of scholarship, vetted over a longer time with more care than peer-reviewed journal articles. When approved, your faculty are saying that they are original and significant. Those are exactly the kinds of works that ought to be available to others. Even when dissertations are for sale from services like ProQuest, there's rarely a way to preview them for relevance before spending your money. Most libraries don't buy dissertations and only hold the ones written and approved at the institution. In an article a few years ago, I called them the most invisible form of useful literature and the most useful form of invisible literature. In the same article I argued that an OA requirement would actually elicit better work by asking students to write for a real audience beyond their committee.

http://www.earlham.edu/~peters/fos/newsletter/07-02-06.htm#etds

Recommendation: Extend your OA mandate to apply to ETDs. The fact that they are not publications means there is no publisher to demand payment or permission. Moreover, you start to cultivate the habit of self-archiving in the next generation of scholars. You send the message that green OA should be the default for significant works of scholarship.

Contrary to student fears, sometimes fed by faculty advisors, the evidence shows that OA dissertations do not reduce the author's ability to publish revised chapters as journal articles. But when a student has a reasonable fear, a dean could grant a temporary delay to the OA requirement. The whole work should be deposited as soon as it is approved, but the affected chapters could be left dark for a time. Similar temporary exemptions could be granted to students who have previously published a chapter as a journal article, and transferred copyright to a publisher, and students who made a patentable discovery and need time to apply for a patent.

A widely discussed controversy at the University of Iowa last year suggests that the period of dark deposit should be longer for creative writings, submitted for fine arts degrees, than research theses and dissertations submitted to other departments.

http://www.earlham.edu/~peters/fos/2008/03/controversy-over-oa-for-fine-arts.html

(18) Who decides?

Until 2008, university OA mandates were all adopted by administrators and one might well have wondered whether they were welcomed or resented by faculty. In February 2008 we saw the first faculty vote on an OA mandate, at the Harvard Faculty of Arts and Sciences. The faculty approved it unanimously. Soon the faculty at Harvard Law School also adopted an OA mandate by a unanimous vote, as did the faculty at the Stanford School of Education and Macquarie University.

It's too early to call this a trend. But if we look only at the 10 university mandates adopted in 2008, five were adopted by faculty themselves (Harvard FAS, Harvard Law, Stanford Education, Macquarie, and Stirling), and most of those were adopted unanimously (all but Stirling). The other half were adopted by administrators (Charles Stuart, Helsinki, Glasgow, Queen Margaret, and Southampton). As a tiebreaker, I can point out that the European University Association voted unanimously to recommend university-level OA mandates for its 791 institutional members in 46 countries.

Recommendation: Let the faculty decide. This method requires time for faculty entrepreneurs to educate their colleagues—sometimes a lot of time. But the result is more secure, more inspiring to faculty elsewhere, and more revealing of faculty attitudes (e.g., that low participation in self-archiving is more about lack of familiarity than informed opposition). However, a good policy adopted by administrators is still a good policy, and a lot better than no policy.

Conclusion

Here's a summary of the concessions to TA publishers built in to the policies I've recommended. The policy requires green OA and may encourage gold OA, but it doesn't require gold OA (#2). It requires gratis OA and may encourage libre OA, but it doesn't require libre OA (#4). It requires immediate deposit, but it doesn't require immediate OA (#7). It requires OA to the final version of the author's peer-reviewed manuscript, not to the published edition (#5). It gives publishers the option to replace the author's manuscript in the repository with the published edition (#5). It puts a citation and link to the published edition in the OA repository copy (#5). It offers to pay publication fees at fee-based OA journals, at least when the funder can afford to do so, directly helping OA publishers and creating a safety net for TA publishers (#11).

Note that many of the recommendations are time sensitive. Some stronger provisions which could backfire today will be wise and justified later. The case for compromise is not fixed and permanent. The balance of considerations will change over time.

Even when authors retain the right to authorize OA, giving publishers no legal ground to block it, publishers retain the right to refuse to publish any work for any reason. If the goal is to maximize OA to peer-reviewed literature, then a good policy depends on accommodation from peer-reviewed journals, and would be undermined by publisher refusals to publish work subject to an OA policy. But publisher accommodation doesn't depend only on the terms of a given policy; it also depends on the number and strength of other policies. If a publisher can refuse to publish work subject a strong OA policy, and still find enough other good work to publish, then it might do so. But this will change as more institutions adopt OA policies and more new work is subject to them. Likewise, as more TA journals convert to OA, and as more TA journals adapt to OA mandates without converting, then funders can strengthen their OA policies without increasing the rejection rates for authors.

Funders and universities should watch the shifting balance of power and seize opportunities to strengthen their policies. But the moments of opportunity will not be obvious and may not even be limned by objective evidence. The reason is that there is some self-fulfilling leadership at work here. Assess the climate created by existing policies and existing journals, but also assess the likely effects of your own action. Every strong, new policy increases the likelihood of publisher accommodation. Hence, every strong, new policy creates some of the conditions of its own success. Policies elsewhere don't just cover research elsewhere; they are implicit invitations to common action for a common purpose. View your own policy not only as a way to bring about OA for the research you control, but as a way to make the way easier for other institutions behind you.

Here are the major points on which the policy I recommend could be strengthened as circumstances change. It's now a green OA mandate but could become a gold OA mandate (#2). It's now a gratis OA mandate but could become a libre OA mandate (#4). It's now limited to the author's peer-reviewed manuscript but could later apply to the published edition (#5).

Postscript

For earlier versions of some of these thoughts, see:

Three principles for university open access policies, SOAN for April 2, 2008

http://www.earlham.edu/~peters/fos/newsletter/04-02-08.htm#principles

Ten lessons from the funding agency open access policies, SOAN for August 2, 2006

http://www.earlham.edu/~peters/fos/newsletter/08-02-06.htm#lessons

While the present article represents my current thinking, I stand by most of what I said in the older articles and they contain more detail on many of the points they cover.

In #18, I said it was too early to call unanimous faculty votes for university OA policies a trend. But now I can call it a trend. I wrote a follow-up essay in June 2010 enumerating 27 cases of unanimous faculty votes. After publishing the essay, I moved to the list to the Open Access Directory (a wiki), where users updated it further. The list now covers 50 policies.

http://www.earlham.edu/~peters/fos/newsletter/06-02-10.htm#votes

http://oad.simmons.edu/oadwiki/Unanimous_faculty_votes

Quality and Open Access

Open Access and Quality

From "Open access and quality," SPARC Open Access Newsletter, October 2, 2006.

http://dash.harvard.edu/handle/1/4552042

If an article is published in a toll-access (TA) journal and then deposited in an open-access (OA) repository, its quality does not change. And conversely, if it's first deposited in an OA repository and then published in a TA journal, its quality does not change. That's the sense in which quality and access are independent. It's obvious and it's basic. But it's not the whole story.

There are other, subtle ways in which quality and access intersect. This is an attempt to disentangle a large tangle of them.

Most of the ways in which access affects quality are very indirect. But there's one family of indirect effects that I won't cover here: the ways in which OA improves the quality of published research by improving the productivity of the researcher. That goes to the heart of the case for OA, but it's more familiar, and actually larger, than the topics I want to explore here.

*

The main factors that affect the quality of journal literature are price- and medium-independent: the quality of authors, the quality of editors, and the quality of referees. We know that these key players can be just as good at OA journals as at TA journals because they can be the very same people. An excellent TA journal can convert to OA and use the same standards and the same people that it used before. An excellent newly-launched OA journal can use the same people as an excellent TA journal. And of course two journals don't have to use the same people to use people of comparable skill and experience.

*

We have to acknowledge from the start that there are strong and weak OA journals, just as there are strong and weak TA journals.

Hence, any analysis focusing on weak OA journals and strong TA journals (as if to show the superiority of TA journals) would be as arbitrary as one focusing on weak TA journals and strong OA journals (as if to show the superiority of OA journals). Without some additional argument showing that the journals on which they focus are typical of their breeds, they would be guilty of cherry-picking and generalizing from an unrepresentative sample.

Moreover, we know that something has gone wrong if an argument for the virtues of either model implies that weak journals using that model do not exist.

*

TA publishers have often charged that OA journals compromise on peer review. The allegation is that if a journal accepts a fee for every paper it publishes, then it has an incentive to lower its standards in order to accept more papers. It sounds plausible but it doesn't stand up to scrutiny.

http://www.earlham.edu/~peters/fos/newsletter/03-02-04.htm#objreply

First, even if OA journals charging author-side fees have an incentive to accept more papers, it doesn't follow that they have an incentive to lower their standards. If they have a large number of excellent submissions, they can increase their acceptance rate without lowering standards. Unlike TA journals, they have no space limitations to hem them in.

Second, OA journals charging author-side fees often waive the fees in case of economic hardship. Not every accepted paper will create revenue, and some will have the opposite effect.

Third, OA journals charging author-side fees have editorial firewalls in place to insulate the peer-review process from business decisions about fees. For example, it's very common for editors not to know whether an author has requested a fee waiver. Many OA journals ensure that at least one voice in the editorial decision is not employed by the journal and has no financial stake in the outcome. At most of the new hybrid OA journals, authors don't even communicate their decision on the OA option until after the paper has been accepted.

Fourth, just like TA journals, OA journals know that their submissions and prestige depend on their quality. Preserving their quality will always be more valuable to them than another fee. This is especially true when we realize that the fees themselves are set at or near (and sometimes below) the subsistence level. A journal gains nothing and loses much if it lowers its quality in order to bring in a fee that does little more than pay the costs of bringing in the fee.

Fifth, the majority of OA journals charge no author-side fees at all.

http://www.earlham.edu/~peters/fos/newsletter/06-02-06.htm#facts

We're hearing less of this objection now that some of the critics (like Elsevier and the Royal Society) are offering hybrid journals and accepting author-side fees themselves. As full and hybrid OA journals spread, the objection will continue to fade away.

*

Is peer review at OA journals less rigorous than at TA journals? In October 2005 the Kaufman-Wills report (The Facts About Open Access) concluded that it was, based on a finding that TA journals used external reviewers, or reviewers outside the journal's editorial staff, more often than OA journals. However, a subsequent addendum retracted most of that conclusion as based on an erroneous interpretation of peer review practices at BioMed Central.

The Kaufman-Wills report (October 11, 2005)

http://www.alpsp.org/Ebusiness/ProductCatalog/Product.aspx?ID=47

Post-publication addendum (October 28, 2005)

http://82.45.151.109/Ebusiness/Libraries/Publication_Downloads/FAOAaddendum .sflb.ashx

For more details on the original criticism of OA journals and the post-publication retraction and clarification, see my interview with Cara Kaufman (November 2, 2005).

http://www.earlham.edu/~peters/fos/newsletter/11-02-05.htm#kaufman

On the other side, there are reasons to think that TA journals face stronger incentives to lower standards than OA journals.

First, the Kaufman-Wills report showed that more subscription journals charge author-side fees than OA journals. Author-side fees needn't cause a lowering of standards at either kind of journal. But insofar as they have that tendency, TA journals are afflicted more often than OA journals.

(Not only do a greater number of TA journals charge author-side fees, but a greater percentage of them do so as well. Of course, at a TA journal, author-side fees are laid on top of reader-side subscription fees.)

Second, TA journals often justify price increases by pointing to the growing volume of published articles. This is the incentive that critics saw in fee-based OA journals: the incentive to increase quantity in order to increase revenue. As with OA journals, this needn't result in a decrease in quality; but insofar as it has that tendency, the problem exists at both kinds of journals. Is it worse at TA journals? Consider the next factor.

Third, subscription fees at TA journals include substantial profits or surpluses, often more than 35%. An EPS report from July 2006 showed that the *average* profit margin at STM publishers in 2005 was 25%.

http://www.econtentmag.com/Articles/ArticleReader.aspx?ArticleID=16942&Category ID=17

http://www.earlham.edu/~peters/fos/2006_07_09_fosblogarchive.html#11528820
6732578292

At fee-based OA journals, the incentive to accept more papers to generate revenue is small, because the fees barely cover their costs. At TA journals, the incentive to accept more papers to justify price increases is much larger, because subscriptions often contain significant profits or surpluses. As I've noted, when a journal has an abundance of excellent submissions, then it can increase quantity without decreasing quality. But when it doesn't have enough excellent submissions, then it can only accept more papers by lowering standards.

Not all TA journals have towering profit margins. Not all are even in the black. However—though no one has yet done the relevant studies—I would bet that subscription revenue exceeds costs more often at TA journals than fee revenue does at OA journals, and conversely, that fee revenue falls below costs more often at OA journals than subscription revenue does at TA journals. If so, then the average TA journal using increased quantity to justify price increases will get a bigger revenue bump from increasing its acceptance rate than the average OA journal will. Hence, the incentive to increase the acceptance rate by lowering standards is stronger at TA journals than at OA journals. Within the domain of TA journals, it's stronger at high-profit journals than at low-profit or non-profit journals.

TA publishers who gloated at the news—last June—that PLoS would have to supplement fee revenue with foundation grants didn't realize that the same news showed that PLoS has no incentive to lower its standards in order to bring in more insufficient fees. Or at least TA publishers with any kind of profit margin have a greater incentive to lower standards, accept more papers, and justify a price increase. Are OA journal fees high enough to corrupt peer review or too low to pay the bills? Critics can't have it both ways.

Fourth, if TA journals have a shortage of excellent submissions, they cannot publish a short issue without shortchanging subscribers. Hence, to fill an issue they must lower their standards. Because OA journals don't have subscribers, they are free to publish short issues limited to their first-rate submissions.

Fifth, TA journals with lower standards, lower submission rates, and (consequently) lower rejection rates have higher profit margins than journals with higher standards and higher submission rates. The reason is that journals with lower rejection rates perform peer review fewer times per published paper. Hence, publishers seeking higher margins have an incentive to lower standards. (This is compatible of course with the existence of other incentives pulling in the opposite direction.)

This is the conclusion of financial analysts at Credit Suisse First Boston, published on April 6, 2004. The report is not online but I wrote a summary for SOAN.

http://www.earlham.edu/~peters/fos/newsletter/05-03-04.htm#creditsuisse

The same Credit Suisse report shows that bundling can protect weak journals from cancellation and thereby insulate publishers from the market forces that would ordinarily punish declining quality.

Note that some of these incentives amplify one another. For a TA journal, lowering standards and lowering the rejection rate not only enlarges the journal and justifies price increases but also lowers the costs of peer review and increases profit margins.

*

There's evidence from TA journals that have shortened their embargoes or converted to OA that OA increases submissions. If it increases submissions, then it allows the journal to increase selectivity and improve the quality of the accepted articles.

From an interview with Elizabeth Marincola, then-Director of the American Society for Cell Biology, which publishes Molecular Biology of the Cell (Open Access Now, October 6, 2003):

http://web.archive.org/web/20031115185846/

http://www.biomedcentral.com/openaccess/archive/?page=features&issue=6

> What happened after ASCB decided to provide OA to all the articles in MBC after only two months, the shortest embargo in the industry? "We have not lost subscription income, our submissions have gone up and our meeting programs have held strong. Financially we have been able to have our cake and eat it."

From T. Scott Plutchak, Editor of the Journal of the Medical Library Association (Lib-License, February 10, 2005):

http://www.library.yale.edu/~llicense/ListArchives/0502/msg00172.html

> The Journal of the Medical Library Association (JMLA) ... has been open access via PubMed Central since September 2001. At present, every article, letter, editorial and feature of every issue, back to volume 1, issue 1, July 1911, is available. The online version is generally up within a day or two of the hard copy arriving on my desk. ... Benefits? Although difficult to quantify, I'd say we're seeing greatly increased readership, a striking increase in manuscript submissions, particularly from overseas, and vastly increased value of the older material, since it is now so easy to get to.

From Sara Schroter (BMJ, February 14, 2006):

http://dx.doi.org/doi:10.1136/bmj.38705.490961.55

> Three quarters (159/211) [of surveyed authors] said the fact that all readers would have free access to their paper on bmj.com was very important or important to their decision to submit to BMJ. Over half (111/211) said closure of free access to research articles would make them slightly less likely to submit research articles to the BMJ in the future, 14% (29/211) said they would be much less likely to submit, and 34% (71/211) said it would not influence their decision.

From D.K. Sahu and Ramesh Parmar (the Neil Jacobs anthology from Chandos Publishing, 2006):

http://openmed.nic.in/1599/

> OA has certainly helped the Indian journals to reach an international audience ... The number of manuscripts submitted to the journals has increased many fold (see Figure 19.1), with increases in the number of articles coming from other countries ranging from 12–44% for various journals (see Figure 19.2).

Finally, here's an argument I made in SOAN for March 2005:

http://www.earlham.edu/~peters/fos/newsletter/03-02-05.htm#coexistence

> For authors, the only reason to submit work to a TA journal is its prestige. In every other way, TA journals are inferior to OA journals because they limit an author's audience and impact. OA journals will start to draw submissions away from top TA journals as soon as they approach them in prestige. And by the time they equal them in prestige, the best TA journals will have lost their one remaining competitive advantage.

There is abundant evidence that OA increases citation impact.

http://opcit.eprints.org/oacitation-biblio.html

I've often argued that citation impact is not the same thing as quality, and I haven't changed my mind. But I can justify talking about citation impact here because for many authors, funding agencies, and university promotion and tenure committees, citation impact is a crude surrogate for quality. Some acknowledge its crudity, or its divergence from a true quality measurement; but at the same time, some act as if they preferred impact to quality, insofar as the two diverge.

Some critics have argued that part of the correlation between OA and citation impact is due to a quality bias: authors preferentially self-archive their best work. Studies by Tim Brody, Chawki Hajjem, Stevan Harnad, and Gunther Eysenbach show that there is a substantial OA citation advantage even after correcting for any effects of this bias. I doubt that the debate is over, but for present purposes we needn't decide the question. Either OA articles have greater impact than TA articles even after we control for quality, or OA articles have a higher average impact because they have a higher average quality.

If self-archiving authors do preferentially deposit their best work, then the reason could be called author pride—the quality filter that costs publishers nothing. All published articles pass through this filter, of course. But published and then self-archived articles pass through it twice.

Just for the record: I'm not saying that author pride suffices; on the contrary, we still need peer review, sometimes to ratify author pride but more often to check it. Nor am I saying that the existence of a self-archiving bias arising from author pride negates the evidence for an OA impact advantage; on the contrary, I accept the evidence that a significant impact advantage remains even after subtracting the self-archiving quality bias.

I wrote about one form of quality bias in BMJ for May 2005.

http://bmj.bmjjournals.com/cgi/content/full/330/7500/1097

This is an editorial commenting on a study by Jonathan Wren, also from May 2005.

http://bmj.bmjjournals.com/cgi/content/full/330/7500/1128

Note that the OA impact advantage centers on the citation tally for individual articles, not the impact factor of whole journals. Insofar as OA increases the citation tally for articles, it will tend to increase the impact factor for journals. But other articles from the same journal might raise or lower the impact factor, muddying the water. In 2004 Thomson Scientific did two studies of the impact factors of OA journals, and both showed that OA journals had competitive numbers. Despite the relative youth of OA journals, even in 2004 there was at least one OA journal in the top cohort of impact factors in nearly every scientific discipline.

First Thomson study: James Testa and Marie E. McVeigh, The Impact of Open Access Journals: A Citation Study from Thomson ISI, April 14, 2004.

http://www.isinet.com/media/presentrep/acropdf/impact-oa-journals.pdf

Second Thomson study: Marie E. McVeigh, Open Access Journals in the ISI Citation Databases: Analysis of Impact Factors and Citation Patterns Thomson Scientific, October 2004.

http://www.isinet.com/media/presentrep/essayspdf/openaccesscitations2.pdf

Journal prices don't correlate with impact or quality. In fact, Theodore and Carl Bergstrom have shown that journal prices are either unrelated to quality or inversely related to it. In their analysis of journal prices and citation impact (Nature, May 20, 2004), they conclude that "libraries typically must pay 4 to 6 times as much per page for journals owned by commercial publishers as for journals owned by non-profit societies. These differences in price do not reflect differences in the quality of the journals. In fact the commercial journals are on average less cited than the non-profits and the average cost per citation of commercial journals ranges from 5 to 15 times as high as that of their non-profit counterparts."

http://www.nature.com/nature/focus/accessdebate/22.html

http://www.earlham.edu/~peters/fos/2006_06_25_fosblogarchive.html#115168252 782138224

Golnessa Galyani Moghaddam confirmed this conclusion in a study published this summer (Libri, June 2006). Not only do for-profit journals cost more than non-profit journals per issue or per volume, they also cost more per citation and per point of impact factor. Moreover, of the top 30 journals by usage at the Indian Institute of Science, 20 were non-profits and only 10 were for-profits.

http://eprints.rclis.org/8547/

http://legacy.earlham.edu/~peters/fos/2006/07/more-evidence-that-journal-prices -dont.html

By hugely enlarging the audience, OA makes authors more careful. If you like, consider this another effect of author pride.

In SOAN for July 2006, I argued that one reason for graduate schools to mandate OA for theses and dissertations is to improve their quality:

http://www.earlham.edu/~peters/fos/newsletter/07-02-06.htm#etds

> All teachers know that students work harder and do better work when they know they are writing for a real audience—large or small—beyond the teacher. The effect is amplified if they are writing for the public. Some teachers try to harness this power by telling students to write as if their work were to appear on the front page of the New York Times. Some arrange to give students a real audience beyond the teacher. In a law course in which I conducted moot court, the quality of student preparation and argument improved dramatically after I started video-taping them. I didn't even have to put the videos online; I just put them on reserve in the library for the rest of the semester. ... OA gives authors a real audience beyond the dissertation committee and real incentives to do original, impressive work. ... [E]ven when grad students think it's safe and easy to fool their committee, it's risky and difficult to fool the world.

The Chronicle of Higher Education quoted a Yale professor to the same effect just last month:

http://web.archive.org/web/20080704211022/

http://chronicle.com/daily/2006/09/2006092001t.htm

> Ramamurti Shankar, a professor of physics who is teaching one of [Yale's new OA] courses, said knowing that his lecture might be watched online by a wide audience keeps him on his toes. "I have to be a little more careful than I usually am," he said.

Here's a variation on the same theme: OA keeps authors honest.

Citing OA articles makes it easy for readers to verify that authors are accurately summarizing the cited work or data. Citing TA articles makes this harder (but clearly, not impossible) and to that extent protects authors who want to blow smoke. The most detailed case I've seen for this conclusion is also the most recent: Mark Liberman, Open-access sex stereotypes, Language Log, September 10, 2006.

http://itre.cis.upenn.edu/~myl/languagelog/archives/003565.html

http://www.earlham.edu/~peters/fos/2006_09_10_fosblogarchive.html#115799535
190633252

Here's another variation on the theme: OA deters plagiarism. In the early days, some authors worried that OA would increase the incentive to plagiarize their work. But this worry made no sense and has not been borne out. On the contrary. OA might make plagiarism easier to commit, for people trolling for text to cut and paste. But for the same reason, OA makes plagiarism more hazardous to commit. Insofar as OA makes plagiarism easier, it's only for plagiarism from OA sources. But plagiarism from OA sources is the easiest kind to detect. Not all plagiarists are smart, of course, but the smart ones are steering clear of OA sources.

For the same reason, they'll avoid OA dissemination for any of their own works containing plagiarized passages.

The first tendency improves the average integrity of work quoting OA literature. The second improves the average integrity of OA literature itself.

Because OA will only reduce plagiarism by smart plagiarists, the effect may be small. And today the effect is small in any case because so little of the literature is OA. But just as we can expect good things from a pest-resistant strain of wheat, even when we've just introduced it in one field, we can expect good things from this plagiarism-resistant strain of research literature.

*

The EC's Study on the Economic and Technical Evolution of the Scientific Publication Markets in Europe (dated January 2006 but apparently not released until late March or early April) recommended that we widen our concept of a journal's quality to include quality of access or quality of dissemination. This is an excellent idea.

http://europa.eu.int/rapid/pressReleasesAction.do?reference=IP/06/414&format=HTML&aged=0&language=EN&guiLanguage=en

http://www.earlham.edu/~peters/fos/newsletter/05-02-06.htm#ecreport

A critic might object that even if adopted, this wouldn't change the fact that the OA/TA status of an individual article is independent of the article's quality. That's true but beside the point. The report isn't trying redefine the quality of articles, but to recognize other kinds of quality. When academic publishers give awards to good journals, they recognize many kinds of quality, including (for example) quality of design. That's the kind of enlargement of our thinking the EC study recommends, but it focuses in particular on quality of access, which publisher award ceremonies tend to overlook. When libraries decide what to buy, renew, or cancel, they consider many kinds of quality, including quality of access. For example, they take price into account, as one criterion among many others, and for TA electronic journals they investigate whether they will still have access to subscribed issues after they cancel.

Now and then someone will suggest that OA is fine for second-rate work but not for first-rate work. This claim is more sniffed than elaborated, so it's hard to tell what the argument is.

If it's saying that high-quality, high-prestige journals will never or rarely be OA, or vice versa, then it's a prediction, not a datum. Moreover, it seems to be a false prediction. There are already high-quality, high-prestige OA journals, for example, the Beilstein Journal of Chemistry, Nucleic Acids Research, and PLoS Biology.

(I pick these three to show that OA, quality, and prestige can exist together under a variety of circumstances: two charge author-side fees and one doesn't; two are from non-profit publishers and one from a for-profit; two are converted TA journals and one was born OA.)

There are more than this list of three, of course. But one reason there aren't already more than there are is that most OA journals are new. Even when new journals are excellent from birth, it takes time for their prestige to catch up with their quality. Another reason is that most of the money to pay for peer-reviewed journals is still tied up in support of TA journals. Since neither of these explanations depends on any intrinsic limitation in the quality of OA journals, we have good reason to think that the numbers of high-quality, high-prestige OA journals will grow as we remove the barriers to their growth.

I can accept one form of the premise, namely, that so far most high-quality, high-prestige journals are TA. But of course, so far, most low-quality, low-prestige journals are also TA. Moreover, the present ratio of excellent TA journals to excellent OA journals is just a present fact about a very dynamic, rapidly changing situation, not a fact about the intrinsic quality of either kind of journal. To mistake it for more would be like arguing in 1980 that more prestigious journals used typewriters than computers, and therefore that computers must have some intrinsic limitation keeping their numbers down.

I can accept another, more important form of the premise, namely, that most authors will seek prestige before OA, if they have to choose. The mistake is to assume that they have to choose.

There are two reasons why there's no trade-off here. First, there are already high-quality, high-prestige OA journals and their existence shows that nothing intrinsic to OA blocks that path. Second, authors can publish in a prestigious TA journal and then deposit their postprint in an OA repository. About 70% of TA journals already give blanket permission for this and many of the others will give permission after an individual request.

http://www.sherpa.ac.uk/romeo/statistics.ph

There's a related argument (related because it's more sniffed than elaborated) that the internet is the proper home for crap, not scholarship. It's really more prejudice than argument, and in 2006 it's more dead than alive. Hence, you may think it no longer deserves a response. But it was common in the early days of the net, and when it was common it was also self-fulfilling. It was one (of many) early obstacles to OA, and we're still struggling to overcome its effects. Moreover, it isn't completely dead.

It's true that the crap/gold ratio was very high in the early days of the net. But even then it didn't follow that there was no gold, let alone that there shouldn't be. And today the only people who can still say that there's no high-quality, peer-reviewed work in their fields on the internet are the ones who aren't paying attention.

Even though scholars generally know that there is good scholarship online, there is still a sense in some quarters that quality work belongs elsewhere, or that good work online is harmed by its association with crap. For example, at universities giving grad students the option to submit dissertations electronically, and where OA for electronic submissions is the default, there's evidence that some professors advise their graduate students against it. They're trying to preserve their students' chances of publishing parts of the dissertation in the future (well-intentioned but uninformed) and trying to make their students look like real scholars rather than camp-followers (ironically more camp-following than scholarly).

The attitude is often accompanied by mutterings about the dislike of reading long or difficult works online or the love of printed books—which I share, by the way, but which are compatible with taking full advantage of the benefits online dissemination. Just as often it's accompanied by mutterings that "you get what you pay for." And of course it's still true that the internet is full of crap, though it's false that that crap/gold ratio hasn't declined steadily in the past decade and false that the tools for finding the gold haven't improved just as steadily. It's true that putting peer-reviewed scholarship online puts it in the same bin as a lot of crap, but the same is true of the bin of print. What's astonishing is that smart people can forget that the low quality of the crap online doesn't affect the high quality of the scholarship online. More critically, putting peer-reviewed scholarship online doesn't add to the crap online; it dilutes the crap online.

If the same squeamishness about online dissemination had infected print dissemination in the age of Gutenberg, on the ground that real scholarship was inscribed by hand on goatskin, then every kind of knowledge would have been held back. What's striking is that those still carrying traces of this prejudice would rather follow the (literally) hide-bound customs of their field than take advantage of new technologies to pursue their own interests.

Thinking about Prestige, Quality, and Open Access

From "Thinking about prestige, quality, and open access," SPARC Open Access Newsletter, September 2, 2008.

http://dash.harvard.edu/handle/1/4322577

I've been thinking a lot lately about how journal quality and prestige overlap, how they diverge, and how their complex interaction affects the prospects for open access (OA). Here are a dozen thoughts or theses about prestige and OA. Some are commonplace, but I include them because they help me build up to others which are not. I start with the rough notion that if journal quality is real excellence, then journal prestige is reputed excellence.

(1) Universities reward faculty who publish in high-prestige journals, and faculty are strongly motivated to do so. If universities wanted to create this incentive, they have succeeded.

Researchers have always been motivated by their research topics. If all journals were equal in prestige, or if all journals were equal in the eyes of promotion and tenure committee, most researchers would happily focus on their research and give very little thought to where it was published. Universities have succeeded at putting journal prestige on the radar of faculty who might not have cared. This is important for at least two reasons. First, the OA movement has to work, or start working, within the existing system of incentives. Second, it means that researchers are not so preoccupied by their research that they can't be induced to pay attention to relevant differences among journals, or at least the differences which universities make relevant. This gives hope to a strategy to get faculty to pay attention to access issues.

Funding agencies can have the same effect as university P&T committees. If they give grants to applicants who have a record of publishing in high-prestige journals, they help create, and then entrench, the incentive to publish in high-prestige journals.

If journal prestige and journal quality can diverge, then universities and funders may be giving authors an incentive to aim only for prestige. If they wanted to create an incentive to put quality ahead of prestige, they haven't yet succeeded. Much more on this below.

Universities and funders can mandate green OA, of course, and a growing number of them do (as of today [9/2/08], 22 universities, 4 departments, and 27 funders).

http://www.eprints.org/openaccess/policysignup/

It may seem sufficient to motivate authors to provide OA to their own work, and that motivating journals to provide OA is unnecessary. That may be true for providing OA. But if more journals don't *permit* OA (green OA), then even successful attempts to motivate authors to self-archive are needlessly limited in their scope. However, if universities wanted to create incentives for journals to support OA (green or gold), they haven't yet succeeded. I know that many universities and funders are thinking about adopting OA policies. But as I argued in an article from January 2007,

http://www.earlham.edu/~peters/fos/newsletter/01-02-07.htm#2006

> While they're deliberating, it would help if universities [and funders] would recognize their complicity in the problem they are trying to solve. By rewarding faculty who win a journal's imprimatur, mindful of the journal's prestige but heedless of its access policies, universities [and funders] shift bargaining power from authors to publishers of high-prestige journals. They give publishers less incentive to modify their standard contracts and authors greater incentive to sign whatever publishers put in front of them.

(2) Most high-prestige journals today are toll access (TA).

This isn't surprising. Most OA journals are new and it takes time for any journal, even one born excellent, to earn prestige in proportion to its quality. But it means that the motive to publish in high-prestige journals leads most faculty most of the time to try TA journals first.

If a journal can be excellent from birth, but not prestigious from birth, or if new journals typically achieve quality before they achieve a reputation for quality, then we have a non-cynical reason to think that quality and prestige can diverge. Quality and prestige clearly overlap, perhaps most of the time. But a significant number of high-quality journals, most notably the new ones, will not be correspondingly high in prestige.

If most OA journals are lower in prestige than most TA journals, it's not because they are OA. A large part of the explanation is that they are newer and younger. And conversely: if most TA journals are higher in prestige than most OA journals, it's not because they are TA. A large part of the explanation is that they are older or have a headstart.

Could the average quality of TA and OA journals be another part of the explanation? For journals of roughly the same age, differences in quality probably correlate closely with differences in prestige. But we don't have a good quality measurement—a problem that will come back again and again—and we can't forget the age variable. No one has done the studies. But if we could compare TA and OA journals of the same age and quality, I suspect we'd find that they had roughly the same levels of prestige.

(3) Most authors will choose prestige over OA if they have to choose. Fortunately, they rarely have to choose. Unfortunately, few of them know that they rarely have to choose.

There are two reasons why authors rarely have to choose between prestige and OA. First, there is already a growing number of high-prestige OA journals. They function not only as high-prestige OA outlets for new work, but as proofs of concept, showing that nothing intrinsic to OA prevents the growth of prestige. Second, authors can self-archive. They can publish in a prestigious TA journal and then deposit their postprint in an OA repository. About two-thirds of TA publishers already give blanket permission for this and many of the others will give permission on request.

http://www.sherpa.ac.uk/romeo/statistics.php

When the OA archiving is mandated by the author's funding agency, the percentage of TA publishers allowing it rises to nearly 100%.

http://oad.simmons.edu/oadwiki/Publisher_policies_on_NIH-funded_authors

Beyond this, there's growing evidence that some scholars actually prefer OA to prestige, when they have to choose.

http://www.earlham.edu/~peters/fos/2005/03/lawrence-lessig-takes-oa-pledge.html

One of the best-kept secrets of scholarly communication today is that deposit in an OA repository is compatible with publication in a TA journal. Of all the damage caused by ignorance and misunderstanding of OA, more may be caused by ignorance of this fact than ignorance of any other. Today, many prestige-driven authors will dismiss the idea of OA because they haven't heard of any OA journals—proof, to them, that OA doesn't carry sufficient prestige. Even if they want to support OA and look up the OA journals in their field, they may not find any with the prestige they could get from certain TA journals and therefore, perhaps reluctantly, dismiss the idea of OA itself as one of those ideas which is good in theory but not yet in practice. But authors who do either of these things are unaware of OA archiving or unaware that OA archiving is compatible with publishing in TA journals.

In my experience, people who don't know about this compatibility assume incompatibility. They assume that there's usually a trade-off between prestige and OA when in fact there usually isn't. If we could enlighten researchers and their institutions on this one point, we'd remove one of the largest single barriers to the spread of OA. But we must be precise: the barrier isn't prestige or the pursuit of prestige. It's ignorance and misunderstanding.

(Note that even in the minority of cases when journals don't allow OA archiving, they don't prohibit dark or non-OA deposits in an OA repository. Authors can always self-archive in that sense, and switch the article from closed to open when the journal's embargo period runs.)

John Unsworth once made the good point that we needn't make OA prestigious if we could only make it cool.

http://www.iath.virginia.edu/~jmu2m/CICsummit.htm

Both prestige and coolness would attract author submissions, and OA does seem to be growing on both scales. We needn't see them as the same thing. Authors want to be associated with a journal's prestige, or reputed excellence, and they want to be associated with a journal's coolness (and even a repository's coolness), or contribution to a good cause. I'd love to explore this in more detail. But for my present purposes, it's enough to say that no one is likely to see an incompatibility between OA and coolness.

(4) Apart from the fact that most OA journals are new, there is no intrinsic reason why OA journals can't be as high in quality and prestige as the best TA journals.

The key variables in journal quality are excellent authors, editors, and referees. OA journals can use the same procedures and standards, and the same people—the same authors, editors, and referees—as TA journals. If this weren't already clear, we're reminded of it every time a TA journal converts to OA.

There are even some respects in which the average OA journal may exceed the quality of the average TA journal, such as the freedom to publish a short issue (without shortchanging subscribers) rather than lower standards to fill it out. I discussed some of these at length in SOAN for October 2006.

http://www.earlham.edu/~peters/fos/newsletter/10-02-06.htm#quality

It's harder to pinpoint the key variables in journal prestige, but any list would include quality, age, impact, circulation, and recognition by promotion and tenure committees. Except for age, good OA journals can match good TA journals on all these parameters. By age, I mean how old a journal is today, not its prospects for longevity. When OA journals have sustainable business models and are as likely as any other journals to survive for the long-term, they are still on average much newer and haven't yet been around long enough to acquire the brand recognition and reputations of venerable TA journals. There is no doubt that their newness works against their prestige, but little doubt that they could possess all the other marks of prestige. In the case of citation impact, OA journals are likely to surpass TA journals of comparable quality, and in the case of circulation, they already surpass all TA journals whatsoever.

If most high-prestige journals today are TA, that's much more a fact about today than about any intrinsic advantages or disadvantages of TA and OA journals. It's a snapshot of dynamic, rapidly-changing situation.

(5) Quality feeds prestige and prestige feeds quality.

Quality ought to feed prestige and generally does. Or prestige ought to rest on quality and generally does. Excellent journals deserve reputations for excellence and, with conducive circumstances, tend to acquire them.

But prestige also feeds quality. Journal prestige is a powerful incentive for authors to submit work, perhaps the most powerful. By attracting submissions, prestige allows a journal to be more selective and actually improve its quality. Journal prestige also attracts good editors and referees, who directly help a journal improve its quality.

Prestige even feeds prestige. Journal prestige attracts readers, and helps justify library decisions to spend part of their limited budget on a subscription. The growth in readers and subscribers directly boosts prestige.

The quality-prestige feedback loop operates as a benign circle for high-prestige journals. The prestige itself helps them maintain both their quality and their prestige. The same feedback loop operates as a vicious circle for low-prestige journals (journals with little or no reputation, regardless of their quality). The lack of prestige itself becomes a barrier to gaining prestige in proportion to their quality. This vicious circle often takes a stark form: a journal needs excellent submissions to generate prestige, but needs prestige to attract excellent submissions.

Prestige enhances quality roughly the way interest enhances wealth, enabling the rich to get richer.

(6) Prestige is a zero-sum game, but quality is not.

On the mountain of quality, there's always room at the top for another journal (OA or TA). But on the mountain of prestige, there isn't. As long as researchers are producing excellent work, publishers can produce excellent journals. But as excellent journals multiply, not all of them can be on a library's must-have list, because budgets are finite. Not all can have a reputation for excellence, because brand awareness is also finite.

Even if all excellent journals could have reputations for excellence—say, when there are very few of them—not all could have a reputations for *superiority* to other journals in the same field. Insofar as prestige is reputed quality, it might attach to all high-quality journals, at least when there aren't too many of them. But insofar as prestige is reputed superiority, it cannot.

This is another non-cynical reason to think that quality and prestige can diverge, and that a significant number of high-quality journals will not be proportionally high in prestige.

I owe this insight to Doug Bennett, President of Earlham College, who makes the point with regard to colleges rather than journals. But it clearly applies to journals, just as it applies to books and movies.

Prestige is only approximately, not strictly, a zero-sum game. There is obviously no fixed limit to the number of prestigious journals or to the total quantum of prestige a system of scholarly communication could sustain. But there are pressures from finite budgets and finite scholarly attention which constrain the number and percentage of prestigious journals, independently of their quality. These pressures don't cap the number of journals that can earn prestige in proportion to their quality, or force new ones to displace old ones, but they burden the new ones that try and jack up the burden roughly in proportion to the number of existing high-prestige titles already regnant in a given field. With this understanding, I'll refer to prestige as a zero-sum game without always adding the wordy qualification.

(7) Because prestige is a zero-sum game, and quality is not, prestige can actually inter-
    fere with quality.

When the journals in a field are few, it might be possible for the all the good ones to have recognizable brands and prestige in proportion to their quality. But when they are many, as today, then it's difficult or impossible for all the good ones to have recognizable brands and prestige in proportion to their quality.

This isn't the kind of interference which directly prevents a journal from becoming excellent. But it does prevent many excellent journals from earning prestige in proportion to their excellence. And because prestige feeds quality, lack of prestige prevents a journal from taking advantage of the feedback effects which could help it sustain and improve its quality, for example, through increased submissions and subscriptions. If two journals are equal in quality, and one has more prestige than the other (say, because of a headstart), then the one higher in prestige will generally become higher in quality at a faster rate than the one lower in prestige.

In short, prestige generates quality, but the zero-sum problem means that quality only generates prestige up to a point or with increasing resistance. This matters for several reasons. Prestige can't keep pace with quality, at least when there are many high-quality journals. If prestige is our measure of valuation, then it will inevitably undervalue some high-quality journals. And this kind of undervaluation will function as an obstacle to the kinds of quality improvements that prestige helps to make possible. It prevents some high-quality journals from earning interest on their quality, the way high-prestige journals do.

When prestige and quality diverge, therefore, it makes sense for journals to choose prestige over quality. Prestige will help them gain quality, but quality won't always help them gain prestige. Note that authors have different reasons to make the same choice. When prestige and quality diverge, authors have a stronger incentive to publish in a high-prestige journal than in a high-quality journal. For journals, this preference reflects the zero-sum problem, and for authors it reflects incentives created by promotion and tenure committees, which themselves favor prestige over quality when the two diverge. But if authors could be made to invert their preference and put quality ahead of prestige (say, because universities did the same), then journals would have a strong reason to follow suit.

For a different kind of evidence that prestige interferes with quality, see the evidence that journal prices are either unrelated to quality or inversely related to it. Publishers can charge what the market will bear, and prestige and monopoly potently affect what the market will bear.

http://www.nature.com/nature/focus/accessdebate/22.html

(8) Universities tend to use journal prestige and impact as surrogates for quality. The excuses for doing so are getting thin.

If you've ever had to consider a candidate for hiring, promotion, or tenure, you know that it's much easier to tell whether she has published in high-impact or high-prestige journals than to tell whether her articles are actually good. Hiring committees can be experts in the field in which they are hiring, but promotion and tenure committees evaluate candidates in many different fields and can't be expert in every one. More-over, even bringing in disciplinary experts doesn't fully solve the problem. We know that work can be good even when some experts in the field have never heard of it or can't abide it. On top of that, quantitative judgments are easier than qualitative judg-ments, and the endless queue of candidates needing evaluation forces us to retreat from time- and labor-intensive methods, which might be more accurate, to shortcuts that are good enough. And perhaps above all, it's easier to assume that quality and prestige never diverge than to notice when they do diverge and act accordingly.

Impact factors (IFs) rose to prominence in part because they fulfilled the need for easy quantitative judgments and allowed non-experts to evaluate experts. As they rose to prominence, IFs became more tightly associated with journal prestige than journal quality, in part because their rise itself helped to define journal prestige.

IFs measure journal citation impact, not article impact, not author impact, not jour-nal quality, not article quality, and not author quality, but they seemed to provide a reasonable surrogate for a quality measurement in a world desperate for a reasonable surrogate. Or they did until we realized that they can be distorted by self-citation and reciprocal citation, that some editors pressure authors to cite the journal, that review articles can boost IF without boosting research impact, that articles can be cited for their weaknesses as well as their strengths, that a given article is as likely to bring a journal's IF down as up, that IFs are only computed for a minority of journals, favoring those from North America and Europe, and that they are only computed for journals at least two years old, discriminating against new journals.

By making IFs central in the evaluation of faculty, universities create incentives to publish in journals with high IFs, and disincentives to publish anywhere else. This discriminates against journals which are high in quality but low in IF, and journals which are high in quality but for whatever reason (for example, because they are new) excluded from the subset of journals for which Thomson Scientific computes IFs. By favoring journals with high IFs, universities may succeed at excluding all second-rate journals, but they also exclude many first-rate journals and many first-rate articles. At the same time, they create perverse incentives for authors and journals to game the IF system.

When we want to assess the quality of articles or people, and not the citation impact of journals, then we need measurements that are more nuanced, more focused on the salient variables, more fair to the variety of scholarly resources, more comprehensive, more timely, and with luck more automated and fully OA.

There is already a number of new measurements available or under development: Age-weighted citation rate (from Bihui Jin), Batting Average (from Jon Kleinberg et al.), the Distributed Open Access Reference Citation project (from the University of Oldenburg), Eigenfactor (from Carl Bergstrom), g-index (from Leo Egghe), h-index (from J.E. Hirsch) and variations on the theme like the Contemporary h-index (from Antonis Sidiropoulos et al.) and Individual h-index (from Pablo D. Batista et al.), the Journal Influence Index and the Paper Influence Index (both from the Center for Journal Ranking), MeSUR (MEtrics from Scholarly Usage of Resources, from LANL), SCImago Journal Rank and SJR Indicator (both from the University of Granada), Strike Rate Index (from William Barendse), Usage Factor (from UKSG), Web Impact Factor (from Peter Ingwersen), and y-factor (from Herbert van de Sompel et al.).

None of the new metrics tries to remedy all the limitations of the IF, when misused as a quality measurement, but they generally have more nuance and lower costs than the IF, and some have wider scope. Because none of them is widely adopted, none yet rivals the IF as a constituent of journal prestige.

We could solve many problems at once if we had more direct and accurate measurements of quality and could stop using citation impact and prestige as surrogates. But I'm very conscious that this is easier said than done. The new metrics are not direct quality measurements either, and quality may always be too difficult to measure directly—too time-consuming, labor-intensive, and subjective. But if we have to settle for surrogates, then at least we can improve the surrogates. If new metrics could reduce the inevitable oversimplification, then we could make more intelligent hiring, promotion, and tenure decisions. We could recognize more first-rate work, not just the subset delivered in certain venerable packages. We could remove some artificial disincentives for faculty to publish in OA journals. We could help more quality journals (OA and TA) use feedback effects to maintain and improve their quality. We could undo some of the ways in which prestige interferes with quality.

Here's a thought experiment. Imagine that we could agree on our judgments of journal quality. Construct two sets of peer-reviewed journals such that the average quality of the journals in the two sets were equal and that the journals in the one set were 1–3 years old and those in the second set 10 years old or older. Then we could check to see whether promotion and tenure committees reward faculty for publishing in the second set more than for publishing in the first set. (I'd bet big that they do.) When there's a quality difference, P&T committees ought to do their best to detect it and let it guide their judgments. But when there isn't a quality difference, steering faculty toward journals with little more than the advantage of age, headstart, or incumbency, and indirectly steering them away from journals of equal quality, only makes sense for the publishers of the incumbent journals. It makes no sense for universities trying to recognize and reward good work.

This point has been misunderstood in the past. I'm not saying that universities should lower their standards, assume quality from OA, give equal recognition to journals of lower or unknown quality, or treat any impact metric as a quality metric. I'm saying that universities should do more to evaluate quality, despite the difficulties, and rely less on simplistic quality surrogates. I'm saying that work of equal quality should have equal weight, regardless of the journals in which it is published. I'm saying that universities should focus as much as possible on the properties of articles and candidates, not the properties of journals. I'm saying that in their pursuit of criteria which exclude second-rate work, they should not adopt criteria which exclude identifiable kinds of first-rate work.

I'm never surprised when OA journals report high IFs, often higher than older and better-known journals in their fields. This reflects the well-documented OA impact advantage. I'm glad of the evidence that OA journals can play at this game and win. I'm not saying that journals shouldn't care about their citation impact, or that IFs measure nothing. I'm only saying that IFs don't measure quality and that universities should care more about quality, especially article quality and candidate quality, than journal citation impact. I want OA journals to have high impact and prove it with metrics, and I want them to earn prestige in proportion to their quality. But I want universities to take them seriously because of their quality, not because of their impact metrics or prestige.

I do want to increase submissions to OA journals, but the present argument has the importantly different goal of removing disincentives to submit to OA journals. I want OA journals to earn their submissions with their quality, and if possible with prestige matching their quality. Universities don't have to help at this, provided they don't hurt. As long as universities encourage or require green OA, they can let the process of rooting gold OA take its own time. But they must stop slowing it down, partly in fairness to new journals which are actually good, but mostly in fairness to themselves, who deserve to recognize and benefit from good work.

(9) Quality is made by authors, often in conjunction with editors and referees. Prestige is made by communities.

Peer review and brand—or if you like, quality and prestige—are the two most valuable attributes of published articles. Publishers contribute essentially to each, of course, but they contribute less to these than to other kinds of journal value such as copy editing, mark up, and marketing. But even if we consider peer review and brand to be "added value" (if only to let us use conventional idioms), peer review and brand are the most valuable forms of added value. They do more than the other forms to attract author submissions and trigger the prestige-quality feedback loop.

Peer review and brand are quite different from each other, however. Peer review is the kind of thing that can be duplicated at the same level of quality somewhere else, for example, at a new startup with no reputation. It's not easy, but it's possible. Brand or prestige is not that kind of thing at all.

Publishers create the conditions for prestige the way farmers create the conditions for a harvest. But weather, not to mention time and chance, happeneth to all. Publishers can't directly add prestige. If they could add it to a new journal, they would. If they could add more of it to an existing journal, they would. If they could create prestige as straight-forwardly as they organize peer review, then there would be as many high-prestige journals as high-quality journals—or in fact, more. But prestige is added by the community of users. After publishers do their part, the rest is added by the recognition of authors, readers, libraries, and promotion and tenure committees. Their recognition responds to a journal's antecedent value, of course, but in turn it creates subsequent value, for example, by boosting the incentive for authors to submit their work. The journal and its external stakeholders are partners in adding this kind of value. Without the contribution of the community, good journals, like good people, would be admirable but not admired.

The respect shown by authors, readers, librarians, and promotion and tenure committees can be a rational response to a journal's quality. But it can also be uninformed, reflect the dearth of high-quality alternatives in the same field, reflect past quality rather than present quality, or be based on quality surrogates like impact factors rather than quality itself. It may take some kinds of quality into account (e.g., local usage, name recognition, circulation) and not others (e.g., originality, importance, reliability), and may disregard the ways in which a journal subtracts value (e.g., password protection, locked PDFs, truncating good articles solely for length, freezing processable data into unprocessable images, and turning gifts into commodities which may not be further shared). But as a journal grows in prestige, for whatever reason, it attracts more submissions, which gives it the ability to pick off the best pieces and improve its quality, creating the feedback loop which enhances both its quality and its prestige.

Prestige is not an illusion, even if it is more shadow than substance. Prestige is not always deceptive, even if it is sometimes deceptive; we know this because prestige feeds quality. Even if some degree of it is unearned, it will work to earn its keep. Nor is prestige irrational, even if it isn't always based on evidence of quality. We needn't draw any of those disparaging conclusions in order to point out the variables that belong to the community rather than to the journal.

In short, quality has a couple of parents and prestige takes a village. This matters for several reasons. Prestige is a more elusive goal than quality and cannot directly be engineered even by a determined publisher. If it weren't for prestige, or if the only forms of "added value" available to a journal were peer review, copy editing, mark-up, marketing, and so on, then the greatest value of existing publications could be duplicated overnight by new startups (OA or TA). But prestige changes the picture, explains why this kind of value duplication is so rare, and helps explains why OA journals, as a class of newcomers, have so much trouble gaining traction against TA journals, as a class of incumbents. (The rest of the explanation is that the money to support OA journals is still tied up in TA journal subscriptions.)

At best, because prestige takes a village, it will take time for OA journals to earn prestige in proportion to their quality. At worst, because prestige is a zero-sum game, many OA journals will never earn prestige in proportion to their quality. In both cases they face this barrier because they are new, not because they are OA. An important consequence is that we must complement slow-moving gold OA strategies with fast-moving green OA strategies.

The corresponding good news for TA publishers is that the existing high-prestige journals, which are mostly TA, are likely to be entrenched for a long time. The only bad news for TA publishers on this front is they don't deserve all the credit for the prestige of their prestigious titles. They must share that credit with the research community.

It's tempting to conclude that the community which creates prestige for the existing prestigious journals could redirect it toward all high-quality journals, OA or TA. But that presupposes that we could agree on quality, that generating prestige is not slow and difficult, and that quality is not a zero-sum game.

(10) Despite its value, prestige may only give TA journals limited protection against the rise of green OA.

If prestige is an important value beyond peer review, could it help high-prestige journals survive the threat of postprint archiving (green OA to peer-reviewed manuscripts)? It could help. I've argued before that high-prestige journals will last the longest on library "must-have" lists and therefore will be the last to lose subscriptions attributable to green OA.

http://www.earlham.edu/~peters/fos/newsletter/03-02-05.htm#coexistence

Nevertheless, there are two reasons why this isn't the whole story. First, postprint archiving in physics doesn't cause any detectable cancellations, at high-prestige journals or low. This seems to be true even though only about half of deposits in arXiv are postprints, and the rest preprints. Second, when a self-archived postprint includes a citation to the journal where it was published, it benefits from some or all of the journal's prestige, not just from its peer review.

Publishers are usually the first to call for self-archived postprints to include citations to the published editions, and I've supported their calls.

http://www.earlham.edu/~peters/fos/newsletter/05-02-05.htm#brand

I wonder whether publishers will reconsider their desires here. On the one hand, calling for archived postprints to cite the published editions is another way to spread the brand, and conventional wisdom says to lose no opportunity to spread the brand. But on the other, this method of spreading the brand extends a journal's prestige to OA editions, cutting into the protection that prestige might otherwise have provided against cancellations. (BTW, I didn't call for archived postprints to cite published editions as a snarky way to hurt publishers; I did it to help authors, readers, and publishers, and am now wondering myself about its net effect on publishers.)

But the news for TA publishers isn't all bad. Their fear that postprint archiving will undermine subscriptions itself oversimplifies the problem. For now, at least, the effect of green OA on subscriptions, and the effectiveness of prestige as a shield, are both unknown.

http://www.earlham.edu/~peters/fos/newsletter/09-02-07.htm#peerreview

On a related front, it's tempting to conclude that any significant added value beyond peer review could support an alternative TA business model: give away the peer-reviewed literature and sell the value-added enhancements to it. That business model may eventually work for some kinds of added value, and I hope it does. But it won't work for prestige. First, as we've seen, OA postprints can incorporate a journal's prestige, not just its peer review. Second, if journals can't significantly add or increase prestige through their own efforts, then the only publishers who can build a business model on it are those lucky enough to have high-prestige titles already, probably the group least in need of an alternative business model. Third, any new business model along these lines presupposes that libraries would willingly pay for the peculiar value of prestige, when all or most of the journal's quality resides in the peer reviewed manuscripts. Finally, even if this model worked for some, it would carry a perverse consequence, giving publishers one more incentive to favor prestige over quality when the two diverged.

Prestige may or may not protect TA journal subscriptions from the rise of postprint archiving, but it's already protecting TA publishers from disintermediation.

Let me approach this one indirectly. The press often depicts the debate between OA advocates and TA journal publishers as a standoff or uncompromising conflict. But I see it as a prolonged negotiation. Both sides are currently making concessions that they need not make. For example, publishers needn't permit postprint archiving and scholars needn't work as authors, editors, or referees for publishers. Publishers could stop experimenting with OA, even where it benefits them, and scholars could stop collaborating with publishers, even where it benefits them. Publishers could slam the door on OA, even if that harmed them, and scholars could disintermediate publishers, even if that harmed them.

We're not at the two extreme positions because each group does benefit from working with the other. Because of the self-interest on each side we needn't call the current positions compromises. But compromises or not, they needn't be as conciliatory as they are now. Or to pick up the stick from the other end, there's still a lot of room to escalate polarization and antagonism. That's why I call the current situation a negotiation.

Publishers need scholars (as authors, editors, and referees) and scholars need publishers (to organize peer review and worldwide distribution). But these needs are not equal and therefore the situations are not symmetrical. Publishers need scholars unconditionally; without scholars to serve as authors, referees, and editors, they couldn't publish scholarly journals at all. But scholars only need publishers as long as publishers are the best current providers of a package of valuable services; it's a marriage of convenience and needn't last. Scholars need peer review and worldwide distribution, but they've always provided peer review themselves, they could find new ways to organize it without publishers, and the internet gives them the tools for low-cost worldwide distribution. If push came to shove, it would be much easier for scholars to do without publishers than for publishers to do without scholars. Or as Richard Smith put it, "I think that you will quickly find that journals (even the arrogant ones) need authors more than authors need them."

http://www.oxfam.org.uk/email/archive/0504_oxdocs.htm

In this prolonged negotiation, scholars benefit from the asymmetry: that publishers need scholars more than scholars need publishers. Publishers benefit from the status quo: that most prestigious journals today are still TA. The prestige of existing prestigious journals, then, is the largest single factor which keeps scholars working with publishers and, therefore, which keeps this a negotiation. If it weren't for the entrenchment of prestigious journals, researchers and their institutions would be cutting TA publishers out of the loop much faster than they are today.

(11) When OA journals approach TA journals in prestige, TA journals will lose their
      only remaining advantage. But this is not just a matter of time.

OA journals reach a larger audience than even the most popular TA journals. OA articles are cited 40–250% more often than TA articles, at least after the first year. Peer
review at good OA journals can be as rigorous as peer review at good TA journals, using
the same standards, procedures, and even the same people. The only advantage of TA
journals over OA journals is prestige, a side-effect of incumbency. Prestige may be more
shadow than substance, but it matters a great deal here and explains the undeniable TA
journal advantage in author submissions.

However, if OA journals approach TA journals in prestige, TA journals would lose
their only advantage in attracting author submissions.

In an article from March 2005, I made this argument:

http://www.earlham.edu/~peters/fos/newsletter/03-02-05.htm#coexistence

> [S]ome OA journals are already prestigious and others are growing in prestige. An OA journal
> has no intrinsic prestige handicap just because it is OA—or if it does (or did), this is a prejudice
> that is rapidly vanishing. However, most OA journals are new. And while new journals can be
> excellent from birth, it takes time for a journal's prestige to catch up with its quality. Now
> here's the key: it's only a matter of time before the prestige of excellent OA journals does catch
> up with their quality. At the same time, as OA spreads, it will be easier to recruit eminent
> scholars to serve on OA journal editorial boards. In addition, we'll see more and more already-
> prestigious TA journals convert to OA, taking their reputations with them. These are three
> reasons to think that OA journals will continue to rise in prestige as time passes.
>
>   For authors, the only reason to submit work to a TA journal is its prestige. In every other
> way, TA journals are inferior to OA journals because they limit an author's audience and im-
> pact. OA journals will start to draw submissions away from top TA journals as soon as they
> approach them in prestige. And by the time they equal them in prestige, the best TA journals
> will have lost their one remaining competitive advantage. As authors lose their incentive to
> submit work, subscribers will lose their incentive to subscribe. This suggests that coexistence
> [of OA and TA] will be temporary.

I still accept the main thread of this argument. But I have to update it with two
retractions. First, I was wrong to say that it's just a matter of time. Or at least OA journals are not marching steadily toward greater prestige at the same pace at which they
are marching toward greater quality. The reason for this shows up in my second retraction: I was wrong to say that there is no "intrinsic prestige handicap" for OA journals.
Or at least there is such a handicap for *new* journals. The handicap emerges from a
cluster of facts: that prestige is a zero-sum game, that most prestigious journals today
are TA, and that most OA journals are new. Quality feeds prestige, which gives hope to
all high-quality OA journals. But prestige feeds quality, which gives an inherent advantage to those with a headstart.

Because journals publish different articles, they don't compete for readers or subscribers. If you need to read the articles in a given journal, then you have reason to consult it, even if it's expensive, and even if there are free journals in the same field. But journals in the same field do compete for authors. That is why the superior prestige of TA journals today gives them an edge in the competition for authors. It's also why, when OA journals have comparable prestige, even the best TA journals will lose their competitive edge and start to suffer from all the competitive disadvantages of being TA.

If someone argued that financial stability is another advantage of TA journals over OA journals, I wouldn't disagree. The problem is not that the claim is untrue, but that it doesn't bear on the balance sheet of intrinsic strengths and weaknesses that I'm trying to sketch here. It's true that most TA journals are on more solid financial footing than most OA journals, today. But that's a fact about the present dominance of TA journals, or the present allocation of funds, not a fact about the business models. If the money now spent on TA journals were redirected toward OA journals, the financial footing of OA journals would be at least as strong as that of TA journals today. In 1980, the typewriter industry was on a more solid financial footing than the personal computer industry, but that said nothing about the superiority or typewriters or their business models.

If OA journals did approach TA journals in prestige, and start to take their submissions, they would also start to take their funding or to accelerate the redirection of funds from TA to OA journals. The institutions that pay for journal subscriptions aren't trying to support the TA business model; they're trying to support research. They won't follow the business model; they'll follow the authors.

Prestige is the flywheel preserving the present system long into the era when it might have been superseded by a superior alternative. Or viewed from the other side, it's the flywheel delaying progress.

(12) Conclusions and recommendations

Quality and prestige overlap significantly. Because quality feeds prestige and prestige feeds quality, this is no accident. But sometimes they diverge, for at least three reasons: because some journals are new and prestige takes time to cultivate, because prestige is a zero-sum game and quality is not, and because prestige can be based on inaccurate or outdated judgments of quality. It's always convenient, and usually irresistible, to use prestige as a surrogate for quality. When quality and prestige overlap, that's entirely legitimate. But when they diverge, favoring prestige harms university hiring practices, research funding practices, and the growth of every kind of science and scholarship represented by new journals (which always lack prestige). Universities have a responsibility to notice when prestige and quality diverge, resist the almost irresistible temptation to favor prestige in those cases, do their best to recognize and reward quality, and give faculty an incentive to put quality first as well.

When we stop discriminating against new journals, then we can recognize more excellent work, not just a subset, and stop ruling out first-rate work in our attempt to rule out second-rate work. Even opponents of OA should see that some new journals are high in quality, and that some new journals explore important new topics (genomics, climate change) and methods (stem cells, nanotechnology), not just new business models and licensing terms. Policies that deter faculty from submitting to new journals as such, regardless of their quality, put an artificial brake on science and scholarship themselves. Don't make this change for OA; make it for quality and research.

But make other changes for OA. Once we remove the disincentives to submit to high-quality OA journals (by removing disincentives to submit to high-quality new journals), we can add incentives to submit to journals that are at least green (permit no-delay no-fee postprint archiving). We can supplement slow-moving gold OA strategies with fast-moving green OA strategies. We can do this as individual researchers: by self-archiving whenever we publish in TA journals. We can do this as universities: by requiring OA archiving for the research output of the institution, and (in P&T committees) by requiring the articles eligible for review to be on deposit in the institutional repository. Likewise, governments and funding agencies can put a green OA condition on research grants. Finally, we can all help publishing scholars understand that publishing in a TA journal is compatible with depositing in an OA repository. Even when authors choose TA journals for their prestige, there's rarely a trade-off between prestige and OA.

University promotion and tenure committees should focus less on journal prestige and journal impact than on article quality and candidate quality. I know that's easier said than done. We'll never have quality metrics that are as easy to apply as our current prestige and impact metrics. But we can stop putting easy judgments of prestige or impact ahead of difficult judgments of quality, and we can find help in metrics which oversimplify less than the one we tend to use now.

When prestige and quality diverge, journals, universities, and authors all tend to favor prestige. It's not hard to see why. When prestige and quality diverge, prestige continues to offer undiminished rewards and create undiminished incentives. Quality is a weaker incentive when it is not accompanied by prestige. Journals have their own reasons for favoring prestige over quality: because of the zero-sum problem, prestige boosts quality more than quality boosts prestige. But authors favor prestige mostly because their universities lead them to, and universities tend to favor prestige because it's easier than favoring quality. If universities could take on the difficult job of assessing quality, they'd change incentives for authors, which would have at least some effect on journals.

Prestige is a real incentive, for journals, universities, and authors. We shouldn't expect that any of these players will nobly rise above prestige. But neither should we underestimate the attraction of prestige or its superior attraction when prestige and quality diverge. Nor should we underestimate either its non-accidental relationship with quality or the non-cynical reasons for thinking it can diverge from quality. Nor, finally, should we underestimate either side in a delicate balance of opposites: our own role in creating prestige and the difficulty of creating prestige where it doesn't already exist.

Prestige is no obstacle to green OA. But green OA suffers when authors make the mistaken assumption that publication in a prestigious TA journal is incompatible with OA. Prestige is a greater obstacle to gold OA, but only because gold OA journals are new, not because they are OA.

Two developments would change everything: (1) roughly equal prestige for OA and TA journals of roughly equal quality, regardless of age, and (2) high-volume green OA across the disciplines. (Funder and university OA mandates are terribly important, but they are merely means to the second of these.) The two developments are compatible, and we can work for both at once. We can make rapid progress on the second as soon as we have the will. But we can't make rapid progress on the first, even with the will, and my main purpose in this article has been to show why. We can describe the impediment from many angles: the benign circle entrenching the high-prestige TA journals, the vicious circle excluding newer OA journals, the zero-sum game of prestige, the slow-changing community attitudes that create prestige, the slow-changing allocation of funds paying for peer-reviewed research articles, and the stubborn fact of age. This impediment doesn't prevent OA journals from becoming first-rate, or even from growing in prestige, but it slows progress, like the slope of a hill, and can deprive OA journals of the feedback effects which boost submissions, quality, and prestige.

The second development is attainable, as advertised. But the first is equivalent to the state in which quality and prestige never diverge, which shows that it's an asymptote. We can increase the prestige of some OA journals, and sometimes even bring their prestige into alignment with their quality, and the same is true of publisher efforts on behalf of new TA journals. But we'll never prevent quality and prestige from diverging.

In my mind, these are reasons to work for gold OA and green OA simultaneously: gold OA, so that we don't further delay the benefits of hard-won, slow-growing incremental progress, and green OA so that we don't miss precious, present opportunities for accelerating progress.

The Debate

Not Napster for Science

From "Not Napster for science," SPARC Open Access Newsletter, October 2, 2003.

http://dash.harvard.edu/handle/1/4455490

If the past is any guide, it will be hard to argue for open access in a month when P2P music swapping is a hot story in the news. Academics and journalists who haven't encountered the idea of open access to peer-reviewed journal articles and their preprints—just the people who need to hear the argument—find it too easy to assimilate this unfamiliar idea to the more familiar one. "Napster for science" is the inevitable, false, and damaging result.

This is such a month. The Recording Industry Association of American (RIAA) sued 261 music swappers on September 8, hoping to scare and deter tens of millions of co-swappers. The lawsuits have greatly intensified the public debate on file sharing and copyright. In fact, the discussion is now broader and deeper, touching on what universities should do, what parents should do, what music lovers should do, what musicians should do, what music companies should do, what courts should do, and what legislators should do.

So this is a good time to say, once more, in public, with emphasis, that open access to peer-reviewed research articles and their preprints is fundamentally different from free online access to music files, despite one obvious similarity.

What makes music swapping interesting is that most musicians don't consent to it and most file swappers don't seem to care. But I don't want to talk about that, really, except as a contrast to the situation with journal articles. Scientists and scholars do consent to publish their journal articles without payment. This has been the rule in science and scholarship since 1665 when the first science journals were launched in London and Paris. Scholarly monographs and textbooks are different, because authors can hope for royalties. For the same reason, most music, film, and software are different. But journal articles are special. Music companies and music lovers would call them peculiar.

The fact that scholars eagerly submit articles to journals that don't pay for them, even journals that demand that authors sign away their copyright, is probably the best-kept secret about academic publishing among non-academics. It's the fact that simultaneously explains the beauty of open access and the mistake of "Napster for science."

This peculiarity of journal articles should draw some of the public attention generated by music swapping. Defenders and critics of music swapping should both hear this intelligence and say, "Really? Scholars do all that work researching and writing, and then give it away to some journal? Either you're lying or free online access to journal articles is completely different from free online access to music." But instead, we tend to hear the opposite. Most people disregard this difference as trifling or technical and equate consensual open access with unconsensual Napsterism.

If "Napster for science" communicates the basic free-of-price idea to a larger public, then isn't it a useful phrase? The answer is No! It's true that music swapping is about free online access to content. That's the important similarity. But it's equally about an army of content creators who resist free online access. It may be about freedom, but it's also about copyright infringement. Careful writers, with careful readers, could successfully compare open access with the first feature of Napsterism and contrast it with the second. But why bother? It's much more effective to define open access in its own right than to yoke it to the better-known but different concept and then try to undo the confusion that results.

Copyrighted scholarship does not face the same mass infringement that copyrighted music does. And yet, like copyrighted music, most copyrighted scholarship is locked away behind economic, legal, and technical barriers. You might think it's ripe for a real Napster attack. But nobody advocates this, least of all the open-access movement. Open access proponents know that the peculiar legal standing of journal articles makes free online access possible without infringement. The simple, sufficient reason is consent. When authors and copyright holders consent to open access, there is no infringement.

With sex, we have no trouble seeing that consent is critical. Sex with the consenting is one of life's great goods. Sex with the unconsenting is a crime. If the public could see this fundamental distinction behind forms of online access and file swapping, then open-access proponents could welcome the comparison to Napster. It would show open access in the best light. "You know that kind of free online access to music that makes most musicians and all studios hopping mad? How cool would it be if they consented to it? Imagine that. That's open access."

Open access is free access by and for the willing. There is no vigilante open access, no infringing, expropriating, or piratical open access.

Of course I'm not saying that all journals consent to open access. Most don't. I'm saying that academic authors consent to write and publish their research articles without payment. The consent to relinquish payment is directly connected to the consent to open access. Musicians would either lose revenue from open access or fear that they would. That's why most don't consent to it. But because scholars have already relinquished income from articles, they have nothing to lose and everything to gain from open access.

We can go further. Scholars don't just consent to relinquish payment and copyright. They are eager to publish—at least journal articles—even on these harsh terms. Nothing shows more clearly that they write journal articles for impact or influence, not revenue. Their interest lies in making a contribution to knowledge, partly for its own sake and partly because advancing knowledge will advance their careers. This explains why open access serves their interests, and why limiting access to paying customers (the traditional model in scholarly publishing and the RIAA model for music) would violate their interests.

Music swapping was practiced in the age of vinyl, but it took digital music and the internet to make it widespread. It's widespread now because something unexpectedly good happened, not because some creeping criminal malice overtook tens of millions of people. We graduated from the age of vinyl in two stages, first by recording music in bits, and then by creating a worldwide network of bit-swapping machines. This was revolutionary progress from every point of view. Now that we can make perfect copies and distribute them at virtually no cost to a worldwide audience, we should find ways to seize this beautiful opportunity, make it lawful, and enjoy the new access to information that it makes possible.

The RIAA and commercial journal publishers both have reason to fear that the internet will make them unnecessary. They both respond to this fear by making their products harder to use, less accessible, and more expensive, which is surely perverse. The RIAA has now gone even further, trying to intimidate users and make them afraid to take advantage of the power of the internet. If it wins, then digital technology will be like sex in the Victorian age. Virtue will be construed as resistance to all the beautiful temptations. This will chill advances even to the consenting.

I know that some fraction of music swapping carries the artist's consent and encouragement. These artists consent to free downloads because for them (as Tim O'Reilly put it in another context) invisibility is worse than infringement. So while most musicians fear losing revenue from open access, some don't. While most don't consent to it, some do. This fact upsets the digital Puritanism of the RIAA and blurs the moral lines it has tried to draw for music swapping.

It may be that open access to music will increase net sales, and that most musicians below the top ranks of superstardom will profit from it. I'm in no position to say. But it is clear that the RIAA is engaged in self-serving oversimplifications about both the economic interests of musicians and the truth about copyright. The comparison to open access helps us draw at least one lesson: copying digital files is not theft.

It's only unlawful when the files are copyrighted and when the copyright holder refuses consent. But many files are in the public domain, and many carry the copyright holder's consent to free or open access. This is true for growing bodies of both music and scholarship. This is more than lawful; it's wonderful.

[...]

Postscript

In my view, Phase One of the open-access movement is to secure open access to journal articles and their preprints. They're the easiest case or low-hanging fruit because their authors already consent to write and publish them without payment.

However, we should imagine a Phase Two in which we persuade authors and artists who do not currently consent to reconsider. Ripe for persuasion are authors of scholarly monographs, who rarely earn royalties and, even when they do, would benefit far more from the wide audience than the meager checks. Also in this category are programmers who might shift from priced to open source code. Novelists might be persuaded by the experience of the Baen Free Library that the free online availability of the full-text stimulates more sales than it kills. Finally, it might include musicians who decide, with Janis Ian, that free access, wide recognition, and good will generate more sales than high-priced invisibility.

We can also imagine a Phase Three in which we enlarge and protect the public domain by rolling back copyright extensions, establishing the first-sale doctrine for digital content, restoring fair-use rights denied by DRM, and letting federal copyright law preempt state contract or licensing law. While all these steps would be advances for the free flow of information, copyright reform is unnecessary for open access. All we need is consent. All we need for the bulk of science and scholarship is Phase One. All we need for music is Phase Two.

If all we need is consent, and our idea is a worthy one, then all we need is a chance to spread the word about it. We should be able to bootstrap this good idea into reality by explaining, educating, and persuading. Spread the word. (How cool is that?)

[...]

Two Distractions

From "Two distractions," SPARC Open Access Newsletter, May 3, 2004.

http://dash.harvard.edu/handle/1/4391169

Proponents of open access should focus their energy on delivering open access. Success may not be easy, but at least we can hope that preserving this focus is easy. However, there are two related distractions nowadays that are making it difficult.

(1) Don't be distracted by the wrong problem.

The problem is to provide OA, through journals and archives, not to undermine publishers who are not providing OA. The problem is to deliver on our vision of what we think is good, not to torpedo those who aren't helping us.
[...]
TA publishers are not the enemy. They are only unpersuaded. Even when they are opposed, and not merely unpersuaded, they are only enemies if they have the power to stop OA. No publisher has this power, or at least not by virtue of publishing under a TA business model. If we have enemies, they are those who can obstruct progress to OA. The only people who fit this description are friends of OA who are distracted from providing OA by other work or other priorities.

One mistake is to aim at undermining the current model rather than constructing the alternative. Another mistake is to think that all publishers are alike. A third mistake, which follows from the first two, is to alienate publishers who might become allies, or who are already becoming allies.

If OA and TA can coexist, then it's clear that advancing OA needn't undermine TA and that undermining TA needn't advance OA. If they cannot coexist, then one day we'll find that out. But the most constructive and effective way to find out is to work for OA and observe the consequences. Even if providing OA is inseparable from undermining TA, there is still an important difference of accent. We have to be motivated by what we love and want to build, by the good alternative we envision and its good consequences for science and scholarship. Otherwise we risk distraction and open ourselves to burnout and ennervation. But of course, in the meantime it's just enlightened self-interest to preserve the option of recruiting new allies.

(2) Don't be distracted by public debate.

Even more than in the previous section, here I want to make a nuanced and two-sided point. Public debate can be very valuable but it can also lead us to forget the primary goal and waste energy.

When publishers object to OA, it's tempting to pause in what we are doing to answer them. If we have time and good answers, then this can be very helpful. Public debate helps the undecided. If we let misunderstandings go uncorrected or objections go unanswered, then we may lose a chance to persuade the unpersuaded and recruit another ally. Moreover, converting existing journals would be progress. It would be better than having to launch all OA journals from scratch.

But to pause in what we are doing to answer objections can lead us to interrupt the primary work in favor of the secondary. If you don't have time to do both […], then stick to the primary work of delivering OA. It helps the cause at least as much.

One mistake is to let secondary work interrupt primary work. Another mistake is to let critics set the agenda. Most objections to OA, for example, come from TA publishers and most of these objections point to alleged problems with OA journals. But it doesn't follow that those alleged problems are suddenly "the front" which must be addressed in order to make progress. OA archiving is a path of equal value and greater convenience. We should pursue it regardless of how we deal with publisher objections to OA journals. Moreover, delivering OA is more important than persuading publishers to join us in delivering OA, and we should pursue it regardless of how we deal with publisher objections to OA.

The latter is the most delicate point: it's true that we could always use more allies, but it's false that we need existing publishers to deliver OA. We should conduct ourselves so that we always invite and welcome new allies, but at the same time we must give primary attention to the primary task of providing OA.

Some publishers will never be persuaded, and some are telling us through their public objections that they are not yet persuaded. That's all right. They don't need to be persuaded for us to continue our work. We can provide OA without their consent, cooperation, or assistance. One constructive response is simply to get back to work on delivering OA.

I don't want to draw a false distinction between persuading and doing. Persuading is part of doing—because the job is large and we need allies to do it. Likewise, doing is part of persuading—because the best argument that OA is feasible is to deliver it, the best argument that it is valuable is to use it, and the best argument that it is sustainable is to build it and watch it survive.

I'm perfectly willing to turn the tables here and have TA publishers take the same attitude toward objections from the side of OA. They have the same dual interest in getting their work done and recruiting new allies to share in it. Sometimes this makes public debate a good investment of energy and sometimes it doesn't.

I believe in public debate even when it doesn't recruit allies. It's a courtesy that we owe our critics. It's also an intrinsic part of intellectual honesty. If we have beliefs on which we're willing to take public action, then we should be willing to defend them in public and show how we deal with evidence and respond to criticism. If we admit that we are fallible, then we need to check our enthusiasms and commitments against other thoughtful judgments. I haven't changed my mind about any of this. For example, I often engage in public debate and make my own attempts at public persuasion. I've tried to persuade subscription-based journals to experiment with OA (most recently in my last issue, SOAN for 4/2/04), and I continue to make this appeal. I've answered publisher objections (for example, SOAN for 11/2/03, 12/2/03, 3/2/04) and, time permitting, will continue to do so in the future. I merely want to remind us of a few truths that we are tempted to forget when we are most driven to participate in public debate. Helping the undecided will help the cause but it can also interrupt primary work with secondary work and shift the focus from our agenda to a critic's agenda. Answering objections will help the cause but it can also lead us to false beliefs about whose cooperation is necessary to build OA. Persuading unpersuaded publishers is not necessary, just as it is not useless; it is only helpful. The unpersuaded are not enemies. Persuasion can fail while OA succeeds. We don't need unanimity; we need OA.

Praising Progress, Preserving Precision

From "Praising Progress, Preserving Precision," SPARC Open Access Newsletter, September 2, 2004.

http://dash.harvard.edu/handle/1/4736612

One sign of OA momentum is that more and more publishers are jumping on the bandwagon. Some are launching OA journals. Some are converting subscription-based journals to OA. Some are offering OA content in subscription-based journals. Some are widening access short of OA. And some are using the now-popular name of "open access" regardless of how well or badly it describes their access policies.

Can we welcome every initiative to widen access without abandoning our goal of fully open access and without diluting the definition of "open access"? I hope so. These goals are perfectly compatible. However, they are sometimes seen as incompatible and that holds us back. I regret that some initiatives to widen access dilute our useful term, and I regret that some attempts to resist dilution and pursue full OA criticize useful progress.

What definition?

More than ever before I'm hearing the complaint that the term "open access" doesn't have a firm, common definition. This is not true, but it could become true if dilution and misuse of the term continue.

The three major public definitions of "open access" are contained in the Budapest, Bethesda, and Berlin public statements. Even though these three definitions differ from one another in small ways (which I explored in SOAN for 8/4/03), they agree on the essentials. Let me refer to them collectively, or to their common ground, as the Budapest-Bethesda-Berlin or BBB definition of open access.

Nearly all OA proponents agree on the BBB definition. When I defend the concept of open access against dilution, I'm defending the communal consensus embodied in the BBB definition, not my own private preferences. The three contributing public statements have unparalleled stature and influence within the OA movement. Only outsiders and newcomers might mistake this. And that, I believe, is part of the problem. Our growing success means that our message in one form or another, clear or garbled, is reaching new people who almost certainly do not know the BBB definition or its centrality for our work.

The best-known part of the BBB definition is that OA content must be free of charge for all users with an internet connection. However, the BBB definition doesn't stop at free online access. It adds an extra dimension that isn't as easy to describe, and consequently is often dropped or obscured. This extra dimension gives users permission for all legitimate scholarly uses. It removes what I've called permission barriers, as opposed to price barriers. The Budapest statement puts the extra dimension this way:

> By "open access" to this literature, we mean its free availability on the public Internet, permitting any users to read, download, copy, distribute, print, search, or link to the full texts of these articles, crawl them for indexing, pass them as data to software, or use them for any other lawful purpose, without financial, legal, or technical barriers other than those inseparable from gaining access to the Internet itself. The only constraint on reproduction and distribution, and the only role for copyright in this domain, should be to give authors control over the integrity of their work and the right to be properly acknowledged and cited.

The Bethesda and Berlin statements put it this way: For a work to be OA, the copyright holder must consent in advance to let users "copy, use, distribute, transmit and display the work publicly and to make and distribute derivative works, in any digital medium for any responsible purpose, subject to proper attribution of authorship."

All three tributaries of the mainstream BBB definition agree that OA removes both price and permission barriers. Free online access isn't enough. "Fair use" ("fair dealing" in the UK) isn't enough.

Note that the three component statements of the BBB definition do not agree on exactly which permission barriers must be removed. There's room for variety here. BBB requires removing barriers to copying and redistribution. It doesn't require removing barriers to commercial re-use; authors can go either way on this. Two of the three BBB component definitions require removing barriers to derivative works.

One danger is the dilution of our term. That's why I'm reminding us of the BBB definition and its place in our history. But another danger is the false sharpening of our term. If we thought that the BBB definition settled matters that it doesn't settle, then we could prematurely close avenues of useful exploration, needlessly shrink the big tent of OA, and divisively instigate quarreling about who is providing "true OA" and who isn't.

The BBB definition functions as a usefully firm definition of "open access" even if it leaves room for variation. We should agree that OA removes some permission barriers (e.g., on copying, redistribution, and printing) even if it leaves different OA providers free to adopt different policies on others (e.g., on derivative works and commercial re-use). My personal preference, for example, is to permit derivative works and commercial re-use. But (as I wrote in FOSN for 1/30/02) I want to make this preference genial, or compatible with the opposite preference, so that we can recruit and retain authors on both sides of this question.

Praising progress

One reason to praise forward steps is that they really do constitute progress, whether or not they reach full OA. If we had to choose between calling them "open access" and criticizing them, that would be a hard choice. But we face no such choice. Let's do both: praise the widening of access and stick to the BBB definition of the term "open access."

There's no contradiction here and no implication that the progress we are praising is all that could be desired. We praise students for improving without implying that they've improved enough. We praise good moves in politics, sports, and science without implying that further progress is unnecessary or impossible. We can speak clearly. If we want to say that widening access is good and open access is better, we can say that.

Time to get specific. [...] [Here omitting six examples.]

You get the idea. In evaluating new access policies, we needn't confuse the widening of access with open access. And we needn't confuse policies that stop short of open access with policies that make no progress. We can praise progress and criticize dilution of our term at the same time. We can praise policies for some progressive elements and criticize them for some regressive elements. If we take the trouble to do these things, then we preserve clarity about our standard, avoid undermining our useful term, and head off quarrels about what counts as open access.

I once wrote to a journal to make this kind of two-sided point, praising it for its steps toward widening access and protesting its use of the term "open access" as a synonym for "free" or "no-fee" access. In defense the editor replied, "I'm afraid that the term 'open access' has so many meanings it has almost no meaning anymore." Of course, if this were really true, then the journal would never want to use the term to describe its new policy. However, the editor's pessimistic assessment can become true by a kind of self-fulfilling prophecy. If enough journals use the term loosely, then the term will become loose.

Let's avoid the self-fulfilling prophecy. "Open access" still means something. We encourage journals to misuse the term if we're only willing to praise the ones that use the term. Let's use the term according to the BBB definition and encourage others to do so as well. But then let's praise access policies that make progress, even if they fall short of the BBB definition.

Educating newcomers, a burden of success

I was at a conference recently where someone seriously contended that "open access" has never been adequately defined, and as evidence cited a professional association that was having trouble defining it.

As a teacher, I was reminded of the many times that I watched students struggling to define a term or concept without consulting the book where it was clearly presented. The difference is that the students know or should know that the concept is well-defined in the book. But the professional association, and the person I heard at the conference, may have no idea that "open access" has a written definition in public documents that reflect, inspire, and shape the open-access movement. We shouldn't blame those who think that "open access" has never been adequately defined; we should blame ourselves for not making the definition better known.

One lesson is that success is not enough if it encourages newcomers and bystanders who, through compound interest on initial misunderstanding, make our clear term fuzzy. Too many newcomers are trying to define "open access" contextually from contemporary discussion. Some by good luck start from informed discussions, but some by bad luck start from uninformed discussions.

It gets worse. Not only is there ignorance and misunderstanding about what "open access" means. This very ignorance and misunderstanding are taken as evidence that the term is only loosely defined. The self-fulfilling prophecy about the term's loose meaning is being fulfilled as we watch.

Not all the news is bad, of course. True understanding is growing alongside this ignorance and misunderstanding. New OA journals and OA archives prove it. A very large number of journal articles and newspaper stories prove it. The US and UK open-access proposals prove it.

The problem is that the meme of OA is spreading faster than accurate information about OA. Too many messages that introduce OA to newcomers, and recruit new allies and critics, define the term loosely or incorrectly. Very few point to the BBB definition.

The term "open source" has the same history of careful definition threatened by loose usage. For that matter, so do "evolution," "self-defense" and "Christmas." We're not unique and we're not doomed. We just have to appreciate that our term is not self-explanatory and that dilution causes and justifies further dilution.

I wrote my Open Access Overview (first posted June 21, 2004) precisely because our successes were bringing in newcomers who couldn't put their hands on a brief, accurate introduction. They could easily find lists of links or essay-length analyses that didn't start at the beginning, but not a primer that defined the basic concept and its major issues.

http://www.earlham.edu/~peters/fos/overview.htm

Let me close with two appeals:

(1) To friends of OA: Praise progress wherever you see it. If it doesn't amount to OA, then don't call it OA, but don't let that stop you from recognizing it as progress. Unless you speak unclearly, no one will mistake your praise for the claim that full OA is not possible or not desirable.

(2) To publishers experimenting with wider access: Keep up the good work, but please don't use the term "open access" for policies that don't meet the BBB definition. If you mislabel a policy as OA, then please don't mistake criticism of the label for criticism of the policy.

The BBB definition of "open access"
Budapest Open Access Initiative (February 14, 2002)

http://www.soros.org/openaccess/

Bethesda Statement on Open Access Publishing (June 20, 2003)

http://www.earlham.edu/~peters/fos/bethesda.htm

Berlin Declaration on Open Access to Knowledge in the Sciences and Humanities, (October 22, 2003)

http://www.zim.mpg.de/openaccess-berlin/berlindeclaration.html

How should we define "open access"? From SOAN for 8/4/03

http://www.earlham.edu/~peters/fos/newsletter/08-04-03.htm

Thoughts on commercial use of FOS. From FOSN for 1/30/02

http://www.earlham.edu/~peters/fos/newsletter/01-30-02.htm

Postscript

We're clearly entering an era of wider and easier access to research literature. This includes full OA in the BBB sense, but it also includes lots of kindred forms of access for which we don't have names. On the one hand, the absence of names will lead many people to call these kindred forms "open access," diluting our term. On the other hand, concocting a family of new names may be at least as confusing and harmful. The names would have to discriminate among fine and constantly changing variations on the theme. We could quarrel about which was the right name for a given policy, especially as the discriminations became finer and finer. Policy innovations could always develop faster than our vocabulary and there could always be more policy variations than names. We would feel pressure to invent ever new names to prevent the dilution of older ones. And as the access vocabulary grew, journals with evolving access policies would have to rename them every quarter.

I don't like that scenario and am certainly not advocating distinct terms for every distinct access policy. There are several alternatives to this ugly scenario. We can use descriptive phrases ("free after six months," "postprint archiving but only in institutional repositories") without trying to compress them into names. We can use a small number of terms (green, gold, OA, delayed OA, partial OA, free access) without trying to name every shade or wrinkle. When definitions differ, and the differences matter, we could use discriminating adjectives ("Budapest OA," "Valparaiso OA," "IFLA OA").

I only mention these alternatives to show that they exist. [...] I don't delude myself into thinking that I could direct the evolution of language. I only want to argue that our central term has a usefully firm definition codified in public documents, that we should appeal to that definition in resisting attempts to stretch or dilute the term, and that we can do this without advocating a host of coinages to describe every different flavor of access.

The many kindred forms of access

http://www.earlham.edu/~peters/fos/lists.htm#incomplete

Who Should Control Access to Research Literature?

From "Who should control access to research literature?" SPARC Open Access Newsletter, November 2, 2004.

http://dash.harvard.edu/handle/1/4725018

Many of the publishers objecting to the NIH plan already provide free online access to their contents after some delay. For some the delay is longer than six months but for others it is not. Some publishers allow postprint archiving without any delay at all, although perhaps they adopted this policy on the assumption that authors would not seize the opportunity in large numbers.

In short, their objection does not seem to be to OA as such. The objection is that the NIH plan will provide OA on the NIH's terms, not on the publishers' terms. The problem is control. Will the timetable and the conditions be set by publishers or by others, such as authors or funding agencies?

In the past, I've tended to focus on the access barriers that stand in the way of OA and the task of removing them one by one. But watching some publishers oppose the NIH OA plan (and other OA initiatives as well) when they are willing to remove some of these barriers on their own, I've shifted in my thinking a bit. The more fundamental question is who controls access, not what barriers stand in the way. Who should decide which access barriers to remove, when, and on what terms?

Publishers opposed to the NIH plan want to make these decisions themselves, not to cede control to anyone else, especially the government. Notice that we're not talking about decisions on what to study, what to publish, or how to conduct peer review. [...] The question is not how to conduct science, but how to control access to the results. Some publishers opposing the NIH policy like to blur this distinction, perhaps deliberately. [...]

Publishers who object to this loss of control are defending the remarkable proposition that they should control access to research conducted by others, written up by others, and funded by taxpayers. More: they claim that they should control access to this literature even when it is given to them free of charge and even though the prices they demand for it have risen four times faster than inflation for nearly two decades.

If we let publishers control access to this knowledge, then the toll will continue to grow faster than inflation. Even if it didn't, or even if the prices were low and reasonable, the present system wouldn't scale, since the growth of published knowledge itself would quickly put the total price out of reach, creating access barriers based on the accident of user wealth. We want to remedy information overload, but we want to do it with smart tools that help us find the subset of information we need, not with crude policies that set off huge swaths of it, relevant and irrelevant alike, as too expensive.

Publishers cannot say that they deserve to control access because their role in the process is the most important. They facilitate peer review, which is critical, and add value in other, less critical ways. But nobody can argue that facilitating peer review is more important than conducting the research in the first place, or writing it up, or even funding it. The peer-review provider is now the access gatekeeper, but not because any rational principle requires it. When we start to replace this inherited system with a more rational one, the former gatekeepers protest, but I have yet seen them offer a principled objection. I've seen principled or evidence-based objections to the economics of OA journals and to the economic consequences of OA archiving; these are constructive, deserve responses, and are receiving responses. But publishers have not been as constructive or coherent on the fundamental proposition, represented by the NIH plan, that publishers should not be the ones to control when or on what terms the public will have access to publicly-funded research. Their objections to this proposition have been naked assertions of economic self-interest at the expense of the public interest.

Four Analogies to Clean Energy

From "Four analogies to clean energy," SPARC Open Access Newsletter, February 2, 2010.

http://dash.harvard.edu/handle/1/4315928

When I think about the political fortunes of open access, I find that I compare them privately to the political fortunes of clean energy. I know there are differences, but I keep returning to the similarities.

I'm not ready to say that the similarities are more salient than the differences. But it's time to get these analogies out in the open.

(1) The gap between breakthrough and uptake

Lots of smart and well-funded people are looking for a source of energy that is renewable, inexpensive, efficient, low-impact to produce, low-impact to use, and doesn't require a police state to keep byproducts out of the hands of terrorists. Suppose they succeed. That would be a momentous breakthrough.

This is already a key difference between OA and clean energy. On the energy side, we're well-embarked but still moiling through primary difficulties of physics and engineering, trying to raise efficiencies and lower prices. But on the OA side, the breakthrough is in hand, and has been since the birth of the internet. We've long since replaced the difficulties of engineering with the difficulties of uptake and persuasion.

As I argued in 2002, "If asked for a precedent for the kind of revolution represented by [open access], we might first mention the Gutenberg Press. But it isn't a very good fit. It's a technological advance, and all the technology required for [OA] already exists. We're trying to bring about an economic change that will take advantage of existing technology."

http://www.earlham.edu/~peters/fos/newsletter/03-11-02.htm#analogies

But suppose we had a clean energy breakthrough. Would it change the world overnight? Or would it need something more like a decade?

We might draw an optimistic distinction: We could recognize the superiority of the new technology immediately, and still need some time to embrace it and switch over.

The experience of OA makes me respond, "Maybe, at best." [...] I wonder whether we'd need serious time even to recognize the superiority of the breakthrough technology. "We" here means everyone in a position to make a relevant decision, from policymakers and manufacturers to consumers.

The question suggests a pessimism that may not be warranted. Some useful new technologies, like cell phones, spread far, wide, and fast. We know that doesn't happen for all useful new technologies, like plug-in electric cars. Rapid adoption is not automatic, and it's not a simple function of the technology's utility or value.

Of course the internet was widely and quickly adopted. But for taking full advantage of the internet in individual domains, such as music or peer-reviewed research literature, we're already in our second decade.

One variable seems to be whether the new technology makes an easy fit with existing business models and businesses. If the cell phone threatened to bankrupt phone companies, rather than enrich them, it would not have spread as quickly. If VoIP were as accommodating or convergent as cell phones, it would be spreading faster.

OA isn't held back because it isn't useful enough, but because a bewildering array of interests and incentives pull against it, by no means limited to commercial business interests (see #2 below). Of course many other interests and incentives pull for it, but that matters much less here. The interests pulling against it clog the path with obstacles, and the mere existence of obstacles slows down uptake and adoption.

A breakthrough energy technology might require widespread infrastructure before it could be widely adopted—for example, neighborhood hydrogen stations for hydrogen-powered cars or capacity to transport and store wind and solar power for use in places that are not windy or sunny. These infrastructure prerequisites are expensive and time-consuming add-ons to the original energy breakthrough and can certainly slow down adoption. By contrast, the infrastructure required for OA is much lighter, at least once the internet is in place. The software for launching journals and repositories, maintaining them, and searching them, are all in hand, even if all are undergoing constant refinement.

Just a few years ago, publishers who were not ready to adopt OA themselves were often willing to recognize its superiority. Even publishers lobbying against it were willing to say in public that OA was better than TA for research, and that the only problem was paying for it. (Publishers who cheerfully made this concession five years ago have apparently been advised by their PR departments not to do it again.) The real problem has been the slow growth in the group of people paying attention to OA. Even today study after study shows that most publishing researchers know very little about it or labor under misunderstandings.

OA depends on thousands of distributed author decisions. That's an advantage when authors are ahead of the curve and can decide to submit their work to OA journals, deposit it in OA repositories, or retain key rights, without waiting for deep changes in markets, legislation, or institutional policy. But it's a disadvantage when the worldwide growth of OA depends on educating thousands of authors individually.

Clean energy has a way around that problem. If utility companies adopt the breakthrough technology, then their customers and consumers automatically adopt it at the same time. In OA, we can approximate this advantage by recruiting institutions in a position to influence author decisions: funding agencies and universities. When they adopt OA policies, the assistance is decisive. But while the number of funders and universities adopting OA policies is sharply up, and will continue to climb, each new policy is a new struggle, especially at universities which decide (wisely) to adopt OA policies through faculty votes rather than administrative edicts.

But I'm still wondering: will it take roughly as long to persuade the world's utility companies to adopt a breakthrough energy technology as it's taking to persuade the world's funding agencies and universities to adopt OA? I don't know the constraints on utility companies, but I imagine there are many: from legacy facilities optimized for coal or oil to long-term contracts with suppliers and the skills in the local labor market.

When I'm pessimistic, Howard Aiken captures the mood perfectly: "Don't worry about people stealing your ideas. If your ideas are any good, you'll have to ram them down people's throats."

(2) Putting obstacles in our way

Imagine the same breakthrough in efficient, inexpensive, clean energy. Now imagine that during the age of dirty energy we had adopted laws and practices which turn out to deter the development, uptake, and use of the spectacular new technology. Some of the obstacles clogging the path to adoption are of our own making.

We might have provided subsidies to dirty energies, which in turn created jobs and revenues, which in turn elected politicians and enriched corporations who now fight to protect those jobs and revenues at the expense of any energy breakthrough. We might have grown to depend on cars, which spawned suburbs, which not only elected politicians but changed the landscape of life for millions of people and now make almost irrelevant any energy breakthrough that doesn't work in cars. We might have grown to depend on cheap oil, which nurtured whole industries and lifestyles which we find it inconceivable to abandon.

During the age of print, the first stirrings of digital allowed us to dream about OA. But now we find ourselves obstructed by laws and practices that evolved during the age of print. University promotion and tenure committees steer authors to high-prestige journals regardless of their access policies. Universities could easily reward publishing in the same journals and require green OA, but few do.

The same committees are addicted to journal impact factors, which they know or ought to know discriminate against new journals, even excellent new journals, and disregard the merits of individual articles, even excellent articles. They could easily distinguish the average citation impact of a journal from the actual quality of the individual articles by candidates up for renewal or tenure, but few do.

Copyright law prevents the wholesale adoption of new technologies for sharing perfect copies with a worldwide audience at zero marginal cost. We could all lobby for copyright reforms to support research and education, but few do. Universities and funders could adopt policies to keep key rights in the hands of those who will consent to OA; but while this position is spreading, it's still the minority position.

We have the technology to abolish information scarcity, but we are reluctant to use it even to advance our own professional interests. Sometimes we're stalled by inertia and overwork. Sometimes we consciously put the professional interests of another industry ahead of our own. We could support our favorite journal and publisher brands, even if TA, and insist on green OA at the same time, but few do.

If we were only obstructed by law, we could work for the vote that would change everything, even if took years and years. But the law is the least of our problems, since we already know how to implement OA lawfully. The problem is that we're also obstructed by our own customs and practices. There's no direct path through this thicket.

What should we do when law and custom prevent us from taking rapid advantage of a momentous boon? Unfortunately it's a serious question.

(3) Slowing down to protect the incumbents

Imagine the same breakthrough technology producing efficient, inexpensive, renewable, clean energy. Imagine that the only downside seemed to be that it would jeopardize the revenue streams of oil companies and coal mines.

Should we hesitate to use it? Should we wait until we can find a way to ensure the survival of the threatened industries? When policy-makers weigh the advantages and disadvantages of the new technology, should the effect on oil companies and coal mines count as a disadvantage? If so, how much environmental and economic good are we willing to forgo in order to prop up the old industries?

When people argue that OA will likely harm existing publishers, this is one thread of my thinking. Maybe they're right about that harm. (And BTW maybe they're not; I've written extensively about this and won't pause here to recap the state of the evidence.) But why should the effect on publishers be a criterion? What about the benefits for authors and readers, researchers and research?

Of course publisher prosperity is a criterion for publishers. It is and it ought to be. The question is whether it should be a criterion for other stakeholders, especially funding agencies and universities. Funders underwrite research in order to advance knowledge or realize social benefits. Allowing publishers to limit the circulation of that knowledge would undermine those goals. Public funding agencies are structured to put the public interest ahead of private interests, and private funding agencies are charities. In both cases, for similar reasons, they generally decide that if research is worth funding, then it's worth making available to everyone who could make use of it.

Sometimes funders needlessly compromise their public or charitable missions in order to prop up publishers. In this category I put all the "loophole policies" or "loophole mandates" which require OA except when publishers do not allow it, giving the opt-out to publishers rather than authors. However, this problem is more common among universities than funding agencies.

Let's focus on universities for a moment. Should publisher prosperity be a criterion for universities, whose mission is to generate, share, teach, and preserve knowledge?

An undeniable part of the background is that publishers have played a central role in generating, sharing, teaching, and preserving knowledge. So the question is nicely complicated, and we shouldn't oversimplify it. (Hence, before you write in, I'm not saying that slowing down the progress of OA to protect publishers is like slowing down the progress of green energy to protect oil companies, or that publishers are to knowledge what oil companies are to the environment.) One tempting answer, then, is that institutions like funders and universities should try to preserve publishers, as acknowledged allies, even if the same funders and universities are determined to put knowledge ahead of profit. But that position doesn't answer the original question. What if we had efficient, inexpensive, renewable, and clean energy whose *only* downside was its threat to the revenue of oil companies and coal mines? What if the *only* downside to OA was its threat to the revenue of existing publishers?

If the question itself carries dubious assumptions, drawing on analogy and conjecture, let's put it to one side. Publishers are allies in the distribution of knowledge. But publishers who require access barriers for cost recovery have interests which actually limit the distribution of knowledge. Hence, to support them is not like supporting other kinds of allies who pull with and never against the forward motion. And there's now clear and convincing evidence that publishers needn't require access barriers for cost recovery.

There are shoals to avoid on both sides. We oversimplify if we don't acknowledge the role of publishers in the distribution of knowledge. The past role has been indispensable, and the future role could be as large and central. But it doesn't follow that we must compromise the progress of OA in order to prop up publishers. We oversimplify on the other side as soon as we say that the only viable business models for publishers is to erect access barriers, that solicitude for existing brands is better for research than removing access barriers, or that the valuable role of publishers can only be provided by TA publishers.

Just last month BioMed Central put the position lucidly in its submission to the Obama White House Office of Science and Technology Policy:

http://blogs.openaccesscentral.com/blogs/bmcblog/entry/biomed_central_s_comments_in

> BioMed Central supports both the goal of open access and the goal of ensuring that the value added by publishers is properly recompensed. ... [W]e do not feel there is a need to 'balance' these two goals as we do not feel that they are in opposition. ... [O]pen access need not threaten the role of STM publishers. The open access publishing model, in which publishers are paid directly for the service of publication, is proving in practice to be just as viable a business model ... as the traditional model whereby publishers recover the costs associated with publication by taking exclusive rights and then selling access via subscriptions. Given that there is a viable business model for publishing scholarly research that does not depend on restricting access, we do not feel that the US government needs to arbitrarily limit the extent and reach of its open access deposit requirements attached to its research funding. We therefore recommend that the mandatory Public Access Policy which has operated successfully with respect to National Institutes of Health funding since 2008, be extended to cover all federally funded research. ...

OA publishers are not threatened by the rise of OA, and at least two different OA business models are already producing profits or surpluses: the no-fee model at Medknow and the fee-based models at Hindawi, BMC, PLoS ONE, and the Optical Society of America. Only the publishers who choose to meter out knowledge to paying customers, or to depend on artificial scarcity, are threatened by the rise of OA and can call for compromise.

As Tim O'Reilly pointed out, OA doesn't threaten publishing, just (some) existing publishers. We can add the converse: OA would have to compromise to protect (some) existing publishers, but not to protect publishing.

Some publishers are adapting while others are resisting. That difference makes all the difference, and here the advantage belongs to OA. It may be easier for TA publishers to adapt to OA (not necessarily to adopt OA themselves but to coexist with it) than for oil companies and coal mines to adapt to the new world of clean energy. But if oil and coal companies could adapt to a world of clean energy, and perhaps even take a leadership role in it, then full steam ahead for clean energy. If they resist, and if we allow their survival and prosperity become criteria for public policy, then we will run out of steam. Or whatever takes the place of steam.

What if oil companies only wanted temporary shackles on Wonder Power to give them time to adapt? The delay would be hard to justify, given the urgent need for clean energy and the mounting harm of doing without it. But there might be a case for it if the transformed companies could give more material aid to the energy metamorphosis than they would subtract by slowing it down.

The Canadian Library Association took a similar position in May 2008 when it called on Canadian libraries to support OA: "If delay or embargo periods are permitted to accommodate publisher concerns, these should be considered temporary, to provide publishers with an opportunity to adjust, and a review period should be built in, with a view to decreasing or eliminating any delay or embargo period."

http://www.cla.ca/AM/Template.cfm?Section=Position_Statements&Template=/CM/ContentDisplay.cfm&ContentID=5306

But to slow down Wonder Power to prop up incumbent industries without any expectation that they will adapt is the worst of both worlds.

(4) Some pay for all

The economics of wind power are peculiar. The benefits are global (reduced reliance on oil, reduced greenhouse gas emissions) but the costs are local (expense, sight, sound, wildlife damage). The costs and benefits largely affect different groups. Some other clean sources of energy, and some dirty ones, share the same peculiarity.

So do OA resources, and especially OA journals. The benefits are global (barrier-free access for everyone, increased research productivity) but the costs are local (expense, labor). Moreover, the costs and benefits largely affect different groups. The costs are borne by the publisher and those who support it through publication fees or subsidies. The benefits are enjoyed by researchers everywhere.

I often point out that not all (and not even most) OA journals charge publication fees ...

http://www.earlham.edu/~peters/fos/newsletter/11-02-06.htm#nofee

... and that there are many different business models for OA journals,

http://oad.simmons.edu/oadwiki/OA_journal_business_models

But one thing that all OA journal business models have in common is the "some pay for all" principle.

http://www.earlham.edu/~peters/writing/acrl.htm

"Some pay for all" (SPA) applies equally to fee-based and no-fee OA journals. It also covers green OA as well as gold OA. The cost of a repository is borne by the institution hosting it, and perhaps a few benefactors elsewhere such as foundations or consortial peers. But the benefits are global.

SPA has the obvious advantage of allowing free access for end users. The paying subset pays, of course. But if it pays all the production costs, then the journal or repository can meet its expenses without charging end users. Broadcast television and radio proved that SPA can work. OA is simply applying or adapting the model to research literature, a domain where costs are far lower than news and entertainment, and where the creative talent even gives away its work.

The major disadvantage of SPA is that members of the subset asked to pay may be unable or unwilling to pay, a problem that is more serious for gold OA than green OA. We've evolved a family of solutions and partial solutions to this problem: for example, funders paying on behalf of grantees; universities paying on behalf of faculty; waiving fees in cases of economic hardship; discounting fees for authors affiliated with institutional members; at hybrid journals, discounting fees for authors affiliated with institutional subscribers; and eliminating fees in favor of institutional subsidies. Some sophisticated variations on these solutions are still evolving, such as the Rowsean flip and CERN's SCOAP3.

http://www.earlham.edu/~peters/fos/newsletter/10-02-07.htm#flip

http://www.scoap3.org/

On the bright side, SPA can deliver OA research and wind power, when the local groups that would bear the costs are willing to bear them. On the other side, SPA can halt OA research and wind power when those local groups are not.

Is SPA easier to pull off for OA than clean energy? I don't know, and of course there's need to know. We only have to know whether to keep trying when we've been unsuccessful. A locality might welcome a wind farm, despite the local costs, because it will make its own energy green—and, under the hypothesis, less expensive. Important players in a locality might pony up the money to support an OA journal or repository because they want to see the research disseminated—because they paid for the research, because the research was done at their institution, because it advances their field, or because it promises important social benefits.

If a wind farm really can lower the local price of energy, then there are local costs and local benefits to weigh against one another. OA resources may be in the same boat: there are local costs (to pay for the resource) and local benefits (if it advances the interests of the people or institutions paying for the resource), entirely apart from the global benefits.

Broadcast TV and radio made SPA work because they could find deep-enough pockets with an interest in disseminating the shows: advertisers. OA projects make SPA work, when it works, because they can find stakeholders with an interest in disseminating the research: authors and author sponsors such as employers or funders. Economically, an OA journal or repository is like a lighthouse: supported by local ports because it benefits local ports, but also benefiting everyone who sails nearby, even those who don't use local ports.

It's tempting to say that even TA journals use SPA, since those paying the subscription fees are just a subset of users. (They may not even be users at all.) But this would change the meaning of "all." Subscription fees may cover more users than the subscription payers, but they don't pay for "all" the way OA business models do.

By contrast, dirty energy uses SPA, just as wind power does. The pollution from a coal-fired power plant may spread far and wide, and the greenhouse cases may cause global harms. But there's no doubt that the local harm is even greater than the global harm. Yet the electricity can be enjoyed as widely as that generated by a wind farm. Hence the shift from dirty to clean energy is not a shift from non-SPA to SPA. It's a shift from burdening one locale in a certain way to burdening another locale in a different way. It's a gain not by lifting all burdens, or by shifting them, but by lightening them.

Here's another difference: It's hard for the public to share the particular burden of wind power. The windmills can't be in *everyone's* back yard. But it's easy for the public to share the burden of green and gold OA. It's just a monetary cost, which can be spread as evenly as we like. For example, the cost of implementing the NIH policy (about 0.01% of the NIH budget) is spread among all US taxpayers. The cost of arXiv, which was formerly borne by Cornell alone, is now spread among Cornell and 20+ other universities.

http://communications.library.cornell.edu/news/arxiv

The monetary cost of wind power can be spread widely, since everyone who uses the power can be asked to pay for it. Only the effects on sightlines and wildlife remain stubbornly local. Unfortunately that local increment can be enough to derail a project. By contrast, most OA resources are spared this problem. They impose local costs, but these are almost wholly monetary. If we spread those costs far enough to succeed in raising the needed funds (which sometimes needn't be far at all), then there need be no stubbornly local residue to go without support. However, many OA projects launch before their fees or subsidies are adequate to cover their costs, and the unpaid portion becomes a local burden which, unfortunately, can be enough to derail a project.

A year ago this month, the US Congress agreed to fund the State Children's Health Insurance Program (SCHIP) with a new tax on tobacco.

http://www.cms.hhs.gov/home/schip.asp

http://content.nejm.org/cgi/content/full/NEJMp0900461

This is an SPA program in which the payors—smokers—are not volunteering. There is a slim argument that it makes sense to fund health insurance by charging smokers, who create ill-health for themselves and others. But since most American children today grow up in smoke-free households, relatively few smokers endanger the health of children covered by SCHIP. We may just have to admit that SCHIP subsidizes a good thing (children's health insurance) by taxing an unrelated or marginally related bad thing that we want to discourage for independent reasons. If the logic transferred, then we could support OA by taxing scientific ignorance.

(I'm sorely tempted to explore this playful hypothesis further, and already have a few ideas for carrying it out that are more than half-serious. But there are better SPA models for OA than SCHIP.)

Even if you support SCHIP, as I do, we can admit that it rests on some slippage between the "some" who pay and the "all" who benefit. It would be more elegant if the "some" were a subset of the "all," so that all who paid were at least beneficiaries of the program they were funding.

Can we find a way to charge all and only those who *benefit* from energy or research, and minimize SCHIP-style slippage?

Unfortunately, as long as wind farms impose unavoidable local costs, then we can't follow this model except perversely by limiting the benefits to the same locale. (Otherwise some beneficiaries would be spared the costs.) That might work for wind farms in windy places, but it would foreclose the possibility of sending wind-generated electricity elsewhere. The problems are even worse on the OA side. Since authors and readers both benefit from the distribution of knowledge, we'd have to charge both. But as soon as we charge readers, we give up on OA. Hence, spreading the costs among all the beneficiaries could fund restricted access to knowledge but it couldn't fund unrestricted access.

Note that the problem doesn't lie in trying to charge *only* beneficiaries, but in trying to charge *all* beneficiaries. If we retreat from trying to charge all of them, then there are two large families of solutions: author-side charges and reader-side charges. Both charge a class of beneficiaries, both leave a class of beneficiaries uncharged, and hence, both ask one class of beneficiaries to pay for others. But if we don't retreat, then we can't apply the model to support of clean energy or OA.

The question then becomes whether the benefits of OA are worth the asymmetry in which some beneficiaries pay for others. My answer is yes, certainly, and for four reasons. First, the two major classes of beneficiaries in this domain—authors and readers—overlap significantly. Second, nothing in the model prevents the beneficiaries who do pay from getting their money's worth. (Clearly there are ways for some to pay for all in which the "some" don't get their money's worth, but we needn't defend them.) Third, nothing in the model or in the asymmetry itself requires an injustice. For example, there's nothing unfair or unjust in having advertisers rather than viewers pay the costs of broadcast TV, even though both groups are beneficiaries. (Clearly there are unjust ways to make some pay for all, but we needn't defend them.)

Finally, the benefits are huge. We're not talking sitcoms and talk shows here, but the research on which our health, safety, technology, and prosperity depend. That includes the research which will bring us closer, if anything can, to efficient, inexpensive, clean energy.

More on the Landscape of Open Access

Promoting Open Access in the Humanities

From "Promoting Open Access in the Humanities," originally written for oral presentation on January 3, 2004, at the Annual Meeting of the American Philological Association in San Francisco. I wrote the section on diagnosis for the SPARC Open Access Newsletter, February 2, 2004, and revised the combined edition for publication in the proceedings of the APA meeting, *Syllecta Classica*, 16 (2005) 231–246.

http://dash.harvard.edu/handle/1/4729720

[…] [Here omitting an introduction to open access.]

Diagnosis: Why is open access moving so slowly in the humanities?

Open-access archiving took off fastest in physics and open-access journals took off fastest in biomedicine. There are fascinating cultural and economic reasons why these disciplines opened first. But let's focus on the other end of the pack where open access is moving the slowest. Why is it moving so slowly in the humanities?

Here are nine differences between the humanities and the sciences that help explain their different rates of progress.

(1) Journal prices are much higher in science, technology, and medicine (the STM fields) than in the humanities. The pricing crisis is not the only reason to consider open access, and not the primary reason for researchers themselves, but it's a major one for libraries and universities. In the humanities affordable journals defuse the urgency of reducing prices or turning to open access as part of the solution. Researchers have the same motivation to consider open access in the humanities and the sciences—to enlarge their audience and increase their impact. But the sciences see a convergence of motives, and hence a partnership of stakeholders, missing from the humanities.

According to the 2002 *Library Journal* pricing survey, the average subscription prices for journals in STM fields were 10–20 times higher than the average prices in the humanities. For example, compare biology ($1,097.01), chemistry ($2,143.22), and physics ($2,218.82) with history ($126.35), literature ($110.51), and philosophy ($146.60).

http://lj.libraryjournal.com/2002/04/ljarchives/periodicals-price-survey-2002 doing-the-digital-flip/

(2) Much more STM research is funded than humanities research. Hence, in the STM fields there is much more money to pay the processing fees charged by open access journals. In the humanities, there are fewer open access journals, and nearly all of them operate without processing fees.

(3) At least in the U.S., the government funds far more STM research than humanities research. Hence the taxpayer argument for open access (that taxpayers shouldn't have to pay a second fee for access to the results of taxpayer-funded research) is stronger in the STM fields than the humanities. The taxpayer argument isn't the only argument for open access, but it's one of the strongest and certainly one of the first to appeal to policy-makers and the public. It may only apply to a fraction of STM research, but that fraction dwarfs the comparable fraction of humanities research.

http://dash.harvard.edu/handle/1/4725013

Total U.S. federal funding for university research in fiscal 2001, in all fields, was about $19 billion, which constituted about 60% of all funding for university research. Of this, eight federal agencies, all in STM fields, provided 97% of this funding, and two of the agencies alone, NIH and NSF, provided $14.2 billion or 75%. By contrast, the National Endowment for the Humanities (NEH) budget for 2002 was $124 million, less than 1% of the STM funding from the 8 leading federal agencies alone.

(Sources, GAO report of November 14, 2003 and NEH budget request for 2004.)

http://www.gao.gov/new.items/d0431.pdf

http://web.archive.org/web/20040203233951/

http://www.neh.gov/whoweare/2004budget.html

If we don't limit ourselves to university-based research, then the total research budget of the U.S. is much greater, $110 billion in 2003. All the funding beyond the

subset for university-based research was for the STM fields, including defense, none for the humanities.
(Source, Rand Corporation, Federal Investment in R&D, 2002, Chapter One.)

http://www.rand.org/pubs/monograph_reports/MR1639z0.html

(4) On average, humanities journals have higher rejection rates (70–90%) than STM journals (20–40%). This means that the cost of peer review per accepted article is higher in the humanities, lower in the STM fields. Hence, for open access journals that cover their expenses through processing fees on accepted articles, the fees would have to be higher at the average humanities journal than at the average STM journal. This combines badly with the fact that the humanities receive much less government and foundation funding than the sciences.

H.A. Zuckerman and R.K. Merton first showed this disparity in rejection rates in the 1970s, and ALPSP confirmed it in the 1990s. See the discussion thread on this question from January 2001 in the American Scientist Open Access Forum. See H.A. Zuckerman and R.K Merton, "Patterns of evaluation in science: Institutionalization, structure and functions of the referee system," Minerva, 9 (1971) 66–100. Also see a brief online summary of the 2001 data collected by ALPSP.

http://users.ecs.soton.ac.uk/harnad/Hypermail/Amsci/1127.html

(5) There is more public demand for open access to research on (say) genomics than Greek grammar, which is one reason why genomics has more federal funding than Greek grammar. Of course research can be worth funding and making openly accessible even in the absence of public demand, but public demand tends to create funding, policy, incentives, and lobbyists. Note that public demand ranks some scientific research topics above others (medicine above field biology, for example), just as it does in the humanities (American history above Roman history, for example).

I can acknowledge this even though my own field (philosophy) is in the humanities. But a more contentious way to make a similar point is to say that STM research is more socially useful than humanities research, at least in the way that attracts funding. This is what makes foundations and governments want to pay for it, and what makes them receptive to the argument that the subsidy for open-access dissemination is worth paying too since it makes a useful research project even more useful.

Before fellow humanists write me angry letters, I'm not saying that humanities research isn't socially useful, or is less useful than the sciences, merely that this is the perception of most funding agencies. There are two kinds of usefulness, which is why the sciences and humanities coexist wherever civilization takes root. But each kind of usefulness tends to be dismissed or misunderstood by champions of the other. The most succinct wisdom on the usefulness and fundability of humanities research was uttered by Aristippus, a Greek philosopher who sought patronage from one rich Athenian after another. Dionysius once asked him, "Why do I always see you philosophers knocking on the doors of the rich, but I never see the rich knocking on the doors of philosophers?" Aristippus replied, "Because philosophers know what they need and the rich don't."

(6) Preprint exchanges meet more needs in the STM fields than in the humanities. STM researchers need to know quickly what is happening in their microspecialization, partly to build on it in their own work and partly to avoid being scooped. Moreover, they need to deposit their own preprints quickly, partly in order to influence fast-moving research and partly to establish priority over others who might be working on the same problem. Preprint archives are very common in the natural sciences, very rare in the humanities.

Of course humanists build on one another's work too and worry about scooping and being scooped. But there's no doubt that the urgency of timely notification of other work is greater in the STM fields than in the humanities. The explanation may lie deep, for example, in their different ways of being socially useful and their different ways of recognizing and rewarding the solution of problems.

(7) Demand for journal articles in the humanities drops off more slowly after publication than demand for articles in the STM fields. This means that humanities journals will worry more than STM journals that offering open access to articles after some embargo period, such as six months after publication, will jeopardize their revenue and survival.

There are three differences here: objective rate of decline in demand after publication, objective risk of lost revenue from delayed open access, and subjective fear of lost revenue from delayed open access. But none of these means that delayed open access will really jeopardize revenue and survival, either in the sciences and humanities. The revenue from selling access to old issues is miniscule, and losing that revenue will not harm a healthy journal, especially when offset by enhanced access, visibility, and impact that can be translated into increased submissions, advertising, and (if they still exist) subscriptions.

(8) Humanities journals often want to reprint poems or illustrations that require permission from a copyright holder. It's much harder to get reprint permission for open-access distribution than for a limited-circulation, priced and printed journal. And when permission is granted, for either kind of distribution, it usually costs money. This is why open access will come last to art history.

(9) Journal articles are the primary literature in the STM fields. But in the humanities, journal articles tend to report on the history and interpretation of the primary literature, which is in books. STM faculty typically need to publish journal articles to earn tenure, while humanities faculty need to publish books. But the logic of open access applies better to articles, which authors give away, than to books, which have the potential to earn royalties.

Summary: open access isn't undesirable or unattainable in the humanities. But it is less urgent and harder to subsidize than in the sciences. Progress is taking place, and as more humanists come to understand the issues, and the strategies that work, we should expect to see progress continue and accelerate. For example, humanists may have fewer reasons for preprint archiving than STM researchers, but most of the advantages of preprint archiving still apply in the humanities and they are starting to have an effect. Humanists may feel less urgency to launch peer-reviewed, open-access journals, and find it harder to do so without funding for processing fees. But there are still reasons to launch such journals and other funding models to sustain them. Humanists may be more skittish about offering open access to their books than to their journal articles, but there are reasons why informed authors will choose to try the experiment. In the next section I sketch some of the strategies to facilitate these advances.

Recommendations: How can we advance open access in the humanities?

Most of these are recommendations for keeping costs down without sacrificing quality. One goes beyond journals to archives, and one goes beyond Phase 1 [OA for royalty-free literature like journal articles] solutions to Phase 2 [OA for royalty-producing literature like books].

(1) Use journal-management software to reduce the costs of peer review. Use open-source journal management-software to reduce the costs about as far as possible. Currently, Open Journal Systems (OJS) from the University of British Columbia Public Knowledge Project (PKP) is the only open-source journal management software. (I have no financial ties to OJS or PKP.)

(2) Do without copy editors. At most journals with both copy editors (who improve language) and disciplinary editors (who supervise peer review), the copy editors are paid salaries and the disciplinary editors donate their labor. Hence, dispensing with copy editors will reduce costs without interfering with peer review.

   Someone might object that much writing in the SSH fields is atrocious and needs scrupulous copy editing. I couldn't agree more. (Don't get me started.) But copy editing wouldn't help much with this problem because journals that publish atrocious writing seem to think that it's professional or sophisticated and wouldn't employ copy editors who favored mere clarity. I feel free to say this because the average writing in my field—philosophy—is much more atrocious than the average writing in classics.

Many STM journals dispense with copy editors in order to save money. But when they do use copy editors, it's often because they receive many submissions from non-native speakers. This is much less of a problem at humanities journals.

Just so that I am not misunderstood: I regard copy editing as a valuable service. I don't want to discard it unless there is no other way to lower costs enough to provide open access. Dropping copy editing is not a way to improve a journal, just a way to cut costs without reducing a journal's essential service of providing peer-reviewed research to a scholarly community.

The best solution—as long as we can't teach scholars to write clearly—is to find enough revenue to pay for copy editing alongside essential services like peer review. This is happening at the Public Library of Science journals, for example. However, we must admit that the shortage of funds makes this unlikely in the humanities. If we have to choose, then I would definitely prefer open access without copy editing to copy editing without open access.

(3) Get universities to pay processing fees. Major public and private funding agencies in the sciences have declared their willingness to pay the processing fees charged by open-access journals. But I don't know of any foundations supporting humanities research that have followed suit. One reason, clearly, is that there are virtually no such journals today and no constituency seeking foundation support for them. This might change slowly, if open-access journals in the humanities can overcome the chicken-and-egg problem and survive long enough to ask for continued support. But the National Endowment for the Humanities (NEH), for example, is unlikely to help here. It conceives its grants more to subvene a scholar's salary than to pay for a specific piece of research. Nor could it give a grant to a journal to redistribute to scholars to cover the processing fees on accepted papers, since the NEH does not "regrant" or give grants for others to distribute.

Is it hopeless to expect universities to pay the fees for their humanist faculty? Perhaps today it is. Most universities are not only strapped, but perpetually strapped—or at least that's how it seems from the hallways of the humanities. But as open access spreads, university library budgets will realize large savings from the conversion, cancellation, or demise of subscription-based journals. The first priority for this savings should be to pay the processing fees to support the superior publishing model that made the savings possible.

No doubt, however, this kind of solution is more long-term than short-term. But while I admit that, I also want to suggest that visionary leadership in universities will understand that investing in the open-access alternative today, before subscription savings make it easy, will not only share knowledge and accelerate research, but also save the university serious money in the long run.

(4) Even if universities can often pay the upfront processing fees, open-access journals in the humanities will have to explore other ways to cover their expenses.

For example, *Philosopher's Imprint* is an open-access philosophy journal from the University of Michigan. It's motto is, "Edited by philosophers, published by librarians." Because the philosophers and librarians are already on the university payroll, the journal charges no processing fees. The result is that authors don't pay for dissemination and readers don't pay for access. The same model works for STM journals in fields with low funding. The *Journal of Insect Science* is published by the library of the University of Arizona at Tucson. For more on libraries as journal publishers, see recent reflections by Harry Hagedorn and Eulalia Roel.

http://docs.lib.purdue.edu/cgi/viewcontent.cgi?article=1590&context=iatul

http://www.ala.org/acrl/issues/scholcomm/crlnews/electronicjournal

Another model that works where funding is minimal is the overlay journal, which is essentially just an open-access archive plus an editorial board. The board takes submissions through the archive, makes its judgments, and deposits approved (perhaps revised) articles back in the archive. By using open-access archives as the publishing infrastructure, overlay journals reduce expenses about as far as possible without skimping on peer review. The University of California recently launched a series of overlay journals in all disciplines, based on the UC eScholarship Repository.

(5) Experiment with retroactive peer review. In retroactive peer review, a journal starts with unrefereed submissions on an open-access web site, subjects them to its own favored method of vetting or review, and then either copies the approved articles to a different site or marks them somehow as approved. The reason for experimenting with retroactive peer review is not that open access depends on peer-review reform or vice versa; they are independent. The reason is simply that retroactive peer review costs less than traditional, prospective peer review, and this fact matters in fields that are not well-funded. There are many kinds of retroactive peer review, some more rigorous and adequate than others. This universe has barely been noticed, let alone explored. The importance of experimentation is to find the more rigorous and adequate forms of it, not just ways to save money. If we can find these rigorous and adequate forms of retroactive peer review, then there is no academic loss, and much financial gain. There might even be academic gain, especially if you think that peer review as currently practiced leaves considerable room for improvement.

(6) Work for price reductions and open access (two different things) for STM journals. High STM journal prices harm the humanities as well as the sciences, and the savings from lowering these prices can be the salvation of the humanities.

One expensive STM journal can cost more than $20,000/year, more than 100 middle-tier humanities journals. Moreover, we know that the rising prices of STM journals cause libraries to cut into their book budgets, which hurts the humanities much more than the sciences. When libraries buy fewer books, university presses accept fewer manuscripts. Open access in the STM fields would produce savings that could be spent on both (1) monographs and (2) processing fees for open-access journals.

Quoting Kenneth Frazier in *Library Journal Academic Newswire* for November 20, 2003: "A lot of library directors won't admit this, but often the STM increases [in journal subscription prices] come out of the hide of the humanities." (Not online.)

(7) Notice that all the recommendations so far have concerned open-access journals. If their costs can be kept sufficiently low, or if savings elsewhere in university budgets can subsidize them, then they can thrive. But journals are only one of two major avenues to open access. The other is open-access archiving. Every university in the world can have an institutional archive built from open-source software, and should. It can be installed in a weekend at essentially no cost, and even if very successful would use fewer resources than the MP3 traffic generated today by students. If there were no open-access journals in the humanities at all, scholars could still deposit their preprints in their institutional archives, and in most cases their postprints as well. This would not only provide open access to those articles, but also give the authors freedom to publish in any journal of their choice, open access or not.

This model works just as well with disciplinary archives (dedicated to all the eprints in a field) rather than institutional archives (dedicated to all the eprints produced by the institution). Here are some examples of disciplinary open-access archives in the social sciences and humanities.

• Arts and Humanities Data Service (general)

  http://www.ahds.ac.uk/index.htm

• Digital Library of the Commons (interdisciplinary research on the commons)

  http://dlc.dlib.indiana.edu/dlc/

• dLIST (library and information science)

  http://arizona.openrepository.com/arizona/handle/10150/105067

• E-LIS (library and information science)

  http://eprints.rclis.org/

• History and Theory of Psychology (psychology and the history of psychology)

  http://web.archive.org/web/20030201100600/

  http://htpprints.yorku.ca/

- Open Language Archives Community (linguistics)

  http://www.language-archives.org/

- PhilSci Archive (philosophy of science)

  http://philsci-archive.pitt.edu/

- Theoretical and applied linguistics (linguistics)

  http://web.archive.org/web/20031215094730/

  http://archive.ling.ed.ac.uk/

- UK Data Archive (the social sciences and humanities generally)

  http://www.data-archive.ac.uk/

(8) Finally, all the recommendations so far have been "Phase 1" recommendations—ways to provide open access to the texts that scholars already consent to give away. But we should consider the obvious "Phase 2" recommendation: humanists could consent to open access for their monographs, not just their journal articles. There are two reasons for an author to consider this possibility.

- Free online full-text might increase net sales. This is the experience of the National Academies Press (for research monographs) and the Baen Free Library (for science fiction novels). For some of the explanation why, see reflections by Michael Jensen, director of the National Academies Press, and Eric Flint, co-founder of the Baen Free Library.

  http://books.nap.edu/

  http://www.baenebooks.com/c-1-free-library.aspx

  http://web.archive.org/web/20070807233913/

  http://chronicle.com/prm/weekly/v48/i03/03b02401.htm

  http://web.archive.org/web/20070202111951/

  http://www.baen.com/library/palaver6.htm

- Even if open access doesn't increase net sales, the benefits of open access are significant (greatly enlarged audience and increased impact) and the royalties on an average humanities monograph between zero and meager.

  Book authors who are still nervous could consent to open access after they think the majority of purchases has already occurred. During the time that the monograph is toll-access only, the author could still provide open-access excerpts and metadata online to help scholars find the book and learn whether it is relevant to their own research projects.

Helping Scholars and Helping Libraries

From "Helping scholars and helping libraries," SPARC Open Access Newsletter.

http://dash.harvard.edu/handle/1/4552051

Scholars and librarians are close allies in the campaign for open access, but they pursue OA for different reasons. For scholars, the primary benefit of OA is wider and easier access for readers and larger audience and impact for authors. For librarians, the primary benefit of OA is saving money in their serials budgets.

(I've argued in the past that OA will help libraries solve both the "pricing crisis" and the "permission crisis." I haven't changed my mind about that, but here I'll focus on the library interest in solving the pricing crisis.)

http://www.earlham.edu/~peters/writing/acrl.htm

We like to say that OA is a goal to which there are many means. But scholars and libraries in effect treat it as a means to their separate but related, professionally-specific goals. It's not surprising that some OA initiatives help scholars more than they help libraries, or that some OA initiatives help libraries indirectly but don't help them save money in their serials budgets. Here are four quick examples.

(1) Self-archiving, at least at its current low levels: Every new article in an OA repository helps its author and all of its readers. But it doesn't justify librarians in canceling journal subscriptions and it doesn't convert subscription journals to OA journals. As self-archiving spreads, there may be a tipping point after which it helps libraries save money. Or there may not, if the experience in physics transfers to other disciplines. But what matters here is that self-archiving helps scholars even before we get to that tipping point.

Similarly, libraries that host institutional repositories have an important new institutional responsibility and they can benefit from taking on that role. But self-archiving helps scholars even at universities that don't yet have institutional repositories.

(2) Hybrid journals offering OA at the author's choice (the "Walker-Prosser" model): When only a fraction of authors take advantage of the OA option, then libraries cannot justify canceling subscriptions. But scholars benefit when even a fraction of a journal's content goes OA.

(3) Non-OA journals offering OA to sufficiently old back issues: OA to back issues may help libraries save the cost of buying access to the back run, but it doesn't help them save the larger expense of subscribing. If the embargo is sufficiently long, then libraries will not be able to justify cancellations. For journals, of course, this is the point. Finding an embargo period that is short enough to serve research needs in the field without subverting subscriptions (i.e., without helping scholars enough and without helping libraries in the primary way) is an art that many journals are trying to master.

(4) The NIH public-access policy: I've often argued that there are good reasons to think that it won't undercut journal subscriptions. That's the flip side of arguing that libraries won't cancel subscriptions on account of this policy, even if they continue to cancel subscriptions for other reasons, such as rising prices. The best reason to think that the NIH policy will not cause cancellations, and would not have done so even in its earlier and stronger form with only a six-month embargo, is that libraries themselves said so. In its comment on the NIH policy, the Association of College and Research Libraries (ACRL) wrote:

> We wish to emphasize, above all, that academic libraries will not cancel journal subscriptions as a result of this plan and that it will therefore not produce economic harm to publishers. Since biomedical journals publish research that derives from many sources other than NIH funding, the articles made available in PubMed Central will not substitute for the content of individual journals. Even if libraries wished to consider the availability of NIH-funded articles when making journal cancellation decisions, they would have no reasonable way of determining what articles in specific journals would become openly accessible after the embargo period. The six-month embargo also provides substantial protection of publishers' interests. Because most biomedical research is time sensitive, libraries will make every effort to maintain the subscriptions they already have as a way of providing needed access to the most current research.

Eight reasons to think the NIH public-access policy won't undercut subscriptions

http://www.earlham.edu/~peters/fos/nihfaq.htm#subscribers

The ACRL comment on the NIH public-access policy, November 16, 2004

http://www.ala.org/ala/acrl/acrlissues/scholarlycomm/nihsupport.htm

We know what kinds of OA initiative will help scholars—namely, every kind. But what kinds of OA initiative will help libraries save money in their serials budgets?

I want to approach this question from the side. It looks as though helping libraries has to hurt publishers. It looks as though helping libraries save money in their serials budgets means canceling subscriptions. That is not quite true. It's true that canceling subscriptions is one way to help libraries save money, but it's not the only way. Libraries also save money when subscription-based journals convert to OA. Conversions are voluntary and can come about through persuasion, experimentation, or changing market conditions.

I want us to achieve the kinds of OA that help scholars *and* the kinds of OA that help libraries. I want to help libraries in part because I'm in a symbiotic relationship with them. Healthy libraries are necessary to support healthy research and education. I want to help libraries because they are committed allies in the campaign for OA. More importantly, I want to help libraries because the best source of funds to pay for the long-term sustenance of OA is the savings from library serials budgets. If the rise of OA literature lets us spend less on priced literature, then the best way to spend the savings is on the OA alternative that made the savings possible.

Finally, I want to help libraries because we can't take the last steps toward helping scholars without helping libraries as well. For example, low-volume self-archiving may help scholars without helping libraries, but high-volume self-archiving will help both, at least in fields where the experience in physics does not transfer. I want high-volume self-archiving. I want OA to 100% of research literature, through some combination (it doesn't matter what combination) of OA archiving and OA journals.

The inevitable question is whether I, and all others who want to help libraries, want to harm publishers. The answer is no. That is not the goal. The goal is OA to 100% of the research literature. Achieving that goal is compatible with subscription-based access to some considerable percentage of the same literature. (These percentages can add up to more than 100% because some literature can be both free and priced, such as an article in a subscription journal deposited by its author in an OA repository.)

Progress toward the goal of OA to 100% of research literature will eventually help libraries reduce their serials expenses. It may create the quality and quantity of OA literature that justifies them in canceling some subscription journals. Or it may persuade some subscription journals to convert, e.g., by answering fears about conversion or by changing market conditions so that conversion becomes a survival strategy. Or both.

I don't know *how much* this progress will help libraries. That depends on how much priced access is compatible with 100% OA. Last month I looked at some of the variables that affect this kind of long-term co-existence and some of the reasons why predictions are difficult.

http://www.earlham.edu/~peters/fos/newsletter/03-02-05.htm#coexistence

I'm sorry if all of this is obvious. During the long campaign for the NIH policy, I argued that this particular policy would not harm publishers. I made the argument so often that I began to wonder whether it created a false impression about my larger position or at least drew attention away from two equally important parts of it. First, the NIH policy won't do much to help libraries, and second, other initiatives that I do support will certainly help libraries and could threaten subscriptions.

I will never support an initiative whose direct purpose is to undermine publishers. I've argued before that OA does not require publisher setbacks, and that publisher setbacks do not necessarily advance OA. Hence, to pursue publisher setbacks is to mistake the goal. It's harmful and wrong. I haven't changed my mind about that.

http://www.earlham.edu/~peters/fos/newsletter/05-03-04.htm#distractions

But I definitely support initiatives to enlarge the body of OA literature, rapidly and systematically, even if a foreseeable side-effect is that libraries cancel subscriptions. I want to say this in public. One reason is to refocus on the needs of libraries, overlooked in the NIH campaign. Even if libraries benefit indirectly from every OA initiative that benefits scholars, they need more direct forms of relief as well. Another reason is simply to admit that not all OA initiatives will be as innocuous for publishers as the NIH policy.

For example, I support voluntary self-archiving of journal articles by all authors. I support policies at every funding agency, public and private, to mandate OA to funded research. I support policies at all universities to mandate OA to royalty-free research, like journal articles, produced by faculty. Each of these policies will lead to high-volume OA archiving. I support OA archiving for full-text articles, not just abstracts. I support full-text archiving for postprints, not just for preprints. I support postprint archiving immediately upon publication, not just after some embargo period. I support postprint archiving in OAI-compliant repositories, not just on personal home pages. I support these policies for all disciplines, all countries, and all languages. High-volume, full-text, immediate and interoperable OA postprint archiving will help libraries by leading to some combination (I don't know what combination) of journal conversions to OA and library cancellations of selected journals that do not convert. To supplement high-volume OA archiving, I support more peer-reviewed OA journals in every field, whether they are new launches or conversions from TA journals.

As we approach 100% OA, through archives and journals, I'm sure that the responses of subscription journals will differ from discipline to discipline. So I don't know *how much* this progress will undercut subscriptions. If most disciplines are like physics, or if some TA journals can survive in a high-OA environment, or if TA journals that lose subscribers can survive by converting to OA, then the answer is not much. But I don't want to be evasive. Even if the answer is that progress toward 100% will be more rather than less harmful to existing publishers, I still believe that 100% OA is a goal worth pursuing. Certain services, like peer review and wide and easy distribution, are indispensable for science and society. But no particular journal or publisher is indispensable.

Unbinding Knowledge: A Proposal for Providing Open Access to Past Research Articles, Starting with the Most Important

From "Unbinding Knowledge: A proposal for providing open access to past research articles, starting with the most important," in Giandomenico Sica (ed.), *Open Access, Open Problems*, Milan: Polimetrica, October 20, 2006, pp. 43–58. It's an expanded edition of an article first published in SPARC Open Access Newsletter, June 2, 2004.

http://dash.harvard.edu/handle/1/4317663

1. Imagining a Way to Accelerate Research

Most open access projects focus on new literature and leave open access to previously published literature an open problem for the future. This made sense in the early days of the open access movement, when helping hands, funding, and acceptance were all less common than they are today. Providing open access to new research articles is generally easier and less expensive than providing it retroactively to older articles. New articles are born digital; copyright holders are available for consent or persuasion; the benefits of increased audience and impact are most compelling at the time of publication; and a subsidy from the author's funding agency or employer is often available at that time and not later. There are still good reasons to make new literature a higher priority than older literature. But today, when open access has significant support and momentum, there are good reasons to include older literature in our strategic vision.

Some universities are asking their faculty members to deposit all their research articles, new and old, in the institutional repository. Some journals are digitizing their back runs and providing open access to them. PubMed Central will digitize and provide open access to the back runs of selected medical journals, and the Wellcome Trust spearheads a similar project.[1] These efforts are all critical and should continue. But many journals cannot afford to digitize their back issues; many are not eligible for PMC or Wellcome digitization (if only because they're not in biomedicine); and, most importantly, many are still *unwilling* to offer open access to their back issues. For those journals, here's a step in the right direction.

The basic idea is for an authoritative scholar or organization to compile a bibliography of the 500 most important previously published research articles on a subject of urgent public interest, such as the treatment and prevention of HIV/AIDS. Then a hardworking soul asks the journals that published those articles to provide open access to them retroactively.

Let's say that the person compiling the list of articles is the *bibliographer*. It won't be hard to find a credible bibliographer. It could be a scholar with a track record in the field or a respected organization like the International AIDS Society.

Let's say that the person who contacts the journals is the *facilitator*. The facilitator might be a volunteer, but I expect that the work will be extensive and that foundations will be willing to fund it. The facilitator will have many tasks. First ascertain which articles from the bibliography are already open access and temporarily put them to one side. Then organize the remaining articles by journal. Contact each journal, identify the articles it published from the list, and ask it to provide open access to those articles. As needed, explain the request, answer questions, and negotiate details.

Some journals will accept these open access invitations and some will not. When the responses are in, the bibliographer and facilitator, or the organizations sponsoring them, will publicly thank the participating journals as well as the providers of the articles that were already open accessible. The sponsors will produce a revised online version of the bibliography with links to open access editions of its articles.

Articles published in journals that decided not to cooperate will not appear on the list. The project purpose is to open the literature and applaud cooperation, not to publicize or shame non-cooperation. (More on this in Section 3, below.)

For lack of a better term, let's call such initiatives *unbinding projects*. I'm hoping that unbinding projects will be tried first in medicine, where the public good is easily recognized, the need is urgent, and open access is already familiar. However, the strategy is general and could be applied wherever there is clear social utility in accelerating the pace of research. Open access to the most important papers on artificial photosynthesis, fuel-efficient engines, or pollution-scrubbing smokestacks will advance research and development on these beneficial technologies.

2.   Why Would a Journal Agree?

Most journals receiving these requests will not be open-access journals, but most will have electronic editions. Providing open access to the articles identified by an unbinding project will not require peer review, editing, or manuscript preparation. It will only require moving a copy of the electronic file to an open-access Web site.[2] At the same time, the journal might add some boilerplate text about the article's open-access status, and add an icon or annotation to the journal's table of contents to indicate that the article is now openly accessible.

Participating journals will help a good cause. They will help understand, treat, and prevent HIV/AIDS. To doubt this one must believe that good science is ineffective, that communicating scientific results does not make them more useful, or that the best scientific literature is already accessible to all those who can make use of it.

Participating journals will generate good will for themselves. They will become more visible as journals that published landmark articles. They will also become visible as journals willing to share knowledge and accelerate research on a matter of public importance. It shouldn't take an expensive marketing department to convert this kind of reputation into advantage in the competition for submissions, advertising, and subscriptions.

What about unbinding proposals on non-medical topics? Will journals feel the same moral force behind these requests? We won't know until we try the experiment, but it seems safe to assume that the journals publishing important articles on (say) wind power will be the same journals most receptive to the message that accelerating research on wind power is an important public good.

Peer review, editing, and manuscript preparation cost money, of course, but for almost every article included in an unbinding project, the journal will already have recovered these costs. Even if the journal sells access to its back run, this revenue is usually a very small part of its overall revenue stream. Moreover, participating in an unbinding project will only open up access to handful of its articles, not to the entire back run. The project does not ask a journal to accept or publish new articles, but merely to lift the protective barrier from previously published and previously amortized articles so that more people can make use of them.

The journal needn't release the articles into the public domain. If it is the copyright holder, then it can retain copyright.

Finally, the journal needn't worry that this kind of open access, even if extensive, would cause subscribers to cancel. That may be a worry with a general policy to provide open access to all new articles, or all past articles after an embargo period, but it does not arise with the selective, unpredictable, and retroactive opening of access to articles that turn out to be landmarks in their field.

It would be wonderful if all journals agreed to this offer, giving researchers, physicians, and the general public open access to 100% of the identified articles. But we can't expect that and we don't need that in order to justify the effort of trying.

Now imagine that similar bibliographies are compiled, and similar requests made, by the American Cancer Society, the Alzheimer's Association, the Royal Blind Society, the Epilepsy Foundation, the Leukemia and Lymphoma Society, the Malaria Foundation International. ...[3]

3. Applauding, not Shaming

Although the purpose is to open access to important science, and to applaud cooperation rather than shame non-cooperation, some important science journals may feel
that a decision not to cooperate will be accompanied by a stigma. Working scientists
will know that any list of important articles in their field will include some from that
journal; hence, the journal's omission will be a sign of non-cooperation.

I see no way to avoid this perception. It will exist no matter how scrupulous the
sponsors are to avoid any criticism of journals that do not cooperate. Different journals
will give this perception different weights, but care and honesty in running the program will not eliminate it. Moreover, because this perception may be intrinsic to the
decision not to cooperate, there may be no special reason to counter it.

But here are a few possibilities for countering it in case they are attractive to journals. All articles on the original list of 500 could be included in the published bibliography. This will give due recognition to the scientists who did the important work and
the journals that published it. The drawback to this plan is that the bibliography could
not link to open-access versions of articles from non-cooperating journals, and that
could highlight their decision not to cooperate even more than omitting them. Another
possibility is for the bibliography to link to priced or toll-access copies of these articles,
at the journal web sites, in order to facilitate access for those readers who are willing to
pay or who happen to have access privileges through their institutions. But these links
would have to be labeled as toll access (or conversely, the rest would have to be labeled
as open access) in order to help the sponsors identify the journals they wish to applaud
for their cooperation. Since the balance of advantages and disadvantages for non-
cooperating journals is a close call, the choice about these options might be left to the
journals themselves.

A third possibility is to encourage the authors of the articles published in non-
cooperating journals to provide open access to their articles themselves, through an
institutional or disciplinary archive or their personal web site. Then the bibliography
could link to that open-access copy. The drawback is that some journals still do not
consent to postprint archiving. However, some journals that might not provide their
own open-access copy of an article might consent to postprint archiving by the author.[3]

4. How Much Would This Cost?

The sponsoring organizations would pay for identifying the most worthy 500 articles,
discovering which are already available in open-access form, contacting the journals
publishing the non-OA articles, making the request, explaining it, and conducting any
follow-up negotiations. The sponsoring organizations would also bear the cost of preparing and hosting an online version of the resulting bibliography with active links.

All these costs could be paid by the same organization, or they could be split roughly as suggested between a disease advocacy organization (compiling the bibliography) and a research or humanitarian foundation (facilitating the rest). This is a natural opportunity for collaboration between scientific and philanthropic organizations and for cost-sharing between organizations with common interests.

The journals would pay the cost of copying a few files to a new location, adding boilerplate open-access licensing information to each one, and making minor revisions to a few tables of contents. When the electronic file is already prepared and the server costs are already part of the journal's overhead, then there is zero marginal cost in providing worldwide open access to the file, i.e., letting more people view the file that has already been created and is already online. As noted, the journals would already have paid the costs of soliciting, vetting, editing, preparing, and publishing electronic versions of the articles, and these costs were already recovered from the journal's subscription and licensing revenue.

Journals might be very proud that their articles were identified in the bibliography, and proud to enhance their usefulness by providing open access to them. If so, then they might take on the small additional cost of a press release, or even a press conference, to announce the unbinding.

If the journal sells access to its back run, then it might lose something by providing open access to a very small but very important fraction of that back run. If it offers pay-per-view access to individual articles in the back run, rather than all-or-nothing access to the back run, then it may lose revenue from some of its best-selling articles. This is a real cost that should not be denied, although its amount will be difficult to ascertain and almost certainly small. A journal will naturally take this cost into account when deciding whether to agree to the unbinding request.

Because journals need not worry that this form of selective, unpredictable, retroactive open access will cause subscribers to cancel, their decision on the unbinding proposal will turn almost entirely on lost revenue from future sales of access to the identified articles and whether this is outweighed by the resulting benefits for public health and the journal itself. Since typically the lost revenue will be vanishingly small, the public good large, and the good will generated for the journal considerable, we can predict that many journals will agree to participate.

The costs to the sponsoring organizations will certainly be greater than the costs to any single journal (from unbinding), and probably greater than the unbinding costs of all the participating journals combined.

5. Moral Suasion v. Money

Because a journal's costs in complying with the unbinding request are so low, it is reasonable to ask journals to make this gesture for the sake of assisting an important cause.

If moral suasion does not work and the sponsoring organizations have the means, then journals could be paid to release the selected articles into open access.

Moral suasion is preferable to money for two reasons. First, participating in an unbinding project costs a journal very little. Second, the sponsoring organizations would not have to pay an extra cost to bring about this public good, freeing them to pursue similar projects on other fronts and do more for the public good with its limited resources.

The publishers participating in the HINARI program, for example, are providing free online access to entire nations in the developing world without asking philanthropists to pay their costs. They are producing the journals in electronic form anyway. Giving access to new readers who couldn't buy subscriptions costs the journals nothing, generates good will, and enfranchises huge segments of humanity. It's definitely win-win.

Someone might object that the HINARI analogy isn't entirely apt because some of the researchers who would read the articles on the HIV/AIDS bibliography would be in a position to pay for access. That is true. But extending the same line of thought shows how to answer the objection. Many of the researchers, perhaps most of the researchers, who would want to read and use the articles in the bibliography will be affiliated with institutions that already subscribe to the relevant journals. They're not just in a position to pay; they're already paying. So instead of losing more revenue, the journal gets the best of both worlds: good will for providing open access and paid access by most researchers at the same time.

Another reason why moral suasion might work here is that the journal approached to unbind a given article is the only journal that can make this particular contribution to the public good. That makes the unbinding request very different from the request for a monetary donation, no matter how good the cause. Money is fungible and anyone else could give it. This well-known fact dilutes the moral force of the request and leads many good people to hope that their neighbors will make up for them. By contrast, scholarly journals are notoriously non-fungible. This fact is normally an obstacle to open access: if journals were fungible, then journals in the same research niche would compete directly with one another, and (assuming comparable quality and prestige) affordable journals would kill off the expensive ones, and free journals would kill off everything else. But an unbinding project turns the non-fungibility of journals to advantage. People asked for help are most likely to give it when they are in a unique position to do so. When a journal is asked to provide open access to one of its articles, then it can't assume that it was targeted in bad faith (as if the article were really unimportant) or that anyone else could provide this public service.

There's no reason to rule out the possibility that some requests will be accompanied by money and some will rely on moral suasion alone. The two can coexist. If the only way to free up the most important articles on superconducting ceramics, Dutch elm disease, or human-powered flight is to pay for them, then possibly someone could be found who would pay for them.

6. Variations on the Theme

- Free up the 500 most important papers on HIV/AIDS in 2004. Two years later liberate the most important 100 published during those two years. Repeat every two years or until all new research is open access.
- To save time and money, the group funding the bibliographer could start with existing bibliographies in the field.
- To increase the acceptance and authority of its bibliography by researchers in the field, at the expense of some time and money, the group funding the bibliographer could poll experts in the field, or even assemble an eminent editorial board just for this purpose. It could also post the draft bibliography online for a comment period.
- Journals that appreciate the logic of this project might spontaneously offer open access to articles in their back run that have somehow been identified as important. For example, when a scientist receives an award for a research breakthrough, a journal publishing some of his or her past articles could instantly provide open access to them. At the same time, it could issue a press release announcing that these important articles are now free to the research community and general public.[5]
- Likewise, individual scientists who appreciate the logic of this project might ask the journals that published their articles on matters of public importance to provide open access to them retroactively, or even immediately. Journals might be more responsive to organized projects than individual initiatives, but a groundswell of individual requests might be as effective as an organized project. Neither scientists nor journals need wait for brokers or philanthropists to mediate the unbinding requests.
- Participating in an unbinding project, or simply witnessing other journals participate, will demonstrate how open access can benefit journals and publishers, and not just their authors and readers. By making a journal's brand more visible, and cementing its reputation as a journal publishing important articles and serving important public needs, participation can help a journal compete for the next generation of important articles, not to mention advertising and subscriptions. As journals learn more about these benefits, some will move other articles from their toll-access back run to their open-access back run. Some will realize that they gain more from increasing the visibility and accessibility of their articles, at least after a certain time, than from selling access to them.
- There is clearly nothing magical about the number 500. It would be better for HIV/AIDS patients if all articles useful for treatment and prevention were openly accessible than just 500. And on some new or narrow topics, there may be far fewer than

500 useful articles already published. The bibliographer can set this number in accordance with the topic and size of the body of published literature. When scientists bypass the bibliographer and facilitator, and take their requests directly to journals, they will clearly have no particular number in mind, and journals shouldn't feel constrained by a number.

- The sponsors could create a wide-ranging web site devoted to their unbinding project. In addition to the bibliography with active links, and perhaps the archive of papers, the site could contain the sponsors' press release of public thanks and some background on the project's purpose and method. If the project's beneficiaries (for example, article authors, other researchers in the field, and AIDS patients, their families, friends, and physicians) want to offer public thanks and testimonials, this web site would be the natural place to do so. The site could also provide information for donors willing to help offset the project's costs.

- When one or two of these projects have been brought to a successful conclusion, advocacy organizations will be eager to propose new projects and scholars will be eager to nominate articles for them. If the early projects are difficult, we can expect some of the difficulties to disappear as the idea becomes more familiar and we gain experience in implementing it.

7. An Objection from the Side of Open Access

It would be ironic if subscription-based journals liked this idea more than open-access proponents did. Open-access proponents might object that this is not true open access, and that by satisfying journals, authors, and readers, it might delay progress toward true open access.

Here's my quick reply to the objection. As the Bethesda Statement on Open Access Publishing makes clear,[6] open access is a property that belongs primarily to individual articles, and only derivatively or secondarily to journals. An unbinding project will create true open access to the articles from participating publishers. What an unbinding project will not do, on its own, is produce open-access journals that provide open access to all their articles past and future. That is true. But while there are many, highly diverse strategies for persuading conventional journals to offer open access to more of their articles, unbinding projects would not interfere with any of them. On the contrary, the most promising strategy I see for getting subscription-based journals to consider open access seriously is to get them to experiment with it. Unbinding projects are among the easiest and least risky kinds of open-access experiment. Moreover, they do not hinder the launch of new open-access journals or the spread of open-access archiving, and even boost them by directly acquainting more authors, readers, journals, and publishers with the benefits of open access. Finally, while other open access strategies are at work, having their own effects at their own speeds, this one could be enlarging the body of open-access literature, focusing on previously published articles that would otherwise remain behind access barriers, and starting with those that could be most helpful to urgent scientific and social problems.

8. Conclusion

Opening access to important research articles will accelerate research and all the benefits of research, from new medicines and therapies to improved clinical practice. It will also benefit the journals that published the articles by generating good will, increasing their visibility, and enhancing their reputation for scientific excellence and humanitarian assistance, all of which can translate in to bottom-line advantages in the competition for submissions, advertising, and subscriptions. This method of opening access can harness the interests, energy, and resources of groups that normally have little involvement in scholarly publication. It costs journals very little. Many journals will find that it brings them a net gain and many will consent even in the face of a small loss because of the gain it brings to others. Unlike other open-access initiatives, which focus on future literature, this one opens up past articles, starting with the most useful and important. It introduces journals to the methods and economics of open-access publishing, which could lead to more experimentation with open-access publication. It doesn't ask journals to convert to open access, but limits the request in scope and risk, making it easier for journals to assess and accept. It is a frank business proposition, with true benefits for the journal to weigh against the costs. It invites deliberation, not confrontation, and moves the open-access question from sometimes obstreperous conferences to the quiet of the journal's business office. Finally, it is likely that many journals will see it as a win-win proposition, agree to it wholeheartedly, and thereby enlarge the body of open-access research literature, make their own important articles more useful, and accelerate research on a matter of vital public need.

I thank Barbara Cohen, Helen Doyle, and Debra Lappin for comments on an earlier draft of this article. I give special thanks to Darius Cuplinskas for the stimulating conversation in which this idea emerged almost fully formed. He is certainly its coauthor. [...]

Notes

1. For some of the best university policies encouraging or requiring faculty to deposit their research output in the institutional repository, see the Institutional Self-Archiving Policy Registry.

http://www.eprints.org/signup/fulllist.php

Unfortunately there is no definitive list of non-OA journals with OA back runs. But a good collection of such journals is available at Highwire Press.

http://highwire.stanford.edu/

PMC Back Issue Digitization Project

http://www.pubmedcentral.gov/about/scanning.html

Medical journals backfiles digitisation project, sponsored by the Wellcome Trust, the Joint Information Systems Committee (JISC), and the National Library of Medicine (NLM)

http://library.wellcome.ac.uk/node280.html

2. There are several ways to do this. The journal could move a copy of the electronic file to a newly-created open-access directory on its own web site. An open-access directory is simply one that is not password protected. Or the journal could deposit a copy of the file in PubMed Central or another open-access repository for that discipline. Since both acts are trivial, and take only minutes of someone's time, a journal could do both.

The leading open-access publishers today do both. BioMed Central and the Public Library of Science host their own open-access copies of their articles, and deposit copies in PubMed Central.

BioMed Central

http://www.biomedcentral.com/

Public Library of Science

http://www.plos.org/

PubMed Central

http://www.pubmedcentral.nih.gov/

3. For a partial list of disease advocacy organizations, see the membership roster of the U.S.-based National Health Council,.

http://www.nationalhealthcouncil.org/aboutus/membership_index.htm

4. "Preprint archiving" is the deposit of an unrefereed preprint in an open-access archive. "Postprint archiving" is the deposit a refereed version, or a version approved by a journal's peer-review process. For a searchable database of publisher policies on preprint and postprint archiving, see Project SHERPA,.

http://www.sherpa.ac.uk/romeo.php

5. When a scientist wins the Nobel Prize, clearly the journals that published his or her work would benefit science as well as their own standing if they provided open access to the break-

through articles. But the stimulus might come from a turn of events, not just the rising star of an author. For example, after the September 11 attacks, McGraw-Hill offered open access to a full-text book, Glenn R. Schiraldi's *The Post-Traumatic Stress Disorder Sourcebook: A Guide to Healing, Recovery, and Growth.* The fact that the McGraw-Hill was helping victims of post-traumatic stress disorder and advertising itself at the same time did not undercut the usefulness of its action. On the contrary, it is precisely by mixing self-interest with public service that public service becomes more likely and more sustainable.

Details on the McGraw-Hill offer

http://www.mcgraw-hill.com/media/news/2001/09/20010928b.html

6. See the Bethesda Statement on Open Access Publishing, June 20, 2003,.

http://www.earlham.edu/~peters/fos/bethesda.htm

Open Access to Electronic Theses and Dissertations (ETDs)

From "Open access to electronic theses and dissertations (ETDs)," SPARC Open Access Newsletter, July 2, 2006.

http://dash.harvard.edu/handle/1/4727443

I finished my dissertation in 1977, before the web, before the internet, and even before personal computers. I typed it on an Olivetti typewriter and, when my committee accepted it, I paid the department secretary a dollar a page to retype it according to the formatting specs of the university. I was honored when the university made a copy on acid-free paper, bound it in boards, and put it on the open stacks in the main library. It even had a card in the card catalog. I was also honored when I discovered a week later that someone had stolen the copy from the library.

In addition, I sent a copy to University Microfilms International (UMI), which produced priced paper or microfilm copies on-demand. (UMI is now owned by ProQuest.) As far as I know it's still accessible for a price from UMI. I have no idea whether anyone has ever ordered a copy, let alone how many.

Unlike some other Ph.D.s (the majority? the minority?) I never mined my dissertation for publications. I was too eager to get on to other projects to publish it as a book or turn any of its chapters into articles. So it's only accessible today from UMI, on UMI's terms. If I had the text in digital form, I'd certainly want to make it OA through a suitable repository, but I honestly couldn't tell you whether that would violate the agreement I signed with UMI back in 1977. I'd have to research that question, and I don't expect that the research would be easy. But I don't have a digital copy of the text and am not likely to make one any time soon.

The Quality of Dissertations

I know firsthand that dissertation literature is valuable, and not only because my mother and I think I wrote a good one. I wrote on a fairly obscure topic for which there wasn't much existing literature—a fairly common phenomenon, given the assignment. But I found a handful of dissertations on neighboring topics in the UMI catalog and one was better than every book I found on the same subject. Unfortunately, I had to buy these dissertations in order to read them. I had to buy them even to look at them closely enough to evaluate their relevance.

Dissertations are longer than journal articles and cover their topics more comprehensively. They are more responsive to past literature than journal articles and are usually researched, refined, and revised over a longer period of time. And they're not yet salami-sliced into meaningless or trivial snippets. Indeed, they're a prime brand of the salami itself.

Dissertations are more like preprints than postprints in the sense that they're not formally peer-reviewed. But they undergo a kind of review that's at least as rigorous. If you've ever refereed a journal article, you know that the job can be done in an afternoon, and often is. Moreover, your name is rarely associated with the published (or rejected) work, and rarely known to the authors or readers. This frees referees to criticize powerful authors of flawed articles—but it also frees referees to trash powerless authors of brilliant articles. It frees referees from accountability. By contrast, your dissertation was vetted by your faculty committee for months or even years. You know who they are, and so will most readers of the final product. They feel that their own reputations are on the line, almost as much as yours is. That's why they willingly devote time and care to reviewing a dissertation and why they rigorously, almost jealously, enforce a high standard. When they certify that you have satisfied the university's requirements for originality, contribution to knowledge, and mastery of the relevant literature, their judgment is at least as well-considered, authoritative, and useful as a thumbs up from a journal referee.

Instead of devaluing dissertations because they are not formally peer-reviewed, we should see a beautiful win-win situation here. They undergo a review that is sufficiently rigorous to make them good, or to make them worth disseminating and using. But at the same time, their review is sufficiently unconventional (or sufficiently unlike journal review) to carry no publisher's investment and therefore no publisher's resistance to OA.

The Invisibility of Dissertations

Dissertations are not just good, they're largely invisible. Libraries rarely hold dissertations not written by their own students. Dissertations are not well indexed. They're available for purchase, but difficult to evaluate before purchasing. Moreover, many details from dissertations never make it into journal articles, and many dissertation topics are too narrow to justify book publication.

In short, dissertations are high in quality and low in accessibility, In fact, I'd say they constitute the most invisible form of useful literature and the most useful form of invisible literature. Because of their high quality, the access problem is *worth solving*.

You know what I'm building up to, but let me get there step by step.

Three Degrees of Difficulty in Achieving Open Access

Because OA to copyrighted literature requires the copyright-holder's consent, we can rank different bodies of literature according to the ease or difficulty of obtaining that consent. The low-hanging fruit—in the words of the BOAI—is the literature that "scholars give to the world without expectation of payment." Let's say that Phase One of the OA movement is to provide OA to this kind of royalty-free literature. Because its authors don't expect to be paid, and write for impact rather than money, they can consent to OA without losing revenue. That makes it much easier for scholars to consent to OA than musicians or movie-makers.

Phase Two is to provide OA to royalty-producing literature like books. This is harder because the copyright holder must be persuaded that OA will either increase sales or bring benefits that outweigh the loss of sales. If you've been following the book-digitizing wars, you know that some authors are persuaded and some are not.

Phase Three is to reform copyright law in order to reduce permission barriers. It would help to shorten term of copyright, extend the first-sale doctrine to digital content, restore fair-use rights, nullify clickwrap licenses as contracts of adhesion, and safeguard the public domain from further prospective or retroactive enclosure. But because these steps require legislation, and are opposed by well-funded industries, they are the most difficult of all. Fortunately, they're merely desirable and not necessary for OA. We can get all we need from Phases One and Two. For cutting-edge research published in journals, we can get all we need from Phase One.

First point: Dissertations are Phase One literature, just like journal articles. Graduate students are not paid for their dissertations and can consent to OA without losing revenue. Their consent is even easier to obtain than the consent of faculty members, since dissertations are already subject to the terms and conditions of the university.

If there's a difference, it's that authors of journal articles know they'll never be paid for those texts, but some grad students plan to turn their dissertations into books that generate (or could generate) revenue. I'll return to this possibility. But note that it's the future book that's Phase Two; the dissertation is still Phase One.

Mandating OA for ETDs

I've read about 30 university web pages on ETD policies. What's remarkable is the way they list the benefits of OA (wider visibility and greater impact) among the benefits of ETDs as if OA were a natural consequence of creating the work in digital form.

In principle, universities could require electronic submission of the dissertation without requiring deposit in the institutional repository. They could also require deposit in the repository without requiring OA. But in practice, most universities don't draw these distinctions. Most universities that encourage or require electronic submission also encourage or require OA. What's remarkable is that for theses and dissertations, OA is not the hard step. The hard step is encouraging or requiring electronic submission.

For dissertations that are born digital and submitted in digital form, OA is pretty much the default. I needn't tell you that this is not at all the case with journal literature.

There are two lessons to draw from this. First, anything that fosters ETDs (as opposed to paper TDs) fosters OA to ETDs. Second, the call for OA to ETDs is not new. It's been part of the ETD movement since the beginning. If there's anything new here, it's that I'm arguing for an OA mandate, not just for OA.

Notable, explicit calls for OA to ETDs have already been made by Edward Fox and Gail McMillan (1997), Edinburgh's Theses Alive project (2004), JISC's Electronic Thesis project (2005), Richard Jones and Theo Andrew (2005), and Arthur Sale (2006). UNESCO's ETD project called for "equal access" to ETDs in 1999, but this is just another way of calling for OA, since priced access cannot be equal access. The international Digital Access to Research Theses (DART) project is committed to OA for ETDs but is just starting up its advocacy efforts.

Nine Reasons to Mandate OA for ETDs

(1) Nowadays most theses and dissertations are born digital. They're already ETDs even if the university only wants to deal with printouts.

(2) ETDs are Phase One, royalty-free works of research literature. Their authors lose no revenue by consenting to OA.

(3) ETDs are not formally published. Hence there are no publishers in the picture to resist or oppose OA. There are no publisher fears of lost revenue to answer. There are no publisher permissions to seek. There are no publisher negotiations to delay or deter OA archiving.

(4) Mandates work and exhortations don't. This is the universal lesson from OA mandates to date, whether at funding agencies or universities.

   The US National Institutes of Health (NIH) has encouraged but not required OA to NIH-funded research since May 2005. It hoped that the increased flexibility would increase participation, but it had the opposite effect. In February 2006, the NIH reported to Congress that the compliance rate by its grantees was only 3.8%.

The low rate led the agency's own Public Access Working Group to recommend a mandate (November 2005). The Board of Regents of the National Library of Medicine reaffirmed the call for a mandate in February 2006. And last month, the House Appropriations Committee instructed the NIH to adopt a mandate. [...]

By contrast, the Wellcome Trust has mandated OA to Wellcome-funded research since October 2005 and has enjoyed a nearly 100% compliance rate.

Australia registers all accepted dissertations, giving it a good sense of the denominator, or the number of dissertations eligible for OA. The OA repositories themselves give a good sense of the numerator, or the number that are actually OA at a given time. In April 2006, Arthur Sale summarized the results of different university policies on OA for ETDs: "[V]oluntary ETD deposition results in repositories collecting less than 12% of the available theses, whereas mandatory policies are well accepted and cause deposit rates to rise towards 100%."

(5) OA solves the invisibility problem for ETDs. Without OA, there is almost no access, visibility, or indexing for dissertations. They are hard to retrieve even if discovered, and they are hard to discover. When they are OA, ETDs are not only searchable by cross-archive search tools that index the ETD repositories, they are also indexed (in growing numbers but jerky stages) by Google, Yahoo, and Microsoft. Scirus already indexes the ETDs held by the Networked Digital Library of Theses and Dissertations (NDLTD).

By making ETDs visible, OA helps the readers who wouldn't otherwise have ready access. But it also helps the ETD authors, boosting their visibility and impact just as it does for the authors of journal articles. I don't believe that anyone has studied the OA citation advantage for ETDs, but for journal articles it ranges from 50% to 250% and it's likely to be comparable (not necessarily identical) for ETDs.

(6) Universities are in a good position to mandate OA. They can make it a simple condition of submission and acceptance.

In fact, if universities mandate OA for ETDs, their compliance rates should be higher, and grumbling lower, than mandating OA for faculty research articles. Graduate students are not as anarchical as faculty, or at least not tenured; graduate students won't be subject to countervailing pressures from publishers, at least not as often; and graduate students more likely to see the benefits of OA and the obviousness of taking advantage of the internet to disseminate research.

Universities that don't have institutional repositories can still mandate OA. The best way is to launch their own IR. But they could use a consortial or regional ETD repository, or they could have their students submit ETDs directly to NDLTD, which functions as a universal or fall-back OA repository for universities without their own. They could use the universal repository I'm setting up with the Internet Archive (delayed but still coming). Or they could use ProQuest's UMI, which will offer OA to ETDs when the authors or institutions request OA.

(7) Mandating OA for ETDs will educate the next generation of scholars about OA, when they don't already know about it. Young scholars are already more familiar with OA than older ones, at least in the sciences. But even knowledgeable young scholars may not have much experience providing OA to their own work, let alone support and reinforcement from an important research institution. An OA mandate will teach new scholars how easy it is, how beneficial it is, and how routine and expected it ought to be. It will teach them that OA is not incendiary and countercultural, but mainstream and simply useful. It will help create lifelong habits of self-archiving.

The greatest obstacle to routine self-archiving is unfamiliarity with the process, including groundless fears of the time it takes. Familiarity removes this obstacle.

(8) An OA mandate will elicit better work.

All teachers know that students work harder and do better work when they know they are writing for a real audience—large or small—beyond the teacher. The effect is amplified if they are writing for the public. Some teachers try to harness this power by telling students to write as if their work were to appear on the front page of the *New York Times*. Some arrange to give students a real audience beyond the teacher. In a law course in which I conducted moot court, the quality of student preparation and argument improved dramatically after I started videotaping them. I didn't even have to put the videos online; I just put them on reserve in the library for the rest of the semester.

OA gives authors a real audience beyond the dissertation committee and real incentives to do original, impressive work.

I wrote my dissertation on Kierkegaard's dissertation. The members of my committee were strong on Kierkegaard in general, but comparatively weak on his dissertation. There were many spots in my dissertation where I could have bluffed if wanted to. But even when grad students think it's safe and easy to fool their committee, it's risky and difficult to fool the world.

(9) Finally, an OA mandate shows that the university takes the dissertation seriously.

The university asks for a new and significant work of scholarship and most students deliver one. But because the university doesn't disseminate the dissertation publicly, it sends a subtle signal that it doesn't take it seriously as a work of scholarship. Of course the dissertation committee takes it very seriously as a work of scholarship, but the university itself doesn't do what it normally does when its scholars produce new and important work: it doesn't apply its publish-or-perish policy. This policy not only proclaims that research good enough for internal recognition is good enough for external distribution. It also proclaims the stronger converse that only research good enough for external distribution is good enough for internal recognition.

Universities have the same interests in promulgating excellent research by grad students as they have in promulgating excellent research by faculty, the same reasons for taking pride in it, and the same reasons for applying a publish-or-perish policy or public dissemination mandate. It wants the world to know about the quality of the work done there and it wants other researchers to benefit from it. By adopting a serious public dissemination mandate for faculty and not for doctoral students, universities invite students to draw the cynical inference that the dissertation is not so much real scholarship as a hoop to jump through, a final piece of disposable "student work," an admission ticket to the profession, or a rite of passage.

Of course the dissertation is *also* an admission ticket and a rite of passage. Writing a dissertation is a lot like entering the wilderness alone, fasting to delirium, killing a wild animal, and then returning to civilization where one is welcomed as an adult. But universities should do more to send the signal that it's an admission ticket and rite of passage *because* it's a significant work of scholarship, not the other way around.

Students may regard the dissertation as fodder for some truly significant, adult scholarship they might publish in the future. But if so, the incentive to make it significant, adult, and public comes from a future employer, not from the institution that assigned, supervised, and approved the research.

Without an OA mandate, the university is saying that it doesn't care whether the dissertation is publicly disseminated. But if the dissertation is really a new and significant work of scholarship, then the university should care.

The message should be: If we approve a dissertation, then we think it's good. If we think it's good, then we want others to be able to find it, use it, and build on it.

Note that this message is about the purpose of universities and the value of scholarship, not about coercion. The school doesn't have to say "we're requiring OA for your sake" or even "we're requiring OA for our sake." It's saying, "We'll do all we can to help you do good work, and then we'll do all we can to make your good work available to others." It's about the mission of a research university.

Mandates, Coercion, and Consent

Our experience in advocating and implementing OA comes largely from the world of faculty, not the world of grad students. In the world of faculty, the best rationale for an OA mandate is to get the attention of authors. Authors control the rate of OA growth, but they're not paying attention to OA. We can't appeal to them as a bloc because they don't act as a bloc. It's not hard to persuade them, or even excite them, once we catch their attention, but it's very hard to catch their attention because they are so anarchical, overworked, and preoccupied. So we have to work through the institutions that have the greatest influence on authors.

These arguments apply even more easily to grad students than to faculty: the benefits are just as valuable and the barriers much lower.

One objection is that a mandate paternalistically coerces students for their own good. If true, this would be a serious problem for me, though perhaps not for everyone who defends mandates. I cannot support paternalism over competent adults, and I certainly put graduate students in that category. Fortunately, the paternalism objection misses the target and is easily answered. (The answer also applies to faculty mandates but here I'll elaborate it only for grad students.)

First, I only support mandates that are conditions on voluntary contracts. They might be funding contracts: if you take our money, you'll have to provide OA to your research; if this bothers you, then don't take our money. They might be employment contracts: if you work here, you'll have to provide OA to your research; if this bothers you, then don't work here. An OA mandate for ETDs would belong to the same family. If you attend this university, you'll have to provide OA to your dissertation; if this bothers you, then don't attend this university. Students who see this as a threat will go somewhere else; students who see it a promise are getting the idea.

Second, I only support mandates with reasonable exceptions. Grad students who have good reasons to be exempt from the mandate should be exempted, not coerced. (More on the exceptions themselves in the next section.)

Third, an OA mandate for ETDs advances the university's interest, not just the student's. The student interest is greater visibility and impact. The university interest is that an OA mandate will elicit better work, better show students that the university is taking the dissertation seriously as scholarship, better fulfill the university mission to share the knowledge it produces, and better assist researchers elsewhere who could benefit from this knowledge.

In short, the paternalism objection doesn't apply because the kind of OA mandate I'm talking about is fundamentally consensual, not coercive, and aims at benefits far beyond the student-authors themselves.

An OA mandate for ETDs is no more problematic than other academic requirements and considerably more mission-critical. Today universities seem more interested in mission-trivial details like the margins and font sizes of a dissertation than in its availability to others who could use it, apply it, or build on it.

Arthur Sale argues that the OA mandate should apply to all dissertations submitted as of a certain date rather than all dissertations by students who enroll as of a certain date. The two methods differ because students finish their dissertations at different rates. The first method jumps instantly to 100% compliance while the second phases in compliance over a few years. If the primary goal is rapid growth in the body of OA ETDs, then Sale is right to recommend the first method. The drawback of course is that it would change the rules for students who are already enrolled. Hence, if it's important to preserve a consent or contract basis for the OA mandate, then it's better to use the second method, announce the new policy to all new applicants, and apply it only to those who choose to enroll. On the other hand, the possibility of exemptions (see next section) may introduce a sufficient consent element to let us take Sale's recommendation as well.

Snags and Solutions

(1) Some students fear that providing OA for their ETD will disqualify it for future publication. In the world of journals, the policy to disqualify works that have already circulated as preprints is called the Ingelfinger rule. I haven't heard a special name for the analogous rule applied to ETDs but for convenience I'll use the same name here. Some students fear the Ingelfinger rule. Some fear it even though for decades most universities have submitted dissertations to UMI, which distributed copies on demand by xerography or microfilm to paying customers, a process that certainly counts as "publication" for journals that still follow the Ingelfinger rule.

The fear is justified in a small number of cases and unjustified in most. But we shouldn't harm the students whose fears are justified or simply override the fears of the rest. The solution is straightforward. Universities should require students of approved dissertations to deposit the full-text and metadata in the institution's OA repository. This should take place immediately upon final approval (say, within a couple of days or a week). The university should require immediate OA to the metadata. For the text of the dissertation, immediate OA isn't necessary, although it should be the default. Students may apply to the relevant dean for permission to delay OA to the text. They can seek a delay for the whole dissertation, when they plan to publish it as a book, or for specific chapters, if they only plan to publish journal articles. Deans should approve delays only for the affected chapters and require immediate OA for the rest of the dissertation. Deans should only approve temporary delays and make them as brief as possible. During the period of the delay, deans may temporarily block access to outside users, but they should not block access to everyone. For example, access should still be open to the student, the dissertation committee, the administration, and perhaps all authenticated users affiliated with the university.

The OA metadata helps the dissertation become known to others working in the field and could even help the author gather citations, impact, and reputation while submitting chapters to journals. More critically, most Ingelfinger fears are groundless. In 2001, Gail McMillan reviewed the literature and concluded that "if one looks at the results of the Dalton and Seaman surveys in combination with Virginia Tech's surveys of graduate student alumni, the ready availability of ETDs on the Internet does not deter the vast majority of publishers from publishing articles derived from graduate research already available on the Internet."

(2) Some students make patentable discoveries during their doctoral research and want time to apply for a patent.

We don't have to force students to disclose their research before they've had a chance to patent it. We can use the same solution that we used for students who fear the Ingelfinger rule. The only difference may be the length of the approved delay.

(3) Some sections of the dissertation may be under copyright by others.

In one kind of case, students quote extensively from a copyrighted work, or reproduce a copyrighted illustration, and don't have permission to redistribute it. In another kind of case, a student has already published a chapter as a journal article, has transferred copyright to the journal, and doesn't have the journal's permission to redistribute it.

Here we can use the solution to the Ingelfinger problem with a few tweaks. Some OA delays may have to be permanent rather than temporary—i.e., for the life of the copyright rather than for some fairly short period like six months. Universities could require students to seek permission to reproduce the copyrighted material rather than to give up without trying. They could also require students who publish articles before finishing their dissertations either to retain key rights or to give up hope of using the articles in their dissertations. Students who would like to use the articles in their dissertations should retain the right of OA archiving. Students who try and fail to retain these rights could be required to delay journal publication until after their dissertation is approved. This would not be as onerous as it may look. Students could publish and get the rights they need either by publishing in an OA journal (gold journal) or in a non-OA journal that permitted postprint archiving (green journal), and about 70% of subscription journals already fall into the latter category. Or, with the dean's permission, students could include published articles in the version of their text used for internal review and approval, but replace the articles with citations and links in the version used for distribution and storage.

(4) Finally, a snag of a different kind. The largest obstacle to mandatory electronic submission and OA for ETDs seems to be faculty opposition. When universities give students the option to submit their dissertation electronically, well-meaning faculty advisors often caution students against it. They are thinking of the Ingelfinger rule and preservation. They want to protect their student's shot at future dissertation-based publications and they want to be sure the student's dissertation is well-preserved.

The best solution here is education for the faculty advisors. They need to know that their own Ingelfinger fears are usually groundless. They need to know that whatever anecdotal evidence they may have is negated by Gail McMillan's systematic survey evidence. (I quoted her above: "... the ready availability of ETDs on the Internet does not deter the vast majority of publishers from publishing articles derived from graduate research already available on the Internet.")

The preservation objection is equally groundless. Paper dissertations are not like published books that exist in hundreds or thousands of copies (benefiting from the LOCKSS principle). They're usually unique and therefore vulnerable—like mine, which was stolen from the Northwestern University library. Universities could lock them up in special collections, but this is exactly the wrong model of stewardship, as if preservation and access were incompatible when the purpose of preservation is precisely to increase, facilitate, and perpetuate access. Moreover, OA to the ETD is perfectly compatible with the existence of paper copies in the university library and elsewhere and perfectly compatible with microfilm copies at UMI.

Beyond education, the university can use its policies to counteract this bad advice. First, the availability of temporary exemptions should fully answer the Ingelfinger fear. And if necessary, universities could require both electronic and paper submission in order to satisfy everyone that dissertations will be no more vulnerable in the digital future than in the paper past.

BTW, it's because faculty advisors show themselves so backward on these issues that I recommend that exemptions from the OA requirement be sought from a dean rather than from the dissertation committee.

[...]

Bibliography

Apart from the web pages of university ETD programs and ETD repositories, here are the sources I found most useful.

Paul Ayris, Chris Pressler, and Austin McLean, The DART-Europe Project: Toward Developing a European Theses Portal, presented at the 2005 ETD meeting, Sydney, Australia, September 28, 2005.

http://web.archive.org/web/20060808210040/

http://adt.caul.edu.au/etd2005/papers/066Ayris.pdf

Charles W. Bailey, Jr., Electronic Theses and Dissertations: A Bibliography, DigitalKoans, July 8, 2005.

http://web.archive.org/web/20051217134214/

http://www.escholarlypub.com/digitalkoans/2005/07/08/electronic-theses-and -dissertations-a-bibliography/

Charles W. Bailey, Jr., ETD Policies and Procedures at ARL Institutions, DigitalKoans, July 21, 2005.

http://web.archive.org/web/20060514180324/

http://www.escholarlypub.com/digitalkoans/2005/07/21/etd-policies-and-procedures -at-arl-institutions/

Tim Brody, Registry of Open Access Repositories (ROAR).

http://archives.eprints.org/

Also see the page of ETD repositories (listing 70 as of June 25, 2006).

http://archives.eprints.org/?country=&version=&type=theses&order=recordcount&submit=Filter

Edward A. Fox and Gail McMillan, Request for Widespread Access to ETDs, October 1997.

http://web.archive.org/web/20060511213415/

http://www.ndltd.org/info/pubrequest.en.html

Edward Fox, It is easy for universities to support free culture with digital libraries: The NDLTD Example, presented at the MetaScholar Initiative (Emory University), May 5, 2005. Only the abstract is free online.

http://web.archive.org/web/20060222082257/

http://metascholar.org/events/2005/freeculture/viewabstract.php?id=22

Richard Jones and Theo Andrew, Open access, open source and e-theses: the development of the Edinburgh Research Archive, Program: electronic library & information systems, 39, 3, March 2005, pp. 198–212.

http://www.ingentaconnect.com/content/mcb/280/2005/00000039/00000003/art00002

OA edition

http://www.era.lib.ed.ac.uk/handle/1842/811

Joan K. Lippincott, Institutional Strategies and Policies for Electronic Theses and Dissertations, Educause Center for Applied Research Bulletin, June 20, 2006. This came out after my June 8 talk in Quebec, but I wish it had come out earlier.

http://www.educause.edu/LibraryDetailPage/666?ID=ERB0613

http://www.earlham.edu/~peters/fos/2006_06_18_fosblogarchive.html#1150929 01136590442

Gail McMillan, Do ETDs Deter Publishers? Does Web availability count as prior publication? A report on the 4th International Conference on Electronic Theses and Dissertations (Caltech, 2001), College and Research Libraries News, v. 62, no. 6 (June 2001).

http://scholar.lib.vt.edu/staff/gailmac/publications/pubrsETD2001.html

Arthur Sale, The impact of mandatory policies on ETD acquisition, D-Lib Magazine, April 2006.

http://www.dlib.org/dlib/april06/sale/04sale.html

Arthur Sale, Unifying ETD with open access repositories, in Tony Carneglutti (ed.), Proceedings 8th International Electronic Theses and Dissertations Symposium, Sydney, Australia, 2005.

http://web.archive.org/web/20060105065646/

http://adt.caul.edu.au/etd2005/papers/037Sale.pdf

Nancy H. Seamans, Electronic theses and dissertations as prior publications: what the editors say, Library Hi Tech, March 2003.

http://www.ingentaconnect.com/content/mcb/238/2003/00000021/00000001/art 00006;jsessionid=4g9lr4xw0wj0.alice

Brian Surratt, ETD release/access policies in ARL Libraries: a preliminary study, presented at the 2005 ETD conference in Sydney, Australia, September 30, 2005.

http://web.archive.org/web/20051230043249/

http://adt.caul.edu.au/etd2005/papers/055Surratt.pdf

—Data for this article

http://web.archive.org/web/20060502031540/

http://besurratt.com/ETDPolicies/index.htm

I want to thank Richard Fyffe, Arthur Sale, Brian Surratt, Scott Walter, and above all, Sharon Reeves, for answering my many questions about ETDs over the past many months.

This article is based on my keynote address, "Open Access for ETDs," at the 9th International Symposium on Electronic Theses and Dissertations (Quebec City, June 7–10, 2006). My slides will be online at the site soon.

http://web.archive.org/web/20051124203318/

http://www6.bibl.ulaval.ca:8080/etd2006/pages/index.jsf

With one exception, everything from my slide presentation and talk is present and more fully developed here. The exception is that I had two slides in the talk listing universities with different policies on electronic submission and OA for ETDs. To see which universities have which policies, see the slides.

Open Access for Digitization Projects

Reprinted from *Going Digital: Evolutionary and Revolutionary Aspects of Digitization*, ed. Karl Grandin, 70–93. Stockholm: Nobel Foundation, 2011. Based on an article of the same title, *SPARC Open Access Newsletter*, July 2, 2009.

http://dash.harvard.edu/handle/1/14976387

When should digitization projects commit to open access (OA)?

I want to focus this question on public policy, not law or utility. If it were a question about law, the answer would be easy. As far as I know, there is no legal obligation in any country to make the results of any kind of digitization project OA. If it were a question about utility, the answer would also be easy, though the reverse. The results of a digitization project would always be more useful if they were OA.

Yet there may be good policy reasons to make some digitization projects OA even when not legally required, and there may be good reasons to change the law. Likewise, there may be good policy reasons to allow some access decisions to be made by stakeholders who will not choose OA.

Worldwide, more than 30 public funding agencies now operate on the principle that the results of publicly-funded research should be OA.[1]

I started this essay to see how far I could defend the analogous principle that the results of publicly-funded digitization projects should be OA. The presence of public funding supports an OA argument in both domains. But digitization projects differ in OA-relevant respects more often than public funding agencies do, and even when they seem to be similar in all relevant respects, they frequently differ in their access policies. There's very little discernible pattern, and no matter what perspective we take, some of the policy divergence will be justified and some will not. This is a good reason to step back and think about the principles that ought to guide access policies for digitization projects.

Let me start with two relatively simple cases.

Case 1. *When a digitization project uses public funds, and digitizes works in the public domain (PD), then the results should be OA.*

For example, when Ontario digitizes the print editions of its historical statutes, it should provide OA to the digital editions.[2]

Case 2. *When a project uses private funds, and digitizes works under copyright, then it should follow the wishes of the copyright holder. The results needn't be OA.*

For example, when a private journal uses its own money to digitize recent back issues, still under copyright, it needn't make them OA. It may put them online behind a paywall and sell access to them. Or it may keep them offline for its own private research purposes.

When *The Atlantic* digitized all 151 years of its backfile at its own expenses, chose to provide OA only to the most recent 15 years' worth, and toll access (TA) to the rest, then both the OA and TA parts of its project were entirely within its prerogatives.[3]

I'm sure you already see the supporting arguments for these two outcomes, but let me sketch them anyway. The principles behind them will help us navigate the issues in the more complicated cases.

The first case depends on the principle that public funds should be spent in the public interest. OA provides public access, and anything less than OA, or any access and usage restrictions, would compromise the public interest. The use of public funds obliges us to serve the public interest, and when we're digitizing PD works we encounter no barrier in the form of a copyright holder demanding access or usage restrictions. Taxpayers shouldn't have to pay again for access to the digital editions. They shouldn't pay to create an asset for the private enrichment of one citizen, one group, or one corporation, especially at the expense of the general public. Nor should they pay to create a digital asset which can only be accessed offline by the lucky few who are able to travel to a certain physical library or archive.

The second case depends on copyright law. Copyright holders have enforceable rights in their works, even if those rights are limited and temporary. Whatever the limits happen to be at a particular place and time, copyright holders should be free to exercise their rights up to the edge of those limits. They may waive or transfer their rights, of course, and it will be important that they might be asked to do so in order to enter a certain contract or use someone else's funds, especially to use public funds. But when copyright holders are using their own funds or the funds of a willing partner to digitize their own works, they should be free to offer the digital editions on any terms they please. The copyrighted backfiles of a journal might be more useful if they were OA. But I don't want to defend the idea that everything useful should be free, which would entail the abolition of copyright.

The principle of the first case leads us to applaud Ontario for providing OA to its digitized statutes, which are all in the public domain.[4]

Likewise, it leads us to criticize Oregon for falsely claiming copyright in the digital edition of its statutes and threatening to sue anyone who copied them. (This was Oregon's position until challenged by Carl Malamud in June 2008.)[5]

It leads us to criticize Pakistan for making the digital edition of its statutes freely accessible only to the country's lawyers rather than OA to all users.[6]

The British Library Digitisation Strategy 2008–2011 tells us that the BL plans to use public funds to digitize a mixed collection of PD and copyrighted works. Some of the digital editions will be OA and some will not. We can praise the library if the plan is to provide OA to the PD works. In Case 3 we'll ask whether the use of public funds is enough to require OA even for works under copyright.[7]

JISC used public funds to digitize the backfiles of Oxford journals, which had already been supported by Oxford's own public funds. Whether JISC and Oxford should provide OA to issues still under copyright will be explored in Case 3. But under the principle of our first case, they should at least provide OA to any issues old enough to have passed into the PD. However, Oxford provides OA to none of the digitized backfiles—as opposed to more recent back issues which may have been OA from birth. (More below.)[8]

The principle of our second case leads us to conclude that *The Atlantic* didn't have to provide OA to any of its backfile, not even the oldest part which had passed into the PD. Its decision to provide OA to the most recent 15 years' worth is beyond the call, even if based on self-interest. Its decision to provide TA to the rest, especially to the PD issues, may prove difficult to enforce. (At least in the US, users may lawfully treat any copies which escape the paywall as works in the PD.) But as long as the journal avoids copyfraud, or the false claim of copyright, it should be free to try.[9]

The Dutch medical journal, *Nederlands Tijdschrift voor Geneeskunde*, is like *The Atlantic* except that it chose to provide OA to the oldest issues rather than the newest, using a five-year moving wall. Like *The Atlantic*, it paid for the digitization of its 150+ year backfile with its own funds (as far as I can tell). Like *The Atlantic*, it didn't have to provide OA to any of it. Unlike *The Atlantic*, it doesn't have to try to restrict access to PD digital editions of PD back issues, which once online, may be copied and redistributed at will.[10]

Precisely because public funding pulls toward OA and private funding pulls toward the interests of the private funders, participants at the October 2007 LIBER/EBLIDA meeting in Copenhagen noted (in Recommendation 23) that "Private funding of digitisation activity may restrict access by the user, which is not in the interests of the European citizen. LIBER and EBLIDA do not see this as the preferred route for funding the digitisation of content."[11]

Someone might object that some publicly-funded agencies should follow a cost-recovery model. The agencies have a mission to serve the public (the objection would continue), but they can best serve the public by charging for access, recovering their costs, and making their budgets go further. For example, this is the model of the Ordnance Survey, the UK mapping agency.[12]

In reply we can point out that several independent empirical studies conclude that OA stimulates significant economic activity, and that governments can generate much more revenue through taxes on that economic activity than through access fees on public data. In the case of research, this has been well-documented in several studies by John Houghton.[13]

For example, Houghton's first major study concluded that "With the United Kingdom's GERD [Gross Expenditure on Research and Development] at USD 33.7 billion and assuming social returns to R&D of 50%, a 5% increase in access and efficiency [Houghton's conservative estimate] would have been worth USD 1.7 billion; and … With the United State's GERD at USD 312.5 billion and assuming social returns to R&D of 50%, a 5% increase in access and efficiency would have been worth USD 16 billion." [14]

In the case of public data of the sort collected and sold back to the public by the Ordnance Survey, the UK Office of Fair Trading concluded that the cost-recovery model "cost the UK economy £500 million [per year] in lost opportunities."[15]

Even if Cases 1 and 2 are not themselves very simple or non-controversial, I want to use them to mark the two poles of a spectrum of cases which are even less simple. Here are three of those less simple cases.

Case 3.　*All the funds are public, but all the works to be digitized are under copyright.*

In this case, the use of public funds pulls in favor of OA. But the copyright pulls in favor of the copyright holder. Should one side have its way at the expense of the other? If not, what compromise should we seek?

This case arises, for example, when a public agency like the US National Library of Medicine (NLM) or the UK Joint Information System Committee (JISC) funds the digitization of a journal's backfile, including issues still under copyright. When the NLM funded the digitization of the *BMJ* backfile, *BMJ* was willing to make the backfile OA without delay. The entire *BMJ* backfile to 1840 has been OA since May 2009.[16]

When JISC funded the digitization of the Oxford journal backfiles, Oxford was not willing to make them OA, apparently even with a delay, although JISC did buy a license to the Oxford backfile for UK citizens. (The license will expire in July 2011. I can't tell whether UK taxpayers, through JISC, paid once for the digitization and then paid again for the national license. Of course if the license is renewed in 2011, taxpayers will pay yet again; and if it's not renewed, they will lose their access.)[17]

For now let's focus on the case of a journal seeking a grant from a public funder, hoping to use the grant to digitize its copyrighted backfile and hoping to sell access to the online digital edition. It's the Oxford case, but artificially tidied up to eliminate the national license (close to OA for UK residents), TA for those outside the UK (one way in which the license falls short of OA), the limited duration of the license (another way in which it falls short of OA), and the possibility of multiple payments from the public funder.

We can imagine many kinds of compromise between the public and the rightshold-ing publisher. For example, we could make the works free of charge but not free for any sorts of use or reuse beyond fair use or fair dealing (see Case 5). We could make the OA copies low-res and the TA copies high-res. We could put ads on the OA copies. I men-tion these in order to stimulate the imagination. Over time the stakeholders may find many acceptable ways to strike the compromise, even if they also find many unaccept-able ways to do it.

Here I want to focus on a compromise suggested by the analogy to publicly-funded research.[18]

In the case of publicly-funded research, the US National Institutes of Health (NIH) pioneered a compromise later followed by all other funding agencies with OA policies: a period of temporary exclusivity for the publisher followed by OA for the public. When NIH grantees publish articles based on NIH funding, they must deposit the peer-reviewed manuscripts in the NIH's OA repository (PubMed Central) as soon as they are accepted for publication. But the manuscripts are not made OA until after an embargo period of up to 12 months.

The delay is a compromise with the public interest, just as it's a compromise with the publisher's private interest. Because the embargo exists, publishers have a period in which to sell access to their priced editions without competition from OA editions. Because it's temporary, the public eventually gets public access to publicly-funded research.

Publishers who believe the NIH policy is not a fair compromise should seek a different compromise, for example by tweaking the embargo period, rather than demand a no-compromise position which could deprive the public of OA for the full duration of copyright. While publishers have their reasons to lengthen the embargo, many other groups have reason to shorten it, among them researchers, practicing physicians, patients, non-profit organizations, and for-profit manufacturers. If both sides acknowledge the need for compromise, then their engagement on the length of the embargo, or on the precise terms of the compromise, is much more likely to be fruitful and constructive.[19]

The analogy of publicly-funded research and publicly-funded digitization should not leave the impression that the embargo compromise works the same way in both domains. We must note an often-overlooked aspect of the NIH policy. The NIH requires grantees to retain the right to authorize OA through PubMed Central. Hence, grantees are not in a position to transfer the full bundle of copyright to publishers. Publishers never acquire the right to deny permission for OA or claim infringement, and therefore cannot be called "the copyright holders" without qualification. Publishers who oppose the NIH policy understand the incompleteness of the transferred bundle of rights very well, and protest it. Nevertheless, in their lobbying rhetoric they call themselves "the copyright holders" without qualification, misleading many observers and policy-makers.[20]

By contrast, in a digitization project we are often dealing with the full copyright holders. Nevertheless, the embargo compromise can be extended naturally to publicly-funded digitization projects.

Suppose a private journal applies to a public funder for funds to digitize its back run, and suppose that the entire back run is still under copyright. The funder would be justified in awarding the grant. At least the fact that the journal is private and under copyright needn't stop it. The funder would also be justified in putting an OA condition on the grant. The grant needn't require immediate OA and could allow the publisher a temporary period in which it could charge for access to the digital edition without competition from an OA edition.

More importantly, the public funder would *not* be justified in awarding the grant *without* the OA condition, or in using public funds to create a privately-owned asset which would exclude the public. Similarly, Oxford may use public funds to digitize the backfiles of Oxford journals, and it may sell access to the copyrighted issues for a temporary period. But after that the backfile must become OA.

How long should the embargo be? That should be decided by public debate and negotiation. But I have two rough criteria: First, the deal should give us OA sooner than we'd otherwise have it. The publicly-funded digitization and OA condition will accelerate OA, while the embargo period will delay it. These conflicting trends should net out in favor of the public. If we could get OA faster some other way, then there's no reason to spend public money on the project.

Second, the longer the proposed embargo, the lower the project falls on the priority list for public funds. If the funder had to choose between two projects, one requesting a one-year embargo and another requesting a two-year embargo, then (other things being equal) it should pick the one with the shortest embargo. It might even ask the applicant proposing the shortest embargo to cut it even further to qualify for public funds. The US National Endowment for the Humanities follows the rule that, other things being equal, it will favor funding applications that promise (immediate) OA over those that don't promise OA at all.[21]

If the funder thinks a journal's proposed embargo period is too long, the journal might argue that it will still provide OA sooner than otherwise. For example, if the oldest articles it wanted to digitize would remain under copyright for another 50 years, and then it might argue that publicly-funded digitization with a 49 year embargo would give the public OA sooner than otherwise. As the copyright holder, it's in a position to insist that in the absence of public funding it will not allow OA until the expiration of copyright. The public funder needn't deny the publisher's prediction or its good faith. It need only reply that it has better uses for its limited public funds than to create a 49 year monopoly for a private interest at the expense of the public.

The journal might object: "You can't require OA to our copyrighted articles!" The public funder would have several responses. "We can put conditions on our grant. You needn't apply for publicly-funded grant. You can call this is an 'OA requirement' if you like, but it's really just a condition on a voluntary contract. Moreover, of course, we are a public agency and must spend our money to benefit the public."

A government would not be justified in making an *unconditional* requirement that journals provide OA to their backfiles, or at least not until it was ready to abolish copyright law. But it's fully justified in telling those who seek public funds for digitization projects, "If you take public money for this project, then you must provide OA to the results. If you don't like that, then don't take public money."

A member of the public might object: "You can't allow toll access to a publicly-funded work of digitization!" Again, the public funder would have several responses. "It's temporary. Moreover, we only funded the digitization, not the original work, and the original work is still under copyright. But above all, in our best judgment, the public investment will make the work OA sooner than otherwise."

Someone might object that under this rule many journals will not seek public money to digitize their copyrighted backfiles. Yes, that might happen. But it's no calamity, especially when the unpursued projects would have used public funds while excluding the public from access to the results. There's no reason why public funds should be spent on private interests unwilling to provide even delayed OA.

On the other side, for what it's worth, the prediction that many journals would rather reject both the compromise and public funds than accept both seems less likely than the opposite prediction. Allowing the private grantee a temporary period of exclusivity will invite many journals to seek public funds when an uncompromising OA principle would have scared them off.

Someone might object that I haven't been consistent. I've said that copyright holders should be free to exercise their rights up to their limits (Case 2). But here I'm recommending that copyright holders waive one of their rights in order to benefit from public funds.

The two positions are entirely consistent. I'm not arguing that copyright holders don't have the right to insist on TA, or that they couldn't exercise the right if they wanted to. I'm saying that they might choose to waive that right in exchange for the benefit of public funds. If they don't think it's a good deal, they don't have to take it. The deal doesn't limit their freedom; it merely offers something of value which they might or might not find worth the price of waiving their right to block delayed OA. Publishers themselves should understand this situation very well. It's exactly the kind of deal they offer to authors: give up some set of your rights in exchange for the benefit of publishing in our journal.

To obtain this kind of waiver, the public funder must deal directly with the rights-holder. The case gets more complicated when the rightsholder isn't the one desiring digitization or applying for funds. For example, consider the microfiche digitization project of the publicly-funded US Education Resources Information Center (ERIC). ERIC wanted to digitize and provide OA to about 340,000 microfiche documents, some of them up to 40 years old. The documents were written by hundreds of thousands of different authors and might have hundreds of thousands of different rightsholders. Some of the documents might, after diligent inquiry, turn out to be orphans, and some might not. ERIC undertook the enormous job of trying to hunt down each copyright holder. In the end it was able to clear permissions for about 55% or 192,000 of the documents. The rest may never be OA, despite the willingness of the US Department of Education to spend public funds on their digitization.[22]

Even if we adopt OA-friendly rules for orphan works, we must first go to the trouble of trying to locate the copyright holders. Otherwise we won't know whether or not the works are orphans. For more, see Case 10 in the appendix.

Case 4. *The funds are provided by a public-private partnership, and all the targeted works are in the public domain.*

First consider a much easier related case. If Penguin Books digitizes an early PD edition of *Pride and Prejudice* with its own funds, it should be free to sell it. It needn't give it away just because the original was PD. If you agree, then it seems that public funding is a more critical variable than PD status.

The difficult case here is when we pay for the digitization of a PD work with a mix of public and private funds, a common practice. Many public funders are unable to pay for a certain project on their own, or try to stretch their budgets by recruiting private partners. The use of public funds pulls the project toward OA, and the use of private funds pulls the project toward the wishes of the private funders, which may be TA.

Consider the Digitizing American Imprints program, which is using public funds from the Library of Congress and private funds from the Sloan Foundation to digitize 100,000 PD books.[23]

Another example is the Medical Journals Backfiles Digitization Project, co-sponsored by the Wellcome Library (private), JISC (public), and the US National Library of Medicine (public). (The project includes some copyrighted but orphan works, which it promises to remove if the copyright holder steps forward and asks it to; more in Case 10.)[24]

A third is the World Digital Library, with public partners like 13 national libraries and UNESCO, and private partners like the Brown University Library, Yale University Library, and the Wellcome Trust Library.[25]

The private partners in these three projects want OA as much as the public partners. That's good for the public and good for the working harmony of the partnership.

But what if the private partners oppose OA, and want to sell access to the digital editions without competition from OA editions? In that case, we can use the embargo compromise that we used in the previous case. The private funder could erect a temporary toll gate on access to the digital editions.

If members of the public object that the digital editions are temporarily TA, we answer as we did in the previous case. A private funder made an essential contribution to the project and without its contribution OA would be delayed even further.

If the private funder objects that its period of exclusivity is only temporary, our replies are variations on the theme of our replies in the previous case. First, the public made an essential contribution to the project and must benefit as well. Second, the partnership is voluntary and the private partner did not have to join.

But beyond these, we have two additional replies we couldn't have used in the previous case. First, the private partner has no rights in these works, which we've stipulated are PD. Second, if the embargo period never expired, then for a fraction of the cost of digitization we would allow a private company to buy permanent exclusive rights to works in the PD (not the PD originals but the PD copies produced by the project).

If the private partner objects that the embargo period isn't long enough to recoup its investment, and that it can't afford to take the risk of not recouping its investment, then it needn't participate. If it has enough money to do the digitization by itself, without public partners, then it can proceed on its own and follow its own rules, turning this into the related, simpler *Pride and Prejudice* case. If it doesn't, then it should understand the need to allow all the investment partners to get something out of the deal.

In setting the length of the embargo, we must remember that it's a compromise with the public interest. The purpose is to give the private partners something, not everything, just as the public partners are only getting something, not everything. The compromise gives the private partners a chance to recoup their investment, not a guarantee. To give them all the time they need to recoup their investment could require a permanent embargo and eviscerate the very idea of compromise.

Someone might object that under this policy we could lose the contributions of profit-seeking private companies willing to invest in digitization projects. Yes, we could. But as before, it's no calamity to lose the chance to spend public funds on a project which excludes the public, or to lose the chance to spend public funds collaborating with those unwilling to provide even delayed OA.

Nevertheless, if governments wanted to do more to encourage the participation of private partners, without giving up on timely OA for the public, they could combine a fixed deadline on the embargo with a tax deduction for any part of the private partner's investment not recouped during the embargo period.

(This could part of a larger plan to use tax deductions to get private companies to open up access to their research and data.)[26]

Public institutions taking on private partners for digitization projects should advertise their needs openly. If they accept a secret, no-bid, or unsolicited offer from a private company, they might end up agreeing to a longer embargo than necessary. Before accepting any private partners or at least any private partners who will resist OA and require a compromise, public agencies should undertake a transparent process of public consultation and competitive bidding. The rationale is simply that it's bad public policy to compromise the public interest more than necessary.

All three of the projects mentioned earlier, the Digitizing American Imprints program, Medical Journals Backfiles Digitization Project, and the World Digital Library, provide OA without any embargo at all. The private partners in all three cases came to the projects with the same purposes as the public partners, making compromise unnecessary. That's worth noting for two reasons. First, it shows that the principle here is that embargoes are permissible, not mandatory. The embargo is a compromise and is only necessary when a compromise is necessary. Second, it reminds us that the private partners in public-private partnerships don't always oppose OA.

(Conversely, public funders don't always support OA, as we've already seen in Case 1, on cost recovery, and will see again in Case 5, on the database right and sweat-of-the-brow doctrine.)

But some private partners do oppose OA. In January 2007 the US National Archives and Records Administration (NARA) announced a partnership with Footnote.com. Under the deal, Footnote would digitize millions of pages of PD documents from the National Archives, including the papers of the Continental Congress and Matthew Brady's Civil War photographs. The deal gave Footnote non-exclusive rights to sell access to the digital editions for five years. During that time, the digital editions could be viewed without charge from terminals in NARA reading rooms in 16 states. After five years, the digital copies would be OA at the NARA web site. [27]

During the five-year embargo period, Footnote's online access fees are $1.99 per page or $100 per year.[28]

The non-exclusivity of the deal meant that other companies could sell access to their own digital editions, if they could make their own digital editions. But NARA is only willing to deal with Footnote. Moreover, the Footnote deal wasn't publicly announced until the contract was already signed and Footnote had already digitized 4.5 million PD documents.

There are several problems here. One is the length of the embargo period. Five years is very long. Footnote might argue that the combination of its money and embargo will speed up OA more than slow it down. But that seems unlikely in light of NARA's February 2006 deal with Google. Under that deal, Google funded the digitization of 101 PD films from NARA and provided immediate free online access to all of them.[29]

In any case, the long-embargo problem is inseparable from the secret, no-bid contract problem. We'll never know whether other private partners would have done the work with a shorter embargo period, lower access fees, or both.

In July 2007, NARA made an even worse deal with CustomFlix, a division of Amazon. The deal allowed CustomFlix to digitize films from the National Archives and sell DVD editions through Amazon. Members of the public who visit the NARA facility in College Park, Maryland, could copy the films without charge. In contrast to the Footnote deal, nothing in the CustomFlix contract or press release mentions an embargo period, suggesting an effectively permanent embargo.[30]

The NARA-CustomFlix contract was secret until Rick Prelinger forced its disclosure with an FOIA request in August 2007. The contract gave Amazon perpetual nonexclusive license to sell the digital editions and gave NARA its own copies of the digital files and the right to use them in any lawful manner. Hence, it allowed NARA to provide OA at any point. But in striking contrast to the Footnote deal, NARA never promised to provide OA, on any timetable.[31]

In May 2008, NARA released a set of principles to guide its future digitization projects. Interestingly, it requires public comments on proposed private partnerships and highlights the importance of minimizing embargo periods. It seems that NARA heard the public criticism of the Footnote and CustomFlix deals and resolved to fix at least some of the problems.[32]

Case 5. *All the funds are public and all the works PD. So far, this is Case 1. But suppose that the host or funder wants to restrict the use of the digital editions.*

Let's say that a work is gratis OA when it's digital, online, and free of charge, even if it's still subject to copyright or licensing restrictions. A work is libre OA when it's gratis OA and also free of at least some copyright and licensing restrictions. Gratis OA allows no uses beyond fair use (or fair dealing etc.), and libre OA allows at least some. Gratis OA removes price barriers and no permission barriers, while libre OA removes price barriers and at least some permission barriers.[33]

Using these terms, we can restate Case 5 more succinctly: All the funds are public, all the works are PD, but the funder wants to make the digital editions gratis OA, not libre OA. The Oregon statutes from Case 1 fall under this description, and the issues raised by Oregon-type cases deserve a closer look.

Legally, the least complicated way for a digitizer to restrict use of a digital work is to keep it offline. Fair use and the public domain give us the right to use certain works in certain ways, but they don't give us the right to enter buildings where copies may be under lock and key.

But if the digitizer puts the digital edition online and still wishes to restrict usage, then the requested restrictions might have any of these four grounds:

(1) *Copyright.* The work might be under copyright; but if so, we've dealt with the major issues in Case 3.

(2) *Sui generis or database right.* The European Database Directive creates a kind of legal protection, outside copyright law, for databases that require substantial investment but lack the originality required for copyright. Ordinary digitization lacks the originality required for copyright, and individual examples lack the database element required for the sui generis right. But when many digitized files are brought together into a database, and when the effort requires substantial investment, then the collection may qualify for the sui generis or database right. If so, however, then Case 3 covers the major issues. If we can put an OA condition on public funds for holders of strong copyright, then we can do the same for holders the weaker sui generis right.

(3) *Unenforceable request.* The online host might acknowledge that it has no legally enforceable right to restrict usage. But it might make an admittedly unenforceable request, appealing to courtesy or respect rather than law. For example, in the downloaded copies (but not the online copies) of Google-scanned PD books, Google asks users to retain attribution and avoid commercial use and automatic querying.[34]

(4) *Copyfraud.* The host might falsely claim copyright and attempt to ground its requested restrictions in copyright law.[35]

Consider The European Library (TEL). This is an online collection of exhibits digitized from the national libraries of Europe. TEL didn't do the digitizing or set the copyright and licensing terms for the individual exhibits. It coordinates the separate efforts of the separate contributing libraries. In most cases, it doesn't even host the exhibits but links to digital editions hosted by the separate libraries.[36]

It appears that all of the works on display through TEL were digitized with public funds, and that some of the digital editions are under copyright, some under the sui generis right, and some fully PD.

TEL provides no item-level rights or licensing information. See for example the image-scan of a handwritten letter from Napoleon I to Joachim Murat, King of Naples, from October 7, 1813,[37] or the image-scan of the Heiberg translation of the Marseillaise into Danish, published in Copenhagen in 1793.[38]

TEL does provide item-level metadata, even if they don't include rights or licensing information. But the deep links to individual exhibits (which I used above) don't include the metadata. To find the metadata for the Napoleon letter or Heiberg translation, you have to locate the exhibits within this larger exhibition, click on them, and read the metadata off an unlinkable pop-up window.[39]

But since that method doesn't tell us about rights or licensing, we can only learn the status of the Napoleon letter or Heiberg translation by consulting the TEL "terms of service," which tell us that[40]

> The Conference of European National Librarians and its licensors hold the copyright for all material and all content in this site, including site layout, design, images, programs, text and other information (collectively, the "Content") held in The European Library. No material may be resold or published elsewhere without the Conference of European National Librarians written consent, unless authorised by a licence with the Conference of European National Librarians or to the extent required by the applicable law.

Even on the most charitable reading, this statement is false for many or most exhibits in the TEL. For the PD exhibits, it's entirely false. For the exhibits under the sui generis right, it falsely states the rights are based on copyright instead. (This matters, among other reasons, because copyright lasts more than five times longer than the sui generis right.) The attempted restriction on the sale and publication of the exhibits is groundless for the PD content, even if lawful for the other two categories. But TEL says that all the contents are under copyright, and none merely under the sui generis right and none in the PD. If it's true for some exhibits, it's copyfraud for others.

TEL might have intended the copyright statement to apply to the web site's apparatus, not to the exhibits themselves. But nothing in the statement suggests that distinction, and the clear language of the statement ("all content in this site …") suggests the opposite. Moreover, the absence of item-level rights and licensing information on individual exhibits forces us to turn to the general terms of service for that information. The statement might apply only to TEL-hosted content, rather than to content at the separate national libraries to which TEL merely links. But even the TEL-hosted content seems to fall into all three categories, not just the category of copyright, and in any case TEL points to the same terms of service for TEL-hosted exhibits and for library-hosted exhibits.

TEL might have intended the statement to be part of a clickwrap license, under which visitors agree to waive their rights to use and reuse any of the contents which happen to be PD. But the site does not ask users to click their assent to any licensing terms before viewing exhibits, and the terms of service claim to base the reuse restrictions on copyright, not contract. In any case, even if TEL used a clickwrap license to create a contract with the user, and even if the contract was enforceable, users who redistributed files that are actually PD would be making them available to people who were not bound by the contract.

The copyfraud creates several problems. First, for the PD content, the claimed restrictions are unenforceable. Anyone selling or publishing the digital edition of a PD work would be exercising protected rights under copyright law. Second, for content under the sui generis right, the copyright claim implies rights for the full term of copyright rather than the much shorter (15 year) term of the sui generis right.

Third and most important, the false claim of copyright might deceive or intimidate some users into giving up rights they are entitled to exercise. It inhibits the lawful and legitimate use of this valuable historical content.

Even the onerous NARA-CustomFlix contract acknowledged that "Content obtained by researchers through public access [via a NARA reading room] is in the public domain" and its uses could not be restricted.[41]

TEL should drop the false claim of copyright. It should acknowledge that much of its content is PD, and that users may use and reuse the PD content without restriction. If any of the exhibits are under the weaker sui generis right, rather than copyright, it should acknowledge that as well.

I don't want to underestimate the difficulty of adding item-level rights information to each exhibit in a large collection. It can be one of the larger costs in a large digitization project. But if TEL can't add accurate item-level rights information, it should at least stop using inaccurate site-level information in its place.[42]

The TEL can't do much more than that, since it didn't digitize the works in the collection. But the national libraries of Europe who participate in TEL can do more. They are using public funds to digitize PD works. Even if the EC Database Directive allows them to claim a sui generis right in the digital editions, they needn't take advantage of the option. On the contrary, there are good policy reasons why they should not. It's hard to imagine how their purpose in trying to restrict usage could outweigh their mission to serve the public, promote access to the historical materials in their collections, and foster research, scholarship, art, education, and cultural development. (We know that the libraries' purpose is not cost-recovery, since they are already consenting to gratis OA.)

Finally, they should understand that libre OA facilitates preservation, among other forms of use and reuse. Long-term preservation requires making copies and migrating them to new media and formats to keep them readable as technology changes. Copyright and the sui generis right both raise the barrier to those useful copies, either by blocking them altogether or by requiring the expense or delay of seeking permission.[43]

Until recently, Cornell University took a position roughly similar to TEL's for the PD books digitized from its library. It posted the works online, without a clickthrough license, but required users to seek permission for any commercial use. In May 2009, however, it reversed course. It acknowledged that the books are PD, stopped trying to restrict usage, and explained why in an exemplary public statement. In the statement, Cornell said it did not wish to "limit the good uses" of these works. On the contrary, it "decided it was more important to encourage the use of the public domain materials in our holdings than to impose roadblocks." Moreover, Cornell recognized that claiming the right to restrict usage was copyfraud, and that the criticism of copyfraud was justified.[44]

Cornell would have been within its rights to put the digital editions behind a password, require users to assent to a clickthrough license, and then charge for access or impose usage restrictions. Likewise, it could have put the works online without a click-through license and made an admittedly unenforceable request to restrict usage. But in May it chose not to do either of these things, and not to rest on copyfraud either. The Cornell solution is especially commendable because Cornell is a private university. Either it used its own, private funds for the digitization or it used Google's. (Cornell has been a partner in the Google Library Project since August 2007.)

The US doesn't recognize the sui generis database right and Cornell could not have relied on it. But even institutions in countries which do recognize the right can use the Cornell solution. They simply have to decline to use the right available to them, and (in Cornell's words) decide to put "good uses" ahead of "roadblocks."

Cornell is a private university, but its solution is compelling even for public institutions. Indeed, if a private institution can drop copyfraud and support the full use and reuse of PD works, then public institutions using public funds should be able to do so as well.

Appendix

Here's a quick summary of the five cases I've discussed:

Case 1. *All the funds are public, and all the works to be digitized are PD.*

Case 2. *All the funds are private, and all the works to be digitized are under copyright.*

Case 3. *All the funds are public, and all the works to be digitized are under copyright.*

Case 4. *The funds are provided by a public-private partnership, and all the works to be digitized are PD.*

Case 5. *All the funds are public, all the works PD, but the funder only wants to allow gratis OA, not libre OA.*

Here are five more hard cases that will have to wait for another day:

Case 6. *All the funds are private and all the works to be digitized are PD. So far this is the easy* Pride and Prejudice *case. But now add that the targeted works are rare, unique, or fragile.*

The *Pride and Prejudice* case is easy in part because it's easy to get a copy of the print book for digitizing. If one digitization project offers the digital edition on onerous terms, then others can digitize the same book and offer their editions on more liberal terms. But the realistic odds of re-digitization plummet when the original is rare, unique, or fragile.

Consider the *Codex Leicester*, a volume of Leonardo da Vinci's handwritten journal which Bill Gates bought from Armand Hammer in 1994 for $30.8 million. It's the only original da Vinci now in private hands.[45]

Gates has been generous with its display: the original is on loan to a different museum every year; high-res photos of every page have been published in a book (a priced, printed book, not an OA book); and OA thumbnails are available online at Corbis. But as far as I know, he has not allowed OA to high-res images.[46]

Is there a strong policy argument for asking a private individual like Gates to provide OA to this kind of unique PD work? If not, does the argument become stronger if the owner is a private university like Cornell?

What if the digitization of the Dead Sea Scrolls is funded by private donors?[47]

Case 7. *All the funds are private and all the targeted works are PD. So far this is either the easy* Pride and Prejudice *case or the hard* Codex Leicester *case. Now add that all the targeted works will be provided to the project by a public institution, which acquired and curated them with public funds for public benefit.*

A typical example is Google's project to digitize PD books from public university libraries, such as the University of Michigan library. Should Michigan put an OA condition on its collaboration with Google?

Case 8. *All the funds are private, all the targeted works are PD, and all the works will be provided by an institution which has acquired and curated them at some expense. So far this is Google-Michigan case. But instead of a public institution using public funds, let it be a private institution acting for non-commercial purposes and with public subsidies through untaxed property and tax deductible contributions.*

A typical example is Google's project to digitize the PD books from private university libraries, such as the Harvard and Cornell libraries. Should Harvard and Cornell put OA conditions on their collaboration with Google?

Similar issues arise when a PD digitization project is funded by private philanthropy, such as the Mellon Foundation, with no public partner.

Do the policy arguments for OA that apply to public funders also apply to all institutions with non-commercial purposes and tax breaks, even if private?

Case 9. *The funds are from a public-private partnership, and the works to be digitized are PD. So far, this is Case 4. But instead of mere digitization, the project extends to editorial work* *and copyrighted commentary. The plan is to integrate the PD texts and the copyrighted commentary. The private partners and copyright holders want to publish the results in print books or TA web sites and oppose any attempt to make them OA, even after an embargo period.*

See the NARA plan for a digital edition of papers of US Founding Fathers:

- The case for OA.[48]
- The case for TA (though misleadingly called "open access").[49]
- The case for a middle position (including an embargo period followed by libre OA).[50]

Case 10. *Take any of the variations above in which the works to be digitized are still under copyright (for example, Cases 2 and 3). Now add the variable that they are orphan works.*

Should the digitizer follow the Wellcome Library and make the digital editions OA, promising to take them down if the copyright holder steps forward and objects?[51]

Should it follow the Google book settlement and sell access?[52]

For a middle position, see Peter Eckersley's argument that all Google-digitized books, and especially the orphan works, whether based on originals from public or private institutions, should become OA after an embargo period.[53]

If we diligently look for the copyright holders, fail to find them, and responsibly conclude that we are dealing with orphan works, then should we assume the lack of permission for OA until we have explicit consent from the copyright holders or national legislature? Or should we assume permission for OA until we have explicit dissent? Even after responsibly concluding that we're dealing with orphan works, should we adopt a compromise like an embargo period?

Or should we start to rethink the very idea of *permission* in cases like this? Normally, medical care without consent is battery, just as full-text copying of copyrighted texts without permission is infringement. But when an unconscious person is wheeled into an emergency room, and we're unable to get an explicit "yes" or "no," then we start to talk about "implied consent" to receive care and "privilege" to render care. When diligent effort fails to turn up a copyright holder, and we're equally unable to get an explicit "yes" or "no," then should we also start talking about implied consent and privilege? The stakes are not the same, but the consent quandary is the same. Do we only want to solve the consent quandary in matters of life and death, or might we also want solve it in matters of scholarship, research, art, culture, and education?

An earlier version of this article was published in the *SPARC Open Access Newsletter*, July 2, 2009.[54] For helpful feedback on that edition I thank Frode Bakken, Klaus Graf, Sebastian Krujatz, and Sanford Thatcher.

Notes

1. http://www.eprints.org/openaccess/policysignup/

2. http://www.earlham.edu/~peters/fos/2009/04/oa-to-historic-ontario-legislation.html

3. http://www.earlham.edu/~peters/fos/2008/01/free-online-access-to-12-years-of.html

4. http://www.earlham.edu/~peters/fos/2009/04/oa-to-historic-ontario-legislation.html

5. http://public.resource.org/oregon.gov/

6. http://www.dailytimes.com.pk/default.asp?page=2006\12\09\story_9-12-2006_pg11_4

   http://www.earlham.edu/~peters/fos/2006/12/free-access-to-pakistani-law-for.html

7. http://www.bl.uk/aboutus/stratpolprog/digi/digitisation/digistrategy/index.html

   http://www.earlham.edu/~peters/fos/2008/08/british-library-digitization-plans-some.html

8. http://www.oxfordjournals.org/access_purchase/archives.html

9. http://www.earlham.edu/~peters/fos/2008/01/free-online-access-to-12-years-of.html

10. http://www.earlham.edu/~peters/fos/2007/11/dutch-medical-journal-opens-backfile.html

11. Paul Ayris, "LIBER-EBLIDA Digitisation Workshop," *Liber Quarterly*, April 2008, p. 17.

    http://liber.library.uu.nl/publish/articles/000222/article.pdf

12. http://url.ca/5yms

13. http://www.cfses.com/EI-ASPM/

14. http://www.cfses.com/documents/wp23.pdf

    http://www.earlham.edu/~peters/fos/2006/08/oa-increases-return-on-investment-in.html

15. http://www.freeourdata.org.uk/blog/?p=86

16. http://dx.doi.org/10.1136/bmj.b1744

    http://www.earlham.edu/~peters/fos/2009/05/169-years-of-bmj-now-oa.html

17. http://www.oxfordjournals.org/access_purchase/archives.html

18. I'm not the first to suggest this compromise. See the High Level Expert Group on Digital Libraries, Sub-group on Public Private Partnerships, *Final Report on Public Private Partnerships for the Digitisation and Online Accessibility of Europe's Cultural Heritage*, i2010 European Digital Libraries Initiative, May 2008.

    http://ec.europa.eu/information_society/activities/digital_libraries/doc/hleg/reports/ppp/ppp_final.pdf

In Recommendation #9 at p. 22, "The sub-group recommends that public domain content in the analogue world should remain in the public domain in the digital environment. If restrictions to user's access and use are necessary in order to make the digital content available at all, these restrictions should only apply for a time-limited period."

19. http://www.earlham.edu/~peters/fos/newsletter/08-02-07.htm#embargo

20. http://www.earlham.edu/~peters/fos/newsletter/10-02-08.htm#nih

21. http://www.neh.gov/grants/guidelines/editions.html

22. http://www.eric.ed.gov/ERICWebPortal/Home.portal?_nfpb=true&_pageLabel=Digitization

    http://www.earlham.edu/~peters/fos/2009/05/eric-microfiche-digitization-project.html

23. http://www.loc.gov/today/pr/2009/09-10.html

    http://www.earlham.edu/~peters/fos/2009/01/loc-digitization-program-crosses-25000.html

    http://www.earlham.edu/~peters/fos/2009/03/oa-book-scanning-program-from-library.html

24. http://library.wellcome.ac.uk/doc_WTD037630.html

    http://library.wellcome.ac.uk/doc_wtx043243.html

    http://library.wellcome.ac.uk/doc_wtdv025956.html

25. http://www.worlddigitallibrary.org/project/english/index.html

    http://project.wdl.org/project/english/partners/

26. http://weblog.infoworld.com/udell/2006/06/12.html

    http://www.earlham.edu/~peters/fos/2006/06/tax-breaks-to-support-oa.html

    http://www.earlham.edu/~peters/fos/newsletter/07-02-06.htm#nih

27. http://archives.gov/press/press-releases/2007/nr07-41.html

28. http://www.dancohen.org/blog/posts/national_archives_footnote_agreement

    http://www.earlham.edu/~peters/fos/2007/01/digitized-public-domain-docs-from-us.html

29. http://www.archives.gov/press/press-releases/2006/nr06-64.html

    http://www.archives.gov/digitization/google-agreement.pdf

30. http://www.archives.gov/press/press-releases/2007/nr07-122.html

31. http://blackoystercatcher.blogspot.com/2007/08/national-archivesamazon-agreement.html

    http://www.panix.com/~footage/NARA_Amazon.pdf

32. http://www.archives.gov/digitization/strategy.html

33. http://www.earlham.edu/~peters/fos/newsletter/08-02-08.htm#gratis-libre

34. Here's an example, though the link may only work from IP addresses in the United States:.

http://books.google.com.ph/books/download/Pride_and_Prejudice.pdf?id=2_S8xAws2G4C&
hl=en&output=pdf&sig=ACfU3U36yL_-URJJlcMilNPjhX7LOkUgfA

35. http://papers.ssrn.com/sol3/papers.cfm?abstract_id=787244

36. http://www.europeanlibrary.org/

37. http://www.theeuropeanlibrary.org/exhibition/Napoleonic_wars/images/texts/_large/
ennw22_l.jpg

38. http://img.kb.dk/ma/nybrev/12-05/spalvor-mars.pdf

39. http://www.theeuropeanlibrary.org/exhibition/Napoleonic_wars/

40. http://www.theeuropeanlibrary.org/portal/organisation/footer/termsofservice_en.html

41. http://blackoystercatcher.blogspot.com/2007/08/national-archivesamazon-agreement.html

http://www.panix.com/~footage/NARA_Amazon.pdf

42. Disclosure: I'm on the advisory board for TEL and have made my objections known. I'm still
hoping to resolve the problem.

43. http://www.ippr.org.uk/publicationsandreports/publication.asp?id=464

http://www.clir.org/pubs/reports/pub135/sec6.html

http://www.pocket-lint.com/news/news.phtml?newsId=3566

44. http://url.ca/6lew

http://www.earlham.edu/~peters/fos/2009/05/cornell-allows-unrestricted-use-of-its.html

45. http://en.wikipedia.org/wiki/Codex_Leicester

46. http://www.amazon.com/Leonardo-Da-Vinci-Leicester-Notebook-Genius/dp/1863170812/
ref=sr_1_2

http://pro.corbis.com/Search/SearchResults.aspx?q=%20"Codex%20Leicester%20by%20
Leonardo%20da%20Vinci"

47. http://www.earlham.edu/~peters/fos/2007/11/digitizing-dead-sea-scrolls.html

http://en.wikipedia.org/wiki/Dead_Sea_Scrolls#Digital_copies

48. http://blog.librarylaw.com/librarylaw/2008/06/free-the-foundi.html

49. http://www.archives.gov/nhprc/publications/founders-report.pdf

50. http://www.earlham.edu/~peters/fos/newsletter/08-02-09.htm#update

51. http://wellcomelibrary.blogspot.com/2009/06/orphan-works.html

52. http://books.google.com/booksrightsholders/

53. http://www.eff.org/deeplinks/2009/06/should-google-have-s
    http://www.earlham.edu/~peters/fos/2009/06/another-idea-for-building-oa-into.html

54. http://www.earlham.edu/~peters/fos/newsletter/07-02-09.htm#digitization

Bits of the Bigger Picture

Analogies and Precedents for the FOS Revolution

From "Analogies and precedents for the FOS revolution," SPARC Open Access
Newsletter, March 22, 2002.

http://dash.harvard.edu/handle/1/4727449

If asked for a precedent for the kind of revolution represented by FOS [Free Online
Scholarship], we might first mention the Gutenberg Press. But it isn't a very good fit.
It's a technological advance, and all the technology required for FOS already exists.
We're trying to bring about an economic change that will take advantage of existing
technology.

If we want an example of an economically sustainable industry which gives away its
product to end-users because the costs of production and distribution are paid by others,
then we need look no further than television and radio. I've used these examples more
than once recently to argue that the long-term sustainability of FOS is not problematic.

http://www.upi.com/view.cfm?StoryID=15022002-015414-4119r

http://lists.topica.com/lists/fos-forum/read/message.html?mid=903623859&sort=d&st
art=111

But television and radio were "born free" (for end-users). From the start, those wanting to make a profit in these businesses needed a funding model compatible with open
access for users. But most scholarly journals were born priced. If future journals are to
be free for end-users, then we must transform their business model.

Are there precedents for this? Can you think of a product that was unfree for end-
users at one time, and became free at a later time, because an intervening economic
revolution shifted the costs from end-users to others?

Leave aside products now paid for by the governments (like roads), because that isn't
the only model we seek for FOS. Let's also put self-archiving to one side, since it didn't
exist in some pre-FOS form needing transformation.

I've thought of one precedent: mail. The postage stamp allowed us to change the funding model for letters, newspapers, and other mail, from "recipient pays" to "sender pays."

When this example first occurred to me, I thought it minor and stretched. But as I've learned more about the postal revolution, I've changed my mind. It was an important social and economic transformation, and its similarities to the FOS transformation are real, even if there are important dissimilarities as well. Bear with me now.

Before stamps, writers sent letters free of charge. Recipients had to pay to take their mail home from the post office. If they couldn't afford to pay, they couldn't read their mail. Stamps were introduced precisely to allow senders to pay in advance and lift the burden from recipients.

The revolution was launched by Rowland Hill (1795–1879), in his 1837 pamphlet, *Post Office Reform: Its Importance and Practability*. The idea of shifting costs to senders was instantly popular. A group of businessmen interested in implementing the idea collected four million signatures—more than 15% of the British population at the time. Parliament gave Hill a temporary position in the Treasury so that he could put his theory into practice. In 1840, England adopted the postage stamp and the "sender pays" rule. Switzerland and Brazil made the change in 1843, and the U.S. followed suit in 1847.

The primary similarity holding up the analogy is the switch from "access fees" (paid by recipients) to "dissemination fees" (paid by senders). That's precisely the change we need to make scholarly journals free for readers and their institutions, and the internet makes it easier by radically reducing the cost of dissemination. This suggests a secondary similarity as well. Before stamps, postage rates depended on weight and distance, which required separate calculations and record-keeping for every letter. Hill realized that his reform would not only make access to mail free for recipients, but would significantly lower the overall cost of delivery. Likewise, providing open access to journals costs much less than disseminating journals on paper or even disseminating them online through DRM software that blocks access to non-subscribers.

There are limits to the analogy, of course, and exploring what they are helps to illuminate the problems facing FOS. If universities agree to support open-access journals by paying a dissemination fee for every outgoing article, then during some indefinite transition period they will still have to pay access fees for desirable journals using the older business model. This forces them either to increase their overall serials budgets or cancel subscriptions to cover their new costs at the other end. (I sketched this dilemma in FOSN [Free Online Scholarship Newsletter] for 1/1/02, and pointed out several possible solutions that make the situation more complex but also more hopeful.) But when nations adopted Hill's funding model for mail, there was no transition period in which users faced the dilemma of greater net outlays or lost content. The only people who didn't save money from the start were those who sent much more mail than they received.

http://www.earlham.edu/~peters/fos/newsletter/01-01-02.htm

This highlights another difference. With mail, essentially all senders are receivers. Mail senders consented to the change, and even clamored for it, not because they would be relieved of costs as receivers but because they would pay less as senders than they were currently paying as receivers. Libraries are similarly situated, and this explains why librarians tend to support FOS. But libraries are not the most likely sources of dissemination fees for FOS journals, and the more likely sources tend to be senders who are not receivers, breaking the symmetry that creates one incentive for the change. These are foundations and government agencies, the funders of research who are not always readers or consumers of research literature. These potential payors have been slower to show up at the revolution and many still need persuading.

Moreover, journal subscribers are always volunteers, while mail recipients are not. While both revolutions want to put costs only on volunteers, postal costs were previously borne by non-volunteers. So the postal revolution had at least this one incentive missing from the FOS revolution. [...]

England loved Hill for his reform. This son of a schoolteacher who painted landscapes and built scientific instruments was knighted in 1860, commemorated with a statue outside the General Post Office in London, buried in Westminster Abbey—and of course he had his face on a postage stamp.

Dwight Rhodes, History of Postal Systems

http://www.aretek.com/POSTHISTORY.html

Biographies of Rowland Hill

http://members.tripod.com/~midgley/rowlandhill.html

http://web.archive.org/web/20011026185310/

http://www.fortunecity.com/marina/armada/367/hillrowl.htm

http://web.archive.org/web/20011205083545/

http://www.glassinesurfer.com/f/gsrowlandhill.shtml

Postscript

I don't claim that the postal revolution is the best analogy or precedent for the FOS revolution, only that it is good enough (in Robert Nozick's words) to be worth surpassing. I hope you'll post your thoughts to our discussion forum, especially proposals for better analogies and precedents.

Here are some questions. Are there better analogies or precedents than Hill's postal revolution for the transformation of scholarly journals sought by the FOS movement? One reason to have a precedent is to show that the transformation we seek for scholarly journals is economically possible, even feasible and realistic. Does the postal transformation show this for journals? If not, again, are there other precedents that might show it better?

Another reason to have a good precedent is to study it and learn to learn how the transition was managed. What were the obstacles and how were they overcome? What were the opportunities and how were they seized? Are there lessons in the postal revolution that the FOS movement should take to heart?

Thoughts on First and Second-Order Scholarly Judgments

From "Thoughts on first and second-order scholarly judgments," *SPARC Open Access Newsletter*, April 8, 2002.

http://dash.harvard.edu/handle/1/4727447

What do search engines, web filters, current awareness services, and peer review have in common? They all help us churn haystacks and find needles, or process noise and find signals. They help us navigate the wilderness of information. Pick your metaphor, or try this non-metaphorical way to look at it.

Let's say that first-order scientific or scholarly judgments are judgments about what is true or probably true in astrophysics, organic chemistry, French history, epistemology, or any other field of academic research. First-order judgments are what scientists and scholars primarily produce in their roles as scientists and scholars. Let's say that second-order judgments are judgments about which first-order judgments you ought to read.

Search engines, web filters, current awareness services, and peer review give us second-order judgments. They are just a few of the many sources of second-order judgments, alongside card catalogs, book catalogs, tables of contents, spam filters, and informal networks of pointers and recommendations by trusted friends and authorities. Of course there are important differences among discovery, retrieval, evaluation, recommendation, and blocking. But there are also important similarities, namely, their second-order parasitism on first-order judgments and their ability to assist or distort research.

Second-order judgments are not necessary for researchers who personally know all those likely to make contributions worth reading, or for disciplines in which literature is sparse or disagreements are shallow. But as the universe of first-order judgments relevant to our research interests becomes unmanageably large, and as the disagreements within this universe increase in number and depth, then we need help avoiding the intellectual provincialism and risk of error that arise from reading only what it is ready to hand. We need the assistance of second-order judgments. (One recipe for crank literature is devotion without this assistance.) This isn't assistance in formulating our own first-order judgments or even in assessing those of others, but in making intelligent decisions about how to allocate the finite resource of our time and attention. As time passes and science grows, the need for second-order judgments will only increase.

There are two reasons to celebrate. The first is that the need for second-order judgments is a sign of the flourishing of the sciences and scholarship producing first-order judgments. Information overload and the need to manage it may be obstacles and irritants, but they are clearly side-effects of success. [...]

The second reason to celebrate is that free online scholarship is free online data for increasingly sophisticated software that generates second-order judgments. In the age of print, second-order judgments had to be produced by trained human scholars. When scholarly literature is digital but priced, then only its owners can experiment with software to help us find what is relevant, what is worthy, and what is new. Some of these owners have the means and will to code tools of this kind, and some are creative. But when scholarly literature is digital and unpriced, and even networked so that it can appear on every desktop [...], then the fetters on innovation will fall away and the pace of development will accelerate.

I'm tempted to put it this way. Computers have triggered more than one revolution in scholarly literature, apart from their assistance with first-order judgments. The first revolution was simply to digitize text, which permitted flexible writing and free copying. The second revolution was to network the digitized articles, which spread them to all connected users. At first these networked articles were all free, but as the technology evolved to block access to non-paying customers, more and more of the new literature came online only behind passwords where most readers could not reach it. The third revolution will be the return to free online access as the default for scientific and scholarly research articles. This will increase the accessibility of every article, helping readers, and increase the audience and impact for every article, helping authors. This is the FOS [Free Online Scholarship] revolution and we're still fighting for it. But it will not be the end of the line. The fourth revolution will be to write increasingly sophisticated software that takes FOS as data and returns increasingly intelligent and customizable second-order judgments about what is relevant, what is worthy, and what is new. Making online scholarship free of charge makes it universally accessibly to connected human researchers, a major plateau in the progress of the sciences. But making it free and online also makes it universally accessible to software and programmers, which has the potential to create an even higher plateau further out.

Today there are several incentives for publishers to make scholarly literature freely available online: to respond to competitive pressure from other free journals, to increase their citation rate and impact factor by reaching a larger audience, to sell auxiliary services, to accede to demands by scholars, and to assist in the dissemination of knowledge. One incentive that is weak today and will become stronger over time is to provide scholarly content to the far-flung, distributed swarm of services processing FOS and turning it into second-order judgments on which scholars rely to learn what is relevant, what is worthy, and what is new.

If the flourishing of first-order science produces information overload, and if information overload increases the difficulty of discrimination, then tools to discriminate according to my own standards will be among the most essential tools in my research toolkit. As the scholarly use of these tools becomes routine, then literature will only be visible if it is made visible by these tools. Free and online won't be enough, just as ready-to-hand isn't enough if my desk is so littered with photocopies that I can't find what I want. If the best tools or the free tools take FOS as data, then publishers will have to produce FOS in order to make their articles visible. It follows that one strategy to accelerate FOS is to write good second-order judgment software that takes FOS as data.

Commercial publishers will still produce second-order software in-house and apply it to their priced content. Insofar as their tools are good, users will have an incentive to pay for them. This not a problem for FOS. First, it is compatible with the growing number and quality of free tools taking free literature as data. Second, many publishers will choose to give away their first-order literature and sell their second-order tools and services, which is entirely compatible with FOS. Third, users and research benefit when second-order tools proliferate and compete.

The beauty of second-order tools using first-order scholarship as data is that there can never be too many of them. If proliferating first-order judgments creates information overload, then proliferating second-order judgments creates competition, and this competition will be beneficial for users and self-limiting. Second-order judgments are valuable even when they conflict, because different users have different needs, interests, projects, standards, and approaches. You should have a choice among services competing to help you decide what deserves your time and attention. Of those services that know what you want, some will be faster, cheaper, or friendlier in providing it. Of those that are fast, cheap, and friendly, some will know better what you want. If putting priced paper literature online free of charge accelerates research, then a robust market of sophisticated, competing second-order tools will accelerate it again.

Part of academic freedom is to have a free market in first-order judgments. By this I only mean that scientists and scholars need the freedom to take a stand on what is true or probably true in their field, and be immune from every kind of retaliation, except disagreement and criticism, for doing so. (I know that I've returned to metaphor by calling this a free market.) As first-order science continues to flourish, and as information overload worsens, an essential part of academic life, as vital as academic freedom, will be a free market of second-order judgments. Yes, there will be neo-Nazi filters on historical literature and fundamentalist filters on biological literature, but these will merely be electronic reflections of methodological and ideological divisions that today show up in different journals or different conferences. Yes, second-order judgments will evaluate other second-order judgments. (For more on this, see FOSN for 11/16/01.) But without the discriminating power of second-order tools, we will be at the mercy of information overload. And without the choice of different discriminating standards, first-order academic freedom will be ineffectual.

http://www.earlham.edu/~peters/fos/newsletter/11-16-01.htm

Postscript

One of the sillier objections to FOS is that it will increase information overload. Either this objection is an inept way of saying that FOS will dispense with peer review (which is untrue) or a prediction that making peer-reviewed literature free and online will increase its quantity (which may be true but unobjectionable). The standard response is to point out that the growth of peer-reviewed literature is a sign of progress, even if it creates information overload. While that's true, it may not address the part of the objection that bemoans the information overload it predicts and might otherwise value. A better response is to point out that FOS will inspire the development of second-order tools that take FOS as data. These tools are not only a remedy to information overload. They are the only remedy that doesn't require reducing the output of science and scholarship.

Saving the Oodlehood and Shebangity of the Internet

From "Saving the oodlehood and shebangity of the internet," *SPARC Open Access Newsletter*, July 4, 2003.

http://dash.harvard.edu/handle/1/4552009

The internet makes open access possible. Open access wasn't physically or economically possible in the age of print. These commonplace assertions are true but slightly out of focus. Let's be more specific. The internet has many properties (it's digital, it's packet-switched, it has end-to-end architecture, it has a certain number of nodes, a certain throughput capacity, a certain level of traffic at a given time, a certain degree of saturation, and so on), but one property above all others makes open access possible. It's the capacity to disseminate perfect copies of a digital file to a worldwide audience at virtually no cost. [...]

Notice that this is the very same property that makes spam and large-scale digital piracy or mass infringement possible. I wish this property had a name. That would do a lot to advance the discussion of open access, spam, and mass infringement. In the absence of an accepted name for it, and for lack of a better term (like oodlehood? shebangity?) let me call it the "prodigality" of the internet.

Open access proponents like to focus on the revolutionary potential of the prodigality of the internet for the public good. But our strategic thinking must address the fact that the same prodigality also has revolutionary potential for mass infringement, economic harm, loss of privacy, and spam hell. The forces at work to curb these harms are powerful and well-funded—and not especially cautious about the goods they destroy in order the crush the evils they fear. It's time to realize that the obstacles to open access don't lie merely in the inertia and ignorance of scholars, and the dysfunction of the journal market. [...] We could be collateral damage in the war against piracy and spam.

I've written often in the past about how the reaction to mass infringement has given up on surgical responses to online crime and turned to crude remedies that threaten the prodigality of the internet. For example, we see this in the denial of the first-sale doctrine to digital content, in retroactive extensions of copyright, in the hardware mutilations contemplated by Hollings' SSSCA [Security Systems Standards and Certification Act], and in the DMCA [Digital Millennium Copyright Act] ban on circumvention even for fair use or other non-infringing purposes. New question: will the reaction to spam be equally harmful?

It may be. [...]

If my keyboard had a key that sent a non-fatal electric shock to the sender of a piece of spam, then I confess: mine would be worn out. I'm ominously attracted to a direct, Skinnerian remedy that combines text and voltage. ("Thanks for the spam. Here are 100 volts just for you.") People who hate copyright infringement hate it even more than I hate spam. On June 19, Senator Orrin Hatch said in public what many no doubt think in private, that the music industry needs a method to destroy the computers of copyright infringers. If executives at the RIAA [Recording Industry Association of America] and MPAA [Motion Picture Association of America] had remote detonation keys on their keyboards, they would be worn out.

You may not hate mass infringement, but you probably hate spam, and that's enough to put you on both sides of this problem. The prodigality of the net carries the potential for momentous good and the potential for momentous harm. [...]

Watch the campaign against spam and mass infringement. You don't have to love either one to love the prodigality of the internet that makes them possible. Fight to defend it and to prevent remedial overreaching. Don't hastily blame only the defenders of indefensible intellectual property theories. All of us who hate spam are now implicated. So while watching others, who might encroach on the prodigality that makes open access possible, we should also watch ourselves. Can we hate spam surgically?

Finally, let's watch for escalations of mischief and harm that create excuses to sacrifice the good potential of the net in order to block the bad. Will the dream of open access live only as long as the internet's prodigality is endurable, and die when terrorist viruses (let's call them Hatchlings) can be delivered to every desktop?

On the threat from challenge-response spam systems

http://news.com.com/2010-1071-1009745.html

http://web.archive.org/web/20030811223019/

http://www.wired.com/news/culture/0,1284,59156,00.html

http://www.canada.com/technology/story.html?id=E5F01452-1B4B-4B33-B94A-F4E71
9E3C874

Sen. Charles Schumer's Stop Pornography and Abusive Marketing (SPAM) Act
http://thomas.loc.gov/cgi-bin/query/D?c108:1:./temp/~c108a62RGp::

Orrin Hatch's remote detonation fantasy
http://www.washingtonpost.com/wp-dyn/articles/A12441-2003Jun19.html
http://money.cnn.com/2003/06/19/commentary/wastler/wastler/

[...]

What's the Ullage of Your Library?

From "What is the ullage of your library?" SPARC Open Access Newsletter, January 2, 2004.

http://dash.harvard.edu/handle/1/4723856

What percentage of the journals or articles needed by the faculty at your university are unavailable except by interlibrary loan or private emails to lucky colleagues elsewhere? Let's call this the "ullage" of the library, after the word for the empty space at the top of a wine bottle. The ullage of a library is the gap between what is directly available and what is needed.

I bring this up, of course, because rising journal prices increase ullage, and spreading open access decreases ullage.

The Los Alamos National Laboratory (LANL) library has made a start in measuring the ullage at 13 major research libraries in the U.S. Instead of looking at all the journals that an institution might need, it looked only at the ISI list of the 100 most-cited journals for 2002. Fair enough, since we can assume that all research institutions would want access to these journals. Instead of counting any kind of subscription, it counted only electronic subscriptions revealed on the library web sites. This seems to be a methodological shortcut to save counting time, but insofar as research universities want electronic access to their most-used titles, it should not distort the measurement.

Kathy Varjabedian published the resulting bar charts on in the December 2003 issue of the *LANL Research Library Newsletter*.

http://lib-www.lanl.gov/libinfo/news/2003/200312.htm#jourbench

Bottom line: even the best-stocked research libraries have regrettable ullage. If we look at all the e-journals studied, then the best-stocked library is at the University of Illinois at Champaign-Urbana, which holds 98% of them. For this body of literature, it has an ullage of 2%. If we look only at the journals outside clinical medicine (a fairer measurement for universities without medical schools), the best-stocked library is Princeton's, which holds 70 of the 70 most-cited journals outside medicine. It has an ullage of 0%.

Postscript

There are two ways to bring ullage to zero. We could provide open access to still-needed resources or find enough money to buy access to them. Because OA isn't the only way to do solve the problem, ullage doesn't measure the progress of OA so much as the itch that OA or money can scratch. We could say that ullage measures the problem, not the solution, but we have to bear in mind that it only measures the reader-side problem (need without access). We need another way to measure the author-side problem (contribution without audience or impact).

Erratum [added in 2004]: I misread the LANL article. Princeton has 70 of the *70* most-cited journals outside medicine, not 70 out of 100. Hence it has a ullage of 0. The figure I cited for the University of Illinois at Champaign-Urbana is correct. I apologize for the error and thank Greg Price for alerting me to it.

Can Search Tame the Wild Web? Can Open Access Help?

From "Can search tame the wild web? Can open access help?" SPARC Open Access Newsletter, December 2, 2005.

http://dash.harvard.edu/handle/1/4727442

Which is growing faster, the size of the web or the power of search engines? No one knows, but it matters for all of us. If the power of search is growing faster, then it will eventually overtake the web's wildness and tame it—all of it. If the web is growing faster, then it will forever outpace our attempts to map, navigate, explore, and understand it.

The problem reminds me of the critical density of the universe. If there is enough matter in the universe, then gravitational attraction will eventually slow down and reverse cosmic expansion. The universe will end in a big crunch. If there isn't enough matter in the universe, the expansion will continue unimpeded indefinitely. The universe will end in heat death. When I was a student, I don't think we knew which outcome was more likely. But the recent discovery of accelerated expansion, perhaps due to dark energy, means that expansion is outpacing gravity.

We may not have a preference between the big crunch and heat death, especially if they're both billions of years in the future. But we should definitely root for the power of search to overtake the wild and rapid expansion of the web. If it does, then as readers we'll be able to find what we want and as authors we'll have a chance of being found by readers. But if search can't keep up with expansion, then as John Alan Paulos put it, the web will be the world's largest library, but its books will be scattered all over the floor. [...]

Unfortunately it's difficult or impossible to make a direct comparison between the rate of web growth and the rate of search improvement. One reason is that web growth and search power are not forces of nature (limiting my analogy). Either or both may suddenly speed up or slow down. We aren't surprised when they fluctuate because we know they are functions of a thousand variables that we do not yet fully understand.

There are many reasons why search may not keep pace with the expanding web. One is limited scope. What percentage of the web does a search engine index? A critical part of search scope is the dark web, a.k.a. the deep or invisible web stored in databases and closed to search engine crawlers. By one estimate the deep web is 500 times larger than the surface web.

Another is the adequacy of the relevance algorithm. How good is the search engine at guessing what you want and giving it a favored position in the search returns? Another is search spam. How good is the search engine at resisting attempts to manipulate its index and ranking algorithm? Another is lack of personalization. Even if the search index is complete and the relevance algorithm top-notch, different users may have different needs when searching on the same search term. Some will find what they want at the top of the relevance-sorted list but others won't, and it doesn't help them to know that what they seek is listed somewhere among the millions of other sites further down the list. (If you insist that search spam and lack of personalization are problems within the relevance algorithm, not separate problems beyond it, then I'll agree.)

The dark web is like dark energy, which accelerates expansion, not dark matter, which slows it down. By resisting search, the dark web helps the cause of entropy and hurts the cause of closure and organization.

Some of the literature in the dark web can still be searched by specialty search engines like Copernic, Deep Query Manager, iBoogie, and ProFusion. Moreover, even when dark web content is invisible to outside tools, it is usually hosted by databases that offer their own search functions. But even together these tools don't take us very far. Most of the dark web is still an unmapped region where content expands unnoticed by web-wide search engines.

Price barriers seclude content just as databases do and create a similar kind of web darkness. Some publishers of non-OA content invite major search engines like Google and Yahoo to index them, and I applaud that. And some search engines, like Scirus, already cover segments of the non-OA literature because they are created by the publishers. But most toll-access literature is still invisible to the general search engines.

In this sense, open access contributes to the mapping, taming, organization, and intelligibility of the web, while toll access resists the forces of closure.

Search is the gravity of the online universe that holds everything together, if anything does. As such, open access is one of its greatest allies. One thing we can do to defeat web entropy and help the cause of organization and discovery is to provide open access to a continually growing proportion of research literature. The harder this literature is to index—and price barriers increase the difficulty—the harder it is for search to keep pace with the relentless expansion.

Postscript

I haven't seen other discussions of the analogy between cosmic expansion and web expansion, and the power of gravity and the power of search. But I can't believe I'm the first to notice it. If anyone can point out earlier discussions, I'd be glad to credit the pioneers.

Glossary

Gold OA

OA through journals, regardless of the journal's business model. *Also see* Green OA.

Gratis OA

Access that is free of charge but not necessarily free of copyright and licensing restrictions. *Also see* Libre OA.

Green OA

OA through repositories. *Also see* Gold OA; Repositories; Self-archiving.

Libre OA

Access that is both free of charge (gratis OA) and free of at least some copyright and licensing restrictions. Because there are many possible copyright and licensing restrictions, libre OA is not just one access model but a range of access models. All the degrees of libre OA are alike in permitting uses that exceed fair use (or the local equivalent). *Also see* Gratis OA; License.

License

A statement from a copyright holder telling users what they may and may not do with a copyrighted work. *Open* licenses, such as those from Creative Commons, permit different degrees of libre OA. In the absence of an open license, a copyrighted work is under an all-rights-reserved copyright, its users may not exceed fair use (or the local equivalent), and OA is at most gratis OA. *Also see* Gratis OA; Libre OA.

Open access (OA)

Barrier-free access to online works and other resources. OA literature is digital, online, free of charge (gratis OA), and free of needless copyright and licensing restrictions (libre OA). The term was introduced by the Budapest Open Access Initiative in February 2002.

Publication fee

Sometimes called a processing fee or article processing charge (APC). A fee charged by some OA journals when accepting an article for publication, in order to cover the costs of production. It's one way to cover production costs without charging readers and erecting access barriers. While the invoice goes to the author, the fee is usually paid by the author's funder or employer rather than by the author out of pocket. Hence publication fees are sometimes misleadingly called "author fees". While charging publication fees is the best-known business model for OA journals, only about 30% of OA journals use this model.

Repository

In the world of OA, a repository is an online database of OA works. Repositories don't perform their own peer-review, but they may host articles peer-reviewed elsewhere. In addition, they frequently host unrefereed preprints, electronic theses and dissertations, books or book chapters, datasets, and digitized print works from the institution's library. OA repositories are interoperable when they conform to the Open Archives Initiative (OAI) Protocol for Metadata Harvesting (PMH). Users can find a work in an OAI-compliant repository without knowing which repositories exist, where they are located, or what they contain. *Institutional* repositories aim to host the research output of an institution, while *disciplinary* or *central* repositories aim to host the research output of a field. There are more than a dozen free and open-source software packages for creating OAI-compliant OA repositories.

Self-archiving

Also called OA archiving. The practice of making work OA by depositing it in an OA repository. *Also see* Green OA.

Toll access (TA)

Access limited to those who pay. The most generic term for the opposite of OA.

Index